Hall of the Gods

Hall of the Gods

Nigel Appleby

WILLIAM HEINEMANN LTD : LONDON

First published in the United Kingdom in 1998 by
William Heinemann

1 3 5 7 9 10 8 6 4 2

William Heinemann
Random House UK Ltd
20 Vauxhall Bridge Road, London SW1V 2SA

Random House Australia (Pty) Limited
20 Alfred Street, Milsons Point, Sydney,
New South Wales 2061, Australia

Random House New Zealand Limited
18 Poland Road, Glenfield,
Auckland 10, New Zealand

Random House South Africa (Pty) Limited
Endulini, 5A Jubilee Road, Parktown, 2193, South Africa

Random House UK Limited Reg. No. 954009

A CIP catalogue record for this book is available from the British Library

Papers used by Random House UK Limited are natural,
recyclable products made from wood grown in sustainable forests.
The manufacturing processes conform to the environmental
regulations of the country of origin.

Typeset in Times by MATS, Southend-on-Sea, Essex

Printed and bound in the United Kingdom by
Mackays of Chatham PLC, Chatham, Kent

ISBN 0 434 00501 0

This book is dedicated to my wife Amanda and my children, Rachael, Stephen, Daniel and Shelby, and also to my parents, especially my father for always being there no matter what the problem, place or circumstance; for his example, kindness and unwavering encouragement and support over the years.

'Someday what we thought was myth will be found to contain the true history of the past, while what we always regarded as history will be relegated to a myth of our own making.'

Gerald Massey, Egyptologist

'The mind is not a vessel to be filled, but a fire to be lighted.'

Plutarch

Contents

Contents

Acknowledgements

My sincerest thanks go to Maria Rejt of William Heinemann at Random House for taking the huge risk in pushing ahead with this publication, despite such a very small timescale in which to do so. To Maria I shall be eternally grateful for her calm, professional and, above all, inspired commitment to this book. Special thanks to Simon Trewin, my literary agent from Sheil Land Associates, for his vision and foresight in securing the project in the first place, and to Cherry Norton of *The Sunday Times*, whose article about my team and me led to the publication of this book.

My thanks also go to Chris Ogilvey-Herald, the editor of *Quest For Knowledge* magazine, for all his valuable contacts, pictures and photographs. To Hartwig Hausdorf for supplying me with rare photographs of the pyramids in China. Thanks, too, to Lucien Morgan and Richard Gibson for enthusiastic help with photographs. To Michael Joyce for bringing to my attention so many of the mathematical elements – fadic values and numbers. To Dr Gerald O'Farrell for introducing me to so many valued people whose subsequent help and supply of confirmatory evidence cannot be underestimated. To Roderick Brown, who had to suffer the nightmare of making sense of my manuscript, for his critical appraisal and editing of the text. Without Roderick the manuscript would simply not have been completed on time. Special thanks have to go to Steve Cox, for his critical questioning of my research and presentation that has resulted in a clearer, more defined argument. Thanks to Nicky Nevin who has worked wonders with the shifting sands of the production schedule, and also to Thomas Wilson for his extreme helpfulness, especially in the last stages. Thanks also to the typesetters, Mike Harrington and Allan Ticehurst of MATS, who cheerfully achieved miracles on a well-nigh impossible schedule. Thank you to Patrick Geryl and Gino Ratinckx for their manuscript, *The Prophecy of the Zodiac*, which further validated my own research. A special thank you must go to both Andrew Collins and Simon Cox for the many conversations we have had cross-referencing each other's research, especially in regard to the Egyptian 'Chambers of Creation', which I had thought I was alone in interpreting until discovering that they were in agreement with my findings, having independently made the same connections.

It goes without saying that I thank my wife, Amanda, for all the hardship she has endured over the past seven years with me. It has not gone unrecognised or unappreciated and perhaps I should make that clearer to her. Without her support and sheer hard work to keep us afloat, neither Operation Hermes nor my years researching would have been possible. I shall forever be indebted to her for that.

Saying thank you to my team members would be an insignificant gesture, as I cannot ever thank them enough for the continued commitment and enthusiasm that they have injected into the project. To Bill Shirley I have to say that without him, the project would never have got off the ground in the first place. To Adam Child I have to say that without him, the project would never have continued on track. I thank them both for their unwavering support, even in the face of personal hardship and, at times, immovable obstacles. Thanks also to Grahame Appleby (my brother), for his insightful comments on the text, and to Tom Squires for all his assistance.

I would like to also thank the following whose own research so greatly helped over the years. Robert Temple, whose remarkable book *The Sirius Mystery* started me on a quest that has, to date, lasted just over 20 years. Peter Lemesurier for first bringing to my attention that a Hall of Records apparently exists. John Michell, whose books first introduced me to sacred geometry and gematria. Thanks to Dr A. J. Monty White, whose book *What About Origins?*, and to Dr Andrew Scott, whose book *The Creation of Life* both helped enormously in my understanding of biology, chemistry and evolution. Christopher Knight and Robert Lomas's *The Hiram Key* was an invaluable source for information on Hiram Abif, the Knights Templar and the Freemasons. David Furlong's *The Keys to the Temple* gave me further proofs on sacred geometric alignments. Christopher Dunn's work on ancient technology made very important observations on the ancients' drilling techniques.

A huge thank you to all you unsung researchers out there who have contributed to the wealth of information but received no recognition in return. It is through the likes of you that great leaps in our understanding of the past are achieved. Without the years of dedicated labour and research by these people, I, for one, would not have found myself in the privileged position of being able to piece the jigsaw of information together. And last but by no means least, thank you to the likes of Graham Hancock, Robert Bauval, Adrian Gilbert, Maurice Cotterell, Andy Collins, and Ahmed Osman, whose books have paved the way for a new perspective on our understanding of our past, for their courage in daring to question orthodox academia, in going on public record with their research and in setting the stage for a new generation of up-and-coming academic researchers who are prepared to listen and learn anew.

Nigel Appleby

HALL OF THE GODS

Prologue

The Wait is Nearly Over . . .

When I was 12 years old I looked at the Great Pyramid in Egypt with awe and wonder. I just hadn't been aware how huge this manmade monument actually is. At nearly 500 feet high, it's the size of a hill. I could sense the antiquity of the building. I had no idea of Egyptian chronology or how old it was in years, but I could almost feel its age physically. At once, I had an overpowering affinity with it. I did not know why, but this edifice was somehow familiar to me. There was something very important involved here, a secret. But what *was* that secret? I knew even then that this was no mere tomb for a pharaoh – no mummies had ever been found inside an Egyptian pyramid. This pyramid was unique; I was captivated totally.

Nearly 22 years later I would find myself waiting for news from members of my expedition team who were carrying out an initial on-site survey of the projected location of our quest. It was late in the afternoon, 20 October 1997. I was standing next to the phone, looking out of the window. It rained hard outside. I was waiting for one of the most important calls of my life. I had felt apprehension before – the times I had been present at the birth of my children, or when I launched myself out of an aircraft for a night-time parachute jump – but the nervous apprehension now was making me feel sick as I waited and *willed* the phone to ring. The tension was tangible.

Only three days before I had ensured that five members of my expedition team arrived in Cairo to carry out that vital survey on the specific place that my years of research indicated was the position of the fabled lost 'Hall of Records'. I was initially going to be leading the reconnaissance team with Brian, my reserve, on standby, but rapid developments here in England with this book required me to stay. Right until the night before departure, Brian still didn't know whether he was going or not. As he had taken the time off from his usual job, I felt it only fair that he should go. So after the team arrived in Cairo, I had to leave them and let them get on with the job in hand.

During the previous two days, the team had done a dummy recce of three other sites as they were being closely watched by interested parties eager to find out where our projection of the site was. Today the team was going to the real site. It had taken me 20 years of research to work out the alignments and mathematical codes from antiquity that all converged on the same site, and nearly three years to put together the team. Now was the moment of truth. Our maps had initially shown that the area was clear of buildings, but recent reports indicated a mass of development over the past three years. After all this time and sacrifice, the thought of finding the site under several feet of concrete and apartment blocks was very disconcerting, to say the least. The quest had originally been mine, but over the past few years it had expanded to include my team, who had consequently sacrificed a lot of their own time, money and, in some cases, both jobs and personal relationships for the project. I was proud of them for their continued faith and their tenacity in sticking with the venture, despite what were at times seemingly insurmountable problems. Now everything hung on what they would find. After thousands of years of the secret being buried for safe keeping, we were tantalisingly so very close to it.

The phone rang. My wife Amanda looked at me hesitantly as I paused. Time to bite the bullet; I answered and waited for a reply. There was a long pregnant pause, then Adam, co-director of the expedition company, spoke very slowly and sounded almost melancholic in tone. My heart sank. I wasn't alarmed and didn't shake with nerves. I went into a sort of auto-mode as Adam began to explain what they had found.

Five team members, Adam, Bill, Brian, Andrew and Trish, had set off for the site early in the morning. They were all anxious and nervous as they sped through the streets of Cairo, Adam convinced that they would hit someone as Firgany, their Egyptian guide and mentor, drove them towards the outskirts of Cairo in his usual fast manner. Inside the Nissan 4 by 4, the air was stifling hot and sweat poured from all of them. After all the sacrifices that they had made over the past few years, they were just as hesitant about what they were going to find that morning. Adam was busy re-orientating the map and guiding Firgany as they approached the site. The map showed clear ground, yet as they looked ahead, all they could see were apartment blocks and smaller buildings. Bill looked at Adam disappointedly, full of mixed emotions. Without a word exchanged they all knew that if there was a building on the site, it was over; they would all get back on the next plane to England. The silence in the vehicle was deafening. Adam explained later that he felt as if he were in a dream state as they drove ever closer to the site, only to see more buildings. Trish and Andrew simply felt as despondent as they could ever remember.

Dust began to swirl through the vehicle as they sped down a long dirt track, as marked on the map. At the junction for the projected site, buildings obscured their view on each side, but as they turned, they suddenly saw a large clear patch of land beyond. Their hearts raced as

4

they drove through and into the open area now surrounded by buildings – and a new motorway – on all four sides. Brian stepped out of the vehicle and said that any doubts he might have had before were now gone. Adam and Bill sighed with relief after double-checking their position. Why the area had been left clear is anyone's guess, but it *was* clear, that was all they needed to know. And just as predicted, there was a very slight rise in the middle of the site. Hardly noticeable, but there nonetheless!

The team carried out their survey, the hairs constantly tingling on their backs as they looked at each other realising what lay less than 20 feet beneath their feet. We now had not just one indicator to this position, but four! Four very different independent codes that converge on the same site: codes derived from DNA, the projection of stars upon ancient sacred sites and mathematical alignments.

Adam's initial melancholic tone was due to his exhaustion and relief after the day's activities. After hanging up the phone I stood still and quiet for a moment. I didn't feel excited or ecstatic; just a sense of knowing that we had now entered into another phase of the project. All that remained now was to prove, absolutely and conclusively, that there is indeed something buried at the site. This my team aims to achieve with the very latest, most advanced probing and scanning equipment available in the world today, operated by highly qualified geophysical archaeologists and support members.

We just may be on the verge of answering some of the most perplexing questions that face mankind. If the records contained within the Hall of Records prove to be what the myths and legends claim, then we shall know where we originate from, our true past history, who the gods of antiquity really were and where we are heading.

Only time will tell . . .

5

Introduction

There is a secret that has waited thousands of years to reveal itself. It links the pyramids of Egypt and the Mayan temples of Central America to ancient sites in Great Britain and Europe's greatest cathedrals. It connects the ancient Egyptian, Babylonian and Sumerian myths, the Ark of the Covenant and Moses, Jesus Christ, King Arthur, the Knights Templar, and the Freemasons.

A mathematical and astronomical code has always existed within ancient myths and legends, testifying to the existence of a highly evolved civilisation that flourished on a global scale, thousands of years ago. Till now, however, that message has remained hidden, as mistranslations, errors, misunderstandings and deliberate suppression have caused its voice to be muffled. Decoded, this information reveals the true history of civilisation on Earth – in flat contradiction of the current orthodox dating of its evolution – and pinpoints the location of a carefully concealed 'Hall of Records' believed to contain artefacts and documents revealing the full extent of knowledge available to those who constructed it.

It is vital to realise that from the outset the world's great myths and legends appear to be based upon factual events – despite subsequent distortion – and all have similar origins. The further back you trace them, the more identical they become. Here is one example. The flood story of the Bible is, in essence, identical to the Babylonian flood tale, the *Epic of Gilgamesh,* and those of the Americas; so much so that the earliest Christian missionaries were convinced the direct biblical parallels in Mayan and Aztec religions had to be a bizarre caricature of Christianity designed by the Devil himself. The same thoughts occurred to missionaries studying in Tibet. In countless other respects, the ancient American traditions paralleled to an uncanny degree those of ancient Egypt, Babylon, Greece, Syria, Persia and India. Furthermore, these civilisations shared something else – they were all preoccupied with and obsessed by the cosmos and celestial phenomena. These very same phenomena eventually helped lead to the location of the Hall of Records.

Although this has proved a global investigation, Egypt is unquestionably the key. Accounts millennia old speak of chambers, located beneath the Great Pyramid and Sphinx at Giza and leading off

6

from them, filled with a technological legacy left by a lost civilisation far older than Egypt itself, whose very existence mainstream archaeology denies. Along with clues to its whereabouts, prophecies are preserved foretelling when and how the vanished time-capsule will be opened – and by whom.

The Hall of Records has not been discovered before simply because we have not been able to understand the true meanings of the clues to its location until our present level of technology helped us to do so. Precise astronomical details about certain constellations only became available this century; without that, and the ability to decipher hieroglyphs which has only existed for the past 170 years, we were unable to recognise data clearly encoded within ancient myths and legends. As Gerald Massey, an eminent and enlightened Egyptologist, declared: 'Someday what we thought was myth will be found to contain the true history of the past, while what we always regarded as history will be relegated to a myth of our own making.'

Around 1950 it was generally assumed that the fundamental principles of science were all known and that only specifics were left to fill in. Since then, that perception has changed greatly. We now know that there are signs of recent massive disruptions both on Earth and elsewhere in the solar system, plus evidence that the magnetic poles have repeatedly reversed and the Earth's terrestrial axis with them. Catastrophes on a global scale have affected Earth – and any civilisations that might have been present. This may be comparatively new to us, but it was not so for these ancient civilisations. They had a precise understanding of the upheavals that beset the planet – and they knew that such things would happen again. In our era.

When I set out on my research, I had no particular aim, just an unquenchable personal determination to find things out for myself. I'd developed a keen interest in all things mythological, spiritual and philosophical, but had absolutely no idea that a Hall of Records even existed, let alone where to start looking for it. I had many preconceived ideas and views and initially tried to fit unsettling discoveries into my existing thoughts and ideologies. In time, however, as mounting facts challenged my views, I had no option but to reappraise my beliefs and to probe as deeply as possible into a wider variety of sources. From these a clear and definite pattern began to emerge. As this became increasingly obvious to me, I began to realise that a Hall of Records still existed. Furthermore, I understood why it still existed, and where to find it!

My personal quest for knowledge has been long – as much of my adult life as I could give it – demanding and frequently frustrating. There have been as many chicanes as clear stretches of road ahead of me. Because of this, I have no wish to claim the glory for the discovery of the Hall of

Records. The information that has led to the revelation of its location is drawn from the progress made over many years of dedicated research by countless, and often unsung, scholarly and academic heroes. I am simply like a man with a jigsaw puzzle who, having pieced it together, has been fortunate enough to see the entire picture for what it truly is. I have provided my own interpretations as I understand things and included many of my own discoveries; but these discoveries would not have been possible without the initial research of others, made over the past 200 years.

This book, then, is the tip of a vast mountain of information and research that has taken me nearly 20 years to accumulate and understand. *Hall of the Gods* reaches back to evidence that starts at the very beginning of time. It assesses the origins of life itself, considering the latest scientific research but not accepting it without question. It looks at anomalies from antiquity that orthodox thinking cannot explain. It presents irrefutable facts that refuse to go away, even when subjected to unrelenting scientific and scholarly scrutiny. My argument is undeniably contentious, but I would ask you to maintain an open mind throughout and not let your judgement be clouded by preconceptions – even though much will come as a shock.

I have tried to convey the more technical aspects of my argument in layman's terms, so that the widest audience can understand its contents and work through it, stage by stage, testing its accuracy and sharing in its development. If at times it appears difficult, remember there is no formula, diagram or complex hieroglyph that will stand in the way of those who set out to read it. On the other hand, it isn't meant to be easy; if it were, the Hall of Records would have been found a long time ago.

In *Hall of the Gods*, I am going to take you on a journey that I hope will make you sit up and realise that our present understanding of our origins is totally wrong. You are not being asked to accept my theories without question; rather you are being invited to assess for yourself. You have to make up your own mind.

Measurements

The dimensions of our planet and many other bodies in the cosmos are central to my argument. I have relied upon Fadic numbering (which is defined and explained in due course) for determining distances and values (such as the diameter of the Moon, or the distance between the Sun and the Earth) as opposed to using measurements from encyclopaedias and other standard astronomical works, as these give a considerable variety of figures for any one particular distance. The Fadic system adheres to a mathematical constant, so I feel it to be more accurate than other methods of determination. Furthermore, the Fadic values for the Earth, Moon and Sun's distances are in agreement with orthodox values given in encyclopaedias and other reference works. This tells me that the Fadic system is also correct when applied to other bodies in our solar system, for which other sources also give differing measurements.

As for the dimensions of Earthly structures, such as the Great Pyramid, I shall declare my reasoning for the precise values chosen as I advance my case. This also applies to units of measurement. For example, my use of the Imperial *and* metric systems may seem rather unusual, but I will demonstrate how both are extremely relevant at the appropriate point in my argument.

PART I

IN THE BEGINNING . . .

Chapter 1

The Trigger

As I stared at the creature, I tried to assess what I was seeing. It was the figure of a powerfully built man, yet he was wearing a strange form of headdress identical to a fish's head, with the rest of its body draped down his back almost to his feet. He was holding some kind of round stone implement in his right hand, which was raised, and a strange-looking basket in his left hand. The man was clearly very muscular, as his exposed legs and arms revealed. He wore what appeared to be bracelets on his upper arms and things that seemed identical to modern watches on both wrists, and sported an imposing beard. As I looked intently at the figure before me, its almost frozen, rigid statuesque appearance projected an image of an other-world origin coupled with a serene sense of great wisdom. This clearly represented something far more than a man wearing a fish's head and body; this was symbolic imagery at its best. And so I closed the page on the illustration and began to research the so-called amphibious being, known to the ancients as Oannes, whom I had just been viewing.

Berengaria, Cyprus, Summer 1976

I can easily pinpoint the moment in my quest for knowledge when I started to investigate seriously: the summer of 1976. A year of record weather temperatures, it had been one of the hottest, driest summers ever recorded in England. By then I was living in a village in Cyprus called Berengaria as my father, who was in the Army, was stationed there. School would only last half a day (7.30 a.m. to 1.00 p.m.!) as the heat in the stifling classrooms was too intense in the afternoons; these would then be free for swimming and exploring the countryside.

During the course of our stay in Berengaria, many people had claimed to see apparitions or ghosts of what looked like knights of the Crusades. Two children saw such things and were so badly shocked that they had to be flown back to England for professional counselling to help them through their trauma. Me, I *wanted* to see something like that, and spent many an evening ghost-hunting, with no success. Strange noises of battle were often heard at night, sounds that could have been those of swords clashing, horses screaming and men yelling, which then faded away.

Eventually, the Army began to investigate these strange events. Research revealed that our small village, purpose-built for the British Forces in Cyprus, was in fact built directly on top of a medieval burial ground. The site had been the scene of a savage and bloody battle involving Crusaders and the dead had simply been buried together in a mass grave, horses included. Once aware of this, I began to investigate the battles and the soldiers who had fought them. This in turn led me to become very interested in the Crusades, chivalric orders and knights; an interest that would later have a direct bearing upon my own researches years later.

One evening I babysat for friends of my parents. Once they'd gone out I sat down to watch TV armed with a supply of Coca Cola, crisps and biscuits. It was a hot night and the veranda doors were open to let in a breeze. I must have fallen asleep, as the next thing I remember it was nearly midnight and I was being woken by the returning parents banging on the windows. I felt a little confused; I hadn't touched my snack and couldn't recall closing the windows and veranda door. Worst of all, I had the earache of the century pounding all down the side of my neck and head from where I had lain awkwardly on my hand.

The following day I was in unbearable agony. I was sent to the camp's MRS (Medical Reception Station), where it was discovered that I had a virulent ear infection. Worse, it was spreading very quickly, causing a massive build-up of antibodies around my ear canal, neck and the side of my face. I was prescribed antibiotics and sent home but for the next week saw no improvement. Then I was put on to a powerful penicillin-based drug, and had to have constant supervision. Amongst other things, that meant not being able to attend school. (This was fine by me. I had found school very limiting and as my reports showed, I was always distracted, following my own internal agenda instead of the lesson.)

For the following weeks the ear infection raged undiminished. Test after test failed to reveal its exact cause. Doctors began to fear that it was causing pressure against my skull, as a large lump was developing behind my ear and against the bone. There was talk of surgery if the drugs did not work, but the infection went to an undefined depth, and there were no adequate facilities to do such an operation at the military hospital in Akrotiri; so they pumped me full of more drugs and waited. There was a further complication. The doctors thought that the infection might be a residual effect from very serious medical problems I had had earlier in life, which was only now making its presence felt.

The dream

When I was four and a half, playing 'doctors and nurses', I told my cousin Susan to get me some tablets from the cupboard, so I could take them, just like a real patient. She did so and gave them to me; *all* of them.

I lay down under a blanket to pretend to sleep – and eventually came to several days later, attached to an array of intensive care equipment in hospital.

I had taken an overdose of tranquillisers so massive that my mother was told it was very likely I would not survive. My kidneys, liver and heart would not be able to stand the huge amount of drugs. My mother held a bedside vigil until she was forced to go and get some sleep, and my father, overseas in the Persian Gulf, was put on a plane home, having been told that I would in all probability be dead by the time he arrived. A parent myself now, I cannot imagine what must have gone through their minds.

During this traumatic period in hospital, I clearly remember having a very lucid dream. Subsequently several people have suggested that it was something more – a near-death experience, a phenomenon I would investigate years later. This event had a profound effect upon the rest of my life. It directly influenced the way I have behaved and conducted myself, continued to some degree to this day. It is irrelevant whether or not my experience was imagined or a consequence of the overdose of drugs; what matters is that on the life-support machine I had a dream that has remained in my mind ever since. I do not feel uncomfortable with the idea of a dream inspiring me. Some of the greatest discoveries have been found because of dreams. Einstein, after all, stated that he dreamt of the formula $E = mc^2$.

What *was* this life-changing dream? I was with 5 people I'd never met before, but somehow I was aware that I knew them very well and loved them very much. I could actually *feel* their love and warmth towards me. It was hard to visualise them precisely, but I was certain that they were very learned and wise. I was deeply saddened when I was made aware that I was going to leave them. It was a very emotional experience that words simply cannot explain without appearing melodramatic. Their message to me was, I would have a task to undertake if I wished. I would know what and when at an appropriate time later in life; they would always be there watching over me.* The next thing I knew was when I opened my eyes to see the monitor bleeping away. The doctors were baffled by my sudden recovery, which was complete other than a slight heart murmur which lasted a short while – or so I thought until my late 20s would prove otherwise.

Over the following years I was to experience many major headaches and spells of sickness, possibly as a direct result of the overdose. I endured numerous head X-rays. I was allergic to just about everything under the sun and spent many a long journey with my poor mother visiting specialists all over England. Then, when I was 9, a doctor at

---

* Incidentally, I did not experience the classic image of travelling down a tunnel towards light, etc.

Harrogate General Hospital noted that I had the lowest level of iron in my blood that he had ever seen, so I was instantly put on iron tablets. The positive effect was immediate. My allergies disappeared overnight and my health became normal. Simple as that.

Berengaria, Cyprus, Autumn 1976

Because of my early illness, then, my parents were naturally very concerned with the ear infection and the problems it was now causing. One effect was that I was unable to make my usual expeditions out into the countryside, go swimming or even to Scouts or the youth club. The antibiotics continued to show no signs of working, though painkillers made the pain bearable. Since the drugs often made me feel weak, I spent a lot of time just sitting on the veranda reading books and developing my taste for cups of tea. Our white-walled house in Cyprus was the biggest we had ever lived in, nearly 100 feet long, with a veranda that ran its entire length, and a huge garden filled with subtropical plants, trees and bushes. The house was of a prefabricated design made with what looked like corrugated sheets of metal, but were in fact concrete-mix boards fixed to an inner timber construction. It was roomy and very pleasant all year round. The house had been built so that the veranda was nearly always in the shade and was the coolest place to relax.

I very rarely slept at night as the pain always seemed worse then. In consequence I spent hours in the cool evening breeze sitting at the end of the veranda just watching the stars as they moved through the crystal-clear night sky. I began to learn as much as I could about the constellations in order to recognise them. The first I found was the Plough, then the Orion constellation. I read several astronomy books to familiarise myself with all the data I could. For a better view I would use my father's telescopes. As an armourer he would use these on the ranges for checking hits on targets in the distance, to help zero weapons for calibration tests, and would often come home annoyed because the batteries in the zoom lens telescope had died. Finally he bought a new telescope, convinced that there was a fault in the first one. That was great. I now had *two* that I could set up each night!

Meanwhile my mother decided that she would get me some books from the library. By this time I had read all the adventures of Asterix and Obelix and Tintin, and all the science fiction, so I was rapidly running out of choices. I had read the Bible at 7 but since then I had never put my intention to study it further into practice. Now I could. So I asked my mother to bring me anything relating to the Bible, or failing that, space subjects. Little did I realise the implications of that simple request – based, as much as anything, on a chance encounter with the Old Testament, 6 years earlier.

Ripon, North Yorkshire, 1970

When I was seven I attended Sunday school in the quiet cathedral town where my family lived – but only because my first-ever girlfriend, Sarah, went there, and this was a way of getting to know her better. Little did I realise the effect these visits would have upon the course of my entire life. As I listened to the lessons I was mystified, confused and at times horrified by what I heard about God. The God I had previously imagined was nothing like this one, smiting people, demanding sacrifices, destroying cities, having His chosen people massacre other nations, including women and children. Surely they were all God's children, as He had stated many times? And there was an enormous volume called *Bible Stories for Children* which – surprisingly – contained material on the number of the Beast being 666, and hinted that only the wise would understand what it stood for. As it was connected to the Devil and evil, I was understandably frightened. However, throughout my life, if anything has scared me I have always tried to overcome the fear by learning all about it or mastering it – an attitude which would serve me well later in life. So I wanted to know what 666 meant. Later, study prompted further questions. Why in sacred gematria – the process whereby each letter or character has a mathematical value which we shall later cover in detail – did Jesus equal the value of 888? And what is so significant about the numbers 144,000 from Revelation and the 12,000 furlongs of the New Jerusalem? In time I would discover the answers to these questions. At this point, I was useless at maths, and as I found reading easier I read, for the first time, the entire Bible. From then on I determined to be one of three things: a fighter pilot in the RAF, a medical doctor or a priest; what a combination! (As it turned out I became none of these, as my life took a course that I could never have predicted.) It would be many years before I would finally solve the riddle and meaning of the number 666.

Berengaria, Cyprus, Autumn 1976

So that experience years earlier had stimulated my initial interest in the Bible. Now I was almost into the fourth month of my ear infection. My brothers were all at school and I was enjoying the peaceful atmosphere of the garden sitting near the carob tree at the end of the veranda. My mother returned from the library with four books for me. One was a full-colour book about manned space flight, another a 'boys' own' adventure story with a lousy picture of a submarine on its cover, the third Erich von Däniken's *Chariots of the Gods?*, and the final one was by Robert Temple, called *The Sirius Mystery*. I immediately rejected the adventure yarn and then flicked through the space flight book: seen it all before. *The*

Sirius Mystery looked very heavy and complicated. It was also long – longer than anything I had ever read. Read that last, I thought. So I started with *Chariots of the Gods?*

I turned the first page and was instantly captivated. For the first time in my life a book fired my imagination. I could sense my enthusiasm rise as I read on, hungry for the next revelation. Without realising it I forgot the pain in my ear and read, oblivious of it. I even left my cup of tea. I read all morning and when my brothers came home at midday I removed myself to the far corner of the garden for peace and quiet in order to concentrate. I was too busy to stop for meals so I feigned feeling sick and asked just for a sandwich which I could eat whilst reading undisturbed.

In short, von Däniken was claiming to present evidence that mankind's prehistory was not as we are taught. He tried to explain the sudden appearance of the major civilisations overnight as a direct result of outside intervention by aliens from space who taught early mankind all the sciences and arts of civilisation, including farming. He also stated that the spacemen who had visited us in our earliest history were looked upon as gods.

I did not put the book down until I had finished it in the early hours of the following day, thinking, Wow! Only then was I reminded of the ear infection, as the pain returned with a vengeance. The months of pain had worn me down; this book had been the only real joy I had experienced. Intuitively I felt that the book contained some truths, though something in the back of my mind hinted that it was not all as simple as von Däniken said. (Indeed, I consequently discovered that many of his interpretations were heavily criticised. Nevertheless, that book had served as a springboard for me, and for that I will be forever grateful.)

Now I turned to the fourth book. I opened Robert Temple's *The Sirius Mystery*, took a deep breath and prepared myself for a hard slog. I was going to read it from start to finish; more importantly, I wanted to *understand* it – even though my elder brother, Craig, bet that I wouldn't get even halfway through it. I found that Temple's writing was both structured and persuasive, unlike von Däniken's, which left me guessing. Temple's was, I felt, far superior. Every question his writing prompted me to ask was answered in his following pages; or so it appeared at the time. And of course, it was here that I encountered Oannes for the first time. Only towards the end of the book, when Temple states that in his opinion the beings who visited Earth were actually amphibious, did I think it not quite correct. I will cover Temple's research in detail later. The key thing for me, in 1976, was his assessment of the ancient god Oannes, the water god who resided in the ocean at night, only coming ashore in the daytime to teach mankind the skills of civilisation. The academic consensus was that Oannes was merely a symbolic religious figure: according to Temple, he came from the Sirius star system (see figure 1).

Figure 1. Oannes.

Chapter 2

Confronting the Consensus

When writing this book I was constantly aware of what might lay ahead, the possible repercussions of what I was stating. The academic backlash and criticism that could follow were a potential problem that I would have to deal with as and when it arrived.

I was also made acutely aware of the horrendous treatment that Robert Temple had received after the publication of *The Sirius Mystery* in 1976. He found himself having to apologise constantly for having written about alien contact with mankind in our ancient past, as he believed. Close friends suddenly disappeared from his life, no longer wanting to associate with him, as extraterrestrials were not 'socially acceptable' in those days. Temple was also berated and ridiculed by a number of scholars for his views on such a lowbrow subject as spacemen, and deemed not a respectable person. (History will show, I am sure, that it was the scholars, the so-called experts, who were at fault for their blinkered attitude. Without an open mind, many discoveries will simply never be made.)

The Sirius Mystery did however get favourable reviews in the British press, especially *The Times* and the *Daily Telegraph*. Temple received many letters from across the world and met some strange individuals as a result of his book. Some of the incidents were favourable but others were quite unsavoury, as he explains in the recent revised edition of *The Sirius Mystery*. Perhaps the most alarming repercussion was the virulent hostility shown towards him by certain security agencies, most notably the American ones. This proved very distressing to him, as he was himself of American origin. According to Temple, the CIA interfered with his livelihood directly, and a military acquaintance actually informed him that he had been asked to read *The Sirius Mystery* in order to write a thorough report on it for the British security forces. Furthermore, a police friend of Temple's was even approached by MI5 to prepare a security report on him. Temple summed this up very well:

The persecution went on for nearly fifteen years. It cost me income, career opportunities, advancement, and friends. I often wonder about it, especially the frenzied aspects of it. Why were so many people in high places foaming at the mouth in such an uncontrollable manner? Just what was it that I had done? I have never known.[1]

Of course, as a schoolboy in 1976, I was not then aware of the book's mixed reception. I had simply been inspired by *The Sirius Mystery* and I could not see any reason why I shouldn't use the same approach. I vowed that I would always strive to achieve the same standard of research, giving provable information as Temple had.

I tried to apply scientific processes to my research and initially stumbled around for quite a few years with no success. As I studied anthropology and palaeontology I perceived huge gaps in the historical records, especially the fossil records. Why, for example, was there so much confusion surrounding the demise of the dinosaurs? How come scientists could not establish the missing link in mankind's ancestral tree? Hitherto I had blindly accepted what I had been taught at school as fact. It was a little disconcerting to discover that most of what I had assumed to be fact, based upon hard scientific evidence, turned out to be theory and supposition. I realised that I was going to have to reappraise everything that I had learned and understood if I was ever to have any chance of finding the truth.

There were many times when I could not make head nor tail of what I was reading, especially from the scientific fields of investigation. Biology, chemistry and physics had never appealed to me at school as they involved a lot of maths, of which I was not particularly fond. Unfortunately (as I thought at the time) all the evidence was suggesting that all these areas were vitally important in my quest for knowledge (and, hopefully, wisdom), therefore I had to study them.

It was to prove very beneficial, because without having done so, I would not have been able to make the relevant connections that would ultimately lead to the Hall of Records' location.

Question everything

Apart from the sinister forces of opposition to much free-thinking research, as made clear by Robert Temple's experience, there is something else. Many present-day authorities are either unwilling to set aside the blinkers of orthodoxy, or unable to admit the validity of anything that lies outside their field or offers a challenge to its status quo. Could there also be a kind of modern arrogance that cannot countenance the possible scientific superiority of earlier civilisations? As we shall see, there is an ever-increasing amount of evidence from a wide variety of sources including geology, anthropology, palaeontology, linguistics, ancient history and cosmology, that clearly points to the existence in ancient prehistory of a highly developed civilisation, flourishing many thousands of years before accepted 'recorded' history. Furthermore, this civilisation possessed a technology, especially in construction methods, that far exceeds ours. The archaeological evidence also proves that the

ancient cultures across the globe had an accurate and advanced knowledge of our entire solar system not rediscovered by 'modern' science
until the past two hundred years.

An example of this is an ancient Sumerian clay tablet, depicting all the
planets in our solar system, that was recovered over 100 years ago –
before we even knew all the planets ourselves. (I will say more on this
later.) An archaeologist will frequently try and identify an artefact with
a certain period in time, or with what he knows, with no regard for such
matters as astronomical or mathematical codes that may be evident in his
findings. Why should he? He is not looking for them. This is a peculiar
practice of 20th-century teaching, where just one specific area is studied
as a specialised subject, to the detriment of having a broader perspective
and an ability to see patterns and connections reaching beyond the
boundaries of rigidly defined disciplines.

Birds with rigid wings

A simple example of how we perceive things, and how we are taught, is
made clear by wooden ceremonial 'birds' found in Egypt. When they
were unearthed in the 19th century, aircraft did not exist; hence
Egyptologists didn't understand what they were really looking at. In
consequence the wooden objects were classified as 'ceremonial birds' and
packed away into museum basements around the world. But look closely
at this bird currently in the Museum of Antiquities, Cairo (see figure 2);
notice its straight wings and vertical tail. Aircraft have vertical tails, birds
do not. In addition, when these artefacts are thrown, they function as
perfect gliders. This begs the question, How did the ancient Egyptians
know how to make model gliders? So it turns out that as our
understanding and technology advances, we see that certain artefacts
and monuments start to make sense as we recognise them for what they
are; though it smacks the face of accepted history.

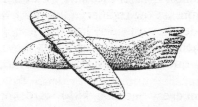

Figure 2.

Then again, look closely at the hieroglyph found recently at Abydos in
Egypt (see plates). One element shows remarkable similarities to modern

aircraft, doesn't it? As for eminent Egyptologists, they have yet to come up with an explanation for this very intriguing motif.

'A whirlwind coming out of the north'

A second example. What should we make of something that, unlike the 'birds' of Egypt, doesn't yet relate to anything we know of? What could be the meanings behind the technological visions of Ezekiel and Elijah in the Old Testament? Ezekiel was a priest amongst the Jews who were deported to Babylon in the first exile of 597 BC. Five years after arriving in captivity, he had the first of a series of visions that would span nearly 19 years. Ezekiel's Old Testament attempt to recount one is quoted below. Because he had only the perceptions of his own era, he had no way of comprehending what he saw. Try and visualise what is described – and bear in mind this is a description of something written by someone who had no experience of modern technology.

4 And I looked, and, behold, a whirlwind came out of the north, a great cloud, and a fire infolding itself, and a brightness *was* about it, and out of the midst thereof as the colour of amber, out of the midst of the fire.

5 Also out of the midst thereof *came* the likeness of four living creatures. And this *was* their appearance; they had the likeness of a man.

6 And every one had four faces, and every one had four wings.

7 And their feet *were* straight feet; and the sole of their feet *was* like the sole of a calf's foot: and they sparkled like the colour of burnished brass.

8 And *they had* the hands of a man under their wings on their four sides; and they four had their faces and their wings.

9 Their wings *were* joined one to another; they turned not when they went; they went every one straight forward.

10 As for the likeness of their faces, they four had the face of a man, and the face of a lion, on the right side: and they four had the face of an ox on the left side; they four also had the face of an eagle.

11 Thus *were* their faces: and their wings *were* stretched upward; two *wings* of every one *were* joined one to another, and two covered their bodies.

12 And they went every one straight forward: whither the spirit was to go, they went; *and* they turned not when they went.

13 As for the likeness of the living creatures, their appearance *was* like burning coals of fire, *and* like the appearance of lamps: it went up and down among the living creatures; and the fire was bright, and out of the fire went forth lightning.

14 And the living creatures ran and returned as the appearance of a flash of lightning.

15 Now as I beheld the living creatures, behold one wheel upon the earth by the living creatures, with his four faces.

16 The appearance of the wheels and their work *was* like unto the colour of a beryl: and they four had one likeness: and their appearance and their work *was* as it were a wheel in the middle of a wheel.

17 When they went, they went upon their four sides: *and* they turned not when they went.

18 As for their rings, they were so high that they were dreadful; and their rings *were* full of eyes round about them four.

19 And when the living creatures went, the wheels went by them: and when the living creatures were lifted up from the earth, the wheels were lifted up.

20 Whithersoever the spirit was to go, they went, thither *was their* spirit to go; and the wheels were lifted up over against them: for the spirit of the living creature *was* in the wheels.

[Ezekiel 1: 4–20]

In 1968 Josef Blumrich, a NASA engineer, set about analysing the suggestion in *Chariots of the Gods?* that Ezekiel's vision was that of a spacecraft. Blumrich, with first-class credentials as a NASA chief engineer heavily involved in the Skylab and space shuttle projects, had the rare distinction of being awarded the NASA Exceptional Service Medal in 1972 for his outstanding contribution to the Saturn and Apollo projects. He read Ezekiel's words in the Bible, and having spent most of

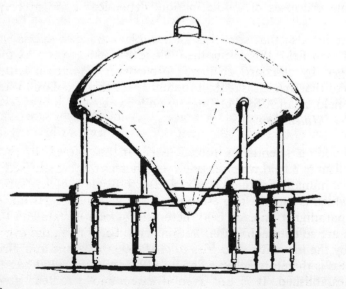

Figure 3.

his life in the construction and planning of rockets and aircraft, felt confident of annihilating von Däniken's claims.

However, after much research, the sceptical Blumrich deduced the shape and size of the craft described. He established key features such as rotor blades, fairing housings, landing legs and retractable wheels (see figure 3). Blumrich concluded that the helicopter devices themselves are distinguished by such features as folding wings, ability to change their position and astute layout for control rockets. All these properties fit together without contradiction; they are unmistakable indications of very sophisticated planning and design.

So convinced was Blumrich that he published his research and drawings in 1973 in his book *Spaceships of Ezekiel*.[2] Now, modern-day space projects are actually developing along very similar lines of design, since the helicopter-like devices are ideal for the purposes of controlled auto-giro descent and inter-atmospheric flight.

The mountains of knowledge

Now you have read these striking examples of the perils of blinkered vision, you will understand my asking you to put aside all of your present perceptions. Approach this book with a clear mind, as if learning from scratch. Most of your beliefs and perceptions of the world and cosmos will have been influenced over the years by books, television, papers and the established academic world-view, as promulgated by the 'Experts'. These experts, you must remember, have likewise been influenced by the very same processes of indoctrination, dependent upon preconceived notions.

Remember also that scientists and scholars are now specialists in a single chosen field; this limits their scope from the outset as they are encouraged by standard academic procedures to remain within the confines of that area. It is almost foolhardy for them to dare to step into another field. Alan Alford eloquently pointed this out in his book *Gods of the New Millennium*:

> The budding scientist is forced, early in his career, to choose a specialism in a field which is becoming increasingly specialised, as the body of human scientific knowledge expands. He becomes expert in a field which is usually long established and which operates under very fixed paradigms. In each field there exist standard texts and theories which are so entrenched that nothing is to be gained (and everything lost) by the maverick who tries to challenge the status quo. Scientific progress is therefore achieved by building on top of what has already been established. It is not a good career move to tear down the 'Mountain of Knowledge' and start again.[3]

25

Whilst undergoing selection training for the reserve Special Forces, the first thing I learned was that sometimes you have to stop, look at what you've got, tear it down, then start totally from the beginning again. This certainly saves time and stops you running around in circles. I applied this simple philosophy in my research.

Over the past few hundred years, a number of specialist fields have evolved that espouse fixed laws and assumptions as if they were fact. One such is the firm conviction that life on Earth is unique; therefore no other life can exist elsewhere in the universe. This single assumption still dominates the fields of biology, geology, genetics and anthropology. When young undergraduates have tried to expand their understanding in these fields, they have suffered for daring to question the accepted view. After the publication of Robert Bauval and Adrian Gilbert's bestseller *The Orion Mystery*, many undergraduates I knew submitted their theses and dissertation projects with references to that work; they were all, without exception, rejected as not suitable and outside the academic criteria required – yet these people had approached their research in a serious scientific manner. (It is, however, encouraging to see that the new generation of archaeologists, Egyptologists and scientists are rather more enlightened in their thoughts and foresight; after all, they will be the academics of tomorrow.) I would like to quote further from Alan Alford's vision of a 'mountain of knowledge', which I think effectively illustrates this problem.

> Let us again return to our 'Mountains of Knowledge' and play a game called 'Honesty'. The man on the highest mountain says to his rivals: 'Come with me and I will show you a higher mountain – the mountain of the Gods!' To the theologian he says: 'You may bring all of your holy books and beliefs with you.' What does the honest theologian say? 'Sorry, but if I come with you to the mountain of the Gods, you will undermine the entire basis of my religion. My Bible is the tool of my trade: if I rewrite it I am finished!' To the scientist the man offers the same invitation. What does the honest scientist say? 'Sorry, but we have been on this planet for 4.6 billion years and that gives me a firm timetable on which to base all of my scientific theories. If I accept interventionism [or new theory] that timetable goes out of the window. How can I then construct my theories and proofs? I will be out of business! I am making a good living out of science so I would prefer to stay just where I am.'[4]

My approach has been to start again on another mountain. This meant seizing the bull by the horns and going back to the very beginning of life itself. I started from a position with no limiting boundaries, and I was free from any obligation to chase around in the current intellectual cul-de-sac. I am confident that my theories are just as valid as those presently doing the rounds, especially as they adhere to a mathematical constant which gives them a firmer base than most.

Bear in mind our final example of how orthodox belief and knowledge changed over time. For over 1,300 years the West believed the Sun and five known planets revolved around the Earth, according to the theories of the 2nd-century Alexandrian astronomer Ptolemy. In 1543 Copernicus overturned this when he published his *De Revolutionibus Orbium Coelestium* ('On the Revolutions of the Heavenly Spheres') which revealed that the Sun is at the centre of our immediate cosmos. Galileo too promoted the idea that the Earth orbited the Sun, not vice versa, and was consequently imprisoned by the Church. The argument that the Earth was not, nor ever had been, the centre of the universe was deemed heretical as it undermined the very tenets of the Church. But rearguard action could not halt the advance of learning. Within a short time, Johannes Kepler demonstrated that the planets travel along fixed orbits determined by scientific laws. With their discoveries, Copernicus, Galileo and Kepler started a revolution that was unstoppable – just as the likes of Graham Hancock, Robert Bauval and Adrian Gilbert are doing in our time. Once the floodgates were open, scientific knowledge about the natural world exploded as a direct challenge to orthodox religious dogma. Earlier authority's opposition to, and oppression of, investigations into the very nature of life that threatened its dominant place in the status quo finds a parallel in the uphill struggle today for those challenging the established academic world.

This struggle is nowhere more fervently conducted than in the 'debate' over the origins of life itself, which is the subject of the next chapter.

Chapter 3

Origins of Man

The diverse – and opposing – theories on the creation of mankind have impassioned supporters, and we must assess their essential elements here and in subsequent chapters.

1) Did we crawl out of the primordial soup millions of years ago to develop and evolve, by natural selection, into what we are today purely by chance, in accordance with the basic principles of Darwin's theory of evolution?*

2) Were we created by a God – an all-knowing, all-seeing and omnipresent being who created the world in 7 days? If we follow the letter of the Bible, this all happened just a few thousand years ago, in around 4,500 to 5,000 BC.

3) Were we biologically created using genetic engineering by an alien race (though the word alien is misleading) which visited Earth thousands of years ago and which took the most highly advanced and intelligent anthropoid ape it could find and designed us from it?

The arguments for the three types of theory – evolution, creation or interventionism – are explored in detail here and in subsequent chapters.

Arriving at a theory

First, though, we need to understand the standard scientific procedures, because when referring to evolution, we should really be referring to the *hypothesis* of evolution, for that is exactly what it is; a hypothesis or theory. A theory is an idea or an explanation which has yet to be proved or disproved. As a scientist learns all he† can about his specialist subject,

---

* Please note: Darwin did not state that mankind is what it is today through evolution and natural selection from the apes. He wisely refrained from including man himself in his published research.

† Or, of course, she. Indeed, for 'he' read 'she' wherever appropriate in this book.

he notes down observations, then studies them at length. From any apparent pattern, he will then form a hypothesis which is really a written statement of this pattern. If he cannot observe a pattern, then we enter into the field of *theoretical* science. From a hypothesis, the scientist will make logical assumptions, then predict what must or must not occur when certain circumstances are applied. If the prediction is false, the hypothesis is wrong and is, in consequence, abandoned or modified. If the predictions are proved correct, then the hypothesis appears correct – even though not proved as conclusive. If the predictions of a hypothesis are repeated time and time again, with the same results, then it becomes thought of as a theory. This approach, known as scientific method, is represented below:

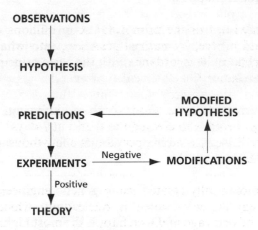

Figure 4. Diagrammatic representation of scientific method.

The Origin of Species

In November 1859 Charles Darwin published his research as *The Origin of Species*, claiming that all living things evolved by a process of natural selection – though as I said, he went to great pains not to mention mankind itself. In one single swipe, Darwin demoted us from our lofty position as divinely created beings to apes that had evolved by a process of natural selection. Today, Darwin's theories continue to win arguments against theologians' opposition, and are backed up with *apparent* evidence of the process of natural selection. It must be pointed out that Darwin's theories were not exclusively his. Erasmus Darwin, Charles's grandfather, was a widely read and respected writer on evolution before Charles was born. Moreover Wells, Pritchard and Laurence, who were all physicians, wrote on evolution and natural selection half a century before *The Origin of Species*. Benjamin Franklin in the United States, Diderot in France and Edward Blyth advanced similar theories. Yet

29

Charles Darwin never acknowledged his predecessors and referred to the origin of species by natural selection as 'my theory'.

Darwin's co-discoverer, Alfred Wallace, was not as reluctant to express his views on mankind and stated: 'Some intelligent power has guided or determined the development of man.' Evidently he suspected the involvement of an outside agency where mankind was concerned, not mere evolution, unaided. Certainly the past 100 years of anthropological research have failed to produce any fossil evidence of the so-called 'Missing Link' (of which more later) to establish categorically the evolution of man from apes. The scant fossil records upon which that theory is based could all easily be laid out on a few tables. Nonetheless, we are expected to accept that they prove that we evolved from the ape by natural selection.

When Darwin put forward his theory of evolution, he had no idea exactly how the mechanism occurred. Only in 1953, with the findings of James Watson and Francis Crick on DNA and genetic inheritance, did it become known. Watson and Crick discovered the double helix structure of the DNA molecule, the chemical that encodes genetic information. Earlier, in 1911, the anthropologist Sir Arthur Keith had listed the anatomical characteristics peculiar to each of the primate species, calling them 'Generic characteristics' – such as the length of a stride, mating rituals, and so on. His results were: gorilla 75; chimpanzee 109; orangutan 113; gibbon 116 and man 312, showing that mankind is nearly three times more distinct than other apes. However, after DNA was discovered, it became apparent that mankind shares 98 per cent similarities with the chimpanzee – i.e. 98 per cent of Man's DNA is found in chimpanzees. How can just 2 per cent of DNA account for the major differences between the two? Chimpanzees (and gorillas) have 48 chromosomes compared with man's (*Homo sapiens*) 46 chromosomes. How could we have evolved from our nearest cousin, the chimpanzee, with such biological differences? In crude terms, the paradigm is: we exist, and the chimpanzee is our closest genetic relative, therefore we must have evolved from it – end of story. Not quite!

Contentious alternatives

One theory, now gaining ground in the scientific community, which explains the change in human DNA is that of genetic intervention by external agents of some kind – perhaps even God himself. Fifty years ago even to propose such an idea would have been unthinkable. But with the discovery of the genetic code, we now have the genetic technological capability to act as gods ourselves. If that's the case, how much more could a civilisation far more advanced than we are now achieve?

Another theory gaining credibility in orthodox circles holds that the

Sun's magnetic polarity reverses at regular intervals over vast periods of time. The resultant electromagnetic discharge is so great that it effects human DNA, causing major changes, as well as inflicting major geophysical upheavals on our very planet. We shall look at this in detail later.

Today, even schoolchildren understand that every cell in the body contains 23 pairs of chromosomes, onto which are fixed approximately 100,000 genes that make up what is known as the human genome (blueprint, as it were). From this we each inherit half of our mother's and father's genes. It is now understood that random changes are passed through each generation; some good, some bad. It takes a very long period of time for a mutation that is beneficial to be passed on through the whole population. Of course, this accords with the Darwinian theory of evolution, but it is a misconception to assume that genes will improve as a direct result of the environment causing optimal adjustments. Such adjustments were *random* mutations that suited the environment they were in – and so they survived.

Missing links?

Evolution and natural selection require very long periods of time. This means that favourable mutations will be diluted, if not lost altogether, in larger populations where, as scientists admit, the process will be even slower. Since the evolution of a species is time-consuming, the separation of one species into two distinct species must be an even longer process. Speciation, which Richard Dawkins has termed 'The long good-bye', is defined as a point when two groups which originated as the same species are no longer able to interbreed. Dawkins likens the genes of different species to rivers that flow through millions of years of time, with the source being the genetic code that is identical in all animals, plants and bacteria. The question is, *why* do these rivers divide into separate streams?

Statistically, the appearance of a new species is very unlikely. Opinions vary, but there are probably between 30 and 40 million separate species on Earth, and estimates of the number that may have previously existed and died out range from 3 to as many as 50 *billion*. It is impossible to pinpoint a single example of an animal species which has recently improved by mutation or divided into separate species within the past 500,000 years. This is where we start to have problems with the orthodox view of the appearance of mankind. It is generally accepted by scientists that a timescale of 100,000 years for the emergence of a new animal species would be regarded as sudden. Thomas Huxley, the biologist, stated that: 'Large changes [in species] occur over tens of millions of years, while really major ones [macro changes] take a hundred million years or so.' So how is it possible that mankind has apparently benefited

31

from not one, but *several* macro mutations, in just 6 million years?

Scientists tell us that mankind's genes split from a common ancestral source with that of the chimpanzee some 5 to 7 million years ago. Then, due to geographical separation and environmental changes, we evolved to what we are today, whilst chimpanzees stayed as they were. As the differences are huge, many scholars have searched for an upright, bipedal ape that is hominid and closer to mankind than the chimpanzee. This elusive creature is popularly referred to as 'the missing link'. A number of fossil remains dating from 4 million years ago have been offered up as evidence but only 3 fully bipedal hominids – all discovered in East Africa – are in any way close to man. Present scientific theory puts the first proto-human hominid at a staggering 14 million years ago; it is named *Ramapithecus*. Nothing then happened for nearly 10 million years, then many animal families (such as dogs) suddenly diversified. At this point, the basic hominid stock branched off into several types of manlike creatures, all of whom became extinct, except the supposed line that led to modern man, *Homo sapiens*.

The first – and perhaps best-known – of these is the hominid known as 'Lucy' (*Australopithecus afarensis*) uncovered in Ethiopia in 1974. Estimated to be 3.6–3.2 million years old (although some prefer 2–3 million years), her skeleton was only 40 per cent complete. This alone caused controversy as it could not be properly established that she was fully bipedal, or even whether 'she' was female or male. Dr Charles Oxnard, Professor in the Department of Anatomy and Anthropology at the University of Chicago, argues that *Australopithecus* was *not* an intermediate between the apes and man, as it is uniquely different from both. His conclusion, reached after careful study of computerised multivariate analysis in comparison with similar analysis of man and modern apes, was that *Australopithecus* was as different from both man and apes as either is from the other.

The second hominid contender is *Australopithecus ramidus*, a 4.4-million-year-old pygmy chimpanzee-like ape, found by Professor Timothy White at Aramis in Ethiopia in 1994. Even though 70 per cent of its skeleton was recovered, it could still not be established conclusively that this was a true bipedal hominid.

The final contender, apparently 4.1–3.9 million years old, is *Australopithecus anamensis*, discovered by Dr M. Leakey in August 1995 at Lake Turkana in Kenya. A single shin bone has been used in claims that it walked on two feet.

'Scientists themselves are confused'

It is only when we reach between 2.5 and 1.8 million years ago that we find any evidence of a type of early man. At 2.5 million years we have the lightly built *africanus*. At 1.8 million years we have the more heavily built *robustus* and then comes the 1.5–2-million-year-old 'Advanced Australo-pithecus'. The latter, being more manlike than the others, is often referred to as 'Near man', or *Homo habilis*, meaning 'handy man'. Most authorities agree that *Homo habilis* was the first real manlike being who could walk and use stone implements.

Suddenly, around 1.5 million years ago, *Homo erectus* appeared with a considerably larger cranium than all its predecessors had. Fossil finds indicate that *Homo erectus* left Africa and spread across China, Australasia and Europe between 1 million and 700,000 years ago. Then, for reasons unknown, the species just as suddenly disappeared altogether, 300,000–200,000 years ago. By a process of elimination, there appears little doubt – so it is argued – that *Homo sapiens* (modern man) descended from this line. In 1995 the *Sunday Times* summarised the evolutionary evidence as follows:

> The scientists themselves are confused. A series of recent discoveries has forced them to tear up their simplistic charts on which they blithely used to draw linkages. The classic family tree delineating man's descent from apes, familiar to us at school, has given way to the concept of genetic islands. The bridgework between them is anyone's guess![1]

Referring to the contenders for the origins of mankind, the paper stated: 'Their relationships to one another remain clouded in mystery and nobody has conclusively identified any of them as the early hominid that gave rise to *Homo sapiens*.'

Whatever fossil records reveal and continuing controversies about the missing link throw up, one thing is clear – the wheels of evolution turn very slowly. So why is it that mankind, *Homo sapiens*, developed a self-awareness and advanced intelligence whilst other apes have spent the last 6 million years in stagnation? If brain size is the answer, is it valid to equate cranial capacity with intelligence? *Afarensis* had a cranial capacity of just 500cc, *Homo habilis* 700cc, *Homo erectus* between 900 and 1000cc. Then *Homo sapiens* jumps in with a sudden cranial capacity increase to 1450cc, an increase defying all presently accepted laws of evolution. To add to the confusion, early *Homo sapiens*, known as Cro-Magnon Man (so called for a cave in the Dordogne area of southwest France), precursor to modern man, appeared to have an even bigger cranial capacity than modern man – some 1700cc. Furthermore, several Neanderthal remains (named for the region in Germany where the first remains were found) have been uncovered with a cranial capacity of nearly 2000cc.

At one point it was wrongly assumed that Neanderthal man died out, to be replaced by Cro-Magnon man, his direct descendants, just 35,000 years ago. Apparently Cro-Magnon man arrived in Europe almost overnight, with building skills, a structured social system, wearing clothes and using tools and weapons. These were the people responsible for cave paintings dated to around 27,000 years ago found across Europe. However, these Cro-Magnons of Europe were anatomically identical to those of 100,000 years ago found in the Middle East. It is now proven that Cro-Magnon man did not evolve from Neanderthal, as originally thought; several recent discoveries have established beyond doubt that they co-existed around 100–90,000 years ago.

It was always assumed that Neanderthal man could not speak properly, and he was portrayed as rather brutish and apelike in appearance, covered in body hair. Then at Kebara Cave on Mount Carmel in Israel, 60,000-year-old Neanderthal remains were uncovered with the intact hyoid bone virtually identical to that of modern man. The hyoid bone makes human speech possible, and scientists have since concluded that Neanderthal man not only had the ability for speech, but used it. Since these discoveries, a further theory has emerged, that both Neanderthal and Cro-Magnon man stemmed from a common source. The whole history of early man is rife with controversy, and the only definite fact we have is that *Homo sapiens* appeared within the last 200,000 years, with no clear record of its origins. The *Atlas of Ancient Archaeology* concludes that: 'The contemporary history of *Homo sapiens* remains bafflingly obscure . . . so little do we know about the approach to one of the great turning points of our global history.'[2]

To add to the conundrum, the puzzling appearance of *Homo sapiens* is, statistically, *impossible*. For millions of years our supposed ape descendants made little progress, using only simple stone tools; then suddenly, around 200,000 years ago, *Homo sapiens* – with a 50 per cent increase in cranial capacity and the ability to speak – appeared almost overnight. Increasing the confusion, he apparently existed for a further 160,000 years in primitive conditions, only to expand suddenly across the entire globe 13,000 years ago. Just 1,000 years later he was using agricultural methods; after a mere 6,000 more years he was forming great civilisations with advanced astronomical knowledge; and 6,000 years on we are probing the depths of space. What happened to the theory of evolution as a process of gradual advancement over very long time periods?

The argument that we evolved from Neanderthal man recently met further obstacles when scientists in both the USA and Germany published results in a Cambridge, Massachusetts journal known as *Cell*,[3] from a revolutionary test that proves once and for all that humans are not descended from Neanderthals. Comparison of Neanderthal DNA (taken from bone marrow remains) with that of modern man indicates far more differences than expected: 27 differences were noted; far more than the 8 that separate modern man from the ape kingdom. It may be that humans and Neanderthals shared a very ancient common ancestor. Svante Paabo of the Zoological Institute at the University of Munich, one of the anthropologists behind the study, is adamant the new data shows that modern man emerged out of Africa fairly recently – around 100,000 to 200,000 years ago – and that Cro-Magnon man and Neanderthal man co-existed, even cross-breeding before the Neanderthals died out. (Note that there are 27 differences; the figure will prove important later.)

However, not everyone is in agreement with these findings. Milford Wolpoff, Professor of Anthropology at the University of Michigan, regards them as hasty conclusions and believes that such large differences in DNA traits or gene sequences do no necessarily indicate a divergence of species, but rather that perhaps the traits simply change over time.[4] In the light of that, my question is: If this happened before, could it happen again, and if so, when? And what causes the change – the Sun perhaps? We shall look at this later.

Brain size and birth canals

Over the past decade and a half (from 1980 to the late 1990s) scientists using new technologies, such as positron emission tomography (a visual mapping process), have been able to discover more about the human brain than ever before. As a result we are now able to see the full extent of the complexity in these billions of brain cells. With its apparently boundless performance, and its ability to handle complex mathematics, art, abstract thought and conceptualisation, the *National Geographic*,[5] rightly described it as 'the most complex object known in the universe'. Theologians have had a field day with this as it proves, in their minds, that we are created. The evolutionist simply sees the brain as no more than a product of evolution created by chance. What of the apparent psychic abilities that seem to make themselves obvious as we probe the mind's mysteries? Moreover, we are faced with the question of whether intelligence is related to cranial size. Are we simply more intelligent and capable because of the size of our heads? If so, would having a bigger cranial capacity improve our intelligence, and therefore, from an evolutionary aspect, improve our survival? If evolution was purely based upon the survival of the fittest and favourable mutations that are beneficial to ensure our continued survival, why haven't we developed an even bigger cranial capacity?

There's another vital question to pose in the debate over evolution and favourable mutation: why hasn't woman evolved a larger birth canal? The smallness of the birth canal is a mystery to many biologists, gynaecologists and anatomists. Simply put, it seems extremely doubtful if natural selection would have favoured a gene that limits the brain size (thus restricting intelligence) and causes a very high risk of mother and infant deaths during childbirth. If natural selection *is* correct, then the gene that gives such a small birth canal would have long since disappeared, deselected in favour of one ensuring a bigger birth canal or smaller skull.

Another factor we have to consider is that we do not use more than 10 per cent of our brain's capacity. Why? Alfred Wallace, Darwin's partner, clearly recognised this contradictory fact: 'An instrument, the human brain, had been developed in advance of the needs of its possessor.' This one comment forced me to address whether we are part of a great plan by some greater outside intelligence who is planning better things for us.

For now, consider the work of anthropologist Dr Geoffrey Bourne, who at the time of his comment given below, was the Director of the Yerkes Regional Primate Research Center of Emory University in Georgia, USA. An Oxford-educated cell biologist and anatomist, and considered by many to be one of the world's top primatologists, he declared *that apes and monkeys are the evolutionary descendants of man; not the other way around.* According to Dr Bourne, individuals very like modern man were in existence long **before** *Australopithecus* and *Homo erectus*. I have included this firstly as it demonstrates the present state of flux characterising scientific understanding of our origins, but more importantly, it contains the intriguing clue that a modern form of man may have existed much further back in antiquity than previously assumed.

Chapter 4

Origins of Life

We've looked at the contradictions inherent in the several versions of the theory of evolution. Now it's time to look at what the often-derided biblical creation story has to tell us. This is the entire account of creation as given in Genesis:

In the beginning God created the heaven and the Earth. And the Earth was without form, and void; and darkness was upon the face of the deep. And the spirit of God moved upon the face of the waters. And God said, let there be light; and there was light. And God saw the light, that it was good; and God divided the light from the darkness. And God called the light Day, and the darkness he called Night. And the evening and the morning were the first day.

And God said, let there be a firmament in the midst of the waters, and let it divide the waters from the waters. And God made the firmament, and divided the waters which were under the firmament from the waters which were above the firmament; and it was so. And God called the firmament Heaven. And the evening and the morning were the second day.

And God said, let the waters under the heaven be gathered together unto one place, and let the dry land appear; and it was so. And God called the dry land Earth; and the gathering together of the waters he called the seas; and God saw that it was good. And God said, let the Earth bring forth grass, the herb yielding seed, and the fruit tree yielding fruit after its own kind, whose seed is in itself, upon the Earth; and it was so. And the Earth brought forth grass, and herb yielding seed after his kind, and the tree yielding fruit, whose seed was itself, after his kind; and God saw that it was good. And the evening and the morning were the third day.

And God said, let there be lights in the firmament of the heaven to divide the day from the night; and let them be for signs, and for seasons, and for days, and years; and let them be for lights in the firmament of the heaven to give light upon the Earth; and it was so. And God made two great lights; the greater light to rule the day, and the lesser light to rule the night; he made the stars also. And God set them in the firmament of the heaven to give light upon the Earth, and to rule over the day and over the night, and to divide the light from the darkness; and God saw that it was good. And the evening and the morning were the fourth day.

And God said, let the waters bring forth abundantly the moving creature that hath life, and fowl that may fly above the Earth in the open firmament of heaven. And God created great whales, and every living creature that moveth, which the waters brought forth abundantly, after their kind, and every winged fowl after his kind; and God saw that it was good. And God blessed them, saying, Be fruitful, and multiply, and fill the waters in the seas, and let fowl multiply in the Earth. And the evening and the morning were the fifth day.

And God said, let the Earth bring forth the living creature after his kind, cattle, and creeping thing, and beast of the Earth after his kind; and it was so. And God made the beast of the Earth after his kind; and it was so. And God made the beast of the Earth after his kind, and cattle after his kind, and every thing that creepeth upon the Earth after his kind; and God saw that it was good. And God said, let us make man in our image, after our likeness; and let them have dominion over the fish of the sea, and over the fowl of the air, and over the cattle, and over all the Earth, and over every creeping thing that creepeth upon the Earth. So God created man in his own image, in the image of God created he him; male and female created he them. And God blessed them, and God said unto them, Be fruitful, and multiply, and replenish the Earth, and subdue it; and have dominion over the fish of the sea, and over the fowl of the air, and every living thing that moveth upon the Earth. And God said, Behold, I have given you every herb bearing seed, which is upon the face of all the Earth, and every tree, in the which is the fruit of a tree yielding seed; to you it shall be for meat. And to every beast of the Earth, and to every fowl of the air, and to every thing that creepeth upon the Earth, wherein there is life, I have given every green herb for meat; and it was so. And God saw everything that he had made, and, behold, it was very good. And the evening and the morning were the sixth day.

Thus the heavens and the Earth were finished, and all the host of them. And on the seventh day God ended his work which he had made; and he rested on the seventh day from all his work which he had made. And God blessed the seventh day, and sanctified it; because that in it he had rested from all his work which God created and made.

[Genesis 1: 1–31. 2: 1]

Genesis and Babylon's creation epic

Is Genesis mythical? I believe it is based upon *fact*, though that factual basis has been obscured by mistranslation. It is vital to bear in mind that symbolism is an essential component of what is being communicated. In other words, the Genesis account is a simplified representation of real events; what those events were we shall investigate later; at this stage the first thing to reiterate is that *all* the ancient myths of creation and the origins of man show a remarkable similarity. For example, the Genesis account of creation by God is almost identical to that in the Babylonian epic *Enuma Elish*, cataloguing the acts of their god, Marduk. During the past 100 years, thousands of clay tablets (similar in size and appearance to the Sumerian one given in the plates) have been unearthed from ancient Mesopotamian sites (in modern Iraq). Only in recent decades have these tablets been seriously studied and deciphered, but it is now widely accepted that the material on them was based upon earlier Sumerian accounts dating to approximately 3,800 BC.

The tablets contain a wealth of controversial information; here it is just the connection with the Genesis story that matters. Thanks to linguistic studies, the many similarities between the events of the Old Testament and those of the *Enuma Elish* have been clearly demonstrated. The early Hebrews spent many years in captivity in Babylon (6th century BC) and were certainly influenced by the *Enuma Elish*, which had been the Babylonians' most sacred text for over 1,000 years. Many of the tablets refer to numerous gods – echoing the plural usage in Genesis, when God talks of creating man in *our* image, and *our* likeness – who directly inter-vened in man's past. One Mesopotamian text describes instructions given to a god in charge of creation: 'Mix to a core the clay, from the basement of Earth, just above the Abzu,* and shape it into the form of a core. I shall provide good, knowing young gods who will bring that clay to the right condition.'[1] The Bible makes the same allusions to using the dust of the Earth to create mankind. This is where I shall introduce you to the first of many meanings attached to ancient words and symbols; as you shall see, a clearer picture begins to emerge.

To claim that mankind was made out of the dust or clay is absurd from a scientific point of view. But what was *really* inferred by dust and clay? The Hebrew word used in Genesis is 'tit'. This is derived from the earliest known language of the Sumerians where Ti.It meant 'That which is life'. This indicates to me that the chroniclers of the Bible were stating that Adam (which happens to mean 'First man', in both Hebrew and Babylonian, as well as several other things) was created from already existing living matter. In Genesis we are told that after man had been created, God created woman: 'And the Lord God caused a deep sleep to fall upon Adam, and he slept; and he took one of his ribs, and closed up the flesh instead thereof; and the rib, which the Lord God had taken from man, made he a woman, and brought her unto the man' (Genesis 2: 21–2).

This seems to stretch the imagination. Even as a child I never felt

---

* The Abzu is the Abyss, or the Deep, usually watery.

comfortable with this idea, that women originated from a single rib. But as I later discovered, in Sumerian the word Ti stood for both 'rib' and 'life'. This made more sense; something dealing with life was involved. Some scholars have recently suggested that this is actually referring to taking the DNA, the life essence, from our original Adam, the 'first man'.

In the Atra Hasis Tablet (convention names tablets after their contents; in this instance, a minor god), over 100 lines are devoted to the creation story. This tablet tells of many gods, including Enki (an important god of creation, and of water as regards its life–giving qualities), who gives instructions to a goddess named Ninti* (which means 'Lady of the Rib'), on how to create life (because of damage to the clay tablet, some of the lines are unreadable):

> Ninti nipped off 14 pieces of clay; 7 she deposited on the right, 7 deposited on the left. Between them she placed the mould . . . the she . . . the cutter of the umbilical cord. The wise and learned. Double seven birth goddesses had assembled; 7 brought forth males, 7 brought forth females. The birth goddess brought forth the wind of the breath of life. In pairs were they completed in her presence. The creatures were people – the creature of the Mother Goddess.[2]

Note the prominence of the numbers 7 and 14. You will encounter these later. Meanwhile, what can be made of this passage? Some researchers have deduced that it clearly describes the production of people by artificial scientific means, possibly some kind of hybridisation process, but nothing conclusive has yet appeared. What's important here is that the new creature was called Lu.Lu in Sumerian, which meant 'The mixed one'.

Further parallels are striking. The Bible states that man was created as 'there was no man to work the ground'. The Atra Hasis text says: 'When the gods, as men, bore the work and suffered the toil – the toil of the gods was great. The work was heavy, the distress was much.' The Atra Hasis text then describes the rank-and-file gods rebelling against their leader, Enlil. The father of the gods, Anu, had to be called down from heaven to resolve the problem. It was Enki, also known as Ea (of whom we shall hear a lot more), who provided the solution: 'Whilst the Birth Goddess is present, let her create a primitive worker, let him bear the yoke, let him carry the toil of the gods!'[3]

Many researchers see this as proof that mankind was created purely as a slave to the gods who came from the stars, but this view is too simplistic and lacks logic. If we were created purely as slaves, we would still be just that – slaves.

---

* Also given as Nintu in some sources.

The chemistry of creation

Having briefly considered ancient accounts of creation, to advance this investigation, we now need to concentrate on the origins of life from a scientific viewpoint. This is more relevant than you might think; certain details are directly related to the codes of antiquity that we shall be assessing later – especially the chemical elements.

Whichever way you view it, the origins of life involve chemical evolution. This term means chemicals reacted and mixed with each other 4,500 to 3,500 million years ago on a primitive Earth before biological processes took place (the accepted term for this is prebiotic), which led to the appearance of the first living cells. Current theory has it that the atmosphere of this prebiotic Earth was essentially composed of methane, ammonia, hydrogen and water vapour, subjected to the Sun's radiation and various cosmic bombardments. Some authorities now believe that life was injected into our planet by debris – meteorites or similar – from elsewhere in the universe crashing on to Earth, in accordance with a process called Panspermia.

Then, it is assumed (and I stress, *assumed*), electrical discharges also occurred. From this, various chemicals in the atmosphere reacted, causing simple organic compounds called amino acids to form. These amino acids are the basic building blocks of proteins, which are, in turn, the building blocks of all living matter. We are usually taught that these amino acids, together with five nucleic acid bases and three naturally occurring sugars (explained in detail later), just happened to fall into the Earth's primeval oceans over a period of 300 million years to eventually form a 1 per cent solution of organic matter commonly labelled the 'primeval soup'. Then, purely by chance, these simple chemical compounds assembled themselves in the course of time to form complex organic compounds which were capable of self-replicating, i.e., able to produce exact copies of themselves. Subsequently (purely by chance again) these compounds arranged themselves into a living cell.

But hold on; even the simplest cell is far more complex than the fastest and biggest computer system. Everything we *apparently* know about the origins of life is based upon speculation about chance occurrences. To me, this demonstrates our limited knowledge and understanding. But far more importantly, it suggested that there is a governing intelligence orchestrating matters in a way we cannot comprehend. As I was to realise, mathematics came to play an important part in answering some of the questions.

If chemical evolution is correct, then modern science should be able to replicate it in a laboratory. One of the most famous experiments – as the first of its kind – showing that under certain conditions, simple organic and inorganic substances can be converted into more complex organic compounds was carried out by S. L. Miller in 1953. Miller produced 4 different amino acids from a mixture of methane, ammonia, hydrogen and water vapour using high-energy radiation. In 1970, Richard Lemmon, a chemical evolutionist, summarised the results of laboratory experiments in synthetic chemical evolution as follows:

> The most important organic molecules (biomonomers) in living systems have been enumerated as the 20 amino acids of the natural proteins, the 5 nucleic acid bases, glucose, ribose and deoxyribose. Of these, laboratory experiments under conditions clearly relevant to probable conditions on the primitive Earth have resulted in the appearance of at least 15 of the 20 amino acids, 4 of the 5 nucleic acid bases, and 2 of the 3 sugars. In addition, representatives of biologically important nucleosides, nucleotides, fatty acids, and porphyrins have been observed. This research has made it clear that these compounds would have accumulated on the primitive (prebiotic) Earth – that their formation is the inevitable result of the action of available high energies on the Earth's early atmosphere.[4]

Impressive though they sound, these results only prove that under certain experimentally controlled conditions, simple organic and inorganic compounds will combine to form more complex organic compounds. They certainly do not *prove* evolution, as some claim. But this needs emphasising: we are expected to believe that life as we know it occurred on a far more complicated level than these experiments – without controlled conditions and purely by chance.

Chance and the laws of probability

As we have seen, we have 20 amino acids of the natural proteins and 5 nucleic acids. It should be possible to examine the hypothesis that we originated by chance by using the mathematical laws of probability. This can be done, since the frequency of occurrence of any given amino acid in naturally occurring protein chains, which have been sequentially analysed, is random. If we have 20 different amino acids and we want to construct just one molecule of a protein, by chance, 100 amino acids long with a particular amino acid sequence, then there are 20 to the power of 100 or 10 to the power of 130 possible different configurations of this protein. Let's keep it simple and assume that only 20 of these amino acids are contained in the primeval soup, and forget the rest. Now, the Earth's hydrosphere (the atmosphere in terms of its water content) contains about 10 to the power of 47 water molecules, so a 1 per cent solution by weight of these 20 amino acids means that there would be something like 10 to the power of 45 amino acid molecules. If all these amino acids linked up to form different protein molecules, just 100 amino acids long, three times every second, it would produce 10 to the power of 50 protein molecules every year. The present scientific consensus is that chemical evolution occurred over a period of 10 to the power of 9 years. This means that our primeval soup would produce 10 to the power of 59 different protein molecules. This is 10 to the power of 71 short of the 10 to the power of 130 possible different protein molecules that could be formed. This means that the chance of one molecule, of a simple protein 100 amino acids long containing 20 different acids, forming in a definite sequence, is 10 to the power of 71 to one against – i.e. 10 followed by 71 zeros. In simple terms, this means that it would take 10 to the power of 80 (i.e. *10 followed by 80 zeros*) years to form the *one molecule* of a desired protein from such a primeval soup.

The other major problem arising from simple probability calculations is that the Earth's primitive atmosphere was such that large numbers of amino acids would have formed – yet *only 20* are found in the building blocks of *all* naturally occurring proteins. Furthermore, every amino acid, except glycine, found in proteins that make up all living organisms, can exist in two forms, each being the mirror image of the other. They have the same relationship as a left hand to the right hand and are hence classified as 'right-handed' (or D, from the Latin *dexter*) and 'left-handed' (L, from *laevus*). The classification is purely spatial, as they have identical chemical composition and properties, along with the same physical melting point and solubility.

If life evolved by chance out of the primeval soup, we would expect to find life forms with protein molecules that had evolved from both D and L sets. However, we only find living organisms with the L variety of amino acids in their proteins. D amino acids are not found in any living systems *at all*. Yet the formation of amino acids from simpler substances *always* produces both D and L amino acids *in equal amounts*. Science has no way of explaining this. Logically, they should be present in equal proportions in proteins. Naturally existing proteins exist as an α-helix because the L amino acids are used to build proteins. If D forms only were used, the protein would be a mirror image of the one containing only L forms. If D and L forms were then linked, the protein would have no helical shape and would exist as a long floppy chain. If evolution had occurred as we are taught, we would expect to find floppy chain proteins – but we don't.

To complicate matters, only the D forms of naturally occurring sugars are normally found in living organisms. If chemical evolution was by chance, then again, both the D and L forms of sugars would be found in living systems, having been formed together in the primeval soup. What's more, only the D forms of the nucleotides are found in living systems; L forms are absent. In short, if D and L forms evolved in equal proportions, as they would have done in the primeval soup, the structure of DNA would not have its double-helix structure. It would be irregular and unable to self-replicate itself as it does. *This implies that some outside agency deliberately chose the foundation building blocks of all living systems. Chance had nothing to do with it.*

E. K. Victor Pearce, in his book *Who Was Adam?*, relates a good analogy which reflects the problems and argument for chemical evolution. I will quote all of it as it is very appropriate.

When the Melanesian* New Stone Age natives were discovered this century, the natives debated the origin of the white man's goods and aeroplanes. Some tribes were unwilling to believe that the white man had manufactured them in his own factories. They had never seen a factory, so why believe in them? They were also unwilling to think that the white man had outwitted the spirits of their ancestors.

Eventually they hit upon an amusing explanation called 'Cargo', as we shall see, but in order to illustrate our point we shall imagine a conversation which might have ensued between a native and a white man. If the analogy seems ludicrous it should be remembered that it reflects the arguments of some 'Origin of life' biologists, but stripped of their technical language, which can often hide fallacies. It is also relevant because we now know that the mechanism of life is made of non-living crystals.

A native stands before the airliner – a native who has only recently been introduced to metals and smelting. The white man, impatient at the native's refusal to believe in the white man's aeroplane factories, ironically dismisses the native's curiosity by saying, 'This is how the airliner originated. One day there was a terrific thunderstorm. Lightning played upon ore bearing rocks, and fused the various ores into lumps of molten iron, copper and bauxite. Again the lightning struck before the metals had cooled, so that the metals formed themselves into patterns inherent in their atomic particles. This resulted in simple components being formed – nuts, bolts, aluminium plates etc. Again the lightning struck and formed more complex components – cylinder heads, pistons, rings, wires ready insulated, turbines, blades, propeller parts, wheels, and melted some rubber trees into tyres and left all these in a heap.

Again the lightning struck and flung the heap high into the air. Some of the nuts were near enough to the bolts to respond to an inherent attraction and screw themselves together capturing another component in the process and so were selected for the developing plane. Other pieces fell uselessly as unwanted debris and so were not selected. After repeated lightning the major units were formed: engines, panel instruments, struts, fuselage, tanks, seats and lavatory pans.

Coincidentally, an earthquake ruptured the strata and released oil

* An island group in the Pacific.

from an anticline.* The oil spouted and poured itself into the tanks, reforming and separating into top grades on the way.

A final burst of lightning flung everything up into the air. There were far more parts than those required by any one aeroplane, but those which were lucky enough to fall into a viable position made up a complete airliner which throbbed into life and made a safe landing.'[5]

The probabilities of the above occurring naturally, by chance, are far higher than the probability of the chemical evolution I outlined earlier in this chapter.

The prebiotic atmosphere theory

Yet another problem bedevils chemical evolution: the assumption of the prebiotic Earth's atmosphere in the first place. The hypothetical prebiotic atmosphere is not supported by scientific evidence; it is purely a speculation. So the very foundation of all chemical evolution is unproven.

What, then, *is* the theory of the prebiotic atmosphere? The argument in favour of the existence of such an atmosphere is based upon the hypothesis that it must have been oxygen-free, as it is impossible to produce organic compounds in living organisms in an oxidising atmosphere (that is, one with oxygen present). A great leap of faith is therefore made, in assuming that the prebiotic atmosphere was composed of methane, ammonia, hydrogen and water vapour – the accepted view for chemical evolution. The problem is, there is *no* geochemical evidence an atmosphere with this composition ever existed on Earth.

The hypothesis is based on the processes involved in the formation of matter in the universe i.e. the predominance of hydrogen and the simpler elements in the early stages of the 'Big Bang'. It is suggested that at the dawn of earth's history, about 4 billion years ago, this predominance resulted in the composition postulated. During the first billion years, carbon dioxide from volcanic activity replaced the methane and hydrogen was lost to space. It is in this period that the 'primeval soup' was produced and simple cell structures in the form of algae appeared in the seas. These started to produce oxygen, which was originally mopped up by volcanic gases and iron rich rocks. Some time in the next billion years free oxygen appeared in the seas and the atmosphere. As a result the ozone layer formed and, protected from the intense ultraviolet radiation, complex living structures began to appear.

This theory makes many assumptions and replication of the conditions

* A fold in the strata of the Earth.

to check it is virtually impossible. To attempt to overcome some of the time problems dealt with earlier, it has been suggested that reactions were accelerated by absorption of simple chemicals on clays, but no evidence of this has been found in the rocks from these clays.

There are also areas of uncertainty as to the stability of the various chemical species in the unusual conditions operating at that period of time, in particular with the effect of intense ultraviolet radiation and heat. We are attempting to forecast the behaviour of a dynamic system in which the balance between build-up and breakdown of molecules is constantly changing because of variations in composition and concentration of reactants and in which there are great fluctuations in the supply of energy, and hence temperature.

Synthesis of complex molecules

Let us assume that the hypothetical prebiotic atmosphere theory *is* correct. Even so, simple organic compounds such as amino acids would not occur so rapidly, as we have already covered. And if they *did,* they would have to be converted to proteins. Proteins are polymers of amino acids and consist of many different amino acids joined together. They are difficult to synthesise from their amino acid constituents. Some scientists have, however, managed to polymerise amino acids in the laboratory by heating a mixture of dry amino acids at 175 degrees centigrade for 6 hours. Water is added and the resulting mixture allowed to cool. The polymers then form spherical globules, or microspheres. These microspheres have properties similar to proteins, but are in fact protenoids (prebiotic proteins joined together in cell-like spherical structures). For polymerisation to occur at all, an energy source – heat – is required. It is argued that this came from volcanoes and lightning.

An alternative theory has it that proteins could have been synthesised from their amino acid constituents in the primeval soup – a concept known as hypercycles. This posits that the primeval soup was rich not only in amino acids but also in nucleic acid bases, which are believed to have joined together *by chance* to form clover-leaf shapes, which then reproduced themselves. The stumbling block for hypercycles is that even their inventor Manfred Eigen, then director of the Max-Planck Institute for Biophysical Chemistry at Göttingen, saw them as purely hypothetical: '. . . creating a hypercycle by chance, required, of course, an astounding coincidence'.

In any case, hypercycles and microspheres are a very long way from even the simplest living cells comprised of a membrane permeable by certain substances, yet not others; such as: mitochondria, where energy is produced so that the cell can function; ribosomes, which play such an important role in the production of proteins; and a nucleus with its

46

chromosomes, composed of DNA which holds the blueprint ensuring the cell reproduces an exact replica of itself. Finally, the simplest living cell possesses life. This itself presents the scientist with such major difficulties that they cannot answer the problem of the origin of life.

Chapter 5

Origins of the Universe

Here I want to go back a stage further – beyond the origins of life to those of the universe itself. To get the most from what follows, bear in mind that there are 6 elements that are essential to our being. They are hydrogen, carbon, nitrogen, oxygen, sulphur and phosphorus, and they constitute the important molecules for life. Other elements required include iron, sodium, calcium and potassium.

A big bang?

The origins of the universe, according to accepted science, started sometime between 10 and 20 billion years ago when a so-called 'singularity' of infinite density exploded. Sounds technical, doesn't it? This eventually settled to create the whole universe, with all its galaxies and star systems that we perceive within our limited visual frequencies. To grasp this, imagine this event as a speck of dust, which we cannot see, and in which all the matter in the entire universe is condensed, suddenly exploding outwards. This is 'The Big Bang' theory. But remember what I said in Chapter 3 about theories, because 'The Big Bang' is just that; a theory.

For now, though, let's continue with this line of argument. After the big bang event, it is thought that the first particles were produced in the initial release of heat. These are called quarks, and later combined to form protons and neutrons. Protons are the positively charged electrical particles that are present in the nucleus of all atoms. A proton can be considered as a hydrogen nucleus, as all it requires to become an atom of hydrogen is just one electron. This can be visually represented by an ordinary hydrogen atom consisting of a central proton and one orbiting electron (see figure 5). Neutrons are uncharged protons.

There are 2 other forms of hydrogen atoms, known as deuterium and tritium. Unlike normal hydrogen atoms, these contain additional neutrons which make them heavier. This means that we have 3 different types (isotopes) of hydrogen. 'Heavy water' contains deuterium which is an essential ingredient for the atomic bomb. Some biblical scholars and

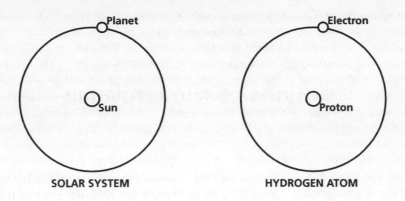

Figure 5.

new-age scientists have seen symbolic elements here, with these 3 isotopes being represented by the Holy Trinity.

At this stage in the universe and for some time afterwards the energy levels in the universe are such that orbiting electrons cannot exist and all elements exist as nuclei; atoms stripped of their orbiting electrons.

The two higher isotopes of hydrogen, deuterium and tritium, are unstable, tritium particularly so. It reacts with a proton to produce a nucleus of helium. The process of nuclei reacting with protons and neutrons continues and larger nuclei are progressively formed. The formulation route is often complex involving unstable isotopes which then split up figure 6 illustrates some of the major steps which occur.

1 .	2 protons	= Hydrogen
2 :	Hydrogen plus a proton	= Helium
3 :	2 heliums	= Beryllium
4 :	Beryllium plus a proton	= Boron
5 :	3 heliums	= Carbon
6 :	Carbon plus a helium	– Oxygen
7 :	Carbon plus a proton	= Nitrogen
8 :	2 Borons plus a proton	= Sodium
9 :	2 Carbons plus a proton	= Aluminium
10 :	2 Nitrogens plus a proton	= Phosphorus
11 :	1 Oxygen plus 6 Heliums	= Silicon
12 :	Silicon plus 7 heliums	= Nickel

Figure 6.

The Big Bang theory proposes that a gas-like soup (just like Earth's apparent primeval soup) of atoms and particles formed, whose components then slowly clustered together, due to the forces of gravitational attraction, to produce the stars and the planets we have today. Put simply, the humble hydrogen atom gave birth to all other atoms in creation, which in turn formed everything else. In the *Veda* (a 4,000-year-old sacred Hindu text), the Bible and various other ancient texts including the Osiris myths of Egypt, you will often find the reference to a notion best expressed by the formula 'As above, so below'. This can equally be applied to the macro and microcosm, as we shall investigate. That is, everything that is created in the Large, is created and reflected in the Small. In this light, the most intriguing thing about the composition of an atom is that 99 per cent of it is empty space.

The study of stars, Astronomy, literally means 'star arranging'. (The Greek component words being *astro*, 'star', and *nomos*, 'arranging'.) It has come to mean the study of the universe, and includes cosmogony (the study of the origin of solar systems and formations such as nebulae and galaxies). When most people gaze up at the stars they cannot help but wonder why we are here; this is one of the reasons that philosophy and astronomy were so closely linked in Egypt, Babylon, Sumeria, Ancient Greece and China. Astronomy as it is understood today only really took off again in 1609, when Galileo used a telescope for astronomical observations; thereafter it developed as a science due to such investigative minds as Copernicus, Galileo, Brahe, Kepler and Newton, followed by such later researchers as John Adams and Urbain Le Verrier. Now we are moving into what is termed 'post-modern astronomy'. This theoretical progress was started by the likes of Albert Einstein and the Russian Aleksandr Aleksandrovich Friedmann (died 1925) and now we have the Hubble space telescope (an orbiting observatory studying Earth, launched in 1990, which is a joint European and American venture). Nonetheless, even with technological advances, we still ask the age-old questions: What kind of Universe are we living in? What is its shape? Where did it come from?

'The universe is not only queerer than we suppose; it is queerer than we can suppose'

Scientist J. B. S. Haldane's famous quote is very apt, as we shall see. First of all, it is important to grasp the sheer size of the universe, starting with Earth. The planet Earth is 7,920 miles in diameter and revolves around its own axis every 24 hours. It travels at an average speed of 66,600 miles per hour and is inclined to its horizontal orbit at 23.4 degrees, or put another way, 66.6 degrees to its obliquity (the level of the equator where the Earth has tilted). (The number 666 is, of course, the often-mentioned number of the beast in Revelation, but we will also be coming across it in other circumstances, as 666 plays an integral part in the codes from antiquity.)

The Earth is 91,402,000 miles away from the Sun at its perihelion (nearest point) and 94,510,000 miles away at its aphelion (furthest point). The distance is often rounded off to 93,600,000 miles average, as an absolute figure is still not agreed upon. It takes the Earth a year, or 365.24 days, to travel once around the Sun. Our Sun, a yellow dwarf star with a diameter of around 864,000 miles, is a huge thermo-nuclear reactor in which hydrogen is continually being converted into helium, at such a phenomenal rate that it loses over 4 billion tons of its mass *every second*. Now, our Sun is just one of many suns that form the galaxy containing our solar system. Our galaxy, shaped like two fried eggs back to back, has over a 100,000 million stars within it. It is rotating at a rate where our Sun, which lies about two-thirds out from its centre, will take nearly 225 million years to make one complete rotation. Our galaxy is approximately 100,000 light-years across, and 20,000 light-years deep. Our nearest star is Proxima Centauri, 4.28 light-years away (that is, 25,200,000,000,000 miles), the nearest galaxy about 2,200,000 light-years away. Having taken on board the vastness of our galaxy, please try to retain these facts. It is estimated that there are *circa* 100,000 million galaxies in the universe. *This means that there are just as many galaxies in the universe as there are stars in our particular galaxy.*

Stars

The sheer number and variety of stars is enormous, ranging from red to orange, to yellow, to white and even bluish-white. Stars vary not only in colour, but also in brightness. Sometimes two stars revolve around each other and are called binary stars. Clusters are very common, too. Furthermore, stars come in various sizes. They can range from the type of our own dwarf star Sun, and Earth-sized dwarf stars that are much heavier, to, at the larger end of the scale, stars such as the red giant star, Betelgeuse. If our Sun was placed at its centre, it would still be many millions of miles from the surface. Then there are neutron stars. These are only about 5 to 19 miles in radius and are composed completely out of neutrons. They are so closely packed that they have a density approximately *100 million million* times that of water. Just one bucket of their matter would weigh roughly 500,000 million tons.

In 1054, Chinese astronomers saw a supernova explosion that was visible in daylight for 23 days and whose remains form the nebula known today as the Crab Nebula. At its centre is a neutron star. The Crab Nebula is 4,000 light years away and about 40 *million million* miles across. The neutron star is spinning very fast – 30 times per second – and has on its surface an area that emits radio frequencies. As it rapidly rotates, this radiation sweeps through space much like a lighthouse beam. This read on a radio telescope gives a reading of 30 pulses a second, hence these stars are called pulsars.

The most enigmatic stars are known as black holes. These are about five miles or so in diameter and are again composed of neutrons, this time packed so densely that a million, million, million tons of matter is packed into a volume smaller than a pinhead. The force of gravity is so great that even light cannot leave a black hole's surface; hence its appearing to be black.

Our solar system

Our solar system is apparently made up of 9 planets which revolve around the Sun: Mercury, Venus, Earth, Mars, Jupiter, Saturn, Uranus, Neptune and Pluto. There are also numerous asteroids varying in size from rocks to objects a few hundred miles in diameter, mainly found between the orbits of Mars and Jupiter. We also find meteors, which are small particles of rock and dust (we often see them burning up as they enter Earth's atmosphere, when they are known as shooting stars), and comets. Our solar system is the only one which we have studied in mankind's recorded history (see Appendix 2).

The solar system has obviously been the focus of human activity for millennia, yet any attempt to make categorical statements about its origins is doomed to opposition. Cosmogonists (those who study the origin of solar systems) have difficulty in producing any rational explanation for the origin of the solar system as we know it now, and many hypotheses are put forward. We cannot even agree on how our Moon came to be in its present orbit; we cannot state with certainty whether the rings around Saturn were the result of a moon that went too close to it, and then broke up into pieces as it entered what is termed 'The Roche Limit', or whether it is just residual debris from when the planet formed. Closer to home is the fact that our very own Moon appears to be a planet in its own right; we should, therefore, refer to our Moon and Earth as a binary planet.

The Moon (i)

Then there is our Moon itself; It is supposed to be 4,500 million years old. If so, such a small body would have solidified from its molten state a long time ago, yet according to geophysicists this solidification would have occurred even before the crust of the Earth had solidified. However:

• Moon-landing samples have proved that the Moon is still cooling and

has a large temperature radiance at its surface.
- It also has a magnetic field, indicating that it must have a fluid rather than solid core.
- The Moon is seismically active – sensitive instruments have revealed 'Moonquakes'.

These points indicate that the Moon is relatively young.

It has recently been argued by an American researcher, Robin Canup[1] of the University of Colorado, that 4 to 4½ billion years ago, a planet at least 3 times the mass of Mars struck the Earth a devastating glancing blow. After it did so, debris ejected from Earth coalesced to form the Moon. Canup and his colleagues drew their conclusions from detailed modelling of the effects of various impactor bodies crashing into the Earth. I would argue that this is not totally accurate, as it does not explain how the Earth 'spun down', to use the current term. During the actual collision the large impactor would cause the Earth to spin rapidly from the swiping impact, which it would still be rotating at today with no visible means of slowing it down. There is, however, an alternative explanation that does fit the geological evidence, as we shall discover.

The Cambrian explosion

It is worth noting at this point that the sudden diversification in the forms of terrestrial life on Earth took place about 520 million years ago, in a small window of time of 15 million years, called the Cambrian explosion. In geological time this is a mere blink of the eye. *Why* this occurred is a complete mystery. Joseph L. Kirshvink, Robert L. Ripperdan and David A. Evans from the University of Puerto Rico, writing in *Science*,[2] claim that a gigantic disturbance in the Earth's plate tectonics occurred during the Cambrian explosion period, resulting in a redistribution of mass inside the Earth and a 90-degree flip of the axis of rotation. This caused the North and South poles to move to the present equator and the equator to become the present poles. Sediment retained on the ocean floor nearly half a billion years old retains the weak imprint of the Earth's magnetic field, thus revealing the positions of the magnetic poles at that time. Such records indicate that continents moved rapidly to the magnetic field for just a short few million years around 520 million years ago, coinciding with the Cambrian explosion. In effect, as the magnetic poles are near the true poles, the continents must have shifted with respect to the axis of rotation as well, i.e. the Earth's crust slid over the lower layers in order to reach a more stable rotational state. The importance of this will be borne out later.

Joseph L. Kirschvink believes that during the pole shift, life on Earth had to cope rapidly with the sudden change in climatic conditions, and as islands of small fragmented eco-systems resulted, rapid evolutionary jumps occurred, of which only the fittest survived. I do not fully subscribe to this idea but it connects to current theories whereby asteroids caused mass extinctions and comets delivered complex molecules, maybe even the seeds of life to the newborn Earth. If a planetoid-sized object collided with Earth, it would encompass all the above theories in one, as we shall see.

The Moon (ii)

On 12 November 1997, the London *Daily Telegraph* carried an article reporting that the Moon was formed from debris from the early forming Earth which resulted after a collision with a planetoid object. This theory was in fact proposed as early as 1974, when it was calculated that a planetoid object the size of Mars would be required to cause the necessary debris to create both the Moon and Earth. Newer calculations show that the impactor planetoid would be three times this size. However, once more the problem is that if this is correct, it *still* doesn't explain the slowing down of Earth's rotation to its present speed, or why the Moon's permanently fixed orbit keeps one side facing the Earth.

Some scientists have argued that the Moon actually was part of the Earth that was ripped away from the present Pacific region, thus explaining its close orbit to Earth. I do not feel that this is the case, as I will explain in the next chapter. Other theorists assume that the Moon was captured into the Earth's gravitational pull millions of years ago. Unfortunately this defies the logic of modern astronomical science. If the Moon was travelling towards Earth, its size would have caused it to smash into the Earth – possibly destroying both in the process. If instead it passed close enough to be affected by the Earth's gravity, without actual collision, the velocity of the Moon as it travelled towards Earth would simply have slingshot it away on to another trajectory, taking it off into the solar system again. The atmosphere and the Earth's magnetic field alone would have ensured that the Moon was repelled.

On top of this, we have evidence that shows the Moon also suffered a major cataclysmic event nearly 4 billion years ago. A large number of breccia rocks, found on the Moon by Apollo missions, had been shattered and then fused together by sudden extreme heat. The Moon's surface layer also melted and its magnetic level declined. Another mystery: the large features on the Moon previously thought to be extinct volcanoes are actually huge craters, formed by massive impacts around 4 billion years ago.

These few points – I could have cited so many more – are intended to show that the origins of the universe and solar system present scientists with many unanswered problems. They simply do not know how long the planets, the stars or the galaxies took to form. Naturally, there is plenty of speculation, but often very little supporting evidence. Astronomical distances alone cannot be measured accurately as they are based upon unproven and unprovable assumptions. This area of debate is far too complex and involved to take further in this book. The point I have striven to make is that not all is as clearcut and factual as it might seem when proffered as fact.

With this in mind, I set out to see if a mathematical formula could resolve some of the anomalies and areas of doubt. I did this because I had come to realise that there appears to be a mathematical set that permeates everything we perceive and understand. In consequence, I started to study astronomy by applying number science to it. As I shall show, mathematical codes do follow a definite pattern. Not only that; my studies of ancient mythology and history revealed that the ancients appear to have known *these very same values, which they encoded within their myths and legends*. It also became apparent to me that a definite universal plan, which accords to a logical and systematic application of numbers, *governs everything*.

We have now covered the modern scientific approach to understanding creation and evolution, so now it is time to look at how our ancient forefathers, within their myths, perceived the same phenomena.

Chapter 6

Ancient Myths of Creation

The biblical account of Genesis has held sway for thousands of years, since the time of Moses, only seriously being questioned during the last 180 years. But is it the only ancient text dealing with the characters and events it depicts?

Beyond the confines of the Old Testament

Thirty-nine books make up the Old Testament, but they are far from being the whole corpus of ancient 'biblical' literature. The version of the Bible we have today was only pieced together from a much wider variety of sources and books after a council held at Nicaea (now Iznik in Turkey) in AD 325 under the aegis of the Roman emperor Constantine. He wished to clarify the muddle of overlapping and contradictory creeds that Christianity had then become, so that one accepted corpus of texts and doctrines could be established. By its very nature, such a council would exclude many gospels and accounts of the activities of Christ and the early apostles. There were – and still are – many books that could have been included but were then considered too controversial or heretical. One such book (familiar to many Mormons as it is contained within their 'Pearl of Great Price') is the *Book of Abraham*, dealing with Moses receiving the Ten Commandments on the Mount of Lawgiving. It also contains details from God about mankind's eternal spirit and his pre-mortal existence, the Sun, the Moon, the stars and creation itself. Then there is the *Book of Moses*. What really caught my attention about this was that it appears to allude to life on other planets. I quote the apposite passage in its entirety – see what you think.

> 32 And by the word of my power, have I created them, which is mine only begotten Son, who is full of grace and truth. 33 And worlds without number have I created; and I also created them for mine own purpose; and by the Son I created them, which is mine only begotten. 34 And the first man of all men have I called Adam, which is many. 35 But only an account of this Earth, and the inhabitants thereof, give I

unto you. For behold, there are many worlds that have passed away by the word of my power. And there are many that now stand, and innumerable are they unto man; but all things are numbered unto me, for they are mine and I know them. 36 And it came to pass that Moses spake unto the Lord, saying; 'Be merciful unto thy servant, O God, and tell me concerning this Earth, and the inhabitants thereof, and also the heavens, and then thy servant will be content.'[1]

The mystery of Nibiru

If such texts, contemporaneous with those now in the accepted Old Testament but excluded from it, have startling and thought-provoking images within them, what of other, even older texts from Sumer?

There is apparently another planet in our solar system that has only recently been discovered by modern science. It appears to have an orbit of some 3,600 years. Now according to ancient Sumerian texts only recently deciphered (see below), their gods came to Earth from a planet in our own solar system called Nibiru, and furthermore, their descriptions of it match precisely those of the 'new' planet being currently given by astronomers. Does this sound absurd? Then what are we to make of another Sumerian clay tablet depicting all of the planets in our solar system, including this extra planet?

The tablet is 4,500 years old; it not only shows all the 9 planets, but also a tenth. In all, it shows twelve major bodies, including the Sun and Moon. In addition to their belief in this 'new' planet, Nibiru, the Sumerians also regarded the Moon as a planet in its own right (see plates). In the light of that it is instructive to note that our Moon is actually *bigger* than one of the planets in our solar system (Pluto); hence my earlier comment that it should rightly be termed as a planet in its own right. The tablet was only discovered 100 years ago, before we even knew about Pluto; the key point is that whoever made it had identified that planet millennia before we had any idea it existed. And, don't forget, Uranus was not discovered by our science until 1781, Neptune until 1846. How come a 4,500-year-old Sumerian clay tablet has them all clearly delineated, together with the tenth planet that we have yet accurately to pinpoint?

The elusive tenth planet

The existence of a tenth planet has become known to science because NASA has recently found deviations in the movements of Uranus and Neptune that have convinced it of the existence of another, as yet unknown, solar body of at least 4 to 8 times the mass of Earth, positioned just beyond 7 billion miles from the Sun; it could, however, be smaller and nearer. NASA is absolutely positive of its existence and has only to give it a name. (These details also coincide with the mathematical formula that I have used in regard to our solar system – but that will be demonstrated later.)

This planet appears to have a very large orbit that brings it close to our Earth every 3,000 to 3,600 years. The last time it passed us would have been around the time of Moses and the Exodus from Egypt – between 1,600 and 1,400 BC. (This we shall look at later.) NASA has yet to confirm its exact size and speed, but estimates suggest that it will become visible to Earth and appear as a new star sometime between 2012 and 2036. (2012 is a very significant date, as I shall reveal later.) NASA's discoveries are momentous, but they are really rediscoveries – the Sumerian tablet showed all along that we have 12 major bodies in our solar system.

As I will discuss later, the Sumerians maintained that 450,000 years ago, people from this planet, Nibiru, came to Earth and taught them all their knowledge about the cosmos, as well as other technical and astronomical doctrines that included the creation of Earth itself. Their texts insist that the Earth was the broken half of a far larger planet. They appeared to be correct about the planets in our solar system; shall we choose to ignore them over this? Intriguingly, modern scientific and geological evidence, especially seismic information, has shown huge scar-like cracks on the Pacific Ocean floor. Computer imaging of the Earth, with all oceans removed, shows something very reminiscent of an apple with a chunk bitten out of it – in this very area. How could such fundamental damage be survived? The answer could lie with the idea of the Earth displacement theory – whereby the Earth's lithosphere (the Earth's crust), with its tectonic plates, floats on the Earth's molten mantle. In accordance with this it would simply cover over the missing area quite rapidly due to the huge spinning forces of its rotational axis and orbit. Look at a globe of the Earth. If you look directly at the Pacific Ocean, you will see something which is not so obvious on a flat map – the Pacific covers most of the visible area. This 'torn-planet' theory also answers the question of continental drift: the remaining landmass would rapidly be pulled apart as the tectonic plates move to cover the damage.

Sumerian names for the planets

Our Sumerian clay tablet is astonishing. It even goes as far as explaining that Pluto was originally a Moon of Saturn, which broke away from its orbit during huge cataclysmic solar upheavals. It clearly states that Neptune's largest Moon, Triton, has a retrograde motion. Perhaps not surprisingly, Triton wasn't even discovered by our science until 1846; it was even later before its retrograde motion was established. In addition, the Sumerians give details of the 5 apparent stages of the solar system's development – now accepted in some of the latest scientific theories. Not only that, they also introduced the 12 signs of the Zodiac based upon the 12 solar bodies. In fact, the Zodiac has what can be described as a Zodiacal cryptogram encoded within it – and this originates from Sumer. (We shall cover this later. It became connected to the Tarot cards that deal with celestial phenomena.) The Sumerians were evidently remarkable in most things. They evolved a highly structured society with advanced medicine and sciences, and laws and administration procedures that we still use today. For example, they employed the symbol of 2 serpents entwined around a staff for medical science, just as we do – it came down to us via the Ancient Egyptians and the Greeks.

The Sumerians called Pluto Usmi or Us Mi, which literally means 'He who shows the way'. The immense significance of this is that Pluto could only fulfil such a function for someone *entering our solar system from deep space*. Earth was called Ki, the 'the seventh planet', represented by seven balls and a crescent-shaped Moon. Again, this is extremely important – Earth is only the seventh planet when counted inwards from Pluto. Neptune was Ea – 'He whose house is water'. Neptune was always thought to be composed solely of gas until scientists were astonished to discover it was actually a small rocky mass surrounded to a depth of 6,000 miles by super-heated rich blue water; this was confirmed by a NASA satellite as recently as 1989. Jupiter was Kishar – 'Foremost of the Firmlands'. This could hardly be more apposite. Jupiter is so large that its body represents over three-quarters of the entire solar system's planetary mass (that is, excluding the Sun).

Only when the planets (including the tenth, Nibiru) are in the configuration as illustrated on the Sumerian clay tablet do the distances between them conform to Bode's Law. Bode's Law, first published by the German astronomer Johann Elert Bode in 1778 (though actually proposed by another German, Johann Daniel Titius, first), comprises a combined arithmetical and geometrical progression which predicts the distances of the planets from the Sun with reasonable accuracy. (It also happens to fit convincingly with something I shall discuss later.) (See figure 7.)

Planet X

Neptune was originally discovered by the use of mathematics due to irregularities in the orbit of Uranus. Similarly, Pluto was located after it was noted that unknown gravitational forces were affecting Neptune's orbit. Following the same line of thought, astronomers have become convinced that the irregularities in the orbits of Uranus, Neptune and

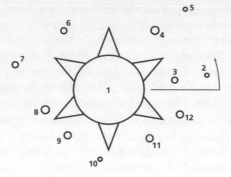

Figure 7. The Sumerian Solar System.
1: Ap Su = Sun. 2: Mummu = Mercury. 3: Lahamu = Venus. 4: Ki = Earth, the seventh planet as counted by Nibiru coming into our solar system from beyond Pluto. Ki also means 'To cut off, to sever, to hollow out'. 5: Duggae = Moon. 6: Lahmu = Mars. 7: Nibiru = Planet of the crossing, coming into our orbit once every 3,600 years. 8: Kishar = Jupiter. 9: Anshar = Saturn. 10: Gaga = Satellite of Saturn before it was knocked to its present position as our outermost planet where it became known as Us Mi = Pluto. 11: Anu = Uranus. 12: Ea = Neptune – 'He whose house is water'.

Pluto (and to a lesser extent those of Saturn and Jupiter) indicate an as yet undetected tenth planet. So certain are astronomers that it exists, they have called it, for now, 'Planet X'.

It was only in 1978 that the theory for Planet X really started to be taken seriously. This was when Pluto's satellite Charon was discovered, allowing measurements of Pluto's mass to be worked out more accurately. It turned out to be far less than expected, so deviations in the orbits of Uranus and Neptune were mathematically worked out to a higher degree of accuracy than before. (There is still debate on the exact details even now.) In consequence, astronomers Robert Harrington and Tom Van Flandern from the US Naval Observatory in Washington DC revitalised the idea of Planet X/Nibiru. In 1982 NASA itself officially recognised the *possibility* of Planet X, which I shall refer to as Nibiru from now onwards. In 1983 the IRAS (Infrared Astronomical Satellite) spotted a large, apparently self-illuminating object in the outer depths of our solar system. The chief IRAS scientist, Gerry Neugebauer from the Jet Propulsion Laboratory in California, interviewed by the *Washington Post*, stated the following:

A heavenly body possibly as large as the giant planet Jupiter and possibly so close to Earth that it would be part of this solar system has been found in the direction of the constellation of Orion by an orbiting telescope. All I can tell you is that we don't know what it is.[2]

The following years saw very little emerging in public regarding Nibiru (which gave the UFO-conspiracy theorists a field day, some claiming it was really a huge spaceship coming in from the Orion constellation). Despite the lack of subsequent disclosures, I was very intrigued as I had already come across Nibiru in Sumerian texts. Furthermore, the linguistic historian Zecharia Sitchin had written voluminous detailed accounts of the Sumerian and Babylonian myths relating to Nibiru. The little information released established that Nibiru was apparently 3 to 4 times the mass of Earth (though I disagree on this point, as will be explained) and that its position was 3 times further from the Sun than that of Pluto. Using a mathematical code (of which more later) that confirms Nibiru to exist, I deduced several years ago that it is in fact about the size of Earth and nearer than anticipated.

In 1987 the American journal *Newsweek* contained this report:

> NASA held a press conference at its Ames Research Center in California last week to make a rather strange announcement: An eccentric 10th planet may – or may not – be orbiting the Sun. John Anderson, a NASA research scientist who was the principal speaker, has a hunch Planet X is out there, though nowhere near the other nine. If he is right, two of the most intriguing puzzles of space science might be solved: What caused mysterious irregularities in the orbits of Uranus and Neptune during the nineteenth century? And what killed off the dinosaurs 62 million years ago?[3]

Then, in the late 1980s two things began to happen; firstly scientific journals started a major 'Nibiru-debunking' campaign, and secondly, NASA started pouring resources into expensive space-based satellite telescopes. Why the debunking campaign? The scientific establishment didn't do this with the other planets when *they* were discovered. This attitude gave rise to theories of some kind of cover-up by the authorities who were deliberately trying to hide something.

The Enuma Elish – *Babylon's creation myth*

Comparison with Egyptian and Sumerian historical facts has demonstrated that the Old Testament was not just a simple collection of stories with moral teachings and laws, but based upon real events, physical in origin, and encoded with symbolism and mathematical codes. Though often incorrectly translated, Old Testament stories still give a good historical account of mankind and its relation to those who apparently came from the heavens. As I will reveal in due course, in ancient Egypt, the basic concepts of astronomy were identical to those of the Sumerians, only later did they begin to differ. Both had systems of dividing their calendar into 12 months consisting of 3 weeks each of 10 days. Each week had a constellation of the night associated with it.

Thirty-six of those weeks added up to a 360-day year, with a further 5 days added at the end. Both cultures possessed knowledge (as did the Mayans) of the Earth's 25,920-year precessional cycle. The Sumerians maintained that this advanced knowledge was a gift from their gods. We shall be looking at these details later.

Babylonian myths were directly descended from Sumerian precursors. In 1876, George Smith of the British Museum translated one of the most important, a 4,000-year-old Babylonian text known as the *Enuma Elish* which I briefly mentioned earlier. It was a sacred epic, and Smith's translation revealed a far more detailed account of creation than that in Genesis. Sadly, as appears to be the norm, the translated story was regarded as meaningless superstition by Smith's peers.

Taken literally, the *Enuma Elish* describes the battle of two Babylonian gods in the heavens, but I do not think we should seriously believe that two so-called gods fought battles in the heavens for the entire world to see. A more plausible explanation of the texts must be sought. Such an explanation was proffered in 1976 by Zecharia Sitchin[4] when he postulated that the text accurately described the formation of the solar system some 4.6 billion years ago. Sitchin, an expert in Near-Eastern languages, realised that the references to 'gods' meant planets and satellites. (Immanuel Velikovsky, of whom we shall hear more, drew similar conclusions to the effect that the myth related to celestial phenomena and had direct links to the Old Testament.)

The *Enuma Elish* is so important that I shall assess its components in some detail. It begins by listing the gods begotten by Ap Su (the name for the Sun, as we have seen); Ap Su literally means 'One who exists from the beginning'. Marduk, the chief deity of the Babylonians, then battles against another god named Tiamat. (The role of Marduk parallels that of the Sumerian planet Nibiru. Marduk is interpreted by Sitchin as a wandering planet on a collision course with the watery planet named Tiamat. Marduk had entered the solar system, passing Neptune and Uranus on the way, indicating a clockwise direction as opposed to the other planets' counter-clockwise direction.) The text says: 'Tiamat and Marduk, the wisest of the gods, advanced against one another; they passed on to single combat, they approached for battle.' It continues that having acquired a 'blazing flame' and various 'winds' (satellites) Marduk 'towards the raging Tiamat set his face':

> The Lord spread out his net to enfold her; the evil wind, the rearmost, he unleashed at her face. As she opened her mouth, Tiamat, to devour him – he drove in the evil wind so that she closed not her lips. The fierce storm winds then charged her belly; her body became distended; her mouth had opened wide. He shot there through an arrow, it tore her belly; it cut through her insides, tore into her womb. Having thus subdued her, her life-breath he extinguished.

After he had slain Tiamat, the leader, her band was shattered, her host broken up. The gods, her helpers who marched at her side, trembling with fear, turned their backs about so as to save and preserve their lives. Thrown into the net, they found themselves ensnared. The whole band of demons that had marched on her side he cast into fetters, their hands he bound. Tightly encircled, they could not escape.[5]

As is apparent from the epic, Tiamat was extinguished. Marduk then became caught in the orbit of our Sun. Writers such as Velikovsky have noted apparent references to major electromagnetic discharges between the planetary bodies being exchanged in 'charging her belly' and 'He shot there through an arrow, it tore her belly'. The above recounts the apparent first encounter between the two gods (or planets), where Marduk's satellites have smashed into Tiamat. Later on, in Marduk's second orbit, he actually collides head-on with Tiamat:

The Lord paused to view her lifeless body. To divide the monster he then artfully planned. Then, as a mussel, he split her into two parts.

The Lord trod upon Tiamat's hinder part; with his weapon the connected skull he cut loose; he severed the channels of her blood; and caused the North wind to bear it to places that have been unknown.

The other half of her he set up as a screen for the skies: locking them together, as watchmen he stationed them. He bent Tiamat's tail to form the Great Band as a bracelet.[6]

The watery Tiamat, now broken in half, is further shunted by one of Marduk's satellites into a new orbit along with Tiamat's previous largest satellite, Kingu (which means 'Great Emissary', i.e. the Moon).* The bracelet has been interpreted as the Asteroid Belt, and Immanuel Velikovsky concluded that the Asteroid Belt was the remains of a single planet totally destroyed by Marduk (however, he assumed that this was the result of Mars). In contrast, I believe the above scenario explains why the Earth has such a disproportionately large satellite, the Moon.

If this is not enough to convince you that the ancients had an advanced knowledge of the creation of the solar system, albeit expressed in simplified terms, note that the account has Marduk/Nibiru creating the Earth and the heavens as outlined in the day one and day two accounts of Genesis. Also, it is worth noting that in the *Enuma Elish*, the elements usually translated as 'winds' are considered satellites because the literal meaning of the original is 'Those that are by his side'.

If the *Enuma Elish* implies that the Earth is the broken half of a larger

---

*This implies that Earth also had satellites smaller than the Moon, which were (presumably) either destroyed, or incorporated into the Asteroid Belt.

planet and the asteroid belt the other half, can we find modern scientific corroboration of this? Yes. In 1972, astronomer Michael Ovenden proposed a sophisticated theory in support of Bode's Law, which predicted the missing planet, if composed of all the material in the asteroid belt, would have been the size of Saturn. This is wrong if one takes into consideration only the combined mass of the asteroids, but it is correct if we combine both the Earth and Asteroid Belt to make one mass; that *would* equal the size of Saturn. For a diagrammatic representation of these events, see figure 8.

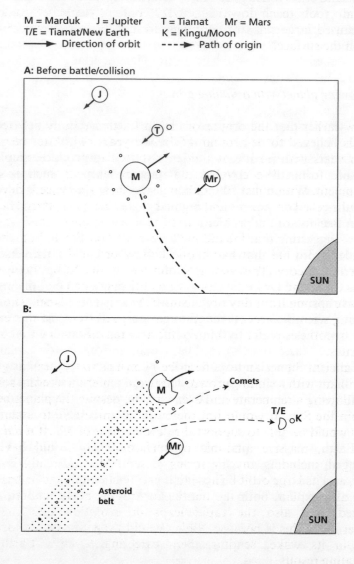

M = Marduk   J = Jupiter   T = Tiamat   Mr = Mars
T/E = Tiamat/New Earth   K = Kingu/Moon
⟶ Direction of orbit   ----▶ Path of origin

A: Before battle/collision

B:

Figure 8.

As we saw earlier, if we remove the water from the Earth's oceans, the hole left by the Pacific covers almost one half of the planet, with the bulk of the Earth's landmass on the other. This feature is unique to planet Earth, alone out of all the planets in our solar system, which all have a uniform distribution of land mass, without a concentration of mass in one area. The Earth displays anomalies. It has less than half the crust it ought to have, relative to its size, compared with other planets. Furthermore, why does the continental crust date to 4 billion years ago, whereas the oceanic crust (which is only five miles thick, in contrast with the dry-land crust which is 20 miles thick, and up to 40 miles thick where mountain roots reach down) is only 200 million years old? And again: what caused large slabs of continental crust to dive nearly 250 miles beneath the surface?

The glowing planet with a shining crown

We saw earlier that the origins of life on Earth are hotly debated. The Earth is believed to be around 4.6 billion years old. After nearly 600 million years with no life, it suddenly started to produce simple one-celled life forms. We covered the improbability of such a sudden development. Within just 500 million years, these simple cells developed into multi-celled organisms and highly evolved genetic material began to emerge. Because of the problems in this theory, many eminent scientists are now suggesting that life did *not* evolve here on Earth, but somehow descended from life that had evolved elsewhere in the Universe – the Panspermia theory. This view is supported by the Nobel Prize winner Francis Crick and Dr Leslie Orgel, who both suggested that life on Earth may have sprung from tiny organisms from a distant planet. The theory is gaining scientific acceptance, though most adherents of the 'external origin' hypothesis prefer to think of life arriving on Earth via a comet or meteorites.

The ancient Sumerian texts describe Nibiru as watery and as glowing and brilliant with a shining crown. This would infer an internal source of heat, allowing a temperate and even climate, despite the planet being so far from the Sun. It would not therefore be unrealistic to assume that Nibiru would be able to support the development of life. If it *did* collide with Earth, massive amounts of surface debris would have been exchanged, including any life forms present. Moreover, if Nibiru is a reality, and its large orbit brings it close to Earth on a regular basis, that would also explain both the many catastrophic mass extinctions that occurred, and also the rapid leaps in evolution on Earth (via Panspermia). This is because Nibiru would drag comets and asteroids along in its wake, sending them careering towards Earth, with devastating results.

Comets

Another bitterly contested area of science is the formation of comets and why they all orbit the Sun in the same direction against those of the planets. If they were simply composed of left-over material, known as Oort clouds (named after the Dutch astrophysicist Jan Hendrik Oort (1900–92)), from the formation of the solar system, as current astronomy informs us, we would have comets coming in from all directions; yet they don't do this. One open-minded astronomer, Tom Van Flandern, recently concluded that comets must have derived from a common source, such as an exploding planetary body.[7] As a result of using mathematical modelling he stated: 'The comets originated in the energetic break-up of a body orbiting the Sun in or near the present location of the Asteroid Belt.'

As per the diagrammatic representation in figure 8, we can see why they follow a trajectory opposite to the other planets in the solar system. If that isn't enough, anomalies in the solar system are now being attributed to an intruder planet as a plausible explanation for the unusual tilt of Uranus, the great red spot on Jupiter (of which we shall have more to say on later), the retrograde rotation of Venus and the eccentric orbit of Pluto.

Chapter 7

Numbers, Sound and Light

I have so far made but brief mention of a mathematical code that is inherent not only in the make-up of the universe, mankind and ancient myths but also in the layout of ancient sites in Egypt, the Americas and England, without fully explaining it. We shall look closely at its details later. However, as it is central to what follows, this chapter will introduce you to some of the relevant numbers and values. The calculations may perhaps be difficult to grasp on occasions, but they are essential to partaking in the evolution of my argument, so I urge you to take a deep breath and dive in – even if you hated maths as much as I did.

Pythagoras

The Greek mathematician Pythagoras (c. 580–500 BC), who was famous for his theory of the relationship between squares and triangles, taught that all things, including the laws of nature, are governed by numbers; this is evident both in the notes of music and in the chemical elements. Furthermore, Pythagoras and Philolaus (another Greek philosopher, of c. 500 BC) held that everything in the universe was linked to a number, each with its own special significance; 1, 2, 3, 4 and 7 were particularly special. Because of this, a device called the Tetraktis, which was composed of a square (4 sides) with a triangle (3 sides) above it ($\triangleq$), was deemed by Pythagoras (and Plato, c. 427–347 BC) to be the representation of a great truth. Pythagoras placed great emphasis on his trinity – air, water and fire – as its 3 components together (or so he maintained) made spirit, which being singular, was equal to 1. This trinity (air, water, fire) added to spirit (i.e. 1) gave rise to the mystic 4. These two concepts, the mystic 4 and trinity of 3, add up to 7. The number 7 was not only important to Pythagoras. It is contained in all major religious doctrines in one form or another. To give one biblical example, in Revelation 12: 3, a beast is described with 7 heads, 10 horns and 7 crowns. Later we shall also see several vital Egyptian connections with 7.

According to Pythagoras, everything was the number 1 and nothing the number 0, so therefore everything and nothing was represented as 10. Then in his reasoning came the primary 3, followed by the secondary 3;

67

these constitute the whole (1), represented as $3 + 3 + 1$ (331), which adds up to 7. This way of looking at numbers in terms of their component digits may seem unusual, as it is hardly modern practice, but once the principle is grasped, you can approach more closely the mind set of the ancients – so the effort *is* worthwhile.

In addition, it is known that 216 was regarded by Pythagoras as a magic number, since (as he said) it is 6 to the power of 3, or $6 \times 6 \times 6$; but beyond that, his reason for singling this number out is lost. However, its importance as a component of the universal mathematical code is easily demonstrated by the following examples (which I give to convey an idea of the all-pervading quality of numbers in the universe).

- Adding a zero to 216 (in numerology, it is acceptable to multiply by the power of 10 or any other figure that merely adds zeros, without changing the inherent value of the original digits) gives 2,160, a very significant number. It is the diameter of the Moon in miles (we'll look at the importance of the mile as a measurement, in due course).
- 2,160 years is the precessional period of each Zodiacal cycle through the heavens (of which, more later).
- $2,160 \times 12$ equals the total complete precessional cycle of all 12 signs of the Zodiac – 25,920 years.
- 2,160 divided by 6 gives 360, the number of degrees in a circle.
- When divided by 24 (the number of hours) the result is 90 – the degrees in a right angle; divided by 12, it gives 180 – and 180 degrees is significant, too.

These key numbers will recur throughout this book, especially in my analyses of ancient Mayan, Sumerian and Egyptian myths, so start getting used to them! If it helps, you could jot them down on a piece of paper for reference later. This may seem like too much work, but I earnestly ask you to take on board as much of this as possible.

Mathematics are the *key* to understanding the message from the past, and a grasp of the principles involved will enable you to share in the gradual unravelling of this great mystery.

Fadic numbers

Now I need to introduce you to Fadic numbers. Fadic calculations are most commonly used today in esoteric numerology, in connection with determining aspects of an individual's personality. However, they have a wider application, as I shall show. To find Fadic numbers, one adds up the component single numbers in a number with more than one digit, to find the lowest value. It sounds cumbersome but an example makes the process clear: the elements of 347 are 3, 4 and 7. When these numbers are added together they total 14. Then, if the 1 and 4 making up that 14 are totalled, the result is 5. So 5 is, by this process, the Fadic number of 347.

In Jewish mystical traditions (the Kabbalah, for example) it is taught that God has 10 faces and that followers of the faith should know them all. In quantum science, where scientists study atomic particles in an accelerator vacuum, a vacuum is basically 'nothing' which consists of particles that spontaneously create and annihilate themselves. Some authorities have given 37 as the suspected number of particle fields. In Fadic terms, this number is 3 + 7, which is equal to 10; i.e. in Pythagorean reasoning everything (1) and nothing (0).

So, according to both a specific religious interpretation and the tenets of scientific quantum theory, there was everything residing in nothing, symbolised by the number 10. From the very start of the universe itself, the basic building-block number was to be 10.

We can build from here on upwards: 1 + 1 could create either 11 or 2; then 1 + 2 became 12 or 3; then 1 and 3 became 13 and 3 + 1 became 4, and so on and so on. Once 3, 13, and 4 had been generated, alternative procedures can make 7: 3 + 1 + 3 or 1 + 3 + 3 or 3 + 4 . . . or just 7 itself once the formula has been followed to that point. An important appearance of the number 5 is when it is concealed in the combination 347, for 3 + 4 + 7 equals 14, and by Fadic addition, that equals 5. By this process, 5 is the Fadic value of 347, a very important number. For a diagrammatic representation of replication, see figure 9.

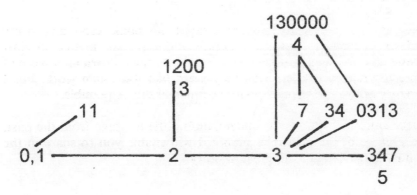

Figure 9.

Pythagoras's reasoning that 3 represents the primary constituents of an entity and 4 the hidden components is tellingly demonstrated by colours. The 3 primary colours, when paired, give 4 subsequent colours (yellow and blue paired make green, for example) and all 7 make up the spectrum. Earlier I pointed out that the Tetraktis was composed of a square of 4 sides, and a triangle of 3 sides. To cite but one instance of its use: the people of the important Jewish religious settlement of Qumran lived in an area with 4 sides that had 3 gates on each side.

Two factors – the number 7, and the numbers 1 and 1 equalling 2 – were of special significance to the unfolding mathematical structure. Because of this, these numbers were subsequently used to set measurements and distances. For example, 720 (remember in numerology the adding of zeros has no effect on the core digits, so 720 has the significance of 72) was used by kabbalists and the esotericists as a multiplier and a divisor on all the numbers that had been created for both the micro and macrocosm. Without an appreciation of the essential value of 72 and its variants, using 720 seems remarkably arbitrary. However, knowing what we now know, the reverse is the case.

Seven and the elements

Atoms whose numbers made Fadic 7 (by which I mean every created element) would be used in the microcosm to construct matter made of different 7s in the macrocosm. By establishing appropriate connections in its 37 (which, remember, was composed as 3 + 7, thereby giving 10 – which in turn is everything and nothing, or thereby the entire universe) energy fields (see below), billions of billions of 331s or 7s were created. Each of these atoms in the periodic table was conceived to be a minuscule particle moving around a spherical object, aided by forces of attraction. An example of this is the electron orbiting the proton in the hydrogen atom. See figure 10.

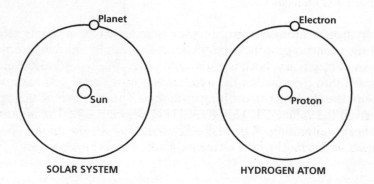

Figure 10.

The number 7 is arguably the most significant of all. This may seem an opinionated statement but I believe it is validated by the following.

The 5 most important 7s from the periodic table are:

Carbon	= 691 (6 + 9 + 1 = 16 = 6 + 1 = 7);
Nitrogen	= 664 (6 + 6 + 4 = 16 = 6 + 1 + 6 = 7);
Oxygen	= 655 (6 + 5 + 5 = 16 = 1 + 6 = 7);
Phosphorus	= 997 (9 + 9 + 7 = 25 = 2 + 5 = 7);
Sulphur	= 934 (9 + 3 + 4 = 16 = 1 + 6 = 7).

These are the prerequisites of all carbon-based life on Earth. So here, then, we have the pattern of small spheres rotating around much larger spheres, that in turn are rotating around even bigger spheres – not only on a subatomic, microcosmic level, but also on the macrocosmic scale of the solar system, galaxy and Universe.

In turn, the numbers 1, 2 (or 11), 3, 4, 347, 1,200 and 130,000 were to become most significant, inherent not only within our atomic make-up, but also in our solar system. The first 4 numbers, multiplied by the divisor 720, convert to 720, 1,440, 7,920, and 2,160. The first 4 figures equal, in miles (I said earlier that we would investigate the history of the mile as a unit of measurement at a later stage), the diameters of Charon (a moon orbiting Pluto); Pluto itself; the Earth; and the Moon. We already encountered 2,160 in this Chapter, and 144, with or without the extra zero, will become very familiar as we progress.

The last 3 numbers convert to 249,840 (347 × 720), 864,000 (1,200 × 720) and 93,600,000 (130,000 × 720) miles respectively. These are: the distance of the Moon from the Earth at their closest point; the diameter of the Sun; and the Sun's average distance from Earth. This has to indicate a structured pattern and planning on a phenomenal scale.

Numbers and molecules

The hydrogen atom consists of even smaller parts: a single electron orbiting a central proton. Invisible forces of attraction (due to opposite charges of electricity, both negative and positive) keep the electron from flying off into the void. In the hydrogen atom a proton (1) has another element, the electron (3), orbiting around it. The diameter of this orbit is also given the value of 3. This gives 331 (Fadic value 7). The importance of 7 bears reiterating: *7 is the Fadic number of all the known chemical elements on Earth.* (For the elements' Fadic numbers, see page 76.)

The periodic table

As pointed out above, scientists have classified the chemical elements in an arrangement of rows and columns known as the periodic table. The hydrogen atom with the value 7 (that is, its periodic table number – 331 – expressed in Fadic terms) encapsulates the blueprint for creating all

71

other atoms, by a sequential and manipulative use of numbers as well as redistributing energy. Helium, the next atom in the table (i.e. below hydrogen in the same row), equals 304 (Fadic 7). Lithium, the next atom, equals 1,114 (once more, Fadic 7). The values for the remaining elements in the same column of the table (labelled period 2) are: Beryllium 781; Boron 700; Carbon 691; Nitrogen 664; Oxygen 655; and Fluorine 628. Neon, the last element in period 2, is 601.

Sodium, which commences the third row (at the top), has a value of 601. The values of the remaining elements in this row (period three) are: Magnesium 1,222; Aluminium 1,132; Silicon 1,042; Phosphorus 997; Sulphur 961; Chlorine 880; and Argon 799.

Links with the solar system

To demonstrate that the connection of the Earth with the Sun is governed by a mathematical constant, I will use the example of the Sun's diameter, showing how it is directly proportionate to the division of time (hours, minutes, etc.) on Earth.

The diameter of the Sun is 864,000 miles. Significantly, there are 86,400 seconds in 24 hours. Not only that; if we then divide 86,400 by 24 we get 3,600. There are 360 degrees in a full circle. One complete spin of the Earth on its axis is 24 hours. As well as containing 86,400 seconds, 24 hours is also equal to 1,440 minutes. We have seen that 1,440 is a significant number; just *how* significant will become apparent later. The Fadic value of 3,600 is 9 (3 + 6), and what's more, that of 1,440 is also 9 (1 + 4 + 4) – again, an important symbolic number.

Let's therefore look at 9 in the solar system. The ninth planet from the Sun is Pluto, with its moon, Charon; these two bodies have diameters of 1,440 and 720 miles respectively. We saw in Chapter 6 that Sumerian creation myths about the Solar system called Pluto 'Us Mi' (literally 'He who shows the way'). This now takes on a two-fold meaning. It can mean that Pluto acts as a beacon showing the way into our solar system (as researchers such as Alan Alford and Michael Joyce have argued); but it can *also* mean that Pluto shows us an example of the mathematical code inherent in all things (using the numerical value of its diameter, and its distance from the Sun, for example). It is the only planet to feature such *essential* numbers, though the others have numbers that are significant in different ways. We saw earlier how the number 720 is used as the mathematical divisor/multiplier for space both on a micro and macro-cosmic scale (see figure 10). In a parallel way, it appears that 1,440 symbolises time, as it is an essential value for accurate time-keeping, related to the Sun's diameter and Earth's time periods of minutes, seconds and hours as given above.

We can establish further connections to the mathematical code in the dimensions of our Moon and Earth. The Moon's diameter is 2,160 miles and the Earth's 7,920. If we were to draw the Earth and Moon as though they were touching each other, then enclose them in a single rectangle that butts against the Earth and Moon, then draw a vertical line from one side of the rectangle to the other so that it passes where the two circles touch each other, we find that the Earth is enclosed within a square box and the Moon inside a rectangle – but both still enclosed within the original rectangle. If we then draw a horizontal line above the Moon, a smaller box appears. When a line is drawn diagonally from one corner to the opposite, two equal-sized triangles are formed. The lengths of the three sides of each triangle are 2,160, 2,880 and 3,600, and these numbers equate to the values of 3, 4 and 5 (Fadic value 12, or ultimately 3.) If we multiply by the 'space' number 720, we get: (3 × 720) 2,160; (4 × 720) 2,880; and 5 × 720) 3,600 (see figure 11).

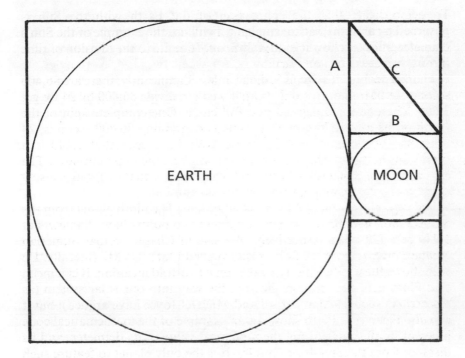

Figure 11. A = 2,880; B = 2,160; C = 3,600.

The Pythagorean triangle

The numbers 3, 4 and 5 have another significance: the length ratios as expressed in the right-angled Pythagorean triangle (a triangle in which two of the sides are perpendicular to each other and meet at an angle of 90 degrees). The ratio is also found in the 5, 12 and 13 triangle.

- $5 \times 720 = 3,600$ (360 degrees);
- $12 \times 720 = 8,640$ (864,000 miles = diameter of Sun, 86,400 seconds in 24 hours);
- $13 \times 720 = 9,360$ (93,600,000 miles = Sun's average distance from Earth).

The Pythagorean triangle of 5, 12 and 13 is of major importance in the quest to pinpoint the Hall of Records' final position – as will be revealed in the final chapters.

A prevalent theory is that galaxies were formed in a spiralling motion after the big bang; remarkably, Pythagoras also suspected the universe spiralled out in all 3 dimensions of space. His theorem states that the number obtained by squaring the length of the longer side of the triangle (the hypotenuse) is equal to the sum of the squares of the other two shorter sides. The 3, 4, 5 triangle represents this as: $3 \times 3 = 9$; $4 \times 4 = 16$; $16 + 9 = 25$; $5 \times 5 = 25$. The sum total of all the values is 50 (in numerological terms 50 can equal 5, which is another number which held special significance in ancient symbology). The 5, 12 and 13 ratio triangle is what we need to look at closely, for when two 3, 4, 5 triangles are contained within it, it gives a diagrammatic representation of how our solar system was contrived. I'll explain more later; meanwhile, see figure 12.

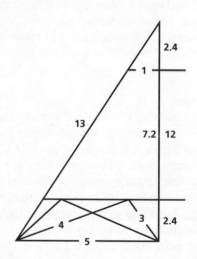

Figure 12.

Squaring the values of the triangle is important in Pythagorean theory. Of the 3 sides, one is equal to (13×13) 169; another (12×12) 144; and the third (5×5) 25; giving a total of 338. In Fadic addition – with which I hope you are now more comfortable – this equals $3 + 3 + 8$, giving 14, which in turn is 1 + 4 resulting in 5. These numbers, 5 and 14, are very important values in ancient Egyptian myths (especially the Osiris legend) and in temple alignments.

Sound, light and frequencies

Everything we perceive in our limited visual and audible world is governed by sound and light. As I worked on my theories about the essential nature of numbers I thought that if a truly universal mathematical plan existed, it would have to be present within these two things. So I started to see if there was a link. As we have seen, the mathematical plan seems to favour the numbers 3, 4 and 7. It would further appear that two 3s were to sustain a further 3 to complete the plan (i.e. $3 \times 3 + 3 = 12$).

Now 12 (Fadic value 3) is not only the value of the Sun (accept this for now; it will be explained in due course), but was also the number of the primary objects in our solar system.* The number 12 would form the very basis, so esoteric sources claim, of the music of the cosmos, generated as the planets rotated and moved around the Sun. In music, each note increases by one twelfth of the previous note, producing 12 frequencies of a musical scale. When I learnt this information I started to study harmonics, as I had read arguments that the ancients were thought to have used sound to move immense pieces of stone, as testified by structures (such as Stonehenge) which are still standing.

The spectrum

We have seen that the numbers 3, 4 and 7 are significant values. As Sir Isaac Newton discovered when he passed a beam of light through a prism, light consists of 3 primary colours: red, yellow and blue. We have 7 colours of the spectrum. Red, yellow and blue are the primary 3, and the additional 4 are green, orange, indigo and violet, giving a total of 7. (This of course fits what we discussed about Pythagoras and 3 + 4 at the outset of this chapter.) Now, an important point to bear in mind is that these 7 colours constitute light. Invisible white – i.e. light – can be made by mixing either the 3 primary colours of the spectrum or all 7 primary and secondary ones. I learnt colour matches during my first year at art college, but at the time I didn't appreciate just how significant this little snippet of knowledge would prove to be. As we shall see later, symbolic

* i.e. the Sun, the planets (Mercury, Venus, Earth, Mars, Saturn, Jupiter, Neptune, Uranus and Pluto, *plus* Nibiru, the tenth planet, *and* the Moon, which the Sumerians, as I have said, considered to be a planet.

references to light made by all major religious teachers have confused scholars for centuries. As an example, how many times have we heard Jesus's statement 'I am the way and the light' and if we wanted to pursue the meanings, found a divergence of scholarly opinion on it?

It could be argued that all the number connections are purely coincidental and adhere to the normal laws of physics. However, whether by coincidence or design, *a mathematical pattern exists* – that's the essential point. What's more, our ancient forefathers were very much aware of its presence, as we will see.

All elements have their radii given in nanometres. 1 nanometre is 1,000,000,000th of a metre (1 thousand millionth). As an example, an iron atom has a radius of 0.1165 nanometres. This means its actual length is 0.0000000001165 of a metre. To convert this metric measure to Imperial, we use a divisor of 2.54 × 63360, which equals 1609344. We do this as 2.54 centimetres equals 1 inch, and 63,360 inches equal 1 mile. We then double the ressult to obtain its diameter.

Example A
We therefore find the space-distance value for iron as follows:
An iron atom has a radius, in nanometres of 0.1165. We can ignore the decimal point, so the calculation is this: 1165 is multiplied by 2: the result is 2330. That figure is then divided by 1609344, giving the answer 0.00144779.

As we have seen previously, on the macro scale we *divide* diameters and distances by the 720 value to convert them to their space-distance values; now, on the micro scale, we *multiply* by 720. In this instance 144779 × 720 = 1042 (only first four digits used). This gives us our space distance value for iron: s-1042. In Fadic terms, of the answer are thus equals 1 + 4 + 2, giving a final figure of 7.

Example B
As a further example, let's consider Hydrogen. The simplest yet most important atom of all has a radius of 0.037 nanometres. Its value is 331, derived by the same method. Therefore, 720 × 0.037 nm = 26.64. As with iron (above), we then multiply this by 2; 26.64 × 2 = 53.28. We then *divide* this by 1609344. 53.28 divided by 1609344 = 0.0000331.

Thus the space distance value for Hydrogen equals s-331, which following Fadie addition, equals 3 + 3 + 1; that is, 7.

This method can be used on all elements using their radii measurements given in nanometres, as given in all good science books. Notice that the Hydrogen radii of 0.037 × 720 equals 26.64. These form two of our most important values, 26 and 64.

Chapter 8

Octaves and Omphalos Sites

I've drawn your attention to the fact that the notes of music play a part in my argument, but how can we be sure that the ancients were aware of the musical scale which we still use today? The best way is to look at ancient sites, known as Omphalos or oracle centres, spread out across the Mediterranean. Omphalos and oracle centres were sacred places of pilgrimage and worship.* The ancients thought it possible to communicate directly with the gods from them. The locations of these centres were originally believed to be set at random, with no particular reasoning involved, but on the contrary as we shall see, they appear to have been very carefully positioned.

The Argo and the Argonauts

Dodona, a major religious centre on the Adriatic coast in Greece connected with Zeus, was remote from other Greek centres of civilisation. However, if we were to take the stars that mark out the celestial representation of the ship *Argo* (figure 13) (since Dodona has links with the Jason/*Argo*/Argonauts myth), and then spread its projection out across the Mediterranean area, the most important stars in the constellation marry up with important ancient religious sites, Dodona being one (figure 14).

The most prominent star in the Argo constellation is that of Canopus, which was known as the 'rudder'. There was a town – now ruined – named Canopus on the northern coast of Egypt which was the most celebrated settlement in Egypt as far as the Greeks were concerned, and which superseded the even more ancient town of Behdet, in existence before 3200 BC and a major capital before the unification of Egypt and the establishing of Memphis as capital. Both city and star are said to

---

* Robert Temple's *The Sirius Mystery* quotes an excellent definition, from Peter Tompkins's *The Secrets of the Great Pyramid*: 'As each ... geodetic centre was a political as well as geographical "navel" of the world, an omphalos, or stone navel was placed there ...' The stones were roughly egg-shaped – assuming an egg with only the top ⅔ visible. Temple's book has several first-rate illustrations of them.[1]

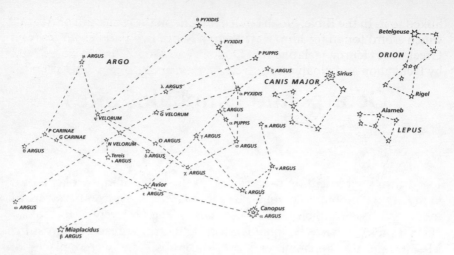

Figure 13.

commemorate Canopus, pilot of the fleet which Menelaos took to Troy. Canopus apparently landed on the Egyptian coast on the return voyage from Troy to Greece, and died there. The naming of the site was a tribute by Menelaos to one who had served him well. However, in the projection, the star Canopus not placed over the *site* Canopus, but over Thebes, to the south. There is a resonance between the Canopus the mariner and Canopus the star, as a sense of guiding or directing is present both in the notion of a rudder and in a fleet's pilot. Behdet was known as an ancient Egyptian version of modern-day Greenwich, in that it was used as the marker of a geographical centre. All this is puzzling, certainly. But is it more than that? (See figure 14).

Odd though it may at first seem, this investigation of the musical scale now needs to look briefly at myths that are surprisingly similar to the biblical account of Noah, his Ark, and the Flood. The Babylonian tale concerning a proto-Noah called Ziusudra (or Utnapishtim) who was warned of a coming flood or deluge by the god Enki, is much older than the biblical account. Depending upon which sources are read, this flood hero sent birds from his ark to seek dry land just as the later biblical Noah did. Here is a link to another legend; in ancient Greek literature, Jason of the Argonauts also sent birds forward from his ship the *Argo* to find the way through clashing rocks. Jason is associated with Dodona, and Dodona (along with Delphi) claimed that the Ark of the Greek Noah (named Deukalion) landed on a mountain top in its vicinity. In *his* legend, Deukalion (son of Prometheus) and his wife Pyrrha (daughter of Pandora) alone survive a heaven-sent deluge which obliterates a degenerate mankind, and repopulate the Earth by casting stones, which become people. Furthermore their union produced Hellen, a boy who founded the Greek, or Hellenic, race. Thus Dodona has 2 boat myths linked to it. In the Bible, Noah landed *his* Ark on the mountain of Ararat, which a bird found for him. Here then, we have two parallel stories (one Greek, one Hebrew) relating that Dodona and Mount Ararat were found by Deukalion and Noah respectively, both in an ark and aided by a bird.

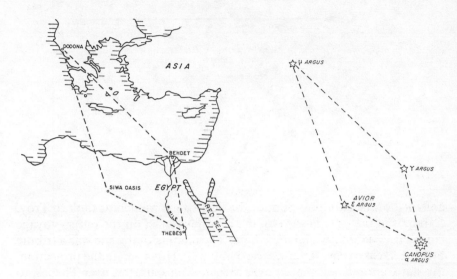

Figure 14. The geodetic pattern (left) and its similarity to the stellar pattern of Argo (right).

The striking thing is that both Dodona and Mount Ararat are on the same parallel of 40 degrees North. What's more, Dodona's religious function and purpose was paralleled by that of a centre at Mount Ararat called Metsamor, where there was an ancient astronomical observatory covered with mysterious kabbalistic signs and hieroglyphs as well as an industrial centre where metallurgy, astrology and primitive magic was performed, just under 5,000 years ago. There is a third connection. If you place a compass on Thebes in Egypt, an arc can be drawn through both Dodona and Metsamor. (See figure 15.)

Dodona is where the oak placed in the middle of the *Argo*'s keel was supposed to have come from, according to the Jason legend. Another mythological character now enters the story – Hercules. Tellingly, Hercules (in Greek, Herakles) was originally a character in Canopic* myths; his visiting Delphi and other acts were additions when the basic story was taken over by the Greeks. The earliest Greek versions of the story of the Argonauts make clear that Hercules was originally an Egyptian. What's more, it was Hercules, not Jason, who led them.

* Canopic is the adjective derived from Canopus.

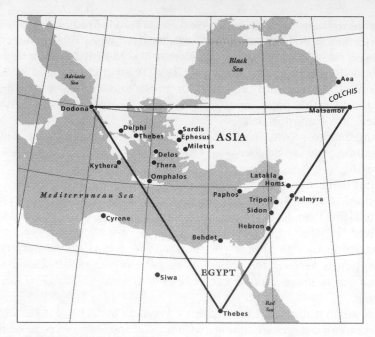

Figure 15. Projection from Thebes in Egypt.

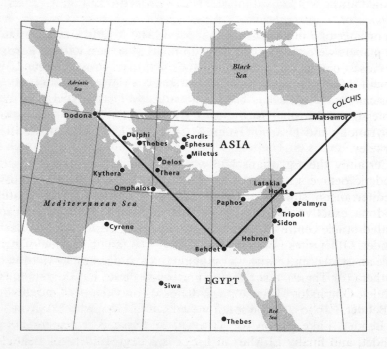

Figure 16. Projection from Behdet in Egypt.

To recap, we have seen the celestial Argo projected on to the Mediterranean world, with its rudder projected over Thebes. If, however, we do a different projection so that the rudder is over Canopus/Behdet and the prow is (still) over Dodona (that is, a *shorter* version of the celestial *Argo*), both prow and rudder are projected over their Earthly counterparts. Then, with this in mind, if we hold the rudder at Canopus/Behdet and swing the *Argo* over a map, moving the prow away from Dodona to the east so that it points towards Metsamor, the angle travelled through is exactly 90 degrees (see figure 16).

What is the significance of all this? Essentially, it shows that a highly advanced understanding of geodesics and projections of celestial constellations on to a sphere, using both latitude and longitude, was involved in the siting of these places – *thousands of years ago*. Remarkable though that is in the abstract, I have demonstrated the above points *because the projection of celestial constellations on to the ground was to prove a major key in helping to locate the Hall of Records' position.*

It is worth noting that the ancient Egyptians thought of distances of 7 degrees as an octave, an analogy with music, and that Egypt is 7 degrees long in latitude, measured from Behdet on the coast to the Southern Cataract on the Nile, in the south of the country. Anyone who has studied music will know that there are 8 notes on the octave scale – *over a space of 7 intervals*, i.e. 5 tones and 2 semitones. Once more the importance of 7 in ancient cultures is evident. A vital component is that the planets were also associated with musical values; what's more, they are closely connected to the Egyptian Isis/Sirius myths and legends. That ancient Mediterranean peoples knew the principles of the modern musical octave scale has been confirmed by Dr Richard L. Crocker, Professor of Music History, and Dr Anne D. Kilmer, Professor of Assyriology and Dean of Humanities, at the University of California, Berkeley.[2]

Certainly the Egyptians laid out their entire country to a precise geodetic octave scale, and this scale is further represented across the Mediterranean, starting at 1 degree north of Behdet and culminating at Dodona, exactly 8 degrees north of Behdet in latitude. Furthermore, the related oracle centre of Delphi is exactly 7 degrees in latitude north of Behdet. Other sites fall into place. Delos, the famous shrine of Apollo, once an oracle centre with an omphalos, is at 6 degrees north of Behdet. Kythera (or Thera), a site on the north-east coast, is 5 degrees north of Behdet. Omphalos (Thenae), near Knossos on Crete, is 4 degrees north of Behdet. Paphos, on the south-west coast of Cyprus, is 3 degrees north of Behdet. Lake Triton (or Tritonis) in Libya is 2 degrees north of Behdet; and finally El Marj in Libya is 1 degree north of Behdet (see figure 17).

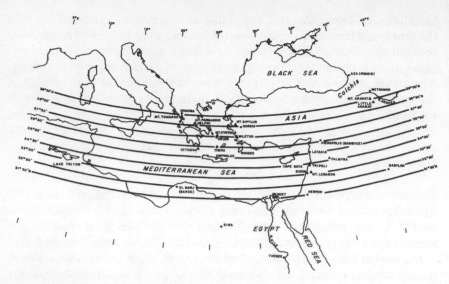

Figure 17. Eastern and Western Oracle Octaves.

The oracle at Delphi

The letter E (epsilon) is associated with Delphi, and featured on the Delphic omphalos stone.* In the geodetic octave scale, Delphi is the second descending centre. This fits well with the 7 vowels that corresponded to each of the oracle centres. They were uttered in succession as the 'Holy unspeakable name of God' by Egyptian priests. There is also an 8-letter version of the name for God in the Bible; Jehovah. Obviously, it has only 7 letters, but the Egyptian 8-letter version was spelt JEHUOVAO. The crux here is that in both cases, the second letter is E, and E, the second letter in descending order on the projection over the Mediterranean, is engraved on the omphalos stone at Delphi. This may seem just an interesting coincidence to the reader, but as we shall see later, the name Jehovah has a direct connection with the Great Pyramid of Giza. (However, perhaps because so much has been destroyed, no other corresponding letters – e.g. J at the first site, Dodona – have yet come to light.)

Nonetheless, from evidence available so far, it would appear that there is a geodetic spelling out, across 8 degrees of latitude, of the unspeakable name of God, known to the Hebrews as Jehovah but in its Egyptian form spelt Jehuovao.

At Delphi itself, during religious rites an immense boat was carried along in procession. Shaped like a crescent, it was variously called an

---

* *The Sirius Mystery* (Temple) reproduces ancient coins showing the E as though at the entrance of the Temple of Apollo at Delphi.

Omphalis, or Umbilicus (the navel link is evident), or the ship *Argo*. In the story of Jason and the Argonauts, it was the Oracle at Delphi that ordered the Golden Fleece to be brought back from Colchis. (Many years after first delving into the mysteries of Dodona, Delphi and the Argonauts, when living in England once more, I would look closely at the connections between Colchis and a major Roman city in southern England . . .)

Oannes and omphalos stones

Sculptural representations of the Sumerian aquatic god Oannes (see figure 1) connect him with omphalos stones. Note that Oannes carries a basket in his left hand. This feature is a constant element of his iconography – it is a sacred basket. Although this is hard to see in figure 1, the basket features two doves' heads turned away from each other at its top, and is covered with a mesh; the same mesh is found on some omphalos stones and is supposed to represent longitude and latitude. A celebrated example of the basket, showing these features clearly, was found at Khorsabad in modern Iraq (see figure 18).

Can ancient Sumerian literature about Oannes provide further insights? Yes. Tablet texts referring to Oannes also mention a vessel known as the Magurru boat. Now the Magurru boat is identified as being the celestial Magan boat of Egyptian mythology, associated with Osiris and Isis, which was later taken into Greek myth as the *Argo*. The Sumerian/Babylonian text the *Epic of Gilgamesh* has so many telling references in it that it is worth quoting pertinent extracts. Line 80 maintains: (1) 'The prow of the Magurru boat was not cut down.' Now read line 98: (2) 'The prow of the Magurru boat was cut down.'[3] These two statements have baffled scholars for years. However, it seems that line 80 (1) refers to the *Argo* as projected from Thebes to Dodona (figure 15), while line 98 (2) refers to the projection of the *Argo* from Behdet to Dodona (figure 16); the latter would require the cutting down, or

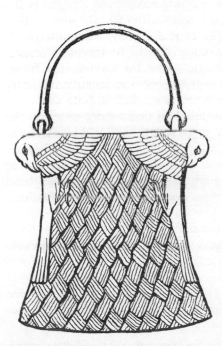

Figure 18.

shortening, of the prow, to avoid the *Argo* extending beyond Dodona. The gist of the poem continues by stating that as long as the prow *was not* cut down, the people of foreign lands were not overwhelmed, i.e. the projection did not fall across them. In contrast, when the prow *was* cut down or shortened, the projection left Mesopotamia/Sumer altogether and then the peoples of foreign lands were overwhelmed. In other words, the projections extended across other countries.

Oannes was often equated with the god Enki (Ea). Enki slept at the bottom of a watery abyss – just as Oannes did by retiring to the sea at night. In early Sumerian and Babylonian myths Enki was responsible for the Ark, from which the biblical Ark was derived. In the Greek version of the Ark story, Deukalion's landing site was claimed both by Dodona and by Delphi. We have also seen that a ship was certainly carried in procession at Delphi. But what of Dodona? We know that Dodona was founded from Thebes in Egypt. Thebes is equidistant from both Dodona (where the Greek Ark may have landed) and Mount Ararat/Metsamor (where the Hebrew Ark landed). The 3 positions, when joined together, form a perfect equilateral triangle – refer back to figure 15. Also, the oasis at Siwa with its Oracle of Amun was founded from Thebes. The Siwa oasis (one of the oracle centres linked to the letters of JEHUOVAO, as Delphi was) and Thebes are both equidistant from Behdet.

When I first came across these compelling details in Cyprus in 1976 as I read Robert Temple's *The Sirius Mystery*, I had no idea where the information they contained would take me; but they certainly remained in my mind. In fact, this led me to investigate further the idea of celestial projections on the Earth in many different historic and prehistoric sites, and eventually proved a vital clue in locating the Hall of Records.

Chapter 9

Global and Cosmic Connections

All myths and legends from across the ancient world, *on all five continents*, contain the same numbers and almost identical stories; the stories just having different names. These names, however, are *practically identical* when converted into mathematical code by the process called 'gematria' – i.e. Alpha = 1; Beta = 2, and so on. By this I mean that each vowel, letter or word has a specific value, and even though names in various legends are different, the mathematical figures contained within them still have the same value. We shall cover this later; in this brief introduction to the principle – which is at the core of my argument – I want to draw your attention to a small selection of examples from several diverse civilisations that will make the use of mathematical codes easier to perceive.

Egyptian gods

Before looking at Egypt, we need to understand the relationships between the key deities in Egyptian theology.

Many ancient Egyptian cities originally had gods of their own, but the gods who play a part in this story are those who originated at the city of Heliopolis and its cult of the Sun, and who came to predominate throughout Egypt. This particular pantheon, called the Ennead (from a Greek word meaning 'group of 9'), was presided over by Atum-Ra (actually a combining of 2 gods, Atum and Ra, the Sun god), who brought himself into existence in the form of a man. From his seed released though masturbation arose 2 cosmic gods, one of each gender: Tefnut, goddess of moisture, and Shu, god of the air. This pair in turn produced Geb, god of the Earth, and Nut, goddess of the sky. The siblings were interrupted by Shu in the act of sexual intercourse, but Nut nevertheless gave birth to 4 deities – Osiris and Seth (male) and Nephthys and Isis (female) – who had human form and lived on Earth. The ninth and final member of the Ennead was Horus, only son of the posthumous sister-and-brother union of Isis and Osiris, who themselves were deemed the first rulers of Egypt.

Osiris was the eldest of the 4, born at Rostau at Memphis (capital of

Egypt). Representations show him as a man, often wrapped as a mummy with his arms left free, allowing him to grasp a crook and flail. On his head was the atef, a white cone-shaped device that was the crown of Lower Egypt, flanked by plumes and the horns of rams. Osiris was the god of grain and is associated with the motif of a sack full of grain that has started to grow, with green shoots; he himself was also sometimes shown with green skin. Seth (or Set) his younger brother was Osiris's enemy, because of jealousy, and was responsible for his death and, in some legends, dismemberment; Isis used her deceased brother's sperm to fertilise her; that was how Horus was conceived. Isis was essentially a mother figure, and her distinguishing emblem was a sun disk encircled by a throne or a circlet of horns, worn on her head, though she was also shown as a kite. Seth was the god of chaos and was associated with violence, strife and discord. After killing Osiris he was later an equally implacable enemy to his nephew Horus, whom Isis had to defend. Seth's characteristic image was as a man with a stylised animal's head featuring a pronounced snout (vaguely like that of an anteater) and ears held upright, though he took many other forms in art, including a crocodile, a hippo and wholly invented animals. Nephthys was associated with death and funerary matters and in some accounts mates with Osiris to give birth to Anubis, a jackal (or merely jackal-headed) mortuary god. Nephthys's 'crown' was the hieroglyph meaning mansion.

Horus was apparently born at Khemmis in the Nile Delta. His main emblem was the falcon – either he took its form completely or was a man with a falcon's head – but the Eye of Horus, a stylised eye accentuated by make-up in a way common in much Egyptian art, is also prevalent, arising from the legend that Seth ripped one of Horus's eyes out, only to find it restored by Isis. This device has several meanings, one of which is a protection against the evil of Seth. Resonantly, accounts tell of his mother Isis hiding the infant Horus in the marsh reeds of the Nile Delta. Depictions of Horus as a naked child are frequent, and he can also be seen as a child with his mother Isis, in a configuration that some have said previsions the later Christian image of the Virgin and Child.

As their cults expanded the iconography of these key characters – Osiris, Isis, Seth, Nephthys and Horus – diversified, while the stories of their relationships, conflicts and areas of dominion grew more elaborate. The above is just the barest outline of their differentiating qualities, and I urge you to commit these to memory, since they will play a vital part in the unravelling of this mystery. Furthermore, I hope it is immediately evident that the important numbers 4 and 9 are integral components of this legend.

The ancient Egyptians

Mathematical figures constantly appear in ancient Egyptian religion and mythology. Their use is especially prevalent in the Osiris myths, which contain many numerical values relating to the Earth's precessional cycles and 'wobble'. This is where the position of the sunrise on the vernal equinox completes one shift of one degree along the ecliptic in relation to its stellar background. It also deals with the time required for the Sun to pass through two full Zodiacal segments equalling 60 degrees and the time for 'the great return', when the Sun shifts 360 degrees along the ecliptic. 72 years equals 1 degree.

How are these numbers – 360, 72, 30 and 12 – linked to Osiris? The myth baldly states certain numbers: it says that there are 360 days (called deacons) in the year, which is divided into 12 months, each of 30 days; in addition Seth, Osiris's evil brother, conspired to kill him, and had 72 conspirators to help him.

When we take the number 30 and multiply it by 72, we get 2,160, which equals one complete Zodiacal precession of 30 degrees along the ecliptic. $2,160 \times 12 = 25,920$ (as shown above, another important number), just as 360×72 also equals 25,920.* This is the number of years in one complete precessional cycle or 'Great Year'. Nonetheless, the most prominent number in the Osiris myths is undoubtedly 72. It often had a zero added in numerology, making 720, a number we will certainly see more of. Furthermore, 72 was frequently added to 36 or 720 to 360, giving 108 or 1,080; again, a number that will recur in the unfolding of my argument. When first studying the Osiris/Orion myths I became immediately aware of the connection between the number 72 and the star Sirius. For example, the Egyptians referred to the time when Sirius rose for a period of 72 days as the 'Dog days', which were scorching.

The Maya of Central America

In the Mayan 'Long Count' calendars, details for calculating precession are found as follows:† 20 kins (days) = 1 uinal; 18 uinals = 1 tun; 20 tuns = 1 katun; 20 katuns = 1 baktun. In this system, then, 1 katun = 72,000 days; 1 tun = 360 days; 2 tuns = 720 days; 1 baktun = 144,000 days; 5 baktuns = 720,000 days; 6 katuns = 43,200 days; 6 tuns = 2,160 days; and 15 baktuns = 2,160,000 days. Is this yet another coincidence or an indication of the worldwide significance of key numbers? Following the progress of my argument will provide the answer.

*2,160 and 25,920 are the times *traditionally* ascribed to complete zodiacal precession of 30 degrees along the ecliptic and to the whole 360 degrees.
†From Adrian Gilbert and Maurice Cotterell, *The Mayan Prophecies*, Element Books, Shaftesbury, 1995.

The Chinese

Ancient Chinese traditions from as far back as 1,400 BC refer to a universal cataclysm, and are written in texts consisting of exactly 43,200 volumes. 432,000 years was attributed by the 3rd-century BC historian, Berossus, to the reign of the mythical kings who ruled Sumer before the great flood. He also ascribed 2,160,000 (obviously based on half of 43,200) years to the time between creation and universal catastrophes. Coincidence once more?

The writers of the Bible

The Hebrew kabbalists in the centuries before Christ were very aware of mathematical values and consequently encoded them within their sacred writings. Later, the mysterious and unknown founders of early Christianity, whose works and ideas were subsequently thoroughly suppressed, expressed their sacred writings in number code to guarantee the persistence of its message across time. As a result, many passages, and whole books, of the New Testament are full of numerical codes. Two of the most prominent numbers in the numerical canon were (and still are) 666 and 1,080. The number of 'The Beast' in Revelation 13, 666, esoterically signifies the positive and active charge of solar energy, while 1,080 represents the opposite and complementary principle in nature, its negative, receptive side associated with the mystic Moon and its influence on the waters.

Other indications

The Moon has another link with 1,080: its radius is 1,080 miles (and remember, I will show there is more significance in the mile as a unit of measurement than you might think), giving a diameter of 2,160 miles. What else is noteworthy where 108 is concerned?

- 108 equals the atomic weight of silver;
- 1,080 is the average number of breaths a human being draws in one hour;
- 10,800 is the number of stanzas in the *Rigveda* – a corpus of ancient Sanskrit writings;
- 10,800 is the number of bricks in an Indian fire altar;
- 108 is the number of beads on the Hindu or Buddhist rosary.

If we add both the positive and negative – the Yang and Yin – values of 666 and 1,080, the result is 1,746. Mystically this is seen as the fusion between good and evil, and perfect balance of unity. This is the number *par excellence*, as we shall discover. Of all the number values in this book, spray this one on your wall if needs be. Whatever you do, remember it, because 1,746 *is of absolute importance in revealing the hidden codes of ancient civilisations and, ultimately, the location of the Hall of Records itself.*

I believe that even so small a sample as this clearly indicates that ancient numerical values must have some significance. We have already seen that they are inherent within the composition of our solar system. My argument is that this shows that the ancients amalgamated complex mathematical values into their myths and legends, but *without knowing the exact reasons why, or what these values signified.* This indicates that the information must have come from an earlier source, one which *did* know and understand what the values represented. From the numerical values, I was eventually able to fit them to the dimensions of ancient sacred sites and temples all across the world. This, I contend, indicates that some intelligence had a unified plan. The spur to my years of research was wanting to know what that plan was. My goal was to reveal the message the ancients intended to convey to us via mathematical codes.

As we shall see, it was not just simply about solar dimensions and Earth statistics. That was just the beginning of the clue

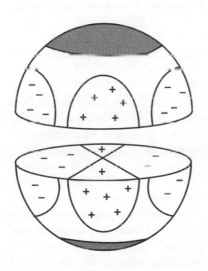

Figure 19. Sectional view of the equatorial region of the Sun, showing idealised magnetic field distribution.

The Sun

As we saw in Chapter 5, the Sun is a yellow dwarf star with a mean diameter of 864,000 miles, 93,600,000 miles away from Earth. It has two very distinct magnetic fields. One extends between the North and South Poles, the other consists of four 'bubbles' of magnetism equally spaced around the Sun's equatorial region (see figure 19).

The Sun's magnetic fields

The Sun spins on its own axis, just as the Earth does. It takes 26 days to complete one rotation around its equatorial region, while the polar regions take longer – 37 days. This movement involving two varying times is known as the differential rotation of the Sun's magnetic fields. Magnetic activity within the Sun causes emission of both negative- and positive-charged particles from its surface, which are scattered into space in the way that a water sprinkler scatters droplets – a phenomenon known as the solar wind.

The equatorial region travelling faster than the polar regions is almost entirely due to the Sun's nearest satellite the planet Mercury, and its gravitational effect. Because of its tilt, the Sun's equator lies at an angle of 7 degrees to the ecliptic, i.e. the posited horizontal value for the solar system (that number 7 again!). Mercury follows this trajectory around the Sun's equator, effectively pulling it with its own gravitational influence, thereby increasing its speed and reducing the rotation period to 26 days. However, the Sun's equator is moving very fractionally faster than Mercury; this discrepancy indicates, according to some researchers, that Mercury cannot be solely responsible for the Sun's increased speed at the equator.

The Sun's differentially rotating magnetic fields also appear to be a contributing factor to its equator spinning faster than its polar regions (though this has still to be proved). The Sun's magnetic fields are certainly thought to be responsible for the huge solar flares and Sunspot activity. The model proposed by Babcock and Leighton shows the basic mechanism responsible for winding up the solar magnetic field by its differential rotation. Sunspots then appear on patches of the Sun's surface, which have been pierced by magnetic loops from the interior. As a result, the Sun spews out huge solar flares that subsequently bombard the Earth with charged particles – the solar wind (see figure 20). The occurrences of winding up and of Sunspot activity are apparently predictable, and as we shall show later, the Mayans went to great lengths to predict these cycles – for good reasons.

As the equatorial region rotates faster than the poles, the magnetic polar fields become wound up to form what is known as a 'toroidal field', which varies in strength depending on latitude. Below the Sun's surface, the magnetic lines of force become tangled up with each other and burst outwards, forming a pair of magnetically linked Sunspots with accompanying solar flare activity.

Sunspots appear in cycles of 11.49 years, on average. These cycles themselves follow a repetitious pattern on a 187-year cycle, eventually causing (it is assumed) the Sun's magnetic field to reverse every 3,740 years (or 1,366,040 days). The Maya carefully monitored this period using the planet Venus: 2,340 revolutions of Venus round the Sun is equal to 1,366,040 days, and to the Maya 1,366,040 was known as 'The Birth of Venus' number. Such awareness shows that ancient cultures had an advanced knowledge of astronomy and astrophysics.

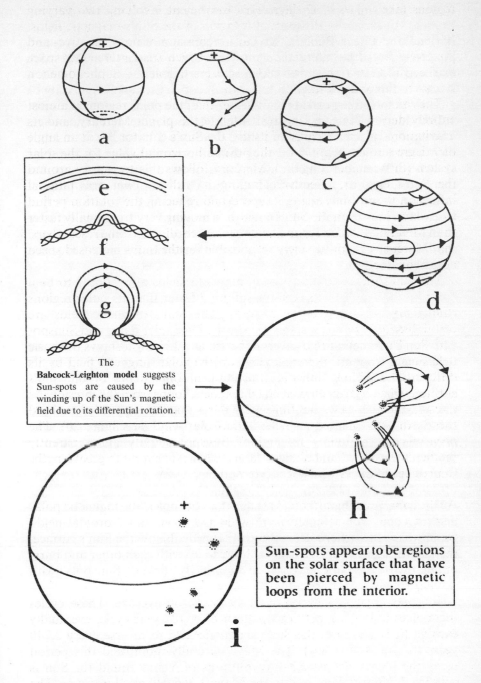

The **Babcock-Leighton model** suggests Sun-spots are caused by the winding up of the Sun's magnetic field due to its differential rotation.

Sun-spots appear to be regions on the solar surface that have been pierced by magnetic loops from the interior.

Figure 20.

Connections with the Great Pyramid

Around the Great Pyramid at Giza, there was once a 26-foot-high limestone wall (the materials came from the quarry at Turah) which enclosed a court (remember the 26-day period of the Sun's equator). Access to this court, known today as the mortuary temple, could only be gained via something called the valley temple causeway – which measures 1,739.8 metres on its inside edge, and 1,746 metres on its outside edge. The important point here is that there were also 5 statue niches, as they have been termed, and a false door that all eventually became standard elsewhere. What the 5 niches were for is open to speculation and it is merely assumed they simply held statues. This is an important piece of information, not only for the number of niches, but also the fact that when referring to niches, Egyptologists assumed that they must have been for statues – what other purpose could they possibly have? We shall see later just exactly what the niche in the Great Pyramid's Queen's Chamber stood for!

Serious implications

The Sun's magnetic fields reverse five times every 18,139 years. As the field swings from one direction to the other, it tends to twist the Earth's crust around its axis – this is recorded in the reversed magnetic fields contained in surface strata of Earth's rocks. In the worst-case scenario, the whole Earth may shift on its axis, if not totally flip over, causing cataclysmic destruction. *Precisely this kind of event is recorded **as having taken place** in every major religion and myth around the world.* As we shall see, both the Maya and ancient Egyptians held that we are now in the 'fourth age of man', which is due to end in the year 2012. After that, the fifth age of man will begin.

We are approaching the next magnetic polarity reversal due in 2012, and solar activity is definitely on the increase; several substantial Sunspot groups have recently been observed. It is probable that this activity will increase further.

What will be the implications for mankind?

PART TWO

EARTH, MOON, SUN
AND PRECESSION

Chapter 10

The Earth, the Moon
and Pythagoras

The Earth remains, at heart, a mystery. Even with all our technology, scientists are not in agreement as to the precise composition of the Earth's interior. Furthermore, as we have seen, there is considerable confusion as to how exactly the Earth was formed. The orthodox consensus has it that the Earth formed from a concentration of gas and particles which, due to gravitational effects from the Sun, swirled together and coalesced into a huge spinning mass. This eventually concentrated itself and slowly began to cool over vast stretches of time to form our planet as we know it. However, everything we *apparently* know about its exact internal composition is based on speculation and theory. We saw in Chapter 3 the problems facing scientists when they formulate hypotheses. On the other hand, there is no reason why a theory based upon known facts, coupled with the all-encompassing mathematical patterns evident elsewhere, should be any less valid as a theory. If anything, it would be *more* plausible, as it deals with numerical values that are never vague and adhere to a set logical pattern (see figure 21; *note*: the use of metric measurements is *not* inconsistent with my overall supposition, as I will discuss at a relevant point. The key thing here is the suggested depths of the layers making up the Earth. Figure 22 will show how my numbers come into play.).

Figure 21 gives the classical view of the Earth's interior, contrasted with that of a new, alternative view. I agree with the new view as regards the Earth's composition, but differ from it over the distances (see figure 22).

Here I have proposed how the mathematical pattern indicates the composition of the interior. It is only where the distances are concerned that I differ. This is not simply a case of making figures fit my theory – as will be borne out later in this chapter.

In the first column are values for the distances in miles for the radius; in the second the total values in miles for the diameter (this means the length of the section within the overall radius or diameter); and in the

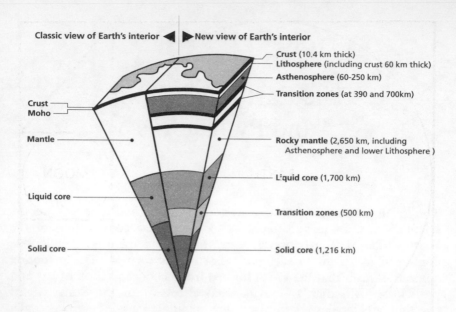

Figure 21.

third the figures are added, to give the Fadic values. Note the total value of *all* the Fadic numbers is 9. This is an important value which we will look at later in the context of all the planets in our solar system.

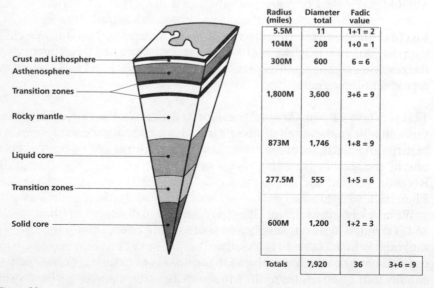

	Radius (miles)	Diameter total	Fadic value
	5.5M	11	1+1 = 2
	104M	208	1+0 = 1
	300M	600	6 = 6
	1,800M	3,600	3+6 = 9
	873M	1,746	1+8 = 9
	277.5M	555	1+5 = 6
	600M	1,200	1+2 = 3
Totals	7,920	36	3+6 = 9

Figure 22.

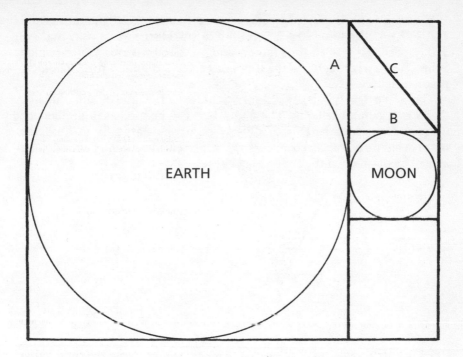

Figure 23. E = Earth's radius – 3,960 miles. M = Moon's radius – 1,080 miles. In the triangle above the Moon: Side A = 2,880 miles or : 720 × 4; Side B = 2,160 miles or : 720 × 3; Side C = 3,600 miles or : 720 × 5.

The Earth and the Moon

I have dealt already with some of the mathematical information yielded by a diagram in which the Moon is placed at a tangent to the Earth, and the resulting figure enclosed in a rectangle (see figure 23) but I want to repeat that image here.

This is a 3, 4, 5 Pythagorean triangle × factor 720 (we shall see later how this actually applies to measuring distances within our solar system and planets). Application of the 3, 4, 5 Pythagorean triangle to data is also one of the methods used to pinpoint the final location of the Hall of Records, verified and substantiated by other methods – as I shall show. Flick back to figure 12.

We already know from Chapter 5 that the diameter of the Sun is 864,000 miles. When divided by 60 (as there are 60 minutes in one hour) the result is 14,400 – and 1,440 equals the amount of minutes in one Earth day of 24 hours, which also has 86,400 seconds. In this case, therefore, we can say that 2,160 relates to the Moon (its diameter), and as we have seen 1,440 relates to time, and 720 relates to a length or space/distance factor.

When each value is divided by its common factor of 720, the results are: $720 \div 720 = 1$; $1,440 \div 720 = 2$; $2,160 \div 720 - 3$. Hence we can say that $1 = 720 =$ space; $2 = 1,440 =$ time factor; and $3 = 2,160 =$ Moon factor (which I discussed earlier; 2,160 is the number of years required for 1 Zodiacal precession cycle).

The value 1,440 is found hidden within stories and legends in just about every major religion. These numbers can be used as multipliers or divisors to convert lengths of objects occurring naturally in both the microcosmic and macrocosmic world, representing either space or time, as will be outlined in the following chapter.

Chapter 11

Meanings within 720 and 1440

I cannot emphasise too strongly how important numbers are in the make-up of my argument. Please therefore remember my earlier request that you work through these numbers now. It's not so complicated as you might at first think. Just take it one step at a time.

To convert the measurements of the Sun, Earth and Moon, plus distances in our solar system, into Fadic values, we divide their respective values by 720 and 1,440. This is where your recently acquired knowledge of Fadic numbers comes into play.

The Sun has a value of 12 – or 3 by Fadic addition of 1 + 2; and the value for the Earth is 11 or 2 by Fadic addition of 1 + 1. The following chart using the two values, 720 and 1,440, will explain where these figures come from. For example: 7,920 divided by 720 gives 11; 7,920 divided by 1,440 gives 5.5, i.e. 1. (See Appendix 3)

	(A) MILES	(B) (A) DIVIDED BY 720 – SPACE/ DISTANCE	(C) FADIC VALUE FACTOR	(D) (A) DIVIDED BY 1,440 – TIME FACTOR	(E) FADIC VALUE FACTOR
Sun diameter	864,000	1,200	1 + 2 = 3	600	6
Earth diameter	7,920	11	1 + 1 = 2	5.5	5 + 5 = (10) 1
Moon diameter	2,160	3	3	1.5	1 + 5 = 6
Earth – Moon distance	250,000	347	3 + 4 + 7 = 1 + 4 = 7	174	12 = 3
Earth – Sun distance	93,600,000	13,000	1 + 3 = 4	65,000	11 = 2

The important values we need to remember are: 1,200; 12 (or 3); 11 (or 2); 347; 13,000; and 13 (or 4). Two further points to note: (a) the Earth's space/distance Fadic value of 11 can give us its diameter when multiplied by 720: 11 × 720 = 7,920. Hence Earth has the Fadic value of 11 (or 2). (b) The average distance to the Moon falls somewhere between 250,000 and 249,000 miles. If we take the Moon value of 347 and multiply it by 720, the result is 249,840 miles.

From these figures we can create a Pythagorean Earth/Moon triangle (figure 24). A-B represents the Moon's diameter of 2,160 miles.

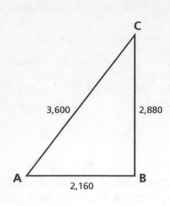

Figure 24.

In figure 24, B-C can be split in 2 significant ways: (a) 1,440 + 1,440 (related to time), or (b) 2,160 + 720 (the Moon and space). Furthermore, 2,880 multiplied by 3 is 8,640; multiplying *this* by 10 gives 864,000, which is the Sun's diameter in miles. That all these apparently 'coincidental' figures and values are able to interchange, and relate to Pythagorean triangles, practically screams at me to look further into them, and into what the ancients knew of them.

The human connection

If everything in the universe is governed by these values, then so important a thing as the gestation period of human females would have to contain them; in fact, we would expect Moon values to occur in this context, as it has been shown that women's menstrual periods are affected by it. We should start with the basics. The period from conception to birth is 9 months, out of the year cycle of 12 months. 9/12 × 1,440 gives 1,080, the diameter of the Moon in miles.* In fact, 1,080 will prove to have even more significance as we progress. The ancient Egyptian coffin text, as will be mentioned in connection with the Chambers of Creation, actually was coffin text number 1080. Coincidence perhaps?

The Sun, Earth and Moon relationship

Having seen the significance of two essential numbers – the space/distance divisor value of 720, and the time value of 1,440 – I started to apply them to the solar system. The results were startling.

- If we take the Earth's mean distance from the Sun of 93,600,000 miles and divide it by the 720 space/distance value, we get 130,000 (or 130 or 13, depending which factor of 10 we use). Fadicly, 13 (1 + 3) equals 4.
- If we take the distance of the Moon from the Earth – 250,000 miles – and divide it by 720, we get 347.† The Fadic value (3 + 4 + 7) equals 14,

---

* During my initial research, I noted that there were 108 elements. As a consequence, I was drawn to the figure whenever I came across it. There are, however, now 109 known elements.
† The actual product of 250,000 divided by 720 is 347.22222, or if the *true* value of 249,840 is used, the result is 347 exactly.

which further reduces (1 + 4) to 5. See figure 25 for a diagrammatic representation of this.

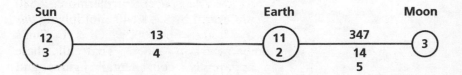

Figure 25.

Here, it appears that the mathematical pattern used a length factor of 10 to the power of 3 in addition to the usual distance factor of 720, thus the Earth was placed 93,600,000 (130 × 10 × 10 × 10 × 720) miles away from the Sun.

As we saw in Chapter 5, after the 'big bang' everything was created from nothing, expressed mathematically as 1 (everything) and 0 (nothing). As I demonstrated in figure 9, there then followed a number replication process. In addition, I demonstrated that *the Fadic number 7 is equivalent to the atoms of the chemical elements that form all matter*. I have further shown how the planet Earth, the Moon and the Sun's Fadic number values, *and* the distances between these bodies, were worked out, and how we arrived at the space/distance value of 720 and time value of 1,440. Now 1 0 + 1 0 can make either 2 or 11; then 1 and 2 produces 12, or 1,200. Consequently 1 + 2 = 3, followed by 1 + 3 = 4 – thus representing 4 solar bodies by Fadic addition. (Mercury, Venus, Earth, Mars and Jupiter are covered in Appendix 3.)

These space/distance values apply to the planets as numbered from the Sun, and their equivalent diameters in miles obtained by use of the factor 720.

I have included Nibiru as all the evidence suggests its presence. It is reputed to be at least 3 to 4 times the mass of Earth, yet as you can see, according to the mathematical pattern it is almost identical in size to Earth. This reduction would help to explain the difficulty in actually sighting it.

Putting the numbers theory into practice

In figure 26, I have listed relevant details of the accepted distances and diameters in miles of the planets, as given in standard works on astronomy. I have then included the Space/distance factor values of 720, and their Fadic values. Note again that all the planets, *including Nibiru*, have a total Fadic value of 9 – *except* Venus, which equals 4. Remember, too, that the Earth's interior, when arrived at using the code, totals the Fadic value of 9.

PLANET	SPACE DISTANCE (MULTIPLE OF 720)	DISTANCE FROM SUN MILLIONS OF MILES	FADIC VALUE OF DISTANCE	STANDARD TEXT DISTANCE	SPACE DIAMETER (DIAMETER ÷ 720)	MY DIAMETER IN MILES	STANDARD TEXT DIAMETER
Mercury	500	36	9	36	4	2,880	3,010
Venus	938	67.54	4	67.24	10.48	7,545.6	7,562
Earth	130	93.6	9	93	11	7,920	7,920
Mars	200	144	9	141.64	5.8	4,176	4,198
Saturn	119	856.8	9	887.13	103	74,160	74,527
Jupiter	670	482.4	9	483.4	1.21	87,120	87,120
Uranus	247	1,778.4	9	1,784	43	30,960	31,763
Neptune	371	2,671.2	9	2,795.6	43.24	31,133	31,363
Pluto	517	3,722.4	9	3,673	2	1,440	1,426
Nibiru	740	53,280	9	?	11.11	7,999.2	?

Notice that Venus has a Fadic value of 4 whereas the other planets all have the value 9. Calculations resulting in answers with 3 decimal places (e.g. 67.536) have been rounded up to 2 decimal places (in this instance, therefore, giving 67.54).

Figure 26.

My workings here were as follows:

- To calculate my space distance values, I began with the generally accepted diameter of the Earth in miles at 7,920. When applying the distance factor of 720, I arrived at 4.
- From this I then looked at the Moon. I already knew the Moon's diameter was a multiple of 720 ($3 \times 720 = 2,160$ miles).
- I began to look for links between Earth and the Moon. I realised that I could also take the Moon's distance from Earth and also divide it by 720 ($250,000/720 = 347$). 347 immediately grabbed my attention because its 3 component digits are of importance, as already shown.
- From the above I felt that 720 could be related to the other planets in the solar system and as a consequence began to test 720 against their diameters and distances from the Sun.
- I then looked at Mars and found that no whole number multiple of 720 went into the text-book diameter of 4,198. 720 did however fit 5.8 times ($5.8 \times 720 = 4176$). 58 was a very significant number, as we shall see.
- As the value of 5.8×720 was so very close to Mars's diameter, I then looked at Venus. Mars and Venus were both very important gods to the Romans and Greeks. Again I applied the value of 720 as a multiple in relation to Venus's diameter. 10.48×720 was the only multiple that fitted very closely, being 7,545.6, and the text book entry was 7,562 miles.
- As I then calculated multiples of 720 into the diameters of other planets, I noted with joy that multiples of 720 fitted Jupiter exactly (121

× 720 = 87,120 miles). When Saturn and Pluto had multiples of 720 that fitted so very closely, only out by several miles, so I was inclined to believe that the other planet values I had calculated as multiples of 720 were probably more accurate than the existing text book entries.

- I could not divide the diameter of Nibiru, as text books do not have this information yet. But working on the basis of 720 as a multiple division and using other planet values, I was able to calculate its diameter and distance accordingly.
- Having established the 720 form, I then applied it to the distances of the planets from the Sun. I used the nearest multiples of 720 to text book entry details, which are on the whole not exact. There is still quite a margin for error. In view of this, I am again more inclined to believe that my values are just as valid, if not more so, as they adhere to a set mathematical constant.
- When I then added all the distance values, I noted that they all equalled (by Fadic addition) 9. This made me feel confident in my assumptions, but also drew my attention to Venus. As a consequence I researched this planet and myths relating to it in detail, which we shall cover later.

To calculate the distance from the Sun and diameter of Mars, we add 10 + 10 (Sun and Moon), giving 20 for its distance, and its diameter 1,100 + 4,000 + 700 = 5,800. Note that 5 and 8 are evident here. Conversion to miles is again by our distance/space factor numbers of 7.2 and 72,000 respectively, but as Mars is past Earth, further from the Sun, the number factors increase by 10 to the power of 3 for distances and decrease by 10 to the power of minus 1, for diameters.

The diameters of the planets and their respective distances from the Sun actually vary depending upon which reference source is consulted. Though this diversity may seem to add confusion, in fact we can discount it, since giving distances and diameters calculated by the above mathematical codes reduces the possibility of error inherent in trying to calculate distances across the solar system, even with modern technology.

The code in the universe

Having used the above codes to work out distances and diameters in the solar system, and the correct number of its planets, I wondered if the same could be done for the formation of galaxies.

The accepted scientific view is that the galaxies formed in a spiralling motion after the big bang, and it appears that this spiralling out is determined by the unfolding of Pythagorean triangles. A spiralling pattern is noticeable as it continues from any spur on the triangles, as long as the Pythagorean rule of right-angled triangles is maintained and using whole numbers for ratios only, i.e. the 3, 4 and 5 triangle. When more than one set of Pythagorean numbers is used to link to a previously formed triangle, directional changes are possible from a single line into three-dimensional space both above and below the plane. So the spiralling could continue branching out, with even more protrusions emerging, on to infinity. See figure 27.

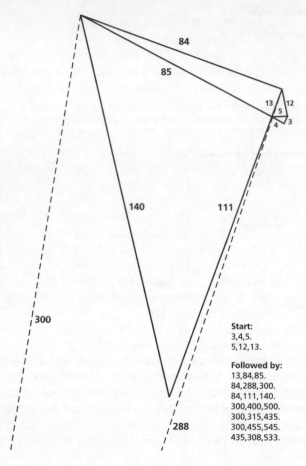

Figure 27.

The first set of numbers have to obey the rule of the Fadic 3 value for the unfolding universe, i.e. the 3, 4, 5 triangle; then follows the 5, 12, 13 triangle, followed by the 13, 84, 85 triangle, and so on. Our solar system can thus be investigated by folding in two 5, 12, 13 triangles into a 13, 84, 85 triangle to obtain the space/distance values.

Finally, the entire solar system is governed by the mathematical code. The planets all orbit the Sun in a circular pattern, and the electrons in an atom also appear to orbit in the same way. Scientists have arranged the chemical elements in a chart known as the periodic table, which consists of rows and columns; the first row contains the 2 elements of Hydrogen and Helium, while the second row contains 8 elements, Lithium through to Fluorine. There are 7 rows altogether (see figure 28).

Periodic/Row arrangement of the elements

Periodic/Row number

Maximum number of
2
8
8
18

The diagram below depicts the atom and its total SEVEN possible orbits or energy levels which will contain electrons. These can be considered to be moving anywhere on the surface of a sphere, called 'a shell', about the nucleus contained at its centre.

Electron arrangement in the atom orbit

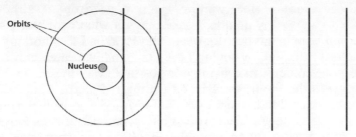

Orbits

Nucleus

Orbit number

Figure 28.

A microcosmic image of our solar system is produced. It has been argued that this is *not* a smaller version of the solar system, as the planets do not jump from one orbit into another as electrons do on the microcosmic scale. However, I argue that they *do* (as our ancient forefathers have told us in their myths and legends), but because the macrocosm is on a bigger scale, naturally the jumps occur at greater intervals – many thousands of years, in fact.

All this is very complicated. But it bears repeating that I believe the ancients knew all about it, and applied key numbers from those codes to the building – and siting – of their most important monuments. Furthermore, such knowledge would include a predictive element, since mathematical patterns are reliable. The importance of prediction will become very clear as you work through this book.

Chapter 12

Hamlet's Mill

One summer's evening in 1983 when I was 19, I found myself dug into a hole in a field in Germany. I was on a major military exercise for the Territorial Reserve (a commitment that seriously ate into my time at technical college, the Colchester Institute, studying engineering design). I was holed up with two other guys, Dick and Roger, and armed to the teeth. We had two GPMG machine guns, two SMGs, three SLR rifles and a Carl Gustav 84 mm anti-tank gun. As I sat viewing the rolling countryside in front of me, waiting for a huge drop of airborne parachutists to arrive any minute, I asked myself what on *Earth* I was doing. We had been in this hole for over 5 days and had seen nothing; as it was a tactical situation, we couldn't even talk and had eaten only cold rations since we couldn't risk giving our position away by smoke from cooking. Every other hour, we kept on getting red alerts. That meant masking up so we couldn't even *whisper* half the time. Suddenly the radio told us it was stand down; enemy forces had been pushed back and the expected air drop was going to occur elsewhere. We could put on a brew and get something warm to eat and drink!

As we sat relaxing in our little home in the ground, Dick started talking about a trip he was planning. He was going to drive across Africa in a team with a 4-ton Bedford truck. Somehow the conversation drifted to the Pyramids in Egypt. Both Dick and Roger were about the most hardnosed and cynical individuals I had ever met, which naturally tempered my enthusiasm for talking about my personal Pyramid theories. Still, as the conversation developed, I started to slip in a few of the anomalies relating to the Great Pyramid and the ancient Egyptian myths that traditional archaeology hadn't resolved, and how certain details relating to the precessional cycles of the Earth and the Sun were encoded within them.

To my surprise Dick said he was quite familiar with these details. How? I inquired. Rather nonchalantly he retorted that he had read all about them in a book called *Hamlet's Mill*.[1] 'What the heck has Shakespeare got to do with it?' I countered. Dick explained that the book (the 2 authors' names escaped him) made claims to prove that the ancients knew all about precessional cycles and various other astronomical facts that they shouldn't have been aware of, according to conventional history. I was staggered. I had assumed that I was alone in my assumptions and theories; now I was hearing about two others who had followed the same path. I felt quite jealous that someone had published the details first. This would not be the first time I thought I had made an exclusive discovery, only to go and find an existing book covering the same details. On the other hand, it was good news, too. It encouraged me to think that I was obviously on the right track, following the clues correctly.

For the rest of the exercise we talked nonstop about various anomalies from antiquity. We certainly had the time, since the big para drop never did arrive. In consequence of our little chats, Dick and I later teamed up many times on various exercises to swap details and research. This time, the first thing I did upon returning home was to hit the college library. Had they got *Hamlet's Mill*? No, but they could order it. When it arrived, I felt like I had found the Holy Grail itself. Though I was due to attend a military training weekend I decided the book was more important. So I spent the weekend taking in the ideas of its authors, Giorgio de Santillana and Hertha von Dechend. As I had expected I got into serious trouble for not attending the training session. Little though I realised it then, that weekend marked the gradual decline of my part-time military career.

Hamlet's Mill was published in 1969, but I had never come across it before. I learnt that even though Santillana was a very highly respected professor of the history of science, *Hamlet's Mill* was attacked by the academic world. Academic publishers would not touch the manuscript and eventually it was published commercially, which was then looked upon as a lesser type of publishing by academics. Because of this, many scholars simply ignored their findings as irrelevant, reasoning if they were worthy of serious attention they would have been published by an academic publisher. Santillana, many decided, had joined the lunatic fringe, so his standards of scholarship were deemed below par.

Before compiling *Hamlet's Mill*, Santillana had been aware for some time that there was a point in history where science and myth blended. He makes it clear that the revelation of his findings overwhelmed him with the sense that he had been entrusted with some great secret from antiquity. In consequence – and regardless of the backlash that would result – he collaborated with von Dechend, an anthropologist, to research further and get their findings published. She had also felt that all the myths of antiquity were more than just nonsense, so was perfectly suited to the joint venture.

Years previously, Santillana had concluded that 'primitive' cultures in the past such as that of the Stone Age had paid a meticulous, almost obsessive attention to measures, counting, astronomy and the seasons, far beyond what might have been expected of simple farmers or hunter gatherers. Santillana explains in some detail that early man not only knew about the precession of the equinoxes (which wasn't 'discovered' again until 134 BC, by the Greek Hipparchus) but also encoded this knowledge and understanding, complete with the actual mathematical values, into myths and legends.

Santillana points out that he is not trying to *explain* the myths in terms of precessional cycles; it is not as simple as that: 'The subject has the nature of a hologram, something that has to be present as a whole to the mind.'[2] In essence, this means that from all across the ancient world, there are myths and legends all carrying the same information and recounting the same story. Santillana even suspects that these myths are much much older than is supposed, perhaps by thousands of years. *Hamlet's Mill* presents myths and legends from Icelanders, the Chinese, American Indians, Hawaiians, Japanese, Persians, Romans, ancient Greeks, ancient Hindus, ancient Egyptians and Eskimos plus dozens of other nations. As Santillana so rightly asks, 'How did all these strange similarities develop unless myths have some common origin?'

Santillana takes as his focal point the corn-grinding mill belonging to the Icelandic hero Amlodhi (which we translate today as Hamlet).[3] This mythical mill originated in the 'golden age' of mankind and ground out peace and plenty. Then the age ended, causing the mill to grind out salt before finally ending up at the bottom of the sea, grinding up sand, causing a whirlpool, the Maelstrom. The symbolic use of the mill is appropriate, as the grinding wheel represents the image of the Sun passing through the constellations in one direction, while the equinoxes move in the opposite direction. Santillana also mentioned the ancient Egyptian god Osiris, of whom I was already aware, so it all made sense to me.

The information embodied within the mill myth is that catastrophic disasters occurred, after which the world had to be rebuilt. As we've seen, most ancient myths talk of catastrophic disasters such as the great flood. The point here is that ages end in disaster (more on ages later: the usage is that of the Age of Pisces, etc) due – somehow – to precession of the equinoxes as we move from one age to the next.

If worldwide cataclysms that destroy most of mankind occur regularly, due to precessional cycles, this would explain why ancient man was so obsessed with observations of the heavens and attached such a great importance to it.

I learnt a lot from this book; more importantly, it convinced me that I was correctly following the clues in ancient myths. It also further instilled the sense of responsibility that I felt to prosecute the matter to its final conclusion as regards locating the Hall of Records. Now I knew I had to try and find it. If what Santillana was proposing was correct, it would be in my interest, as well as my family's, to do so.

Chapter 13

Astrology and the Zodiac

My mother was forever reading her stars in the papers, so ever since I can remember I have been aware of the Zodiac. I never subscribed to the idea that your stars could be read on a daily basis and could apply to everyone born on that day. I did, however, have an intuitive feeling that it could certainly have an influence on personality. I believed this, having learned about the Moon and its effects on the oceans causing tides; if the Moon could do that, what influence must it have upon us, who are made up of 68 per cent water? Scientific results had shown that the Moon's gravitational pull was such that it effected even water in a cup. In addition, I pondered the role of other planets in our solar system, whose magnetic and gravitational fields affect the Earth.

As we shall see, recent scientific research does appear to confirm that the planets exert an effect upon us along with the Sun. Furthermore, the Zodiac not only contains precessional details relating to our solar system, but also carries an encrypted message. The Zodiac is not just a new-age fantasy but a carefully planned message-carrier, permeating the entire ancient world.

Looking for a plausible scientific answer for my intuitive feelings towards the Zodiac and how the Sun affects us was difficult. Eventually I arrived at several conclusions which I would put under scientific scrutiny. My initial workings were met with derision when I approached various scientific establishments to test the validity of my research. This was only to be expected, so I did not lose heart. Then Maurice Cotterell's *The Mayan Prophecies* appeared in the mid-1990s, assessing the effects of the Sun on personality.[1] Here was someone thinking along the same lines as myself, but backed up by a lot more scientific evidence than I had managed to put together. Again this was one of those moments where what had started as an intuitive hunch was independently proved.

I will summarise Cotterell's argument as I think it demonstrates clearly and simply how the Sun affects mankind.

Solar magnetism and the human body

The Sun throws out particles, both negatively and positively charged, that travel towards the Earth. This is known as the solar wind and results in magnetic modulations of the atmosphere, which in turn result in genetic mutation in any life form reproducing by means of conception, at the time of conception. Hence, in humans, personality is determined by astronomical influences; this is often referred to as Sun sign astrology. These magnetic modulations correlate to a 260-day solar cycle. Solar radiation affects behaviour through bio-rhythm regulations from the moment of birth. The link here is that the Mayan sacred year was 260 days long. Each day had a ritual or astrological significance and each day was either lucky or unlucky. Mayan children were named according to the day they were born.

The alignment of planets further influences personality by introducing variations at the time of conception; this is why the Maya followed the movements of the planets to compile their astrological forecasts. Cotterell[2] noted the determination of personality by the influence of the Sun *and planets*, which was termed 'Astrogenetic theory'. The theory argues that personality is a function of genetic mutations caused by modulated magnetic fields acting upon the foetus (egg/zygote) at conception. These modulations are in turn caused by the Solar particle interaction with the Earth. If this is true, it would certainly offer another reason why all the ancients studied astrology. If the Sun's magnetic field reverses at regular intervals, and also increases at certain periods in time, it would affect the people of Earth directly (see figure 29).

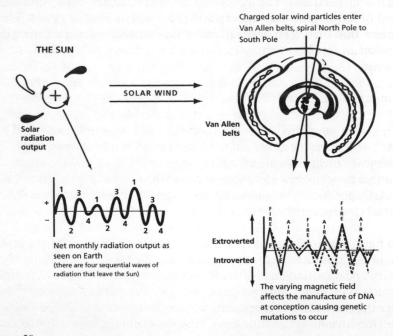

Figure 29.

As can be seen on figure 29, 4 clear sequential codes, or peaks and troughs of radiation, leave the Sun. The varying field affects the manufacture of DNA at conception, causing the genetic mutation to occur. Could this type of genetic mutation be one of the causes for sudden developmental changes in mankind's history, perhaps even causing a jump from one type of hominid to another? Could *this* explain why modern man has 27 differences when compared with Neanderthal man?

In astrology there are four main types of birth sign, known as Earth, Air, Fire and Water. The Sun signs show either extroverted or introverted tendencies. Basic genetic mutations lead to variations in personality. (If this sounds implausible, remember that the menstrual cycles of women are directly influenced by the Moon's magnetic and gravitational effects.) The graphs in figure 29 are the result of two studies undertaken by Jeff Mayo and an Institute of Psychiatry under the aegis of Professor Hans Eysenck. The first study, of 1,795 people, is marked by the solid line; the second study, of 2,324 people, by the broken line. It can be seen that the positive signs are predominantly extroverted and the altering negative signs are predominantly introverted.

The rotating Sun showers the Earth with particles every 28 days (on average), particles which have been shown to affect the follicle-stimulating hormone (FSH) that regulates menstruation and fertility on Earth. Maurice Cotterell demonstrated[3] that the Sun's magnetic perturbations, as reflected in cyclic Sunspot activity, can be seen to align with the rise and fall of civilisations. The Maya in consequence worshipped the Sun as the god of fertility, as they understood the cause of fertility cycles. They also knew that their own civilisation would eventually decline through a disruption in fertility hormones caused by changes in the Sun's solar magnetism.

To sum up, then:

- It has been suggested that the human organism is bio-regulated by solar particles induced by magnetic modulations after conception.
- Changes in melatonin affect bio-rhythms.
- Changes in oestrogen and progesterone affect fertility.
- In Astrogenetics, the magnetic to chemical conversion process is termed electrochemical transduction.

From figure 30 we can see that the pineal gland is affected by magnetic fields in its production of the bio-rhythm hormone melatonin. The pituitary and hypothalamus affect the manufacture and release of fertility hormones, oestrogen and progesterone. As the Sun's magnetic fields shower the same radiation upon all women at the same time, they *should* thus all menstruate at the same time. That this is not the case is due to their birthdays. How this occurs can be likened to a fairground carousel: each

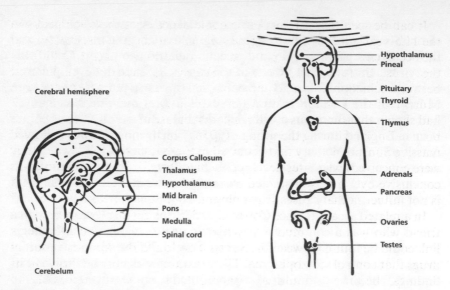

Figure 30.

horse is set at a different height, but is still travelling around at the same speed and direction as the others. The analogy is that each individual woman is set at a different height on the carousel. As the carousel travels a complete revolution, the individual woman will ascend and descend, always returning to the same height at the position she started from. In this way, each is synchronised with the Sun's radiation at their particular point of birth, and hence bio-rhythms and endocrinal activity commence at different times. Each endocrinal system responds to the 28-day solar cycle, which happens to be linked with the Moon's cycle.

Anything that affects the bio-rhythm or the body's metabolic rate will affect the duration cycle: stimulants such as coffee or tobacco; artificial hormones; oestrogen; progesterone; anything which interferes with the signal from the Sun – including overhead power cables and other electro-magnetic interference – will cause a change in the cycle. A case that proves this, cited by Cotterell,[4] concerned a Stefania Follini, an Italian interior designer. She was placed deep underground, totally shielded from the Sun in isolation inside a cave in New Mexico for 4 months; in consequence, her bio-rhythms became disturbed and her menstrual cycle actually stopped. Her waking hours lasted 35 hours and she slept for 10 hours at a time. This experiment has far-reaching implications, as it shows the human reproductive system can be rendered ineffective underground out of the Sun's radiation. Indeed, it has since been postulated (and subsequently proved) that if this is the case with humans, then perhaps the same applies to other species, and even to infections and viruses. A link has been established showing the links between the 'flu virus and Sunspot activity.

It can be seen that a remarkable coincidence exists between peaks in the 11.5-year Sunspot curve, where solar activity is at its maximum, and the occurrence of influenza pandemics associated with antigenic shifts of the virus. In July 1991, the *Daily Telegraph*[5] reported a direct link between schizophrenia and influenza; in the article, Professor Robin Murray of the London Institute of Psychiatry stated that his research had shown that there was an 88 per cent increase in the number of babies born in England during the spring of 1958 (which coincidentally followed massive Sunspot activity that occurred in the summer of 1957, when they were conceived) who later developed schizophrenia. The correlation was conclusive over a period studied from 1939 onwards. This shows that it is not influenza that causes schizophrenia, but Sunspot activity.

In a related area, Maurice Cotterell undertook further research, with a friend who was a community psychiatric nurse, to establish whether a link could be found between the Sunspot cycle and the administration of drugs that control schizophrenia. Their research was not conclusive in its findings, because a multitude of problems made it impossible to complete, but Cotterell did state:

> ... the evidence from Hope Simpson and Robin Murray suggested that schizophrenia is indeed caused by solar activity. Removal of that radiation may therefore provide comfort to sufferers. It also brings a sense of reality to the Biblical phrase in respect to Armageddon, 'the first shall be the last, and the last shall be first', which seems to suggest that when catastrophic destruction frequents the Earth, not only will the poles shift, and fertility decline, but as the magnetic field swings, the sane will become mad as the man become sane.[6]

In view of the above findings on the Sun, I wondered if radiation from other stars could affect humans directly. I couldn't see why not. Perhaps radiation from a given star might have certain beneficial properties, causing positive results. Could this be why so many ancient temples and long barrows were aligned to certain stars – particularly Sirius – and why the star's light shone directly down a sacred corridor or shaft at a particular time, thereby focusing its power/radiation on any person correctly positioned? Could this help to raise the individual's intelligence or psychic abilities? I wondered. (In fact, as my research developed over the years, I concluded that the alignments had many purposes.)

The components of the Zodiac

There are 12 signs to the Zodiac, each represented by a particular animal or symbol (see figure 31). We have seen the importance of 12: the 12 months of the year, and so on. But where did the Zodiac originate from?

113

Figure 31.

Its connection to precessional cycles, spread over many thousands of years, implies that the Zodiac is very ancient in origin, or was at least constructed by an advanced civilisation who understood the mechanics of the solar system thousands of years before accepted history acknowledges that such knowledge was available.

Leo

To the ancient Sumerians, the first age, *c.* 11,000 BC, and sign of the Zodiac are both Leo, 'the lion', known to them as Ur.Gula. This sign symbolically represented their god Enki, the god of the African lands. In ancient Egypt, Enki was known as Ptah, whose goddess wife Sekhmet was represented with the face of a lioness. As we shall see later, the Sphinx (which I maintain is a lion's body with a human head) is thought to represent the period of Leo which would have coincided with the

114

Sumerians' first epoch. Latest geological surveys also prove that the Sphinx has weathering patterns that indicate it was constructed around 10,000 BC or earlier, in marked contrast to orthodox historical dating, which gives *c.* 3–4,000 BC.

Cancer

After Leo came the age of Cancer, around 8,700 BC. This was depicted as a crab, which the Sumerians called Dub, meaning 'pincers'. (The later ancient Egyptians depicted Cancer as the scarab beetle with its huge pincers.)

Gemini

Cancer is followed by the age of Gemini which the Sumerians called Mash.Tab.Ta, meaning 'the twins'. (Interestingly, the Egyptian depiction shows two twins of both male and female.) This ties in with the Sumerian belief that Gemini was associated with another of their gods, Enlil, whose first-born son Nannar (or Sin) had twins, Inanna (female) and Utu (male), who were apparently born shortly after his arrival on Earth.

Taurus

Taurus follows Gemini and was known as Gu.Anna, meaning 'heavenly bull'. The Egyptian Zodiac represents the bull with a disc on its back. (Some scholars have taken this to represent the tenth planet Nibiru, as this time period coincides with an apparent passing of Earth by Nibiru, as well as a visit of the god Anu to Earth.)

Aries

The sign of Aries follows, symbolised by the ram (Sumerian Ku.Mal meaning 'field dweller').

The age preceding the birth of Jesus Christ and the Piscean age was Aries, explaining why stories connected with Moses relate to rams, goats and shepherds. This is also why shepherds were 'watching their flocks by night' on the eve of Christ's birth. The early Christian church symbol was the Vesica Pisces. It has made a comeback in recent years and can, for example, be seen on car stickers as a simplified fish. The Vesica Pisces will play a major clue in the quest, especially its links to the Great Pyramid and sacred alignments in England.

It is also stated in the Bible, that 1,000 years after the return of the Messiah, the Devil will again be let loose to tempt mankind. This equates to the Aquarian age (when the Messiah is due to return) and to the age of Capricorn that follows it. Capricorn was often depicted as a half-man, half-fish or half-man and half-goat. The half-man/half-goat is immediately recognisable as the image of the Devil as he has been portrayed during the past 2,000 years. More on this later.

Pisces

After Aries comes Pisces (Sumerian: Sim.Mah, 'fishes'), represented by two fishes astride a watery stream. Water is symbolic for spirit, so this sign also represents a stepping stone towards a spiritual age to follow – the age of Aquarius.

Aquarius

Aquarius (Gu to the Sumerians) is depicted as the 'Water Bearer'.

Capricorn

Capricorn was known to the Sumerians as Suhur.Mash, meaning 'the goat fish'. It has been associated as a symbolic representation of the Mother Goddess, Ninharsag, who was nicknamed Nin.Mah, meaning 'Lady Fish'. In ancient Egypt she was known as Hathor and depicted as a cow, bearing some similarity to the goat-fish image. Egyptian artists occasionally linked Capricorn with an umbilical cutter; that was also a symbol for Ninharsag, as she was the Mother Goddess.

Sagittarius

Sagittarius is represented by the archer. In ancient Egyptian he is half-animal and half-human with a bow. In Sumerian this was Pa.Bil, 'the Defender'.

Scorpio

Scorpio was called Gir.Tab by the Sumerians. The ancient Egyptians depicted it as a scorpion.

Libra

Libra was called Zi.Ba.An.Na (meaning 'Heavenly Fate' in Sumerian) and was depicted as a god between two scales.

Virgo

Finally Virgo, depicted as a beautiful maiden, was known to the Sumerians as Ab.Sin, meaning 'Whose Father Was Sin'.

Several scholars have claimed that the signs actually refer to real personalities and events in the past. Indeed, Alan Alford opines in his book *Gods of the New Millennium*[7] that all Sumerian myths actually refer to individuals or gods, who visited Earth every time Nibiru passed planet Earth. I believe that they do refer to events of antiquity, but in a very simplified manner. The main point of the original stories was to make them interesting, *thus ensuring the information encoded within them would be carried intact through time.* I repeat what I pointed out earlier, *all things were contrived symbolically.*

To sum up

Each precessional cycle of the Zodiac takes 2,160 years. Each month of the year is represented by one of the signs of the Zodiac. Apparently one's personality is governed by which particular star sign of the Zodiac one is born under. As we have seen that the Sun does indeed affect us biologically, it would not be surprising if a certain part of our personality is determined by the Sun sign we are born under. Certainly, evidence suggests that our moods and behaviour appear to be directly linked to the positions of the planets and the Sun and seasons. In regard to Earth's seasonal changes, this is now recognised in medical circles as SAD: Seasonal Affective Disorder.

Below I have listed the Zodiac signs, starting backwards from now (with their respective dates, as they are of relevance later; I use here the modern symbols of the Zodiac).

SIGN	DATE PERIOD	MYTHICAL IMAGES OF THE TIME
Pisces: The Fishes	148 BC – Present (2012)	Fish symbolism, Fisher men, Disciples, Vesica Pisces
Aries: The Ram	2,308 – 148 BC	Shepherds, Goats, Rams
Taurus: The Bull	4,468 – 2,308 BC	Apis/Bull worshipping
Gemini: The Twins	6,628 – 4,468 BC	Twin Gods/Goddesses
Cancer: The Crab	8,788 – 6,628 BC	No mythical images in this time period, indicating a time of turmoil and chaos
Leo: The Lion	10,948 – 8,788 BC	Lions, Sphinxes
Virgo: The Virgin	13,108–10,948 BC	
Libra: The Scales	15,268–13,108 BC	
Scorpio: The Scorpion	17,428–15,268 BC	
Sagittarius: Half Man/half horse	19,588–17,428 BC	
Capricorn: The Goat	21,748–19,588 BC	
Aquarius: The Water Carrier	23,908–21,748 BC	

As you can see, the period for Leo reaches back to nearly 11,000 BC; an important point to remember. As is indicated, the period of Cancer has been referred to as a time of chaos or turmoil by some scholars, as unusually there simply are no mythological representations in history relating to it.

Chapter 14

Precession

During my years of study, I kept coming across strange documents and articles. One that particularly caught my attention was a comment by the 5th-century BC Greek historian Herodotus. In *Canon of the Kings of Egypt*,[1] Herodotus states that the Sun has twice risen where it now sets, and has twice set where it now rises. This man was far from a fool. Having read Immanuel Velikovsky's book *Worlds In Collision*[2] which gives many references to immense destruction caused by the Earth shifting on its axis, and other cosmic upheaval, I was more than prepared to accept that at times the Sun could shift its position in the skies; this would be only natural if the Earth had tilted on its axis. I had also read many accounts from antiquity (such as the Central American Creation myth *Popol Vuh*) that stated the Sun stood still in the heavens for many days whilst on the opposite side of the globe, and did not appear for several days. All this intrigued me greatly. It also strengthened my conviction that ancient myths and legends referring to such events could be based on facts. What especially caught my attention about Herodotus's comment was the fact that he was stating that *the Sun had changed position several times*. In consequence of reading that, I set about learning all I could about our Sun.

To me, Herodotus's statement (the Sun has twice risen where it now sets, and has twice set where it now rises) did not imply that, due to cataclysmic events, the Sun shifted its position dramatically to set and rise in a different position. If this were the case I am sure Herodotus would have said so. I understood Herodotus's account to infer that *the Earth itself* has transited through a full 360-degree revolution of the heavens against its stellar background; a full precessional cycle of 25,920 years. The implications of what Herodotus was saying struck me immediately. *It meant that one and a half precessional cycles have elapsed since the foundation of ancient Egypt, i.e. 38,880 years.*

If that wasn't enough, Pomponius Mela, the Spanish cartographer of the first century AD, cited 13,000 years for the rule of 330 kings who ruled Egypt. He also quoted Herodotus's statements,[3] adding that the Egyptians, according to their own accounts, were the most ancient of men, and that since the commencement of the Egyptian race, the stars

118

had completed four revolutions. This means no fewer than 4 precessional cycles totalling 103,680 years.

It may be unwise to take these accounts at face value, but they do show that the ancients did not think of mankind as relatively new to the world, and were happy to believe that the history of mankind stretched back many thousands of years. Furthermore the Egyptian historian Manetho, of *c.* 300 BC,[4] maintained that Egyptian records went back as far as 9,000 BC.

Another thing that struck me was that ancient civilisations knew the timescales involved in precessional cycles, especially the Sumerians and Babylonians. In both cases their texts state the information was handed to them by their gods. We shall look at these claims later; for now we need to look at the actual mechanics of precession itself.

It is worth noting that the names of the 7 days of the week still current in many languages come from astronomical sources, derived from Ptolemy's (2nd century AD) incorrect theory that the Sun, Moon and 5 known planets revolved around the Earth. Hence Sunday comes from the Sun, Monday the Moon, Tuesday from Mars (for example the French Mardi), Wednesday from Mercury (the French Mercredi), Thursday from Jupiter (the French Jeudi), Friday from Venus (the French Vendredi), and Saturday is named after Saturn.

Many people, on hearing the terms archaeoastronomy, equinoxes, solstices and precession, wince at them as if they are unfathomable scientific processes and therefore beyond them. I felt the same many years ago when I first started to research this field. In consequence I have spent many an hour poring over astronomy charts, and learning all I could about precession and equinoxes. I felt that it was important to do so, since I sensed that these were directly linked with ancient myths and legends. However, knowing and appreciating many people's fears of the subject, I have made the following piece on precession brief. It is still enough to convey a working knowledge of the subject, which is an essential element of the quest. Please therefore work through it – you must be aware of the actual mechanics behind precession and the equinoxes to follow the trail to its conclusion.

The motion of the Earth

First of all we need to understand that the Earth spins on its own axis, which causes the regular phases of night and day. If the Earth was like the Moon (which offers a face fixed towards Earth) one side of our planet would be permanently exposed to the Sun with the other constantly in total darkness. This would not be good for any evolving life: the constant radiation and build-up of heat would turn the exposed hemisphere into a desert, while the other half would be a cold, ice-bound environment.

The Earth's axis is also tilted at an angle in relation to its orbital plane around the Sun. This tilt is known as the obliquity of the ecliptic. Because of it, the planet has 4 seasons as it travels round the Sun. These features are easily recognised and it only takes 2 years to confirm the effects, with each season occurring twice. The earliest civilisations (such as Sumer) were also quick to learn of this by noting the 4 key observational points where the Sun rises and sets in relation to the horizon. The first 2 points are known as the summer and winter solstices. This is when the Sun reaches its furthermost positions North and South, appearing to remain in a particular point on the horizon before turning back again. The second 2 points are the spring and autumn equinoxes, when day and night are of equal duration on the 2 occasions in the year when the Sun crosses over the Earth's equator.

Moreover, the Earth has what can best be described as a wobble, very much like that of a spinning top. If an imaginary line (which remains fixed, though as we shall see, this is not strictly speaking correct) is drawn through the Earth's axis pointing to the sky above the North pole, over a very long period of time, the Earth's wobble will cause it slowly to change direction, eventually tracing out a full 360-degree circle in the heavens (see figure 32).

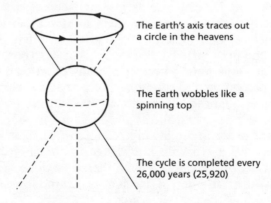

The Earth's axis traces out a circle in the heavens

The Earth wobbles like a spinning top

The cycle is completed every 26,000 years (25,920)

Figure 32.

The time taken to complete this circular motion is 25,920 years. As a direct result of the wobble, which gradually alters the tilt of the Earth, the starting-points for the 4 seasons arrive slightly earlier every year; this is known as 'precession'. The shift is very slow: one month every 2,160 years. From our point of view, its importance lies in the fact that the backdrop of the heavens appears to move, albeit very slowly.

It has been one of the earliest recorded practices of man to note and measure precession from a point taken from the equinoxes. This is termed the 'precession of the equinoxes'. The 360-degree circle 'drawn' in the heavens as outlined in figure 32 over 25,920 years was divided into 12 sections of 2,160 years. Each section was associated with a house of the Zodiac, as discussed in Chapter 13. Because of this, we can use the Sun rising on the day of the spring equinox as a reference point against which to measure the movement of the Earth's axis line – from one section of 2,160 years (or house of the Zodiac) into the next one. We are presently in the last section of Pisces, the fish, and about to move into the first section of Aquarius, the water carrier (see figures 33a and 33b).

At spring equinox, observer at X sees sun rise against stars in the house of Pisces. (Present age) Earth's wobble causes spring equinox to slowly slip forward in time.

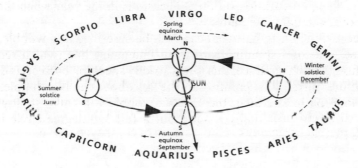

Figure 33a.

13,000 years on, the Earth's axis is halfway through full cycle of 26,000 years. Spring equinox would then occur in September as the sun rises against the house of Virgo.

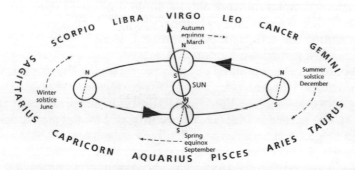

Figure 33b.

The dawn of astronomy

In 13,000 years from now, the Earth will be in the age of Virgo and about to move into the section of Leo, the Lion. The last time that the Earth moved into Leo was around 11,000 BC. Remember, I stated earlier that the Sphinx is a lion with a man's head. This made a perfect sign to indicate the period of its construction – the time of Leo, as I thought when I was 13. Several years after making my simple deduction I read about Sir Norman Lockyer and his theories that ancient sites and temples were astronomically aligned. This really caught my imagination – here was an accredited scholar claiming exactly what I was trying to point out (in vain I might add), with a book on his findings under his belt. Thus began a mini quest, just to locate that book! I was just 15 then and tried *everywhere* to locate a copy, but to no avail. The British Library in London would not get me a copy – I was too young. I had just about resigned myself to the fact that I would have to wait until I was older, when I had a visit from a friend, Denise, who knew about my intense interest. She presented me with a package, insisting that I could have it only if I agreed to go on a date with her; I had to agree prior to opening it. I'm human and I'm inquisitive – I agreed. Inside? A book, *the* book – *The Dawn of Astronomy* by Sir Norman Lockyer.[5] Denise and I consequently dated for quite a while and spent many an hour under the stars talking about history and philosophy. I don't think her parents were too keen, fearing the worst from two young people left alone at night!

The Dawn of Astronomy caused a storm of controversy when published in 1894. Lockyer had initially been intrigued by the repeated realignment of temples over long periods of time, especially at Thebes/Karnak in Egypt, and eventually compiled a comprehensive collection of astronomical alignments on numerous sites, including temples and cathedrals. Not only did he suggest that the ancients had astronomical knowledge hitherto not thought possible for their times, he also maintained that by using various temples' alignments, he could accurately date their construction. This was a revolutionary theory in its day, one fiercely opposed by the scientific and scholastic community. It would be nearly 100 years before his work gained the support it deserved.

In his book, Lockyer pointed out that the tilt on the Earth's axis varies by as much as 1 degree over any 7,000-year period. Later work on Lockyer's theories suggests that the Earth's tilt varies between 21 and 24 degrees to the perpendicular. It is presently at 23.4 degrees. Lockyer's very meticulous measurements and alignments have enabled today's scholars to make very close approximations of the construction dates for temples aligned to the solstices, and in consequence affected by the moving of the Earth's tilt after their erection. By closely examining when the temples' alignments had been celestially correct, he was able to date them. This endeavour developed into what is now termed as Archaeoastronomy. For me, the vital thing was that Lockyer's findings implied the ancients had advanced astronomical knowledge – which, according to accepted history, they shouldn't have had. I was to use Lockyer's argument to date other ancient sites, as I shall reveal later.

'A globe in space'

Here the other essential point is that the ancients were clearly aware of the precessional cycle that lasted 25,920 years. The ancient Maya, Egyptians, Babylonians, Chinese and Sumerians all knew about precession. *How?* It has been argued that the others all derived their knowledge from the Sumerians, as theirs seem the earliest known records of astronomy; but remember, the Sumerians claim *they* received their information from their gods. As we've seen, the first 12 signs of the Zodiac are attributed to the Sumerians. Now, the puzzling thing about the Sumerian Zodiac is that it appeared 'overnight' nearly 6,000 years ago – intact and correct. Instead of then progressing, knowledge of the Zodiac and the cosmos actually went into decline, at least in European cultures; so much so that the later Greeks and Romans believed the Earth to be flat. This view would not change until the 16th-century astronomer Copernicus placed the Sun at the centre of the solar system, and was nearly executed for doing so.

It has been argued that Copernicus drew his insight from ancient esoteric wisdom sources that had been driven underground into secret religious mystery schools. There is certainly clear evidence that such knowledge was kept alive. For example, the 13th-century Rabbi Hamnuna compiled the *Zo'Har*, a key literary work of Jewish mystical wisdom contained within the Kabbalah. In it, it is stated that the Earth turned on its own axis: "The entire Earth spins, turning as a sphere. When one part is down, the other part is up. When it is light for one part, it is dark for the other part; when it is day for that, it is night for the other."[6]

There are other equally percipient comments from elsewhere. The ancient Indian text *Surya Siddhanta* describes the Earth as 'a globe in space'. Our friend Pythagoras taught his students that the Earth was a sphere, and the 5th-century BC philosopher Anaxagoras taught that the Moon darkened the Sun during an eclipse, and that during a lunar eclipse the Earth's shadow fell upon the Moon.

There are countless other facts that demonstrate that the ancients had advanced astronomical knowledge. The biggest question however remains: *why* the obsession? Mankind doesn't require a complex system in order to know when to start sowing crops; simple observation of the seasons and animals reveals that. No. There must have been a *major* factor that caused the ancients to become obsessive to an extreme in regard to celestial phenomena and precessional cycles.

What was it?

PART THREE

NUMBER SCIENCE

Chapter 15

Magic Squares

In ancient times, such as the classical period in Greek history, each planet had a magic square related to it with various numbers contained within it (see figure 34). In addition every letter, especially in the Hebrew and Greek languages, had a mathematical value attached to it – a science known as numerology or gematria. Just what all the values stood for is not clear. However, during the course of my investigations over the years, I have discovered what the meanings and values relate to, and why.

SATURN.

4	9	2
3	5	7
8	1	6

JUPITER.

4	14	15	1
9	7	6	12
5	11	10	8
16	2	3	13

MARS.

11	24	7	20	3
4	12	25	8	16
17	5	13	21	9
10	18	1	14	22
23	6	19	2	15

THE SUN.

6	32	3	34	35	1
7	11	27	28	8	30
19	14	16	15	23	24
18	20	22	21	17	13
25	29	10	9	26	12
36	5	33	4	2	31

VENUS.

22	47	16	41	10	35	4
5	23	48	17	42	11	29
30	6	24	49	18	36	12
13	31	7	25	43	19	37
38	14	32	1	26	44	20
21	39	8	33	2	27	45
46	15	40	9	34	3	28

MERCURY.

8	58	59	5	4	62	63	1
49	15	14	52	53	11	10	56
41	23	22	44	45	19	18	48
32	34	35	29	28	38	39	25
40	26	27	37	36	30	31	33
17	47	46	20	21	43	42	24
9	55	54	12	13	51	50	16
64	2	3	61	60	6	7	57

THE MOON.

37	78	29	70	21	62	13	54	5
6	38	79	30	71	22	63	14	46
47	7	39	80	31	72	23	55	15
16	48	8	40	81	32	64	24	56
57	17	49	9	41	73	33	65	25
26	58	18	50	1	42	74	34	66
67	27	59	10	51	2	43	75	35
36	68	19	60	11	52	3	44	76
77	28	69	20	61	12	53	4	45

Figure 34.

The figures within each magic – or planet – square were very highly regarded by mathematicians of antiquity, who viewed them as paradigms of universal laws. Each temple and ritual centre was accordingly laid out to a cosmological pattern, directly linked to principles of geometrical design inherent within each square; thus the ancient world was set out with smaller patterns within larger patterns – all radiating out from a certain point on the Earth's surface. This is an important point to remember for later.

Each of these ritual centres was also reputed to be a natural point of terrestrial currents and each centre, or cluster of centres, was known by an astrological symbol that related directly to a magic square. The 7 wonders of the ancient world likewise formed an astrological system, each site representing a centre of the influence for which they were famous. Each building was constructed as an instrument for controlling a particular aspect of cosmic energy according to the pattern of magic squares to which that energy responds. Below is a list of the '7 Wonders of the World' and the squares that control them, as written by Eliphas Levi.[1] Again, notice that the all-important number of 7 is present.

WONDER	SQUARE OF
The Colossus at Rhodes	The Sun
The Temple of Diana at Ephesus	The Moon
The Tomb of Mausolus	Venus
The Great Pyramid of Egypt	Mercury (Hermes)
The Towers and Gardens of Babylon	Mars
The Statue of Jupiter at Olympus	Jupiter
The Temple of Solomon	Saturn

As we shall see later, Hermes (to the Romans Mercury, to the Egyptians Thoth) is reputed to be the architect of the Great Pyramid. Also note, for later use, that the total value of any one line in the square for Mercury/Great Pyramid adds up to 64. With magic squares you can add up the numbers vertically, diagonally or horizontally and get the same total value. For example, look at Saturn. Across the top of the square, $4 + 9 + 2 = 15$; diagonally from bottom left to top right, $8 + 5 + 2 = 15$; and from left to right in the middle, $3 + 5 + 7 = 15$.

These details show quite clearly that the ancients related numbers to Earthly projects that were in turn directly related to solar bodies such as planets and the Sun. The magic square for the Sun contains the numbers 1 to 36, with 111 being the sum total of the figures from any one line. The total sum of all the figures is 666, which, as we know, is the number of the beast from Revelation. What's more, 111 equals 3 by Fadic addition, which is representative of the Sun $(1 + 2)$, but also the Moon and God. $6 \times 6 \times 6$ also equals 2,160 (by the process of adding zero without affecting value), which we know is the diameter of the Moon in miles and the precessional period of one sign of the Zodiac in years. It is worth noting that the number 288 equals 216 + the significant number 72. These two figures, 216 (in Hebrew: Gevurah) and 72 (Hesed) are important numbers of the Kabbalistic text *Sephiroth* of ancient Rabbinical origin which were used in esoteric interpretation of the Hebrew Scriptures. They – 216 and 72 – equal (3×72) and (1×72), which parallels in a mathematic sense the holy notion of 3 in 1 (i.e. Father, Son and Holy Ghost).

Chapter 16

Chromosomes, Phi and Pi

As we saw in Chapter 4, DNA is a double-helix-shaped, thread-like material, present in all living cells. It carries all the genetic codes required for cells to divide in the correct sequence to create a living being. DNA has a spiral code of 2 strands, connected together, rather like a twisted ladder, the rungs of which are made up from four chemical bases called Adenine (or A), Guanine (G), Cytosine (C) and Thymine (T). These are strung together in what appears to be a random sequence, i.e. AGTTCGGAA, etc. In fact, this sequence follows a code that determines the colour of your eyes and hair, how tall or short you are, and so on.

When a cell splits in half (which is how it reproduces), the ladder's two 'verticals' come apart and then attract various molecules of the bases, which are floating about free, which grow until they link up, thereby making a new, second vertical. The final result is the formation of two identical ladders. This is how all living matter reproduces itself. Because of my interest in ancient myths and legends, I was aware of the number of 64 that kept on cropping up everywhere (e.g. in the *I Ching*), but it wasn't until I started studying DNA and RNA* that I saw a connection between this number and RNA. I had initially attributed the significance of the number 64 to its Fadic value: $6 + 4 = 10$ – that is, everything (1) and nothing (0) – but I soon realised that 64 is the number which the four bases can form into triplet units of RNA codons (codon means coding unit). I then perceived that these codons corresponded to the 20 amino acids necessary for the production of proteins, which were outlined in Chapter 4. I also noticed, however, that there were two more which are the coded instructions for 'start' and 'stop', meaning that the total number required was 22. As we shall see in the next section, 22 is very important.

(Incidentally, it is worth nothing that the 'start' and 'stop' codes can be directly affected by the Sun, causing cancer. This gives another possible reason why the ancients were so concerned with observations of the Sun's cycles and solar flares; not because they worshipped the Sun, but because they wanted to be warned of potentially lethal doses of radiation.)

Our genes, which we inherit from both parents, are like a packet of

---

* Ribonucleic acids.

chemical information that consists of DNA. It is now known that the individual characteristics of a species are determined by the 4 DNA bases of A, G, C and T (see above). They are further arranged in 'words' of 3 letters that give us the 64 possible combinations of letters; here again I immediately recognised that all-important value of 7, in totalling the values of 4 and 3. Scientists are now beginning to read these letters and words of the genetic code, known as the human genome. To date, they have been able to identify many of them and what their specific instructions are.

The human genome consists of 23 pairs of chromosomes, a total of 46, and it is estimated that there are 3 billion chemical letters within it. As scientists are now beginning to understand DNA and genes, they have started experimenting. They have started what is termed as 'gene splicing' (also known as recombinant DNA technology) whereby a new gene can be inserted or a 'bad' one removed from the DNA strand. This is achieved with the use of enzymes that allow the DNA to be cut in a desired place, and something to be inserted or removed accordingly. We are on the threshold of being able to make ourselves bigger, stronger, faster or whatever we choose. One noteworthy result of this research is that human DNA shows that it has passed through an extremely long and peaceful evolution, which is inconsistent with, and in total contradiction of, the accepted evolutionary theory that posits the split from the apes, as summarised in Chapter 3.

In the ancient Chinese oracle book of changes known as the *I Ching*, the basic unit is a triplet of lines which are either broken or unbroken corresponding to the Yin and Yang principles of opposites: light and darkness, male and female, etc.[1] The *I Ching* is made up of 64 annotated hexagrams (star-shapes – with 6 arms). With RNA, each 'triplet' unit (RNA is shaped like a Y, i.e. with 3 arms) links up with another triplet already contained within the DNA molecule. This means that our double-helix chain of encoded genetic information is made up of 64 hexagrams, just as in the *I Ching*. In the *I Ching* there are also 8 trigrams. If the value of 64 was arrived at purely by chance, then we wouldn't expect to find 8 trigrams within DNA; but we do! (Remember too, I pointed out that the Great Pyramid is associated with the magic square of Hermes/Mercury where the sum value is 2,080 – the sum total of all numbers from 1 to 64. This is not simply yet another coincidence.)

Pythagoras held the value of 22 as sacred for a number of reasons. It represented the 3 musical octaves in music, which the Pythagoreans saw as one of the basic secrets of the universe. The musical scale has the special number of 7 notes (doh, re, mi, fa, so la, ti) and the final doh of the next octave, which then begins the next octave. We have seen the importance of the value 3, so it should be no surprise to learn that 3 octaves begin on doh and end on another doh, 22 notes later.

The numbers 3, 7 and 22 figure prominently within all the major religions and civilisations of the ancient world, and within ancient temples. To give one example, there is an ancient Egyptian decree which appoints a high priest to become the 'Director' of 22 Nomes (districts) in Upper Egypt, and later his son is appointed as a subservient director of only 7 Nomes (the other 15 remain under the father). This symbolism of the dominance of the father over the son (i.e. 22 over 7) is clear. Of course, the ratio is 22 over 7 is an approximation of Pi, as I will explain shortly. The districts of Upper and Lower Egypt were split into two halves, one of 22 Nomes, the other of 20, giving 42. We shall come across the value of 42 again in relation to ancient Egyptian myths.

So, from all the above information it appears that even in the very building blocks of life itself the same values and figures keep appearing. This is further confirmation that all we perceive and understand is governed by a universal mathematical constant.

Pi

Most people are aware of what Pi (π) is – a circle's diameter, when multiplied by Pi, equals its circumference. (As we shall see, the Great Pyramid incorporates the ratios of Pi in its dimensions.) Pi is a complex value to calculate exactly; modern computers calculate it to infinite millions of decimal places. However, a good enough estimation for practical engineering is the ratio of 22/7 or, in decimal form, 3.1428571.

The conventional view of history accords the first accurate discovery of Pi to Archimedes, born in Syracuse, Sicily in 280 BC, who obtained fractional values between 3.142857 and 3.140845. It is significant that Archimedes spent most of his early years in Egypt in correspondence with two notable scholars, Conon and Samos of Alexandria. (Alexandria of course housed the great library of the ancient world, sadly destroyed by the early Christians due to disputes with their Gnostic counterparts of Alexandria in AD 391.) However, the earliest Egyptian records of Pi date back to the 17th and 19th centuries BC. The Ahmes Manuscript at the British Museum and the Golenishev Papyrus in Moscow both deal with mathematical formulae. Although the Pi values achieved were limited to 3.16, this nonetheless shows an understanding of the principle. Indeed, as we shall see, the Great Pyramid used a Pi value of 3.14286 some 1,200 years prior to its supposed discovery.

It has been argued that the Pi ratios in the Pyramids arose through coincidence or accident, by reasoning that the Egyptians had not formed the concept of isotropic three-dimensional space (i.e. had no real understanding of perspective), and could not measure vertically in the way that they could horizontally. However, I cannot accept an argument that maintains that the designer of one of the world's largest buildings was unable to understand three dimensions. It is further argued that in order to overcome the strange, flat, two-dimensional world in which they lived, the ancient Egyptians simply used a wooden roller to roll out the dimensions of the base: the idea was that the roller was marked at one point on its circumference and each full revolution of said mark constituted a unit of measure. (This was before they had discovered the wheel, of course.) They are then said to have rolled out one half of the rolled units along one face of the base to achieve its height ratio. The measuring roller was one cubit in diameter. Using this method would indeed accidentally form a pyramid the same as the Great Pyramid with the same sloping face angles, with a ratio of 2 × Pi × height = circumference. But, if this is the case, how were the original plans drawn? Did the Egyptians simply make it up as they went along? Surely no one could suggest that the construction was made without a plan drawn to scale. No; as we shall see, the ancients did indeed know the value of Pi.

Phi

The Phi (φ) ratio is not so well known. I became interested in it after a school field trip to an ancient Greek temple in 1977 whilst I was living in Cyprus. My teacher drew our attention to the ruins and began explaining the ratios incorporated into them for aesthetic reasons, to be pleasing to the eye. I had two questions: What did aesthetic mean? and, What *were* these ratios? He patiently explained that the ancient Greeks went to great lengths to use the ratios of Phi within their temples as this gave pleasing 'natural proportions'. Many experiments, he said, had been carried out to determine which shapes, sizes and proportions were the most favourable. It turned out that these adhered to the ratios of Phi.

Phi, as I later learnt, was also compatible with human physiology, hence our natural subconscious liking for objects that had Phi ratios. So what exactly *is* Phi? Basically, Phi is a specific ratio of one side of an object to another; an example is the rectangle in figure 35. The length of the longer side in proportion to the shorter side is the ratio of Phi, which equates to 1.6180339.

Figure 35.

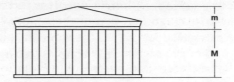

Figure 36.

Phi takes its name from the Greek letter Φ and it was first officially noted in the West by Euclid, around 300 BC. During the Renaissance it was often referred to as the 'Divine Proportion'. It was also used by the Greeks to form a pentagon as a holy symbol, as it contained many Phi relationships. It is more usually known as the 'Golden Section', 'Golden Number' or 'Golden Ratio' – golden simply being a token of approbation. My interest in the ratio really took off when I learnt that all living organisms, including humans and plants, are related to Phi. This was yet another clue that led me to conclude that everything we perceive, including the very structure and proportions of our bodies, conforms to a mathematical constant that is also a law of nature.

Whilst at Art College during my first foundation year, part of my course involved studying fine art from Roman times to the 19th century. Even here I couldn't escape the ratios of Phi. They are important in the composition of landscape paintings; for example the 17th-century masterpiece *Les Bergères d'Arcadie* by Nicolas Poussin, in the Louvre. During the Renaissance and after artists deliberately incorporated this. For example, horizons were positioned on the canvas to divide the

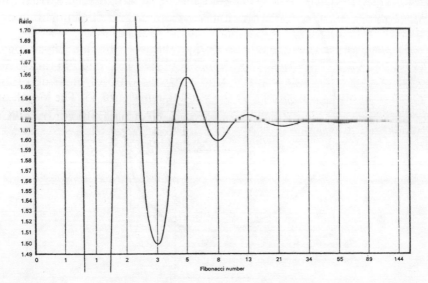

Figure 37.

133

picture in relation to a value for Phi of 1.6 to 1, as the Poussin painting attests. To do otherwise created a picture that didn't look right, even though it might be painted superbly. Furthermore, of course, the Greeks incorporated the ratio of Phi within their temples (see figure 36).

The Fibonacci sequence

In the 13th century, a mathematician named Leonardo Fibonacci discovered a series of figures, all related to Phi, which proliferate in nature. In the Fibonacci scale, each number equals the sum of its two predecessors; 0, 1, 1, 2, 3, 5, 8, 13, 21, 34, 55, 89, 144, etc (see figure 37).

As we move along the scale from left to right, the ratio of any number to the number preceding it comes closer and closer to the precise Phi ratio. The ratio of 2 to 1 is 2 – very approximate. But the ratio of 8 to 5 is 1.6 – much closer – and the ratio of 144 to 89 is 1.61798 – closer still. The

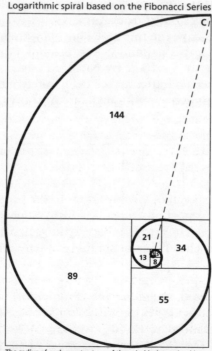

Logarithmic spiral based on the Fibonacci Series

The radius of each quarter-turn of the spiral is determined by the length of the side of the square in which it is inscribed, and the value of this for each succeeding square is in turn determined by the Fibonacci Series

Figure 38.

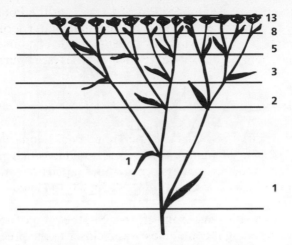

Figure 39. In plants, the branching of the main stem, and subsequent number of buds, follows the Fibonacci sequence.

higher the number, the closer to Phi we get. We have seen the importance of the value 1,440 and 144 earlier. Notice how the Fibonacci line starts to level out once it reaches 144. Also, the logarithmic spiral based on the Fibonacci scale radiates out in the exact same manner as in nature (see figure 38).

For example, the nautilus shell, the petals in a double dahlia flower and even the elements of a pinecone (when viewed from above) radiate out in the same spiral ratio of the Fibonacci scale. A simple plant incorporates the same ratio (see figure 39) as a flowering stem grows and divides – cow parsley and giant hogweed are excellent examples.

Furthermore, Fibonacci values are important to the proportions of man himself. These same proportions subconsciously influence our liking or disliking specific shapes. Those that adhere to the scale are pleasing to the eye even if the observer has no understanding of why this is. (See figure 40, (a) and (b)).

As we have already noted, the value 144 is an important number. The fact that we find it yet again within the Fibonacci scale only serves to strengthen the argument that all is governed by one mathematical pattern. Lemesurier's *The Great Pyramid Decoded* had initially brought the Fibonacci scale to my attention in the context of the Pyramid.[2] In consequence, years later, I was not surprised to discover that the Fibonacci curve matches up perfectly with the three apexes of the Giza pyramids (see figure 41).

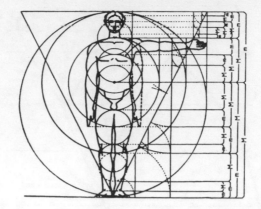

Figure 40a.

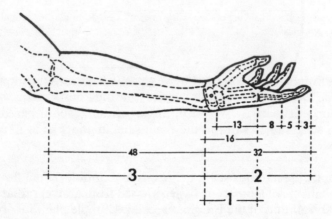

Figure 40b.

The curve matches up not only with the three pyramids, but also with the Sphinx. I didn't realise it at the time, but this simple fact alone was to help pinpoint the Hall of Records' location.

The 22 to 7 ratio

The ratio of 22 to 7 is evidently important. But here, let's examine the use of 22 on its own. Is it another coincidence that the Book of Revelation is 22 chapters long? I doubt it. Within it are many mathematical details that we shall look at later, as they are of direct relevance to the quest. Here are some examples now.

• In Revelation, the New Jerusalem is 12,000 furlongs square. 12,000 furlongs square is equal to 220 yards (220 yards in a furlong) multiplied

136

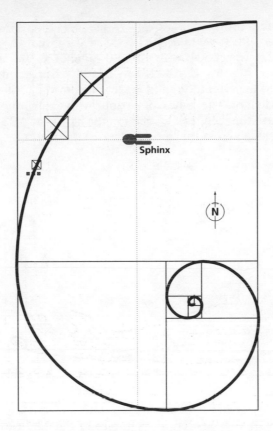

Figure 41.

by 12,000, and that figure is equal to 2,640,000 yards.
- There are 3 feet to a yard; so 2,640,000 multiplied by 3 equals 7,920,000.
- How else does that crop up? – the Earth's diameter is 7,920 miles. As the New Jerusalem *is* square, multiply 7,920,000 by 4; this gives 31,680,000. Now, 7,920 miles multiplied by 4 = 31,680 miles, and 31,680 divided by the significant number 1,440 is 22. (Bear in mind that in Revelation 144,000 is cited as an important figure – we shall look at this in due course.)
- The number 31,680 has another importance: in gematria, certain phrases and words spoken by Jesus (which will be assessed later) total 31,680.
- Here's a further connection: 31,680 divided by 220 gives 144.
- In addition, if we were to draw a square box around the Earth touching the equator, the perimeter of the square would equal 31,680 miles.
- Finally, in Tarot cards, the Major Arcana cards total 22.

In a circle, the ratio of the diameter to the circumference is traditionally expressed as the ratio of 22 over 7, i.e. 3.1428571, which is an approximation of Pi. If we take the height of the Great Pyramid of 482 feet* and add 22, we get 504, with a Fadic value of 9. 50.4 million miles is the distance of the Earth from Mars†. Furthermore, if the circumference of the Great Pyramid is sectioned into 22 equal units, 7 of these fit into its height. The same can be done with the trilithons (literally, 'three stones') at Stonehenge: if we section the height into 22 equal units, we can fit 7 of these across the lintel stone (see figure 42).

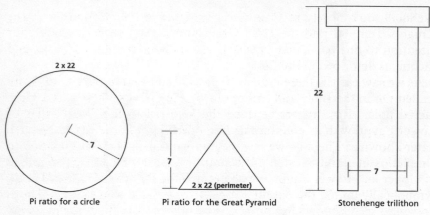

Pi ratio for a circle   Pi ratio for the Great Pyramid   Stonehenge trilithon

Figure 42.

As we have seen many theoretical examples of the 22/7 ratio, it is now time to assess its role in ancient buildings – extant and destroyed – which are central to my quest to find the Hall of Records.

* This is the *total* original height, including the missing capstone.
† If Mars was in an alignment whereby the Sun, Earth and Mars made three points on a straight line, Mars would be 50.4 million miles away.

Chapter 17

Boaz and Jachin

We shall look closely at Freemason lore and its connections with the Knights Templar and the Holy Grail later; here I need to draw your attention to one particular aspect of it – the sacred pillars of Boaz and Jachin, as described in the Bible.

As we saw earlier, there is an ancient tradition that in the city of Annu (called On in the Bible and Heliopolis by the Greeks) there was a great sacred pillar. Researchers believed this referred to the Great Pillar of Lower Egypt, with its counterpart in Upper Egypt in the city of Nekheb (later known as Thebes – we saw the importance of Thebes in relation to Omphalos sites and celestial projections in Chapter 8). These two pillars of Upper and Lower Egypt, which became the Pillars of Hermes/Thoth, symbolically united the nation as one. It was stated that Hermes/Thoth possessed secret knowledge on 36,535 scrolls, hidden under the heavenly vault (the sky), which could only be found by the worthy who would use such knowledge for the benefit of mankind. In the 3rd century BC Manetho apparently uncovered sacred pillars (now lost) that detailed Egypt's earliest history, as we shall cover later.

The Temple of Solomon

Across the ancient world it was common practice to flank the entrance to a temple with two freestanding pillars with no structural purpose (examples included Herod's Temple in Jerusalem). They could occur both outside and inside temple buildings. Why is not known.

In Chapter 16 we saw that it is argued that the Egyptians did not know the value of Pi, even though later Greeks maintained they actually learnt Pi from them. However, we know that Moses was directly linked with the pyramids and Egypt, having been brought up in the Pharaoh's palace. Now Moses obviously figures prominently in the Old Testament, and in the Old Testament we find mathematical details concerning the two pillars that flanked Solomon's Temple. At its gates were two pillars made of brass, each 18 cubits high, known as Jachin and Boaz:

And King Solomon sent and fetched Hiram out of Tyre. He was a widow's son out of the tribe of Naphtali, and his father was a man of Tyre, a worker in brass. And he was filled with wisdom and understanding, and cunning to work all works in brass, and he came to King Solomon, and wrought all his work.

Placed on top of these pillars were two capitals known as chapters or decorative tops, each four cubits high, so the total height equalled (18 + 4) 22. In referring to Hiram of Tyre the Bible states the following:

15 For he cast two pillars of brass of eighteen cubits high a-piece: and a line of twelve cubits did compass either of them about.

16 And he made two chapters *of* molten brass, to set upon the tops of the pillars: the height of the one chapter *was* five cubits, and the height of the other chapter *was* five cubits:

17 *And* nets of checker work, and wreaths of chain work, for the chapters which *were* upon the top of the pillars; seven for the one chapters, and seven for the other chapter.

18 And he made the pillars, and two rows round about upon the one network, to cover the chapters that *were* upon the top, with pomegranates: and so did he for the other chapter.

19 And the chapters that *were* upon the top of the pillars *were* of lily work in the porch, four cubits.

20 And the chapters upon the two pillars *had pomegranates* also above, over against the belly which *was* by the network: and the pomegranates *were* two hundred in rows round about upon the other chapter.

21 And he set up the pillars in the porch of the temple: and he set up the right pillar, and called the name thereof Jachin: and he set up the left pillar, and called the name thereof Boaz.

22 And upon the top of the pillars *was* lily work: so was the work of the pillars finished.

[1 Kings 7:15–22]

It appears that there are two values for the height of the capitals, as it is given twice: once at 5 cubits, once at 4. I believe that the importance of this passage lies in the numerical values contained within it. These can be a pillar 18 cubits high, plus a capital of 5 high (equalling 23), or one 18 cubits high plus a capital of 4 (22). The actual reference to the pillars of the portico of the temple indicates capitals 4 cubits high (18 + 4 = 22). The two pillars are linked together with a netting wound around the top of the pillars twice, and the length of the netting between the pillars equals 7 cubits on either side. Here, then, is the all-important Pi ratio of 22 to 7 (see figure 43).

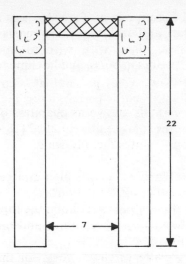

There are other important numbers within the passage.

- Let's look at 18 × 4 = 72. We already know the significance of the value 72 (see Chapter 11); now, 72 divided by the capital height of 5 results in 14.4. Remember, 144 is a significant number.
- This is another vital calculation: 18 × 5 equals 90, and 90 degrees is an essential base for all Pythagorean triangles and angles.
- 18 × 200 (the pomegranates) equals 3,600; 18 (pillar height) × 5 (first capitals height) × 4 (second capitals height) – 360. Two pillars at 18 cubits high are equal to a total of 36 cubits. Now, 36 × 4 is 144, while 36 × 5 is 180.
- What's more, if we take 18 (height of pillars) and multiply it by 12 (pillars' circumference) we get 216. We have seen the significance of 2,160 previously – in Chapter 7.
- In between the capitals were nets and wreaths of chainwork that were 7 cubits long for one capital and 7 cubits for the other, totalling 14. Why indicate this unless 14 was significant? Certainly, as we shall see, 14 is very significant in relation to the Giza pyramids.
- Multiply 14 by 36; you get 504. Mars's distance from Earth (as cited later) is 50.4 million miles, and the sum values of 1 × 2 × 3 × 4 × 5 × 6 × 7 = 5,040.

The two pillars spell out the properties of Pi in the sacred cubit measurements of the Bible itself: 22-cubits high pillars and 7-cubits distance between the pillars – 22/7. This shows that Solomon understood Pi a long time before the Greeks 'discovered' it.

The Masonic link

As I shall show, the two pillars are directly linked with Masonic symbology. In Freemason lore, Boaz was the great-grandfather of King David and represented 'Strength' or 'In him is strength', while Jachin was the high priest who assisted the dedication of Solomon's Temple and represented 'To establish'. Boaz, the left-hand pillar, stood to the south representing the Land of Judah, whereas Jachin, the right-hand pillar, stood in the north and represented the land of Israel. When united by the lintel of Yahweh, the two pillars provided, and represented, 'Stability'. Just as in ancient Egypt, which was united as a nation by two pillars in the two lands of Upper and Lower Egypt, as long as these two Temple pillars remained joined, strength and stability would endure.

In the 'Old Ritual' of Freemasonry, the two great pillars had been hollowed out to conceal ancient and valuable records pertaining to the past of the Jewish people. The two pillars have a central role within Masonic theology, where sacred measurements are evident.

The Qumran Community

I have previously considered Qumran in the light of its layout and the numerical values inherent within that. Qumran is now most famous for the Dead Sea Scrolls, discovered nearby from 1947 on. Very close to the Dead Sea and about 8 miles south of Jericho, Qumran is now a ruined settlement that archaeologists believe had 2 principal periods of occupation: from *c*.150 to *c*.30 BC, and *c*.4 BC to *c*.AD 68. We shall have cause to look closer at Qumran later, but for now I wish to bring other details to your attention. Many think of the Qumranians (or Essenes, a group who it is argued Jesus came from) as just another group of early Christians amongst many then in the Holy Land. However, as Christopher Knight and Robert Lomas declare in *The Hiram Key*:

> This is a hopelessly inadequate assessment of the Qumran Community. Its members were the distillation of everything that was important to the Jews as a nation, the guardians of the covenant with their God and the embodiment of all the aspirations of a people. They were Jewishness in fine focus.[1]

The main debate over the Qumran Community (the word is used here to mean a religious body rather than the general population) has centred on the identity of the first 'Teacher of Righteousness'. Does this refer to Jesus, the Messiah; his brother James the Just, also referred to as Messiah; or John the Baptist? Many scholars believe that there were actually two individuals given the title Teacher of Righteousness. Professors Robert Eisenman[2] and Michael Wise[3] have both independently concluded that the later Teacher of Righteousness, as described in subsequent discoveries, *was* the brother of Jesus, James, who was the leader of the important pseudosect, the Jerusalem Church. If this is correct, then it means that the Jerusalem Church *was* the Qumran Community. It is vital to point out here that another scroll, known as the *Manual of Discipline*,[4] states that the Community consisted of 12 perfect holy men who were 'the pillars of the community'. As this implies, the two pillars were highly symbolic, representing both the kingly and priestly aspects of creating and maintaining the 'Kingdom of Heaven'. These pillars were, of course, 'descendants' of the pillars of the united Upper and Lower Egypt, come down to the Qumran community via Boaz and Jachin of the eastern gate of Solomon's Temple. To the Jews, Boaz and Jachin represented the kingly power of 'Mishpat' and priestly power of 'Tsedeq'. When united, they supported the great archway of heaven, the keystone of the important Hebrew word, 'Shalom' (see figure 44).

This illustrates the twin-pillar paradigm:

- Freemasons know the right-hand pillar as Jachin, who was the first high priest of the Temple. To the Qumranians, this was the priestly pillar, Tsedeq, which embodied all that was Holy. Tsedeq is often translated as 'righteousness' though some have argued that equally, it can mean 'rightness'.
- The left pillar of Solomon's Temple was known as Boaz. For the Qumranians this was the Kingly pillar and stood for the House of David. Freemasons know that Boaz was the great-grandfather of David, King of Israel. To Qumranians therefore, Boaz represented Mishpat, which is often translated as 'judgement'. It also signified the law and rule of Yahweh himself, hence the dispensing of justice was always connected with this pillar. (At this juncture, it is worth noting that the biblical Jacob erected his first pillar at Mizpah, which is simply another spelling of Mishpat; furthermore, Saul was declared the first King of Israel there.)

As Christopher Knight and Robert Lomas further point out,[5] when these two pillars are in place with the Teacher of Righteousness – Tsedeq – on the left hand of God, and the Earthly Davidic King – Mishpat – on his right hand, then the archway of Yahweh's rule is in place, with the keystone of Shalom locking everything together at its centre. Shalom is generally now understood as a form of greeting that means peace, but for the early Jews it had far more complex meanings. In short, it meant establishing the rule of Yahweh with a moral order of government supported by both the kingly and priestly pillars. The whole order of the community of Qumran ensured that the symbolic image of two pillars held together by a supporting cross-member was

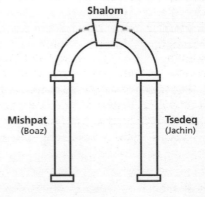

Figure 44.

carried on into the next millennium – as it has been. We have seen how the mathematical values inherent within the pillars of Boaz and Jachin are 22 over 7. However, as Knight and Lomas demonstrate,[6] Freemasons eventually inherited the symbolism, but somewhere along the road of history, lost its true meaning. The Qumranians' pillar ceremonies were the direct forerunners of modern Freemasonry. At Qumran there still survive two round pillar bases outside the East doorway into Qumran's Holy of Holies.

The other biblical reference to twin pillars is intriguing: Samson stands between two pillars and pulls them down. There are too many symbolic meanings behind the Samson and Delilah story to include here, but it does have connections with the later Knights Templar, a consequence of which was that the Knights Templar never cut their hair at the back – just like Samson.

Meanwhile, there is another essential element to take on board. The symbolic representation of two upright pillars joined across the top *is identical to that of Pi*: Π (or, lower case, π). Note also that this amulet (left) in the form of an ancient Egyptian Djed pillar has 5 rings at the top of the column, with a further 4 extended rings above, giving the numbers of the cubits of the 2 types of capital in Solomon's Temple, described in the quote earlier in this chapter (see figure 45).

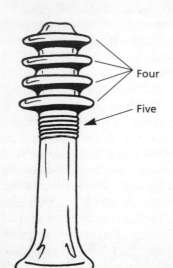

Four

Five

Obviously, then, the numbers given as measurements in ancient descriptions of buildings had considerable significance. Having scrutinised numbers so carefully, I knew I had next to turn my attention to the units of measurements themselves.

Figure 45. Amulet in the form of a Djed Pillar. The sacred nature of the Djed Pillar led to such miniature replicas being used as good-luck charms.

Chapter 18

Pyramid Ratios

Here I need to outline the various units of measure and ratios as used by the ancients so that the argument may be advanced.

We should start by looking at the British Imperial measuring system. This may seem a rather modern system to assess at the outset, given that we have been looking at buildings erected (at least) several hundred years before Christ, but the British unit of measure is reputed to be amongst the oldest in the world; moreover the United States is one of the few countries to maintain this system in use – again, this present-day situation has a direct bearing on my investigation of the distant past.

British Imperial measurements (i)

The British system of measuring is based upon the yard (0.9144 of a metre) and depends on these measurements: 1,760 yards = 1 mile; 220 yards = 1 furlong; 22 yards = 1 chain; and 5.5 yards = 1 rod. Familiar? (In Chapter 10, I pointed out that the Earth's diameter of 7,920 divided by 1,440 equals 5.5.) Moreover, there are 3 feet to a yard and 12 inches to a foot. The exact length of the yard has remained unaltered for nearly 2,000 years. Many eminent people have defended its use against the metre, even though the metric system is easier to use and learn. One was Charles Piazzi Smyth, the Astronomer Royal for Scotland and author of *The Great Pyramid*, published in 1859. In his book, Smyth goes to great lengths with meticulous calculations to prove that British units are inherent within the Great Pyramid itself, and that it was actually built under the divine guidance of God. He added that the British units of measure were sacred, having been supplied by God. Another notable supporter was Sir John Herschel, the astronomer and member of the Royal Society, who was instrumental in preventing the adoption of the metric system in England in 1855. In addition, Sir Isaac Newton (1642–1727) thought along similar lines, as outlined in his *Dissertation Upon The Sacred Cubit Of The Jews*;[1] Newton was convinced that the Jewish nation held the secret to sacred measurements.

It has been argued that a measuring system that uses fractions (as the British Imperial system does with its 5.5-yard rod) would not have been created deliberately with such elements. Eminent metrology specialists have argued that the 5.5-yard rod was a by-product of two different systems being conflated at some remote date. Rather, a deliberate creation would have produced something like the Metric system, using whole numbers exclusively. However, as we saw in Chapter 16 in relation to Pi and Phi, nature dictates her own rules in her ratios; natural ratios *do* include fractions.

Connections with the Great Pyramid

I think it is evident from the above paragraphs that the British unit of measure is based upon the natural constant of Pi – or more precisely Pi's fractional ratio of 22 over 7. As we shall see, the Great Pyramid itself is based upon the very same ratio. This means that the Great Pyramid is intended to be, in its measurements, a representation of the Earth's northern hemisphere (the northern rather than southern simply because the Pyramid is within it); its perimeter being one 43,200th of the Earth's circumference, while the Pi-based height of the Pyramid is one 43,200th of the Earth's radius. The Earth is a sphere divided into 360 degrees. If we take 360, first multiply it by 60 (the minutes of one hour), and then multiply by 2 (there being two half minutes), we get $(360 \times 60 \times 2)$ 43,200. If we take the all-important precessional cycle of 2,160 years and multiply it by 2, we get 4,320. This should remind us of two sets of texts: the sacred Books of Thoth/Hermes totalled 43,200, and so did the ancient Chinese scrolls.

As well as being linked to 43,200, the Great Pyramid is actually set exactly with the Earth's 4 cardinal points – though *now* it is very slightly out of alignment: by 5 minutes of arc, or, more specifically, one 12th of a degree. However, this apparent inaccuracy was caused due to the Earth's own rotational wobble on its axis and gradual movement (as explained in Chapter 14), *not* through the inaccuracy of the original architect. When *did* the Earth align perfectly with the Great Pyramid? The date for that is nearly 10,500 to 11,000 BC – dates we have seen before, since the Zodiacal cycle of Leo (represented by the Sphinx) began between these dates.

What of the site of the Great Pyramid – does that have special meanings? The Great Pyramid is situated at the exact centre of the geometrical quadrant formed by the Nile Delta (see figure 46).

Remarkably, reference to any equal area of projection of the Earth's surface shows that the site lies on the longest land contact meridians and at the geographical centre of the Earth's entire landmass (which has not changed in any major way since the Pyramid's time) including the Americas and Antarctica (see figure 47).

Figure 46. The Nile Delta.

To site the Great Pyramid with such accuracy shows that its builders had a very clear understanding that the Earth was a sphere, and knew its topographical and geological make-up. In turn, *that* means that they must have mapped out the entire globe, *thousands of years before the Americas were discovered*, and must also have understood latitude and longitude. Longitude was not successfully determined with any degree of accuracy in the West until the 17th century. However, as I have said, with their knowledge the ancient Egyptians used the Giza plateau as their equivalent to our modern Greenwich.

The Great Pyramid contains many dimensions relating to the Earth's basic geophysical data and orbital astronomy. The basic measurement used by its architect turns out to be an exact ten millionth of the Earth's mean polar radius. This cannot be attributed to coincidence yet again. It is striking that when the Metric system was devised (during the French Revolution), the basic unit of measure, the metre, was taken to represent a ten millionth part of the mean surface distance from either of the Earth's poles to the Equatorial circumference (see figure 48).

However, this distance is impossible to ascertain accurately as the Earth is not a perfect sphere. The mathematician Collet observed this in 1795. A more accurate standard measure, and one that is verifiable, would have

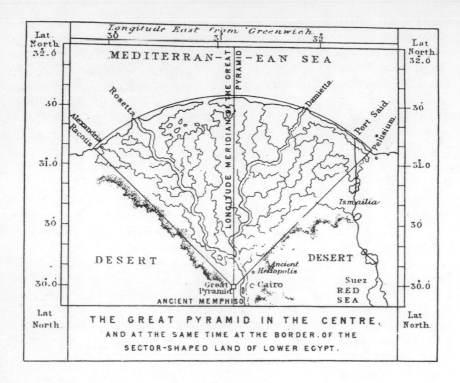

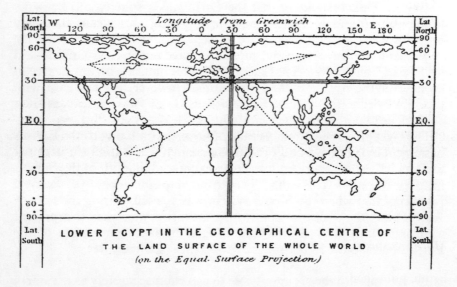

Figure 47. Piazzi Smyth's demonstration of the Great Pyramid's position in relation to the Nile Delta and the land surfaces of the globe.

been the ten-millionth part of the distance from either pole to the centre of the Earth (see figure 49).

Geodetic research using satellites, carried out during the International Geophysical Year 1957, established that the Earth's mean polar radius was 3,949.834 miles, equal to 250,265,000 British inches. British inches

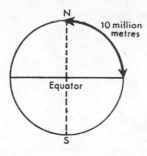

Figure 48.

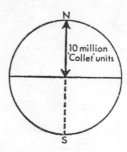

Figure 49.

are amongst the oldest and earliest recorded units of measure in the world, documented since Roman times. The ideal and perfect match for a metric unit equal to a ten millionth of this distance would therefore equal 25.0265. This distance is in fact found, correct to four decimal places, *three* times, *inside* the Great Pyramid:

- the inclined north to south distance between the north wall of the Grand Gallery and the north wall of the well shaft (i.e., the initial section of Gallery floor) equals 25.0265 inches)
- the horizontal distance between the east/west axis of the Queen's Chamber and the east/west axis of the Niche (being a section cut into the wall) equals 25.0265 inches; and
- the distance from the east end of the granite leaf (leaf here is an Egyptologists' term meaning sheet of stone) embedded in the wall to the centre of the raised boss (unadorned and about the size of a man's hand) again equals 25.0265 inches.
- The measurement also figures twice in the Pyramid's *external* design. Many scholars therefore equate 25.0265 inches to what is known as 1 Sacred cubit, with 1 Primitive inch equalling 1.00106 British inch. This is equal to 1/250,000,000 of the Earth's mean polar radius.

More measurements of the Great Pyramid

From published surveys, we know that the Great Pyramid's square perimeter, as defined by still-surviving foundation sockets on the south side, measures 9,140.7 British inches, which is equal to 365.242 Sacred cubits of 25.0265 inches. As you can see in figure 50, the pyramid itself is constructed in a slightly concave fashion (this is exaggerated in the diagram), an enigmatic motif which has puzzled orthodox Egyptologists for decades. However, as such people as Peter Lemesurier, William R. Fix and Charles Piazzi Smyth have pointed out, there was a very good reason for this:

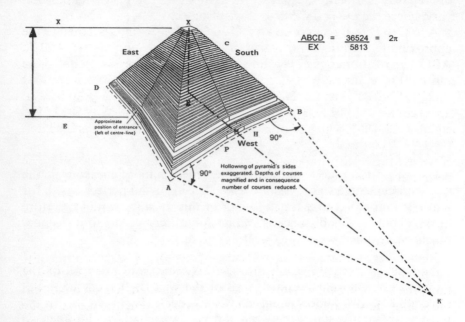

Figure 50.

By constructing the pyramid with the concave feature, the following figures can be obtained which relate precisely to the Earth's solar tropical, sidereal and anomalistic years. Hence: A to B is 365.242 Sacred cubits long, which equals the 365.242 days in the Earth's solar tropical year. A to P to H to B is 365.256 Sacred cubits, which equals the Earth's sidereal year (the time it takes the Earth to complete a circuit of the Sun) of 365.256 days. A to M to B is 365.259 Sacred cubits, which is equal to the 365.259 days in the Earth's anomalistic year (the time it takes the Earth to return to the same point in its elliptical orbit). Even when measured in so-called primitive inches (infinitesimally smaller than Imperial), exactly the same results can be achieved multiplied by 100. Even if these distances are measured in other forms of units, the ratios are the same.

The Great Pyramid is the only major structure with this unique concave feature. In figure 50, if an angle of 90 degrees is marked out from both A and B and a line projected outwards, the distance measured when they finally link from E to K will be 7.4393819 Statute miles, which in turn is equal to 185,984.548 miles divided by 25,000,000. This equals 1/25,000,000 of the average diameter of the Earth's orbit around the Sun, thus giving a theoretical average distance of the Earth from the Sun's surface of 92,992,274 miles. If we add the Sun's diameter of 864,000 miles we get 93,856,274 miles: the difference is just 256,000 miles. This discrepancy is irrelevant as the Earth's elliptical orbit makes its position vary, hence the use of a mean average distance.

A to C to D to B on figure 50 is 25,826.53 primitive inches, equal to the approximate duration, in years, of the cycle of equinoxes: 25,920. ABCD, in relation to the Pyramid's height, is directly proportional to the ratio of Pi (i.e. the ratio of a circle's diameter to its circumference) – that is, 22/7. So ABCD equals 36524.235 and EX (cross section from base to apex) equals 5813.0125. This means that 36524.235 divided by 5813.0125 equals 6.2831853, which in turns equals 3.1415926 × 2 which is 2 × Pi.

If we use the British Imperial units, we can get remarkable results. The perimeter of the Great Pyramid is 3,023.16 feet and its height is 481.3949 feet. (Note the last 4 decimal place figures represent the Earth's centre-to-pole radius in miles.) Using the scale of 43,200 (or, more correctly, a scale of 1/43,200), we can obtain an accurate scale representation of the Earth's northern hemisphere, projected on to flat surfaces.

Remember I stated that orthodox Egyptology argues that the Egyptians did not know how to work in three-dimensional planning? I think the following will refute that. First of all, though, bear in mind that the scaling down cannot now be 100 per cent accurate in relation to the Earth's dimensions because the pyramid is now somewhat eroded and damaged, and most of its outer facing blocks have been removed (see plates). However, the closeness of the figures is too pronounced to allow misinterpretation. For now, let us note that due to modern satellite surveys, we know that the Earth has an equatorial circumference of 24,903.45 miles and its polar radius is 3,949.834 miles. Remember though that the Earth is a spheroid and oblate, not perfectly spherical; so in effect, the architecture of the Great Pyramid is closer to a scale of 1/43,200.

We saw earlier how we derived the scale of 43,200: 360 × 60 × 2. The Earth's circumference of 24,903.45 miles, divided by 43,200, equals 0.5764 of a mile. Multiply this by 5,280 (there being 5,280 feet in a mile), and the result is 3,043.75 feet. This is an error of only 20 feet from the Great Pyramid's perimeter of 3,023.16 feet. However, if we take a closer look at the base of the perimeter, there are what are known as corner sockets that extend out *beyond* the perimeter. These corner sockets have perplexed Egyptologists for centuries, as they seem to be there for no apparent reason. But if we take the base perimeter measurement around the pyramid *and include the extended corner sockets*, we get exactly 3,043.7 feet. This is only .05 of a foot different from our 43,200 scaling down.

Furthermore, if we multiply 3,043.7 by 43,200, the answer is 1,314,878.4 feet. Dividing this by 5,280 feet gives 24,903.45 miles, which is the Earth's equatorial circumference as measured by the best means available today.

If *that* doesn't convince you, let's take the Pyramid's height of 482.75751 feet (remember, we are including the base platform height – most scholars fail to do so), and multiply it by 43,200, and then finally divide by 5,280. We end up with 3,949.834 miles, the Earth's exact polar radius. Not only that, but the Great Pyramid is also located exactly 3,949.834 miles from the North Pole (see figure 51).

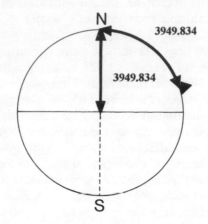

Figure 51.

British Imperial measurements (ii)

Now we need to go back to other British Imperial measurements, to see how they relate to sacred ratios. With the ratio of 22 over 7 in mind, if we section the Great Pyramid's perimeter into 22 equal lengths, we could then fit 7 of these units into its height accurately. If we did this we would have 22 equal units. Fortunately, if we increase the ratio factor, the equal unit measurement will decrease to a smaller, more manageable unit. If we used a ratio of double 22/7 (i.e. 44/14), the cubit unit would be halved. Even smaller measuring units could be obtained by using multiples of 22/7, e.g. 22/7; 44/14; 66/21; 154/49; 198/63; 242/77; 286/91; 506/161; 726/231; and 880/280.

From an engineering and construction point of view, a practical and convenient measurement of around half a yard would be ideal. It would be even better if the multiples were to consist of reasonably even numbers. The most obvious choice would thus be the 880/280 ratio given above, which produces a unit length of 52.35cms. If we multiply the first ratio of our unit of 880 by 2, we get 1,760.* We know that there are 1,760 yards in a mile, so it comes as no surprise to discover that the perimeter of the Pyramid when expressed in Sacred Cubits, is 1,760. We also find that the height of the Great Pyramid is exactly 280 Sacred Cubits – the second ratio figure. In simple terms, this means that the Great Pyramid is a 40-times magnification, as it were, of the Pi fraction of 22/7. It would thus appear, as some have argued, that the British Imperial measurement system is indeed based upon a 1/40 scale of the Pyramid's ratios. Can this be explained away as just *another* coincidence? I think not, as the following demonstrates.

The Great Pyramid measures 1,760 Sacred Cubits around its perimeter; this can be referred to as a Sacred mile. When constructing the Great Pyramid, it would make sense to divide this measurement into smaller units; for example dividing the perimeter by 8 would give a unit of half the base length of the pyramid, which would equal 220 Sacred Cubits. As we have seen, the British Imperial furlong is equal to 220 yards, so by analogy we can name this new unit a Sacred Furlong. As the Great Pyramid is a 40-times scale of the 1,760 yards ratio of 22/7, we can divide 220 by 40, which gives us 5.5 Sacred Cubits. This is highly significant, since earlier we saw the 5.5-yard measurement in the British Imperial system – the rod – perplexing scholars, as a fraction. We can therefore name our 40-scale rod a Sacred rod. This is no mere theoretical measurement: the length of the Grand Gallery to the Great Step inside the Great Pyramid is 16 Sacred rods, while the length of the Queen's Chamber is 2 Sacred rods.

I hope you can see that this demonstrates that the Great Pyramid actually contains a 40-scale ratio of the British Imperial measurement system, one that even includes the enigmatic rod. I think the facts speak for themselves. The ratios and values are derived *as a direct result of the constraints imposed by the constant of Pi*. In consequence, when dividing up a number such as 1,760, a fraction must occur at some point. The smallest unit just happens to be 5.5. In simple terms, this means that when the denominator ratio of Pi, expressed as 22/7, is divided by 4 (since the base of the Pyramid has 4 sides) the outcome is 5.5. Although an Imperial mile is far larger than the Sacred mile, both maintain the same exact ratios – *that* is the important point (see figure 52).

Earlier in this chapter, we saw the significance of the value of 43,200. If we measure the Earth's equatorial circumference in Sacred miles – or simply take the Pyramid's perimeter length – it fits around the Earth

* Each unit = 288 centimetres (2,880 is an important value).

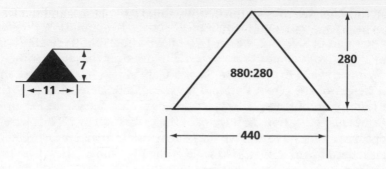

Figure 52. 40 × the ratio of 22:7 was established by C. Piazzi Smyth in the 19th century.

exactly 43,200 times. As for 40, it has been important throughout history, apparently for no special reason. Indeed, it is often thought of as sacred because Moses and the Israelites wandered in the wilderness for 40 years, and Jesus likewise spent 40 days in the wilderness. And, don't forget, the Flood lasted 40 days.

Links with England

How did these measurements find their way from Egypt to England? That question really intrigued me. In consequence, I looked for any connections that could guide me to an answer. (I eventually discovered how, and it was not how I imagined it to have occurred, as I will reveal later.) However, here I shall say that many adepts in sacred geometry prefer to use measurements of feet and inches rather than metres, regarding metrology as nothing more than a fashionable folly because of its adherence to tens and hundreds. As I was to discover, the metric system does have its place for reasons that will be revealed later. At this point in my research, I was struck by the fact that the British Imperial system is often referred to as *sacred.* This might perplex those unaware of the connections laid out above, but once one knows the link with ancient Egypt and later Moses, it is not difficult to see why.

It is evident that throughout the ages, ratios and values have been transmitted as sacred, *as a key,* from generation to generation, *for thousands of years.* The purpose must have been to assist a distant future generation with de-coding ancient secrets.

Other pyramids

Further evidence of the use of the Sacred cubits system comes from 3 other Egyptian pyramids outside the Giza Plateau: the Pyramid of

Meidum (in ruins: see plates); the Bent Pyramid (see plates); and the Red
Pyramid at Dashur (see figure 53).

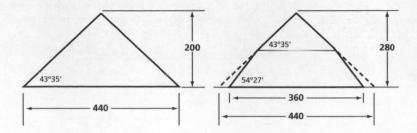

Values in Sacred/Royal Cubits of the above pyramids:

RED PYRAMID		BENT PYRAMID	
First two chambers	$= 16 \times 7$	Northern inclined entrance corridor	$= 140$
Third chamber	$= 16 \times 8$	Lower chamber	$= 12 \times 9.5$
External base length	$= 420 \times 420$	Exterior base length	$= 360 \times 360$
Height	$= 200$	Valley Temple	$= 50 \times 90$

Figure 53.

The resultant geometry matches the Pythagorean triangle of 20, 21, and
29. And remember, the ancient Egyptians, according to orthodox
history, were not aware of these ratios. So I must repeat, if they were *not*
aware of these ratios, why is it that the Great Pyramid contains many Pi,
Phi and Pythagorean values (see figure 54)?

Note the 3, 4, 5 ratio in the King's Chamber and that it measures 17 feet
high by 17 feet wide by 34 feet long. The total of this equals 68:

- Mankind is made up of 68 per cent water;
- planet Earth is 68 per cent covered in water;
- The Earth's average temperature is 68 degrees Fahrenheit; that is
  precisely the average temperature inside the Great Pyramid!

I mentioned earlier the importance of the Pythagorean triangle in helping
to locate the Hall of Records. Look at the angles in the sectional drawing
of the Great Pyramid in figure 55.

Notice that the angles of the descending and ascending passages,
including the Grand Gallery, are of the 26-degree mark. Many theories
have been proffered over the centuries to explain this. However, the
answer is simple if one accepts that the architect, fully understanding
Pythagorean ratios, used a triangle of 89, 80, 39. This not only gives a

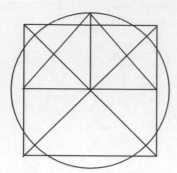

Incorporation of Pi (π)
The Great Pyramid's square perimeter is equal to the circumference of a circle, with a radius equal to the height of the Great Pyramid.

Length of slope: 610 feet
1/2 Base: 377.5 feet
610 ÷ 377.5 = 1.612
(Phi ratio to within 0.3%)

Incorporation of Phi (Φ)
The Phi ratio is approx 1 to 1.618. The length of the slope from top to a corner of the Great Pyramid, and the length of half base are in Golden Section relationship.

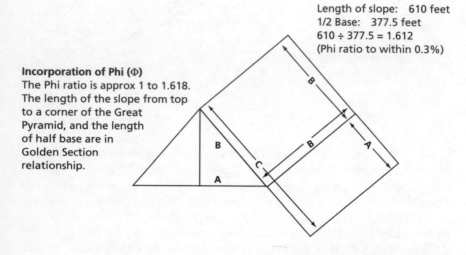

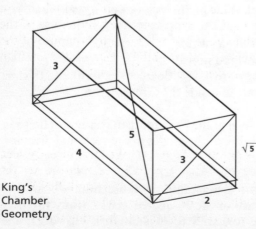

Sir William Flinders Petrie discovered that the dimensions of the King's Chamber encode a 3, 4, 5 Pythagorean triangle and a 2, 3, √5 triangle. The floor is inset from the walls and thus the walls show two heights; one to the floor surface of 17 feet, the other to their true base of 19 ft. The visible dimensions also establish a sound frequency or 'Keynote' of 'C' (65.4 hz, 130.8 hz, etc.).
Height: 17 feet
Width: 17 feet
Length: 34 feet

King's
Chamber
Geometry

Figure 54.

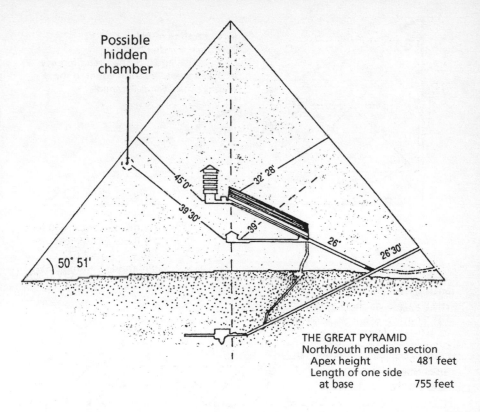

Possible hidden chamber

45°0'

32 28'

39 30'

39°

26°

26°30'

50° 51'

THE GREAT PYRAMID
North/south median section
Apex height   481 feet
Length of one side
   at base   755 feet

Figure 55.

right-angled triangle, but also gives an acute angle of 25.989 (i.e. 25° 59' 21" degrees), which is so minutely short of the 26 degrees that we can safely state that the important value is 26. This is confirmed when you realise that the Grand Gallery roof line represents the hypotenuse of the Pythagorean triangle. The Pythagorean triangle has a hypotenuse of the ratio 89; in this instance, that number occurs in the Grand Gallery, which has a roof line of 89 Sacred cubits (see figure 56).

Clues start mounting up . . .

The angle between 39 and 89 is exactly 64 degrees. We have already seen just how important the value of 64 is, especially in relation to the biological make-up of mankind in regard to DNA and RNA (see Chapter 4). As regards the Pythagorean Fadic triangle of 5, 12, 13, I pointed out earlier that it is of major significance to locating the Hall of Records. This triangle has the same angles 90, 64 and 26 degrees. I added up several tantalising facts:

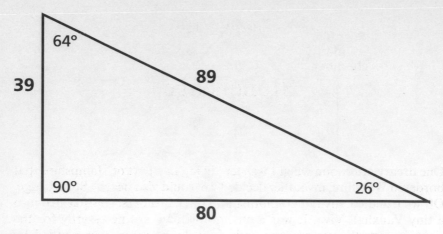

Figure 56.

• the value of 64 and its importance in DNA and RNA (i.e. creation itself);
• the ratios in the 39, 80, 89 triangle;
• that these values are of direct relevance within the Great Pyramid.

Then I began to suspect that someone – or some entity – was trying to communicate something. Initially this was just an intuitive hunch, later it was to be established, as I shall reveal. Reflecting on the notion that the Hall of Records is reputed to contain details about mankind's true origins (as we shall see, the ancient Egyptian Edfu texts refer to it as 'the chambers of creation'), I deduced that this was somehow linked to mathematical values. This would prove a complex and challenging course to pursue, but I was determined not to let go, despite the years of investigation it eventually demanded of me.

Chapter 19

Stonehenge

One dreary afternoon when I was ten, living in a part of Hampshire that bordered Wiltshire, my father decided we would visit nearby Stonehenge. Off we trundled, my father, mother and three brothers, all squashed into a tiny Vauxhall Viva. It was a memorable day, not necessarily for the right reasons. It was pouring with rain; the place was surrounded by barbed wire; and to cap all that we didn't bring enough money for all of us to go in. In consequence, my father decided that none of us would go in, so we each got a souvenir and an ice cream instead, and went back home.

My souvenir was a booklet on the history of Stonehenge, in which I read that scholars had discovered mathematical ratios within Stonehenge, as well as astronomical alignments. This intrigued me immensely, as did the puzzle of the place's construction – how *were* these massive stones moved into position? Hooked, I started to acquire books on Stonehenge. Over the years I developed many theories about it. I assumed that I was alone in my line of reasoning, but as various books appeared, I began to see others making the same connections. This was encouraging – I was not deluding myself looking for nonexistent links.

An Egyptian connection?

How did Π, the Pi symbol, come into use? No one is sure. Nevertheless, the Pi symbol has been evident in England, in solid stone, for countless generations – the Trilithons (literally, 'three stones') at Stonehenge. Think of what we learned about Boaz and Jachin and the twin pillars of Egypt. Is it a coincidence that this image is identical to the trilithons (figure 58) with their two upright stones capped by a slightly overhanging lintel?

As is shown on the figure, if we divide the total height of the trilithons into 22 equal parts, the centre of axis of the 2 uprights is equal to exactly 7 of those units: the 22/7 ratio again! Obviously Π is a Greek letter: superficially it might seem unbelievable that a stone representation of it should be found hundreds of miles from Greece, in England, at this very early date. But what exactly is the history of the Greek alphabet? It was

159

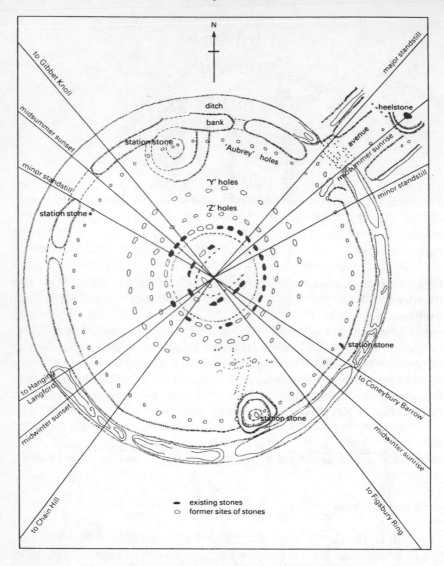

Figure 57. Stonehenge. The 2 barrows that are much discussed in this chapter are the approximately circular motifs at roughly 5 o'clock and 11 o'clock. The Avenue heads out in a north-easterly direction. The Slaughter stone is the long shape immediately left of the words 'midsummer sunrise' top right.

constructed from the earlier northern Semitic script, which is why it has 4 letters derived straight from the Semitic alphabet:

Greek:	A Alpha.	B Beta.	Γ Gamma.	Δ Delta.
Semitic:	⊄ Aleph.	9 Beth.	¬ Gimel.	∇ Daled.

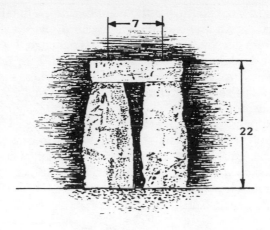

Figure 58.

From various sources on the Internet,[1] it can be demonstrated that the transfer was from the Near East to Greece, *not* vice versa. This view is supported by the fact that the letters themselves tend to have no intrinsic meaning in Greek, but each has a specific meaning in Semitic languages. I maintain that Greek certainly inherited a mathematical code, just as the Hebrew alphabet did; this implies then, that Greek was derived from Semitic languages in Palestine and Egypt. The symbolic shape of the Stonehenge trilithons relates to the gateway of the Temple of Horus at Edfu in Upper Egypt (see figure 59 and plates).

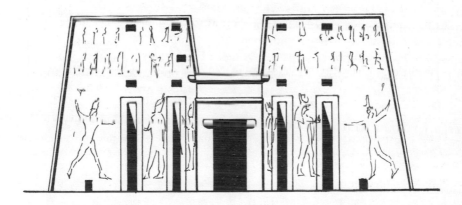

Figure 59. The Temple of Horus at Edfu.

The Temple was built, as it now is, between 237 and 57 BC, but contains earlier work. Its dramatic impact on the visitor arises from its monumental scale, but here, it's the basic pattern of the gateway that matters. The entrance gateway is formed by two massive square towers that taper towards the top (just as the trilithons do); a lintel straddles the two pillars forming an archway. Having been drawn to the Temple of Edfu because of its design, so resonant of Stonehenge, I was curious to know what else I might be able to discover about it. In time, I became aware of many inscriptions on the temple's walls. These hieroglyphs are known as the Edfu scripts or building texts, and relate to the ancient 'chambers of creation'.

Were there other links to Egypt? Yes. The trilithons are actually 6.66 metres in height (I will discuss metres later). We know how important *this* value is. Remember too, the height of the Sphinx on the Giza plateau (see figure 60 and plates) is exactly 66.6 feet. This all seems a little too coincidental, not to have a meaning.

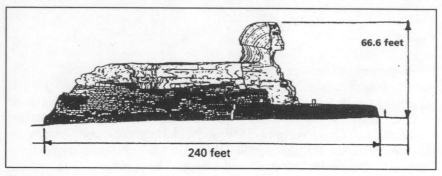

Figure 60.

Because of this one simple link to the Giza complex, I sensed a major connection here, especially where mathematical ratios and values were concerned. Later I noted that the Stonehenge circle stones (sarsens) tend to be set 4 feet into the ground; moreover, they are 7 feet wide and 14 feet high. The Fadic value for 1,760 Sacred cubits (a measurement at the Great Pyramid) is $(1 + 7 + 6 + 0)$ 14. So two of the most important number values occur again. Not only that, the trilithons are 4 feet thick at their base and taper upwards to 3 feet – in Fadic terms, 7.

The Heelstone, sunrise and deviations

Several years later I made other connections. Because Stonehenge has so many elements in its final plan, it is almost impossible *not* to find tantalising mathematical values. The Earth is tilted on its axis by 23.4 degrees. Within Stonehenge there are 2 small barrows (circular enclosures), both north and south; 2 of the 4 station stones are contained within each. The 4 station stones form a Pythagorean rectangle (see figure 61) that defines both the centre of the site and its centre of axis. The axis is 49.3 degrees east of north to the Avenue, which is 1,746 feet long.

(This was one of the very first times I noticed this number.) Both station stones within the north and south barrows are also offset against the site's centre of axis by 23.4 degrees (see figure 61).

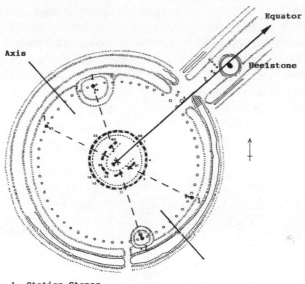

Figure 61. Stonehenge, showing equator and Station Stones.

Now, does the Avenue denote the site's equator? Certainly it is traditionally linked to the Sun as a ceremonial causeway, and has alignment to the midsummer sunrise. Most accounts insist that the midsummer Sun rises over the Heelstone; however, as this actually lies 2 degrees to the south of the Avenue line, such claims are not strictly true. Intriguingly it is known that the Heelstone had a small partner stone that lay slightly to its north. A line running between those two stones together marks the centre line of the Avenue. If this is the case, then where does it point to now?

The midsummer sunrise does not align with either the Avenue or the Heelstone, despite what is usually declared. The midsummer sun actually rises on a bearing of 48.5 degrees east of true north. However, the Avenue is at 49.3 degrees, and the Heelstone at 51.3 degrees, so the midsummer Sun actually rises *3.8 degrees north* of the Heelstone. (Photographs showing the Sun rising over the heelstone are not taken exactly at the moment of the midsummer sunrise.*)

* There is some debate as to when exactly sunrise should be timed from. Is it the second the first rays of sunlight appear on the horizon, is it half the Sun being visible, or is it when the entire Sun is completely visible on the horizon? This point will be explored later.

At the latitude of Stonehenge, the Sun does not rise vertically upwards on the horizon; it rises up in an apparent north-easterly direction, but is in fact moving south as it rises (an invaluable clue to the site of the Hall of Records so keep it in mind!). Once visible above the Heelstone, the Sun is actually 2 degrees above the horizon; this is not *really* sunrise, is it? In my opinion, this feature was deliberately incorporated by Stonehenge's designer. He was telling us something in mathematical terms. Taking into account all other factors (such as atmospheric refraction and aberration, where the Sun appears to look bigger), the Heelstone sunrise is exactly 14 minutes *after* the first limb of the Sun becomes visible on the horizon – that is, when its first rays are seen (see figure 62).

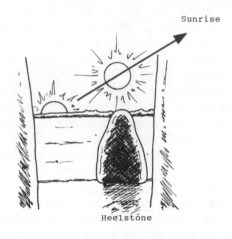

Figure 62. Note that the Heelstone is leaning forward (i.e. *away* from the viewer) by 27 degrees from vertical.

The value of 14 is an important and constantly recurring clue. The reason I feel confident in declaring that this clue was deliberately provided at Stonehenge derives from the fact that it is simple to determine exactly where the midsummer Sun would rise, just by using two people standing a small distance apart. As the Sun starts to break over the horizon, the individual nearer the Sun is simply directed left or right until he stands exactly where the Sun is rising, from the viewpoint of the onlooker. He then marks the ground in some way, so that whatever is required can be constructed on the precise position later. The error margin for this is less than 1/10th of a degree; certainly *not* the 2-degree difference described above. All that is required is that one person furthest away from the Sun tells the person nearest the Sunrise to run either left or right until they are standing directly in front of Sun's image as observed by the first person.

The designer's true intention

What could account for this deviation? The only thing I can think of is the Earth's precessional wobble, analysed in Chapter 14. There are in fact two such wobbles. One, known as nuation, describes the 'nodding' effect of precession on the Earth, caused by the gravitational influence of the Moon; its effect is actually very small. The other, libration, is a kind of oscillation, and has a more pronounced effect. Nonetheless, the deviation that either of these causes is very slow to manifest itself and can be influenced by such factors as the build-up of ice on the poles, the strength of the ocean's currents and so on. Recent scientific calculations posit the wobble from libration as only 1.2 degrees (either way, plus or minus) over a very long cycle – 41,000 years. This is slow indeed.

Now, a tilt in the Earth's angle to make Stonehenge work properly would have to be 22.5 degrees. This would cause the midsummer sunrise to appear at an angle of 51.3 degrees from due north, along the line of the Heelstone. I am convinced that the original designer knew the effects of precessional wobble and incorporated the multi-functional aspects of the Heelstone accordingly, to work both forwards and backwards in time depending on what era you were calculating from. Only now, in *our* time, does the Heelstone give the value 14 as outlined earlier, but only by using the sister Heelstone would the site correctly be aligned *when it was constructed*. This therefore indicates that the designer is telling us that the value 14 applies to our present era.

Stonehenge happens to be situated on a latitude of 51.3 degrees north of the equator. Stonehenge is the only place *on Earth* where the coincidence of latitude position of 51.3 degrees and the midsummer sunrise angle of 51.3 degrees can occur. To work this out clearly required intelligence and very sophisticated technology; it *also* demonstrates that the so-called primitive Neolithic peoples understood longitude and latitude thousands of years before it was discovered again. By assessing the role of such detail in its design, we can calculate exactly when Stonehenge was constructed, as I shall eventually disclose.

If Stonehenge was erected when the Earth's axis was at an angle of 22.5 degrees, over the course of time the Sun would appear further to the right as viewed from inside the sarsen stones. This means that the sister stones to the Heelstone and the Slaughter stones (see figures 57 and 61) would begin to obscure the Sun itself, thereby negating the whole purpose of the site. What's more, as time moved on, one of the large sarsen stones would eventually obscure the view of the sister stones to the Heelstone and Slaughter stone. In effect the two sister stones became unimportant and so were removed. Instead, a small barrow was placed around the Heelstone to signify its new primary importance as the midsummer sun began to pass directly over it. This was just as the original architect planned, with its 14-degree value inherent within it. He therefore deliberately positioned the sarsen stone to eventually block the sister stones from view. If this were *not* the case, the architect would have positioned the sarsen stone *further to the left*, so avoiding the problem completely.

The Avenue and the Aubrey Holes

The original Avenue was not wrong in its alignment. The angles are extremely accurate and remain valid, *regardless of era*. I decided after much thought that the true purpose of the Sacred Avenue is an equator line marker.

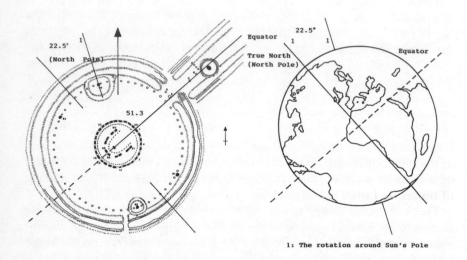

1: The rotation around Sun's Pole

Figure 63.

As we have seen, Stonehenge is located at latitude 51.3 north of the equator. If we wished to mark its location on a cross-section of the Earth, we would have to make a mark at an angle of 51.3 above the equator line. Remarkably, these angles are present in the ring of Aubrey Holes (named after the 17th-century antiquarian John Aubrey, who studied them), where one Aubrey Hole lies exactly on the line of the Avenue and another lies on the axis of the henge. This means that the 56 Aubrey Holes are oriented with the monument as a whole, and *not* the Heelstone. North of the Avenue Aubrey Hole there is another Aubrey Hole, exactly 51.3 north of the henge equator line, that marks the exact location of Stonehenge as positioned on the Earth.

As we saw in Chapter 14, the Earth's poles, or axis, revolve very slowly around the Sun's poles, drawing out an imaginary circle in the sky (figure 32). This is precession and the cycle lasts 25,920 years. I believe that the barrows clearly represent precessional circles. Their design is exactly how

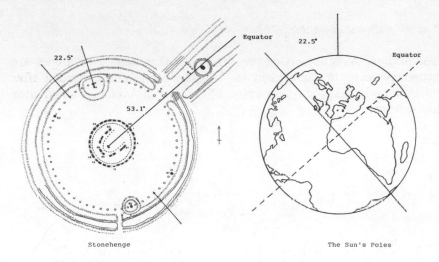

Figure 64.

I would represent them if charged with producing a schematic diagram of the phenomenon. (Stonehenge is not the only henge to represent these details, as we shall see; there is another site that is part of a larger scheme of things, as I shall reveal later.)

The Aubrey Holes served two purposes. They not only marked out the phases of the Moon (i.e. its rising and eclipses), as is generally agreed, but also confirm the theory of the Aubrey Holes as markers just proffered (though some will argue that the theory is very tenuous, as I could have picked any of the 56 Holes). The 56 Holes were eventually filled in with chalk, which guaranteed their positioning would last thousands of years. Using 56 Holes in a circle means that each is (6.4285714 exact, rounded up to 6.43) degrees apart from its neighbours.

Are the positions of the Aubrey Holes significant? Yes. There is one directly in line with the centre line of the Avenue (see above). Then, moving northwest around the Aubrey Holes, we find another in the due north position, the Stonehenge Hole. If we count the number of Aubrey Holes to the Avenue, we find 8. And if we multiply 8 by the angle between each Aubrey Holes (6.43), we get 51.4 degrees. If we move west again, we find another Aubrey Hole situated on Stonehenge's site axis line. There are 6 Aubrey Holes in this segment from due north to the axis, and if we multiply 6 by 6.43, the result is 38.6. Is it *another* coincidence that the remaining distance from Stonehenge to the North Pole is 38.7 degrees?

167

The 56 Aubrey Holes not only confirm the angles found as correct, but also define the *original* 22.5-degree axis of Earth when the site was constructed. Looking at the barrows you will note that their centres lie exactly between two Aubrey Holes (see figure 65).

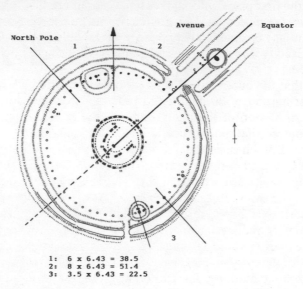

1: 6 x 6.43 = 38.5
2: 8 x 6.43 = 51.4
3: 3.5 x 6.43 = 22.5

Figure 65. Stonehenge alignments.

Using the angle axis of Stonehenge with its original angle of 22.5 degrees, the barrows' positions in relation to the Aubrey Holes are exactly 3.5 segments of 6.43 between the axis (the Earth's pole) and the barrows (the Sun's pole). Now 3.5 multiplied by 6.43 gives 22.5. This is a clear indicator defining the Earth's axis when Stonehenge was constructed. The only figure that would accommodate all the above calculations is 56 – the number of Aubrey Holes.

A pointer to another site?

Having covered the trilithons and the Aubrey Holes, we now need to consider the large circle of sarsen stones. Having realised the significance of the Aubrey Holes and the entire site as a representation of Earth itself, with important latitude markers encoded within it, I wondered if similar calculations could be achieved from the sarsen stones. They form an impressive circle, dominating the site. Surely this indicates that whatever encoded values or latitude markers are contained in their arrangement must be equally important. Besides, why give *latitude* markers without a *longitude* marker as well? Could the trilithons represent a longitude value? I wondered.

The Earth pole, Sun pole and equator line, plus the latitude marker of Stonehenge, together show that this whole site is a map, in stone, of Earth itself. The interesting point here is that there is no need to indicate *Stonehenge itself* on this map. You are already aware of it, as you are on the site in the first place, and all the details so far confirm where you are from a *global* perspective. As I pondered this puzzle I began to suspect that there might be an encoded message that would point to some *other* location. Exactly *why* was irrelevant to me at that stage. I just wanted to know *where*.

I noted that the outer ring of sarsen stones numbered 30. I saw this as yet another marker of 30 degrees latitude. As Stonehenge is marked in the northern section of the plan, and is in the northern hemisphere of Earth, I deduced that the latitude indicated had to be 30 degrees *north* of the equator. But where exactly? I definitely needed a longitude value as well. Then I noticed that the central trilithon horseshoe faced eastwards – according to the site's equator line – following the direction of the Avenue. To me this said, Look eastwards. Now I was doing much of my thinking with only books and photographs in front of me. But at this point a trip to Stonehenge was required, as I simply could not determine a longitude marker value without being in the vicinity. It was only when I was on site, having jumped over the fence in the middle of the night wearing combat clothing for camouflage, that I thought to use the trilithon horseshoe as a possible indicator. I measured it from all angles and returned home, where I applied all the ancient units of measure I could think of, to try and equate a longitude number. I got plenty of numbers but none married up with any known location. Was that the point? I thought. Was the code indicating a position never before revealed? I shook my head. This didn't ring true: after going to all the lengths of encoding all the relevant details, surely the original architect wouldn't be so ambiguous at this final stage?

Then, in the early hours of the night in the summer of 1983, I suddenly made the connection between the trilithon horseshoe shape and that of the Great Pyramid's mysterious, enigmatic seal (see figure 66).

As I hurriedly began to superimpose the two images, I was convinced that the trilithon horseshoe and Great Pyramid boss were clear representations of each other. Could this mean that Stonehenge was a marker pointing to Giza? I took out my maps and rulers and started calculating. I had my 30 degrees north marker, as encoded at Stonehenge. The Great Pyramid is situated at 30 degrees north of the equator. I measured (in both feet and metres this time) the trilithon horseshoe, around its outer perimeter, which mimicked the shape of the Boss of the Great Pyramid. The result, in metres, was 33. Was 33 my longitude marker? I'd already concluded that all the indications were for a longitude somewhere eastwards – the trilithon horseshoe opened to the

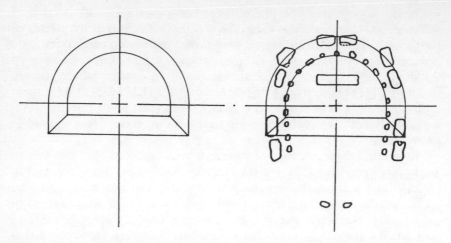

Figure 66. (left) Great Pyramid Boss/Seal on granite leaf. *(right)* Stonehenge trilithons.

east, as did the Avenue representing the equator, when the henge is used as a map. As I quickly grabbed my *Times Atlas* I scanned the Giza complex in Egypt. Not only was it at a latitude of 30 degrees North, *it was also 33 degrees east in longitude from Stonehenge*. That settled it. But *why* was Stonehenge pointing to Giza? I already had suspicions that something important was connected to the Giza Pyramids. Now I felt almost convinced of the fact; so my love affair with Giza really commenced.

But I was still determined to find vital links between Stonehenge and places nearer than that.[2]

Several points in this chapter followed parallel lines of research as those expressed by R. Ellis in his book, *Thoth, Architect of the Universe* (Published by Edfu Books, 1997). I would highly recommend reading his book, as interested readers will see how we were parallel in our research yet reached totally different conclusions.

Chapter 20

Avebury, Giza and Teotihuacan

Avebury and Stonehenge are closely connected, so it did not take me long to start researching the place. Avebury is approximately 18 miles north of Stonehenge, and almost right next to Avebury is Silbury Hill, which we shall also have cause to look at. My reason for looking closely at Avebury, rather than at any of the many hundreds of stone circles dotted across England and Europe, was the horseshoe-shaped arrangement of stones (known as the Cove) in the northern circle. This immediately reminded me of the trilithons and sarsen stones at

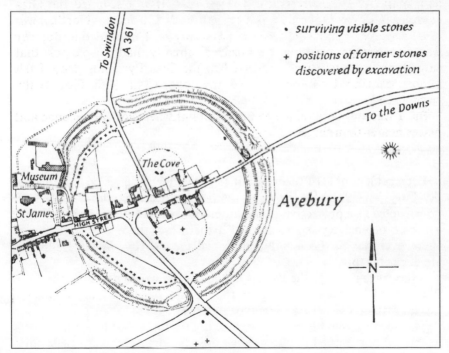

Figure 67.

Stonehenge (see figure 57). One of the first things that I learnt about Avebury is that its enigmas have perplexed orthodox scholars (see figure 67).

In 1720 the antiquarian, William Stukeley, who mapped and measured the site in detail, suggested that the northern inner circle was dedicated to the Moon whilst the southern circle was dedicated to the Sun, as there were no other apparent astronomical alignments or orientations inherent within it.[1] Later scholars did calculate various alignments. It was further postulated that the circles played a symbolic function, used merely for religious ceremonies and festivals. The upright stones were for worshipping the 'Earth Gods' and also formed an enclosed arena in which to perform sacrifices, while the Obelisk in the centre of the southern circle (see figure 67) has been seen as a phallic symbol, associated with fertility rituals supposedly carried out on the site (see figure 68).

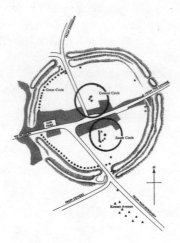

Figure 68.

Let's get a couple of theories out of the way before we go any further. Avebury is surrounded by large ditches but these couldn't have been constructed as a protective embankment and ditch system, as in fact they serve no defensive purpose at all. Furthermore, there is no evidence of there ever having been a Neolithic village nearby. What I think *is* significant is this:

Avebury is perhaps the largest henge* in the world and Stonehenge is likewise the largest *stone* henge in the world. Nearby Silbury Hill is the largest artificial structure of its type in the world.

This seems a tenable reason for looking for links, but to see these sites as part of one unified design goes against the orthodox view of history, which does not accept that they were constructed simultaneously or as a unified system.

* 'Ritual earthwork with a surrounding bank and ditch' – *The Buildings of England* series, Glossary.

If you look in the upper part of Avebury (see figure 67) you will see a small circle, the circle that first made me think of Stonehenge. In the exact centre of the northern circle there were originally 3 large standing stones (only 2 remain). These, the biggest stones within Avebury (apart from the Obelisk), are flat and rectangular, and placed in the ground to form a rectangle, totally unlike other arrangements of stones on the site. They form an enclosure rather like a horseshoe. It points out in a north-east direction, just as the Stonehenge horseshoe does; and east if used as a map with an equator line running through, as at Stonehenge (see figure 69).

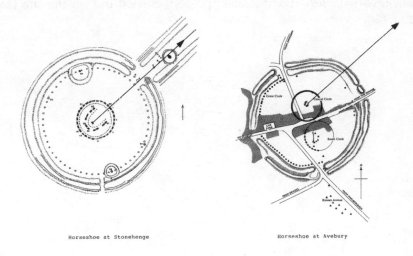

Horseshoe at Stonehenge   Horseshoe at Avebury

Figure 69.

This is why I perceived that Avebury and Stonehenge were connected. The ratio between the Cove stones and the northern circle containing them replicates that of the trilithon horseshoe and its containing circle of sarsen stones at Stonehenge. Later the direction of north-east would prove to be of crucial importance in tracking down the Hall of Records.

Is Avebury a marker?

Having read years previously that the Great Pyramid at Giza was a scale representation of the Northern Hemisphere, as we saw in Chapter 18, I naturally wondered if Avebury served a similar purpose. In view of what I had worked out where Stonehenge was concerned, it seemed a logical step to take. So I compiled a simple diagram of Avebury and an enlarged picture of the Earth, then montaged the two images on my college's magnifier machine. I deliberately offset the Earth image to a 23.4 degree angle of obliquity to be an exact parallel of Earth itself. The actual angle of Avebury's equator line is nearer to 22.5, but is still a close match; and as we saw above, 22.5 degrees appears to have been deliberately constructed into Stonehenge's alignment. There had to be a definite connection here. I knew that even if I was totally wrong, I still had to investigate further, to settle the matter in my own mind (see figure 70).

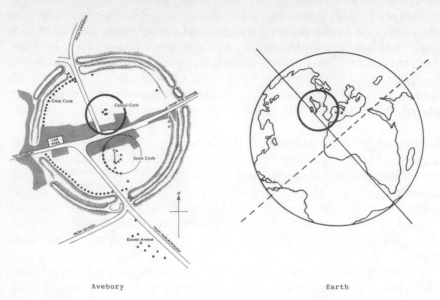

Avebury   Earth

Figure 70.

I immediately noticed that the east/west road cuts across the Avebury ring at the same angle as the Earth's equator. Modern now, the road is built upon a far more ancient pathway deliberately constructed to pass through Avebury (again, this is a further contradiction of the notion that Avebury was a defensive position). I also noted that Avebury is not an exact circle; this is one of the reasons scholars could not achieve perfect astronomical alignments. Avebury is oblate – just as the Earth bulges out at its equator due to its spinning on its axis. This is, I think, a remarkably compelling indication that the architect deliberately included the oblateness to represent the Earth's equatorial bulge. Subsequent henges built to mimic Avebury were constructed with the bulge exaggerated, as though later designers equated this bulge with something sacred, without fully understanding the meaning behind it.

There is much debate over exactly how many stones there were originally in the northern circle. A. C. Smith, a dedicated amateur historian active in the early part of the 20th century, who measured the site in minute detail, judged this circle to contain about 27 stones (27 is an important number, as will be shown).[2] However, only 2 remain upright, 2 more have fallen, and 8 positions for vanished stones have been reliably inferred through geological and archaeological evidence (derived from actual depressions still visible and from resistivity anomalies that pinpoint the remains of the holes). In 1723 William Stukeley also suggested that the northern circle contained 27 stones. One of the fallen stones (known as stone 210) is outside the circle formed by the remains and evidence of the others (directly above the 'o' of 'Cove' on figure 67). This means the suggested circle of 27 stones might not be the correct circle. By drawing a circle that encompasses stone 210, the centre is offset from the horseshoe; if on the other hand we draw the circle from the centre of the horseshoe, while it does encompass the other stone positions in a slightly smaller circle, that circle would only contain *26* stones. It is my belief that the so-called fallen stone was *deliberately* placed. Why? To give both ratios of 26 and 27 respectively.

Having identified a purpose in the horseshoe stones at Avebury (i.e. depicting Stonehenge as positioned in the northern hemisphere), I turned my attention to the southern circle: What could it represent? Was there something in the *southern* hemisphere, in the same position as the southern circle at Avebury? I immediately thought of Easter Island, but a quick glance through my world atlas instantly dispelled that idea. Perhaps I was on a wild goose chase, seeing things that simply were not there.

The small southern circle contains 29 stones which surround another D-shaped group of stones. Every book I have ever read on Avebury drew a complete blank on what these meant, so I knew I had to do some serious investigation.

I wondered if there was some significance in the 8 confirmed stone sites that form the D shape in the southern circle. In contrast with the northern circle, there is no debate about how many stones formed the southern circle, as it is accepted that there were 29. When 29 is added to the 27 of the other circle, the result is 56. So here again, as at Stonehenge, we find 56. I looked again at the southern hemisphere on a globe of the Earth. I looked at latitude 56 hoping to find something significant, but nothing was evident. Then I saw the South Sandwich Islands below, at 58 degrees south. Knowing the importance of 58 from previous research (connections with the Templars, and so on) I was immediately focused on them. This small group of islands in the South Atlantic is made up of 7 major islands – and we know the significance of that number. Nonetheless, I remained sceptical and thought through my findings again. The northern circle is made up from 26 stones if we use the smaller circle dimension, and 2 × 26 equals 52. As we know, this circle contains a horseshoe, just as at Stonehenge. Stonehenge is situated between the latitudes 51 and 52 degrees north of the equator. This seemed a clear latitude pointer to me, so I applied the same process to the southern circle: 29 × 2 gives 58 (see figure 71).

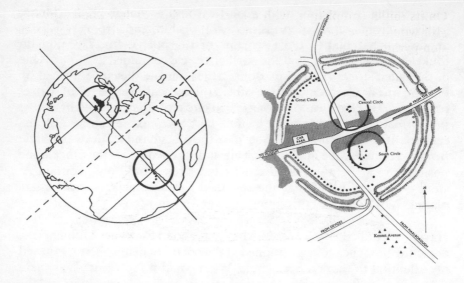

Figure 71. (*a*) Earth Latitudes of 52 and 58: (*b*) Avebury Latitudes of 52 and 58

As we shall see, the value of 58 is recurrent. Here, its occurrence proved that the ancient designers of these sites fully understood latitude and longitude. Their main purpose in letting us know these facts, it appears to me, was to reveal that they knew the dimension of the Earth; and having done so, the *specific* numbers involved (58, 33 and 30) were intended to link Avebury with Stonehenge, with the latter as a pointer to Giza!

A towering prehistoric 'hill'

Silbury Hill (see plates) is so close to Avebury that I had no choice but to research that site as well. I found out that Silbury Hill, the tallest prehistoric manmade structure in Europe at nearly 130 feet, is 1,760 yards south of Avebury and 17.46 miles north of Stonehenge. Carbon dating of organic remains inside the hill gives a rough date of construction of about 4,500 years ago, i.e. *c.* 2,500 BC, which is accepted by mainstream historians. However, this is not correct, as we shall reveal later. After all, carbon dating is not an exact science. The hill is composed of a clay core and flint, and has 6 steps of concentric radial walls composed of chalk with rubble infill; each of these steps is 17 feet high. It has an almost flat top 100 feet in diameter and a base circumference of 520 feet. The estimated volume is 13 million cubic feet (see figure 72).

On its initial completion, with 6 levels of brilliant white chalk, Silbury Hill would have looked identical (in side profile) to ancient Egyptian step-pyramids (such as Zoser's step pyramid at Saqqara, see plates).

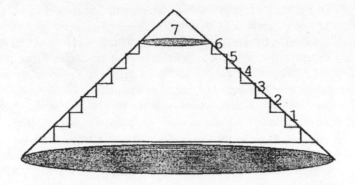

Figure 72.

However, it was subsequently covered in earth to protect its fragile chalk facing. It was constructed just high enough to enable individuals standing on its top to view sacred alignments that we shall look at later. In addition, there are other pyramids constructed in exactly the same manner as Silbury Hill – but on a *rectangular* base. These are the pyramids of Teotihuacan in Mexico, built using the same technique – a clay core faced with stone blocks and covered in earth. This connection led me to investigate the pyramids at Teotihuacan as the parallels were so pronounced. On top of that, the calendar, numbering systems and myths of Teotihuacan were uncannily like those of the myths and legends in the eastern hemisphere. Finally, I also realised that Silbury Hill contains the ratio for Pi if continued to its apex (see figure 73).

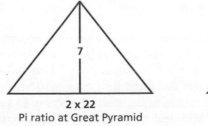

2 x 22
Pi ratio at Great Pyramid

2 x 22
Pi ratio at Silbury Hill

Figure 73.

Constellations and Colchester

At this point I need to draw your attention to certain correlations in relation to Giza, Stonehenge, Avebury, Silbury Hill and Teotihuacan. We shall come back to these details later, but for now I would like to introduce certain aspects of the sites.

Bestselling books by the likes of Graham Hancock, Robert Bauval and Adrian Gilbert have made the world realise that the Giza pyramids appear to be an Earthly image of the constellation of Orion, reproduced in stone. One evening back in 1983, I was plotting ley lines (absolutely straight lines linking ancient sites) on a map of the Colchester area, having read accounts that there were sacred sites in the area. Having learnt about the ancient town of Colchis relating to Jason and the Argonauts story and its subsequent connections to ancient Egyptian myths, which in turn led to Hebrew myths and on to Arthurian legend, I felt compelled to see if there was any kind of connection with Colchester. (As it transpired, I found no link from Colchis to Colchester, other than the linguistic similarity. I *did* learn that Colchester derived its name from the Roman Camulodunum, a Romanised version of its original name, Camulod. The D and the T were interchangeable so it *could* be argued – as some have – that Camulod could be spelt as Camulot.)

The reason I am telling you this now, is that as I started connecting various ancient sites and churches around Colchester, I started to put little orange marker stickers over those that had concentrated lines converging on them. Eventually I stood back to view the mess of lines and orange dots. Being an amateur astronomer, and having had my interest in the Orion constellation sparked off by Robert Temple's *The Sirius Mystery*, I was readily aware of that constellation's pattern. As I stood looking, I suddenly realised that I could see 7 orange dots forming an image of Orion. Just a coincidence, I told myself. Still, knowing the importance of Sirius in relation to Orion and the myths behind it, I calculated where Sirius would be projected, even though there were no lines pointing to the approximate vicinity. As I peered at the projected site of Sirius, I noticed it lay over the ruins of a monastery (Tiptree Priory), set on top of a hill. Bingo! I thought: This means something! (For more details and a map, consult Appendix 1.)

Orion and Giza

A few weeks later I was reading a book from the library – *Pyramid Odyssey* by William R. Fix.[3] In it I came across an aerial photograph of the Giza pyramids. I had seen it before, but now in view of my 'Orion projection' connection, the image took on a new meaning. It was one of those very rare moments in my life, a Eureka moment. Out came my astronomy books to find a photo of Orion. Once I had one, I shot off to college to use the image magnifier machine. As I montaged the 2 images of Orion's 3 belt stars with the 3 apex points of the Pyramids of Giza, a chill ran down my back. It seemed conclusive to me. I mentioned this connection to my parents, brothers and friends, expecting them to be impressed and excited, but no; there was no hint of any such thing. Just a casual, 'Oh really, dear?' from my mother and 'Space cadet!' from my eldest brother Craig. The consensus was that I was 'losing the plot', carried away with all my little intuitive hunches and ideas.

As a consequence of such reactions, I tempered my enthusiasm and sent off for some high-detail maps of the Giza complex. If the Giza pyramids represented the 3 belt stars, I would try and see if there were any other pyramids that married up to the positions of the other 4 stars of Orion. Just getting the maps of the Giza complex was a nightmare in itself, as detailed topographical ordnance maps were nigh impossible to obtain from Egypt at the time, for security reasons and so on. For once, my reserve forces involvement would prove an asset. I was able to obtain several American Military Ordnance survey maps, in full colour and very detailed.

When I aligned my projection of the Orion's belt stars over the 3 Giza pyramids, they again fitted perfectly. The problem was, try as I might, I could not make any connection between the other stars and other pyramids or temples. I had excitedly thought that as I overlaid the projection, Sirius would correspond to some huge temple complex and so I felt highly deflated. There was *nothing* that matched up. It was very near the Nile itself, while the other stars simply projected on to empty desert. Could there be pyramids at these sites but buried under sand? There *were* 2 pyramids, at Zawiyet El Aryan and at Abu Roash, that were *almost* in alignment – but these were a couple of miles off the stars' precise projected position. I desperately wanted the projections to align so I tried stretching, to take the Earth's curvature into account, but to no avail. I even contemplated fudging the star projections at Zawiyet El Aryan and Abu Roash to fit; that way I could show that there were 5 out of the 7 stars of Orion represented in stone. This would surely convince family and friends that I was on to something.

As I jogged home from college that afternoon I was despondent, as I really had thought, with all my heart, that there would be a connection. Perhaps the important 3 stars of Orion's belt were all that mattered. Whatever, I knew I couldn't fudge the facts to fit my theory just to get a short-lived pat on the back. I wanted the truth, real facts; not fudged ones to appease my ego. To accept such things would be being dishonest to myself, and if I followed that attitude I would never get anywhere with my research; certainly not the truth. In consequence, I immersed myself in studying the ancient Egyptian *Book of the Dead* and any other connections to the Orion constellation that I could find.

One of the first things I noticed was that next to the constellation of Orion is the constellation of Leo, the Lion. Next to the Giza pyramids is the Sphinx. Unfortunately the significance of this would not come to me for several years. I also saw that the Red Pyramid and Bent Pyramid (see plates) south of Giza *appeared* to marry up with the Hyades star cluster in the constellation of Taurus; but again, I could not align them perfectly. However, this general pattern did draw my attention back to Avebury, Silbury and Stonehenge, and the connection with both Orion and Giza.* As I drew out a schematic representation of Orion, the Earth's pole and Sun's pole on a planisphere projection, I was immediately struck by the similarity between that pattern and the arrangement of Giza, Stonehenge, Silbury and Avebury – even down to the same angles (see figure 74). This would occur during the year 2,400 BC.

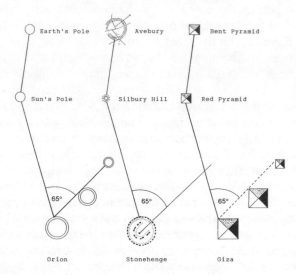

Figure 74.

If the Giza complex replicated both the constellation of Orion (its 3 pyramids representing Orion's 3 belt stars) *and* its near partner Leo (as represented by the Sphinx), would it be unreasonable to assume that the designer of the Stonehenge/Avebury/Silbury Hill complex did likewise and represented a similar constellation related to the English sites?

As I studied my old star charts I immediately noticed on a schematic illustration depicting the 3 belt stars of Orion and the Earth and Sun's poles the constellation of Pegasus. I knew the Zodiac and knew that there wasn't any sign represented by Pegasus. I knew that the ancient Egyptian Dendera Zodiac (carved on the ceiling of a tomb) depicts a *camel*, but I couldn't make a definite connection. Then I turned my attention to maps

* I originally thought that the relationship of Avebury to Silbury Hill was the same as that of the Moon to the Earth.

of the Stonehenge region. What should I see, marked on a map not far from Stonehenge, and *in the same position as Pegasus is to Orion*? The Uffington Horse (see figure 75).

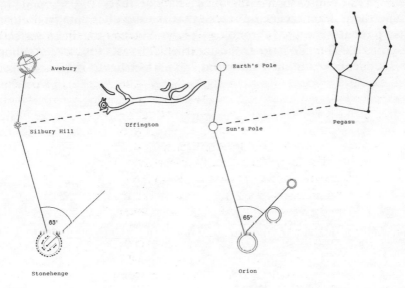

Figure 75.

In my opinion the Uffington Horse has played a dual part, as it represents not only Pegasus but also Leo. I state this, as the Uffington Horse is more feline than equine in its design. It is very representative of early Celtic cat imagery, as my younger brother Grahame (who had studied Celtic myths and art forms) pointed out. If you look closely at the Uffington Horse (see plates) you can easily argue that it is indeed more feline in nature.

Mexican connections

Because of all this I began looking at other ancient sites around the world to see if there were connections to indicate a coherent and deliberate plan, one that showed that someone from antiquity was trying to tell us something. Exactly *what*, I had no idea at the time. I did find connections – not in Egypt, but in Central America.

Teotihuacan, in modern Mexico, was a remarkable city (see plates). Here the pyramids were built by a far simpler method than those at Giza but their scale is enormous. The most notable aspect of the site (*apart* from the obvious pyramids) is the huge 'Path of the Dead' or 'Way of the Dead', a title the Spanish, not the native Americans, bestowed upon it. Teotihuacan was once populated by nearly 200,000 people who lived an organised yet highly complex lifestyle. The entire city complex was laid out in a manner very similar to that of a modern city of comparable size, with many carefully designed canals. The dates of Teotihuacan are debated as radio-carbon dating puts a date of up to 1474 BC on artifacts found there. I am inclined to agree that the site does date back further than presently accepted chronology allows. Some argue that it goes back as far as 3,000 BC. Whatever the arguments over its foundation, the city was suddenly abandoned in around 750 AD (see figure 76).

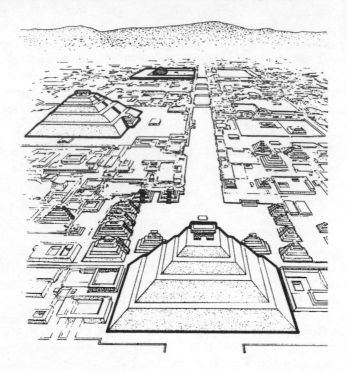

Figure 76.

The 'Way of the Dead' is 7,920 feet long – and the Earth is 7,920 miles in diameter. The 'Way of the Dead' is offset from north by 15.5 degrees north-east. The entire site of Teotihuacan was, for some mysterious reason, totally covered in earth up to 12 feet thick. This phenomenon has also occurred in China, where there are many pyramids that have been deliberately buried in earth and now resemble large hills covered in vegetation (see plates). The pyramids there are verifiable, but they have been off limits to the Western world since the end of World War Two. These deserve a book in their own right, but I bring them to your attention to show that Teotihuacan is not unique in that respect. What's more, of course, Silbury Hill is covered in earth (see plates).

Intriguingly, no one has yet been able to perceive any significant stellar alignments in the design of the place, in contrast to so many other sites. However, the whole of Teotihuacan is set around this avenue, hinting that it must have great significance. Now, if my ideas about the sites of Avebury, Stonehenge, Silbury Hill and the Giza complex are correct, then I would expect to be able to test this theory at Teotihuacan. I therefore estimated with quite some accuracy the positions of two further pyramids located some distance north of the Teotihuacan site – just as at Giza and Stonehenge/Avebury/Silbury Hill.

If a line is drawn through the belt of Orion and another from Orion to the Sun's pole, an angle of 65 degrees is formed. If we take a bearing from the 'Way of the Dead' at an angle of 65 degrees, we end up facing 49.5 degrees west of north. If we travel exactly *65 kilometres* along this bearing, we end up at the pyramid complex of Tula. To date, only one pyramid has been excavated at this site, but the presence of others is very evident and is simply a matter of waiting for them to be cleared (see figure 77).

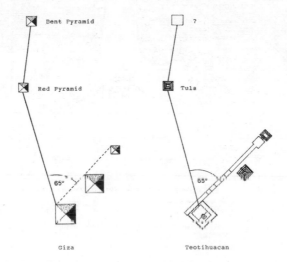

Figure 77.

Another telling feature is that the small pyramid in the citadel at Teotihuacan, dedicated to Quetzalcoatl, casts a shadow at midday that takes precisely 66.6 seconds to move from its summit to ground level across its face. If it had been built anywhere else other than at this precise latitude and longitude, this phenomenon would not take exactly 66.6 seconds. (This pyramid also happens to be 72 feet tall – an all-important number, you'll recall.) Remember, the Earth travels at 66,600 miles per hour around the Sun and is also tilted on its axis to 23.4 degrees – i.e. 66.6 degrees from its obliquity. It has been argued that this pyramid embodies certain calculations that relate to our solar system and its planets.

As a final note in this section on the correlations between Giza, Teotihuacan and Orion, please look at the layouts in figure 78. We shall show later that their respective myths are connected. Need I say more?

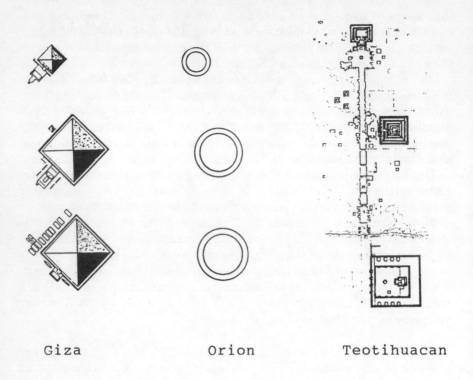

| Giza | Orion | Teotihuacan |

Figure 78.

R. Ellis likewise had drawn many of the same interim conclusions (in *Thoth, Architect of the Universe*) but took the investigation further, thus confirming to me the validity of my own intuitive ideas.

Chapter 21

Taking Stock: Clues in 58 and 64

After these revelations about key ancient sites, I need to convey the significance of two particular numbers before I go on to develop my argument. First I need to draw your attention to some (but not all!) details relating to the value of 58.

During my many years of research into a variety of areas, I constantly came across 58. Why? What was the significance of this number? I intuitively felt that the 58 value *itself* was the important element.

Now, being very fascinated by Arthurian myths and legends, I was determined to research the Knights Templar, reputed to be the guardians of the Holy Grail. As I did so, I became aware of the fact that part of their traditions talked of a head with the value of 58 somehow connected to it. I will have more to say on this matter later; what matters now is that I tried to attach many meanings to the head value of 58. A Templar reliquary for the head was described as follows:

A great head of gilded silver, most beautiful, and constituting the image of a woman. Inside were two head bones, wrapped in cloth of white linen, with another red cloth around it. A label was attached, on which was written the legend CAPUT LVIIIm. The bones inside were those of a rather small woman. [1]

Caput LVIIIm translates as 'Head 58m'. This remains an enigma. What of m? It has been argued this is the astronomical symbol of Virgo.

It is worth noting that an important ancient Egyptian number that has many symbolic meanings (as I shall cover later) is the value of 5. This is the number of the pentagram and the 5-pointed star image that represented Sirius (which I'll elaborate on in due course). Meanwhile, 8 is associated with Isis, who was represented by Sirius in the heavens. The numbers 5 and 8 are also present in the 'Brothers of the Rosy Cross' (known popularly as the Rosicrucians), whose emblem is a rose constructed with a centre of 5 petals, surrounded by 8 petals.

Remember how earlier I stressed the importance of the value of 64? This number plays a multi-functional purpose that helps pinpoint the location of the Hall of Records. As I also pointed out, it is directly connected with human DNA and RNA. By now, it should not surprise you to learn that the Giza complex is set out on an 8×8 grid square system (8×8 obviously equals 64; see figure 79).

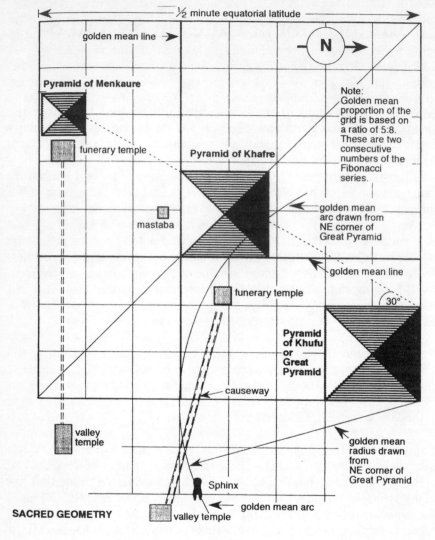

Figure 79.

Not only do we find the important 64 value, but also you will note that the golden mean proportion of the grid is based on a ratio of 5:8. These are two consecutive numbers in the Fibonacci scale, as we saw in Chapter 16. I asked you to make a note of 64 and about multiplying it by 1,440, which has many sacred and esoteric meanings. It happens that each side of the Giza 8×8 square equals 1/2 a minute of equatorial latitude, i.e.

921.44 metres. (Remember, the use of metric in my argument is *not* arbitrary; its purpose will be made clear.) Now, 64 × 1440 equals 92,160 – converting, by gematria, to our metre value, there is a difference of just 0.16 (or 16 cms). Here it is the 921 value we are interested in. I hinted that you need to take a bearing from the Great Pyramid's apex; in this you have a limited choice: 90 degrees, 26 degrees or 64 degrees. Which is it going to be? This is just one clue to lead to the Hall of Records.

Note also that the Great Pyramid sits in the north-east corner of the grid, on just four squares – or more correctly, 1/16th of it. That number 16 is another clue. In addition, notice that the golden mean radius, drawn from the north-eastern corner of the Great Pyramid, passes directly through the Sphinx. Yet another clue.

PART FOUR

THE MYSTERY DEEPENS

Chapter 22

Numerology and Gematria

I shall now investigate the values encoded within these important numbers: 360, 72, 30 and 12. We will also study 1,080. To recap, note that 30×72 equals 2,160 which, as we know, equals the number of years taken by one complete Zodiacal precession of 30 degrees along the ecliptic. Furthermore, $2,160 \times 12$ equals 25,920, just as 360×72 equals 25,920; this is the number of years taken to complete the precession of all 12 signs of the Zodiac – 'the Great Year'. The most prominent number in the Osiris myths is 72. Now, 72 and 720 were frequently added to 36 and 360, making 108 and 1,080 respectively. 1,080 miles is the radius of the Moon.

I also mentioned earlier that in both the Greek and Hebrew alphabets, each letter had a mathematical value attached to it. Below are both alphabets with their respective numerical values (see figures 80a and 80b).

$A\,\alpha$	$B\,\beta$	$\Gamma\,\gamma$	$\Delta\,\delta$	$E\,\varepsilon$	$Z\,\zeta$	$H\,\eta$	$\Theta\,\theta$
1	2	3	4	5	7	8	9
$I\,\iota$	$K\,\varkappa$	$\Lambda\,\lambda$	$M\,\mu$	$N\,\nu$	$\Xi\,\xi$	$O\,o$	$\Pi\,\pi$
10	20	30	40	50	60	70	80
$P\,\varrho$	$\Sigma\,\sigma,\varsigma$	$T\,\tau$	$Y\,\upsilon$	$\Phi\,\varphi$	$X\,\chi$	$\Psi\,\psi$	$\Omega\,\omega$
100	200	300	400	500	600	700	800

Figure 80a: Greek Alphabet.

I will use the Greek values as an example for easier cross-referencing, since more information from this source is available and more up to date. Using numbers as values for words and sounds is known as gematria and when used with magic squares (covered in Chapter 15) it is known as numerology. These methods were applied to the Greek, Arabic and Hebrew languages,* and were regarded as the most sacred of all

* To date, no one has managed to apply these principles to Sumerian and Babylonian. If anyone did, the results could well be of the greatest importance.

LETTERS

Letter	Name (pronunciation)	Transliteration	Numbers
א	aleph (ahlef)	semi-guttural, depends on vowel point	1
ב בּ	veth, beth (vet, bet)	v, b	2
ג	gimel (geemel)	g	3
ד	daleth (dahlet)	d	4
ה	he (heh)	h	5
ו	vav (vahv)	v	6
ז	zayin (zahyeen)	z	7
ח	h'eth (h'et)	guttural h', softer than kh	8
ט	teth (tet)	t	9
י	yod (yohd)	y, i	10
כ כּ	haph, khaph (hahf, khahf)	strong h, kh	20
ך ךּ	haph, khaph*	strong h, kh (at end of word)	20
ל	lamed (lahmed)	l	30
מ	mem	m	40
ם	mem*	m (at end of word)	40
נ	nun (noon)	n	50
ן	nun*	n (at end of word)	50
ס	sameh (sahmekh)	s	60
ע	ayin (ahyeen)	guttural, depends on vowel point	70
פ פּ	fe, pe (feh, peh)	f, p	80
ף ףּ	fe, pe*	f, p (at end of word)	80
צ	tsadi (tsahdee)	ts	90
ץ	tsadi*	ts (at end of word)	90
ק	kuph (koof)	k	100
ר	resh	r	200
שׁ שׂ	shin, sin (sheen, seen)	sh, s	300
ת	thav (tahv)	t	400

* At end of word.

Figure 80b: Hebrew Alphabet.

principles. They were also related to music since that was governed by the same numerical canon. I said earlier that the two universal languages were, and still are, mathematics and music, i.e. harmonics. In gematria, sacred words and music governed by the same numerical canon were used for invocations, the efficacy of which depended on the pitch and vibrational frequency of the sounds made. The same numerical codes and numbers were also used in the dimensions of ancient buildings and temples, which were designed to represent both geometrical shapes and the musical sounds appropriate to the deity invoked and worshipped there. An example is given in the later chapter on sacred geometry.

The ancient Hebrew Kabbalists were very much aware of these facts, as were the contemporaries of Christ. Unfortunately, the mysterious unknown founders of early Christianity had their works and ideas thoroughly suppressed by their supplanters, the fathers of the Christian Church. However, they were known to have framed their sacred writings in the number code in order to guarantee that their message survived across time. Because of this, many passages – and indeed, whole books – of the New Testament are full of numerical codes. Two of the most prominent numbers in the numerical canon are 666 and 1,080 – both of which you are now familiar with. First, 666 was the 'number of the beast' in Revelation 13, and esoterically signifies the positive and active charge of solar energy; second, 1,080 represents the opposite and complementary principle in nature, its negative and receptive side associated with the mystics' Moon with its influence on the waters (water – Latin *aqua* – is symbolic for spirit and spirituality) both within the Earth and human imagination, and thus with prophecy and intuition – as opposed to the solar principle of rational intellect. The Moon, as we know, has a radius of 1,080 miles and a diameter of 2,160 miles.

Now, Christianity was founded upon the inspirational word of Christ and the Holy Ghost. Holy Ghost equals the Holy Spirit, which is written in Greek as το αγιον πνευμα. This equals a total value of 1,080 in gematria and is the representation of the male and female elements of the terrestrial spirit. In gematria, Jesus, spelt in Greek as Ιησυζ, equals 888. Mary, spelt in Greek as Μαριαμ, equals 192. When both are added together, the total is 1,080.

As we have seen, 666 features prominently within Revelation. It was the early Christians who came to associate it exclusively with evil, due in part to the name of the Roman emperor Nero having the gematria numerical value of 666. Certain Protestants during the Reformation of the mid-16th century sought to exclude the number 666 from any consideration of importance as to them it represented the beast, the Devil and an absolute principle of evil, and had no other connotations. As a consequence, such structures as Glastonbury Abbey were destroyed, as its proportions included the measurements of 666 prominently (as we shall see later). Glastonbury is very closely linked with Arthurian myth and Joseph of Arimathea. It is absurd to associate any number solely with evil forces. No number is exclusively representative of a particular moral quality, negative or positive, and in any case, it is inconsistent to relate moral principles to numbers, for numerical relationships are precise and unalterable while morals are neither, being simply adopted by consent in response to prevailing circumstances, time and place. It would therefore appear that Western civilisation today, and over the past 2,000 years, has chosen to ignore what a far wiser, more realistic generation had once found acceptable, understanding that a true cosmology must encompass every credited element.

Referring back to gematria, if we were to add the numerical values of Jesus (888), Mary (192), and the Beast (666), the total is 1,746, a number we have already come across. In doing this we are symbolically joining as one – fusing, so to speak – the physical with the spiritual, the terrestrial with the celestial. Some see this fusing and rejoining as meaning mankind's rejoining with God, i.e. once again becoming true spiritual beings. Others see it as mankind rejoining and uniting with extraterrestrial beings. It could ultimately all prove to be one and the same. (The Hall of Records is reputed to be able to answer this question, but at this stage, we cannot.) We have seen (Chapter 20) that the remarkable pyramid of Quetzalcoatl at Teotihuacan in Mexico (which is 72 feet high) has many of the same numerical values and that it casts a shadow that takes 66.6 seconds to move from its summit to the ground across its face.

The number 1,080 can best be appreciated by studying sacred phrases, the component letters of which, in Greek, add up to that number. They include: Holy Spirit, το αγιον πνευμα; The Spirit of the Earth, το γαιον πνευμα; The Fountain of Wisdom, πηγη σοφιαζ; Tartaros, the Abyss, ή Ταρταροζ; and Cocytos (a god of the Abyss), Κοκυτοζ. By the conventions of gematria, one digit, known as a colel, may be added to or taken away from a phrase without altering its meaning. Therefore we can add: The Abyss, ή αβυσσοζ (1,081). Many scholars (including Peter Lemesurier) have argued that the abyss is a reference to the Great Pyramid's subterranean chamber.

As we know, other correspondences of the value 1,080 include:

- the radius of the Moon at 1,080 miles;
- the atomic weight of silver at 108;
- the average number of breaths drawn in one hour by a human being, 1,080;
- the number of stanzas in the *Rigveda* are 10,800;
- the number of bricks in an Indian fire altar total 10,800;
- the number of beads on the Hindu or Buddhist rosary equals 108.

These are just a few examples. Throughout the entire world, in every tradition, code of architectural proportion, computation of time and wherever else mathematics is used, the number 1,080 is always prominent, and is usually referred to as the Yin side of nature, in contrast to the Yang (or solar significance) of the number 666.

These 2 prominent numbers – 1,080 and 666 – when added together equal 1,746. This number helps to reveal the hidden esoteric meaning in Jesus's phrase 'A grain of mustard seed'. This is written in Greek as Κοκκοζ σιναπεωζ in which the total value of all the letters is 1,746. As we saw above, this represents the fruitful union of two opposite principles in nature. This figure also arises from many other sacred phrases that refer to the product of that union, such as the Spirit of the World, το πνευμα κοσμου (1,746), and the Glory of the God of Israel, ή δοζα του θεου 'Ισραηλ (1,746). The value of 1,746 not only relates to the Great Pyramid but also has direct relevance to the distance of one of the converging alignments of the projected site of the Hall of Records.

Fire, pillars and parables

Jesus used a parable in which faith was likened to a grain of mustard seed by which mountains may be moved. With that in mind, it is striking to note that Plato wrote, 'That solid which has taken the form of a pyramid shall be the element and seed of fire.' The root word 'pyr' in pyramid means fire. The 'seed of fire' was represented by the seed of the mustard plant, because of its colour and hot flavour. I will quote the parable as spoken by Jesus and written in Mark 4: 31–2.

> It is like a grain of mustard seed which when sown in the Earth is less than all the seeds that be in the Earth, but when it is sown, it groweth up and becometh greater than all herbs, and shooteth out great branches so that the fowls of the air may lodge under the shadow of it.

As we have seen, the total value in gematria for 'a grain of mustard seed' equals 1,746.

As we covered earlier, the deity Thoth (alleged architect of the Great Pyramid) was known to the Greeks as Hermes and was not only the god of speech, wisdom and communication, but also the patron of travellers, both physically and symbolically. Roads and paths of stone, with pillars marking their course, were known as 'Hermes' by the Greeks. These 'Hermes' stone roads with pillars (rather like milestones) all pointed to Hermes stones in market squares – only later were these replaced by crosses. In gematria Hermes (written in Greek as Ερμηζ) equals 353. However, as previously mentioned, one digit can be added or removed without altering its meaning so by this convention, Hermes equals the Greek word in the New Testament for the 'Way' (ή όδοζ) which equals 352.

In gematria the value for pyramid (πυραμιζ) is 831. Hermes stones were quite phallic in appearance; in addition, they functioned as apparent instruments of the union between cosmic and terrestrial forces by which the Earth is made fertile. The Greek for phallus (φαλλοζ) also equals 831 in gematria. (It could be argued that certain omphalos stones were also decidedly phallic.) We can see here a direct connection between pillars and the Great Pyramid. Ancient sacred sites located by astronomical projections, then all linked via perfectly straight paths, are found all over the entire world. Often called Ley lines or Paths of the Dragon, such paths in the Mediterranean area were marked out by Hermes stones. They are proof that an ancient civilisation was able to map out the four corners of the globe with an unsurpassed accuracy, thousands of years before the technology was acquired to do so again in the last century.

In Chapter 15 we looked at the magic square of Mercury/Hermes that contained the numbers 1 to 64, the sum value being 2,080. In the light of this, it is interesting therefore to note that the epithet of Christ in Revelation 1: 5, 'The first born' (Greek ὁ πρωτοτοκοζ), also has the value of 2,080 in gematria. Moreover, 2,080 applies to the fire which Prometheus (a type* of Mercury/Hermes) stole from the gods, the 'Artificers' fire' (Greek το εντεχνοω πυρ). Finally, the combination of light (φωζ) and fire (πυρ) totals 2,080.

In his teachings, Jesus used many codes that contained the numbers and key values contained within the Great Pyramid. What's more, the name of his disciple, Simon the fisherman, did not fit the mathematical code (i.e. was not equal to 755); Jesus therefore changed it to Peter. This point has confused and perplexed historians for nearly 2,000 years, but in the context of a mathematical code, it makes total sense. Peter (Greek Πετροζ) equals 755, and 755 feet is the distance across the base perimeter of each side of the Great Pyramid. An ancient nickname for anyone called Peter was Rocky. The Great Pyramid is built out of solid rock. Moreover:

- Rocky in gematria equals 153.
- 153 is an important number within the Great Pyramid. In the New Testament, it was to be Peter who would be the chief cornerstone of Jesus Christ's Church, i.e. the foundation stone.
- Peter was also told by Jesus to cast his fishing nets to the right, the right being symbolic for the way of good; he caught 153 fish. (John 21:11).
- 153 also refers to enlightened souls within gematria (as will be explained later).
- The Grand Gallery in the Great Pyramid rises (at an angle of 26 degrees) exactly 153 feet.
- 153 is the exact number of layers of masonry above the King's Chamber from its base line; and if the 17 steps up to the entrance of the Great Pyramid were continued to its peak, there would be 153 of them.
- Finally, the sum total of digits from 1 to 17 is 153.

Jesus's public ministry has been recorded as lasting 918 days. There is no way of confirming this, but what is significant is that this figure is important: $153 \times 6 = 918$. After his apparent crucifixion, Jesus rose from the dead and ascended to heaven on the third day, so therefore we can add 3 to 918 to get a total duration of 921. This figure is *very* important, as shall be revealed in my final chapters. 921.44 metres equals half a minute of equatorial latitude and is also the length of the 8×8 grid that the Giza plateau complex is laid out upon.

* Someone who foreshadowed a later person.

Codes in Hebrew

For an example of gematria in Hebrew, look at Isaiah 19:19. Isaiah actually mentions a sealed hidden book and various other references to the Great Pyramid, though this is not obvious at first. We shall look at the reference to a sealed book later; for now, note that the gematria numeric value of the Hebrew letters in Isaiah 19:19–20 is 5,449 – and 5,449 is the height of the Great Pyramid, from its base to the platform summit, in inches (see figure 81).

ביום ההוא יהיה מזבח ליהוה בתוך ארץ מצרים ואצבה
אצל-גבולה ליהוה: והיה לאות ולעד ליהוה צבאות
בארץ מצרים כי-יצעקי אל-יהוה מפני לחצים וישלח
להם מושיע ורב והזילם:

Figure 81. The Hebrew of Isaiah 19:19–20.

In Isaiah 19:19, an allusion is made to a pure and prophetic monument, undefiled in its religion though in an adulterous land, as in the monument which was fore ordained as both '"an altar to the Lord in the midst of the land of Egypt, and a pillar at the border thereof" [and] special witness in the latter days before the consummation of all things, to the same Lord, and to what he hath purposed upon mankind' (as Piazzi Smyth chose to express it). The only monument in Egypt that matches this description is the Great Pyramid.*

It would seem, then, that in Isaiah 19:19–20, it is stated in contradictory terms that an altar and a pillar will be at the 'border' of Egypt, at the same time as being in the 'midst' of Egypt. However, the Great Pyramid is positioned at the *border* of Upper and Lower Egypt, as well as at the *centre* of the Nile Delta quadrant. Giza, where the Great Pyramid is located, literally means 'border'.

The 3 Wise Men

Surprisingly, this links to the New Testament. When Jesus was born he was visited by 3 wise men, Magi or kings, who have often been associated with the 3 pyramids at Giza (as in Matthew's account) and the shepherds

---

* In this context, it must be remembered that Moses was an initiate of the Great Pyramid and knew its secrets (though as we shall see, his precise dates are the subject of controversy). As we shall also see when looking at Moses, the actual events during the Exodus were both symbolic and based upon factual events.

(as in Luke's). Tradition maintains that the 3 wise men were of different origins. One was black-skinned, one was yellow-skinned and the third was white, supposedly thus representing the 3 principal races of mankind. Germane to my argument, the 3 pyramids at Giza were similarly coloured: the first, the Great Pyramid, was sheathed in white, polished Lumite; the second (Khafre) was covered in yellow sandstone; and the third (Menkura) was sheathed in red granite, certainly to at least half its height, which when weathered appears black.

The names attributed to the 3 kings by the Armenian *Gospels of the Infancy*[1] are Balthazar from Arabia, Gaspar from India and Melkon from Persia. Gaspar and Melkon appear similar enough to Khafre and Menkura, the reputed builders of the second and third pyramids. Balthazar appears to derive from the Hebrew 'Belteshazzar' meaning 'The Lords' Leader'. This name is also found in the form of Belshazzar, a King whose name later Jews associated with the celebrated Great Ziggurat of Babylon – with which the Great Pyramid almost certainly became identified in the Jewish racial memory. It is arguable that the Giza Pyramids actually took their names from these earlier sources. Furthermore, the geographical origins of the 3 Kings, as attributed by the same gospel, offer an intriguing hint that knowledge enshrined in the pyramids may represent a compilation of ancient wisdom by the pre-Egyptian initiates who constructed them; knowledge, that is, that they had gleaned from India, Persia and Arabia. This in turn would confirm the theory that the pyramids of Giza attest to a worldwide plan of wisdom and knowledge that embraces the essentials of Christianity and Judaism, and Egyptian, Hindu, Babylonian and Zoroastrian traditions.

According to the Armenian Gospels, the 3 Kings bore with them the 'Testament' bequeathed by Adam to Seth. No one has advanced a reasonable explanation for this and it is difficult to imagine, in normal circumstances, what this 'Testament' could be. However, when seen in its true context, the Testament, like the legendary gifts, enshrined a prophecy of things to come, thus constituting the preordained destiny of the new-born Messiah. We may therefore conclude with some certainty that this Testament represents nothing less than the sum of knowledge handed down by the primeval 'Sons of the Gods' (Adam)* to the earliest ancient Egyptian forefathers as personified by Set (who, in some circumstances, was seen as the dark aspect of Horus), and incorporated by them into the Great Pyramid's design.

If the above information is not enough to convince you of the connections between Jesus and the pyramids of Giza, then I will draw your attention to the Great Pyramid's descending passage angle. When the image of the Great Pyramid is projected on to a map over the physical pyramid itself, with its apex pointing due north, a line can be followed in

---

* Adam can mean 'the first of mankind', which has a plural resonance in it.

a straight direction that passes through the one-time ford across the Yam Suph (or Reed Sea*) – the real sea-crossing point of the Israelites during the Exodus – and continues on to Bethlehem, where Jesus was born. It then cuts through the River Jordan in front of Jericho where the Israelites crossed into their Promised Land. See figure 82.

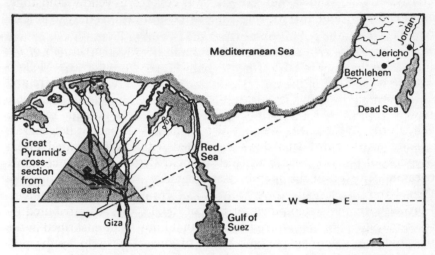

Superimposing the Great Pyramid's passage-angle on the map produces a rhumb-line bearing that marks a former ford across the one-time Yam Suph (or Reed Sea), passes directly through Bethlehem, and cuts the River Jordan in front of Jericho. The Pyramidologists detect in these facts direct links with the biblical stories of the Exodus and the Nativity.

Figure 82.

The path of the Israelites lies exactly on the sunrise line marked out in advance by the Great Pyramid's own passage angle. What's more, nearly 300 years prior to Moses's Exodus (by orthodox chronology, i.e. *c.*1400 BC), a similar sunrise-oriented group from the Preseli Mountains of Wales had migrated a similar distance to their new cultural and spiritual centre on Salisbury Plain, taking with them the sacred Bluestones that were to form the nucleus of Stonehenge.

It is worth noting that just as the Israelites passed over the River Jordan, Moses apparently died at the age of 120 and was buried, his grave being unknown to this day. The age of 120 was commonly applied to anyone who was deemed old and wise, whatever their true age. After Moses died, the hosts of the chosen people, now led by Joshua (the Greek version of which is Jesus), passed through the waters of Jordan that separated them from their divine inheritance. As I have also mentioned, both the Exodus story and those concerning Jesus were not only factual

* Confusingly, the Reed Sea is thought to be a shallow, narrow part of the Red Sea.

events but were also symbolically deliberately arranged and acted out. Paul later put it in 1 Corinthians 10:11 as follows: 'All these things that happened to them were symbolic and were recorded for our benefit as a warning.'

So what can be made of the Exodus with this in mind? The Great Pyramid's passage angle passes through the sites of major importance in the Moses story of the Exodus. One of the first things I learnt about Moses was that he got his name from the Egyptian Pharaoh's daughter. She rescued him as a child from among the river reeds (this is a direct parallel to the story of Isis hiding the baby Horus from Set), and because she 'drew' him out of the water, his name relates to 'Mashah', a Hebrew verb meaning to draw. This is purely a symbolic representation, and it would appear that the Moses story has many deliberate symbolic messages encoded within it that were added later. The word 'Mashah' is almost identical with the Hebrew derivation 'Mashiah' (Mosheh), and even more similar to the Hebrew verb 'Mascheh', meaning 'to anoint'; 'Maschiach' means 'anointed' as well as 'Messiah'. The question is, Why did an *Egyptian* princess use a *Hebrew* name in the first place?

Because of all these compelling details, I decided to investigate Moses more closely. I could immediately see his connection with spirit through the representation of being drawn from the water, since water is symbolic for things spiritual. But that was just the start.

Chapter 23

Moses – the Pharaoh Prophet?

It is conceivable that Moses received the Ten Commandments from the codes within the Great Pyramid, and that it was symbolically the Mount of Horeb specified in Exodus. Moses may have then acted out the symbolism for the benefit of later generations, as detailed in Paul's account regarding symbolism. According to esoteric sources, Moses was 'handed down' 3 slabs of stone with the commandments written upon them. Within the Great Pyramid it is necessary – both physically and symbolically – to take down 3 massive stone blocks of the granite plug before entering the ascending passage (see plan in figure 113).

Before considering Moses in more detail, we need to look at certain aspects of Jesus. Jesus gave all of his parables to his disciples, who were mainly fishermen, *in fish-related symbolism*, as his ministry started at the beginning of the precessional cycle of Pisces, the Fish. The early Christian church used a symbol of a fish as its identifying mark. The esoteric symbol and 'badge' of the Great Pyramid happens to be the shape known as the 'Vesica Pisces', meaning 'symbol of the fish'. When Jesus was born, the Earth had just recently entered into the precessional Zodiac cycle of Pisces, having finished the cycle of Aries, the Ram. Many Old Testament incidents involved goats and rams – hence the shepherds watching their flocks by night on the eve of his birth. The Zodiacal cycle prior to Aries was Taurus, the Bull; hence all the bull worshipping previously, and the Golden Calf incident during the Exodus as Moses received the Ten Commandments. We are now nearing the end of the Piscean age and about to enter the Aquarian or spiritual age.

The close similarities in cosmologies, myths and legends from widely separated parts of the world – such as China; England; Egypt; Sumer/Babylon; the ancient North, Central and South Americas – show that they all originally derived their knowledge from a common source. Early in the last century, the fad was to source it in India, Sumer/Babylon, or the favourite, Egypt. However, it is now becoming increasingly clear that even the Great Pyramid of Giza is far older than current orthodox history credits. I shall demonstrate why later. Like the earliest temples in Mexico and Central and South America, the great riddle that occurs again and again, is that the civilisations that we do know about appeared simultaneously overnight, complete.

Ancient Americans

The mysterious city of Teotihuacan that we looked at in Chapter 20 is situated at precisely 19.5 degrees latitude North. Teotihuacan was a place where, according to legend, men became gods, and has 3 distinctive pyramids dedicated respectively to the Sun, Moon and Quetzalcoatl (Feathered Serpent God of the West – the Central American counterpart of Osiris). The ancients across the world all insisted that the massive monuments of old were built by their forefathers under the guidance of gods, great men who were white, bearded and blue-eyed, such as the mythical gods Quetzalcoatl and Viracocha (a white-skinned bearded Caucasian; the name means 'Foam of the Sea'. He was well versed in science, a master of magic and the art of weaponry). Huge statues of tall bearded Caucasian figures are found throughout Central and South America. However, bearded Caucasians were not to be found in the Americas until the Spaniards arrived.

Many worldwide myths and legends about these great civilising gods maintain that they resided in the ocean whilst here on Earth, or were at least connected to water in one way or another, and water, as we have seen, has become symbolic for the spirit. We are about to enter the Aquarian age or spiritual age, and the symbol for Aquarius is the water carrier. In the name Quetzalcoatl, the last syllable, *atl*, is the Nahua word for water; furthermore the god Atlaua is known as the 'Master of the waters'. According to traditional accounts, Quetzalcoatl apparently descended from the Sun and landed in the Gulf of Mexico with a party of disciples, all priests, who were versed in the arts of astronomy, architecture and music. The Maya give an exact date for this event, making it the start of their year one (in our calendar, 3,113 BC, 12 August). This date is unbelievably close to the ancient Egyptian Year One of the age of Horus, around 3,141 BC, which came immediately after an 'age of destruction'. The ancient Central and South American religions paralleled those of ancient Egypt and the Hebrew Old Testament to an uncanny degree. My explanation for this is that they are all derived from a common source and carry the same message and warning for our benefit. Indeed, according to myth and legend, the contents of the Hall of Records will reveal just who that common source was.

Like the Maya, the Egyptians organised their society as a theocracy governed by complex religious beliefs. Both set down their traditions in complex hieroglyphs and both devoted huge amounts of time and effort to constructing huge pyramids that incorporated solar phenomena. They were obsessed with astronomical observation, symbolic mathematics and the evolution of the human soul. Both built huge boats from reeds, made clothes from cotton, embalmed their dead and told legends of creation, floods, lordly founders of their civilisations and world cycles that ended in worldwide cataclysms. The religious beliefs of the Central Americans were like those of Egypt, Babylon, Greece, Syria, Persia, India and other parts of the ancient world; all mirrored many of the tenets of early Christianity, long before the birth of Jesus Christ. The Maya describe creation in decidedly biblical terms; they practised baptism and also a form of eucharist, the symbolic eating of the god's body and blood. Hermes is identified with the Egyptian Thoth and one of the (rare) alternative names for Thoth was Tehuti – who, like the Norse Odin and Mayan Votan, was viewed by his followers as one of the true founders of civilisation. Remarkably, the Egyptian Tehuti appears to be the same word as the Aztec Tecuhtli, which means the 'grandfather' or 'Lord', as in Yiacatecuhtli ('Great Lord').

For part of their history the Aztecs underwent a period of wandering in search of their promised land called Anahuac, 'The place in the midst of the circle', the source of their inspiration and being. They were led by two brothers, Gagavitz and Zactecaum. Confronted with an expanse of water, these two produced a red staff which they had brought from the 'Holy Land of Tulan' and drove it into the sea, thus parting it to allow the pilgrims to walk across to the other shore. The parallel to the account of the Israelites crossing the parted Reed Sea is extraordinary. What are the implications?

Catastrophe, allegorical and real

I mentioned earlier that as well as having a symbolic meaning, events as described in the Exodus tale were actually taking place across the entire world. This was a time of worldwide upheavals and natural disasters, which included huge floods, hurricanes, firestorms and plagues on a terrifying scale. All the archaeological and geological evidence indicates that in the middle of the second millennium BC – just as the Israelites' Exodus started – there occurred one of the greatest catastrophes in Earth's history. In addition large numbers of ancient documents from various sources across the globe testify to this: for example in the Exodus story, the Sun did not shine for days, and the Egyptian Ipuwer Papyrus (Ipuwer being its author) likewise chronicled the same catastrophes, giving details about the River Nile running red with blood. Mayan accounts tell how the western hemisphere suffered a great cataclysm at the time of the biblical Exodus, that the Earth quaked and the Sun's motion was interrupted, and that the waters were turned to blood.

In his book *Act of God*,[1] Graham Phillips proposes a convincing argument that the disaster described within Exodus was caused by a volcanic explosion on the Mediterranean island of Thera (now called Santorini) far greater than that of Krakatau (often written Krakatoa) near Java which exploded in 1883. As the volcano on Thera erupted, by day it could be seen by the Israelites as a pillar of smoke, just as described within the Bible; by night it was the biblical pillar of fire. Further confirmation comes from the fact that having marched towards the pillar of smoke and fire for so many days *in a north-westerly direction, which happens to be the direction of Thera*, the Israelites turned *eastwards* and headed for the Reed Sea – after which the pillar of smoke and fire would now be at their backs – as also detailed in the Bible.

Archaeological evidence from the Nile Delta shows that during the reign of Akhenaten (around 1380 BC), Thera's eruption blasted a huge cloud of ash high into the skies over Egypt. For days the Sun was obscured by fallout and the fertile plains became a moonlike terrain. Krakatau, the largest volcanic explosion in recent history, was far smaller than the Thera explosion but its effects were identical to the biblical plagues that befell Egypt. Graham Phillips pointed out the following:[2]

Krakatau: A fall-out cloud of ash 500 miles wide darkened the skies for 3 days.
Exodus 10: 21: There was thick darkness in all the land of Egypt for 3 days.

Krakatau: Pellet-sized debris fell like hailstones for hundreds of miles.
Exodus 9: 25: The hail struck down everything that was in the field throughout the land of Egypt.

Krakatau: On Java thousands of the islanders suffered from sores and painful skin rashes caused by acidic fall-out ash.
Exodus: 9: 9: And it shall become fine dust all over the land of Egypt, and shall become boils breaking out in sores on man and beast.

Krakatau: On Java the rivers ran red, stained with the iron oxide of volcanic ash.
Exodus 7: 20: The water that was in the Nile turned to blood.

Krakatau: For hundreds of miles around Krakatau the fish were killed by pungent chemicals.
Exodus 7: 21: The fish in the Nile died and the Nile became foul.

All this occurred during the time of Moses and the Israelites' Exodus from Egypt. Phillips argues that the Pharaoh of the Exodus was Akhenaten; *not* Rameses II, as is often stated. Authors such as Ahmed Osman argue that Akhenaten is in fact Moses himself. We shall look at this in a moment; but one thing is clear, the events certainly convinced the early Israelites that their single God had caused the cataclysm, thus establishing their unshakeable faith, Judaism, that eventually promoted the idea of one God to the entire Western world.

Whoever Moses actually proves to be, another fact is apparent – he was privy to secret doctrines and teachings. If he was aware of the codes from antiquity that are the focus of my research, then he would have been able to calculate with considerable accuracy the forthcoming cataclysm that was to befall Egypt. As the Bible relates, Moses fled Egypt and spent a period in the desert. Then he deliberately came back to Egypt at an appointed time (as commanded by God), just prior to the disaster. It is my firm belief that if the eruption of Thera was solely to blame *by itself*, and Moses predicted it as a one-off event, then he was very lucky or unusually skilled in seismology and vulcanology; we cannot predict an eruption with 100 per cent accuracy, even using today's technology. If, on the other hand, he was more than aware of *astronomical alignments that would cause such disasters on a regular basis*, then it would not have been a case of predicting the unpredictable; Moses would instead have been pinpointing the date of the next cataclysm in an established cycle.

As Immanuel Velikovsky argues in *Worlds in Collision*,[3] the cataclysm actually occurred as a direct result of Mars being shunted by Venus from its previous orbit to one nearer Earth. Venus, according to Velikovsky, was a new planet-sized comet, originally ripped out of Jupiter,* which hurtled out of the solar system, and at this point, careered back into our solar system, before finally settling into its present stable orbit. The resultant gravitational and electromagnetic forces unleashed between Mars and the Earth, coupled with alignments of the other planetary bodies, caused worldwide seismic upheavals. References to red or bloody waters are based on a ferruginous deposit of red dust ejected from Mars as it nearly collided with Earth; across the entire globe this event caused a ruddy pigment to cover the soil and colour expanses of water red.

Here's another vital point. If the events in Egypt were caused solely by the eruption of Thera, we would not expect to find contemporaneous disasters on a similar scale on the opposite side of the world – *but we do*. Not only that, but as the eastern hemisphere remained in 3 days of impenetrable darkness, the western hemisphere remained in 3 days of constant daylight. It is therefore obvious that some kind of disaster befell the entire globe, one that for 3 days caused it to teeter on its own axis before being released to return to its previous rotation. The only thing that could cause this would be another planetoid object (or objects). We shall look at Venus later in this regard. (We have already noticed an unusual thing about Venus: it is the only planet with a retrograde rotation, opposite to that of all the other planets in the Solar System.)

All the information that I have managed to gather indicates that the actual cause of the celestial cataclysm was *predictable*, as events abided

---

*It must, however, be noted that Jupiter is a gas planet, whereas Venus is a solid one.

by the mathematical constants and pattern as outlined in earlier chapters. While I accept the general thrust of Velikovsky's argument, I believe that the events were *also* the result of the passing of the tenth planet Nibiru, which, if its 3,600-year orbit is correctly calculated, would certainly have been in close proximity to both Mars and the Earth at the right time, with its effects being felt for many years. As I outlined, the tenth planet was responsible for breaking the Earth in two. I further believe that as a result of the damage caused to both planets during the confrontation – expressed in ancient Sumerian/Babylonian texts as the battle between Marduk and Tiamat – Nibiru/Marduk was severely damaged, losing some of its mass at the same time. This accounts for why it is *now* almost identical in size to the Earth – it is no longer its original size. Therefore, as it comes close to Earth again, sometime during the early part of the next century, there will be little effect. The above argument is another reason why I feel that the next cataclysm, fortunately, will not be as severe as previous ones.

Links across the Atlantic

The parallels between the Eastern religious myths and those of the Americas are amazing. As was shown above, the biblical Exodus is almost identical to the Aztec legend of Gagavitz and Zactecaum, two brothers who, just like Moses and Aaron, led their people on an epic trek. The Great Pyramid at Giza was originally sheathed in white polished Lumite limestone blocks, forming a smooth faultless slope that reflected sunlight which made it visible for many miles as an artificial golden mountain of light, hence its Egyptian name of 'The light'. Fascinatingly, the Aztecs too had myths specifically related to a white mountain (also described as a white volcano) which Gagavitz entered, then returned full of wisdom, knowledge and power. Remember that the root *pyr* in pyramid means 'fire'? And what is a fire mountain? A volcano. The Great Pyramid fits this symbolism perfectly, especially with its gold-sheathed capstone. As Moses (who certainly grew up in the Pharaoh's household even if he wasn't actually a Pharaoh himself) was an initiate of the Great Pyramid and Egyptian mysteries, it could be argued in effect that he received his commandments from his own White Mountain or fire mountain – i.e. the Great Pyramid – just as Gagavitz had.

It could be further argued – and some scholars have done so quite convincingly – that the two stories are one and the same, repeated with different names, and that the Aztec version came about after one of the 12 tribes of Israel settled in the Americas. This is not a new idea, and is something that all Mormons (Church of Jesus Christ of Latter Day Saints) are certainly aware of and believe; it is covered in *The Book of Mormon*.[4] The Aztecs further maintained that Gagavitz is destined one day to return by emerging in glory from the fire-crowned mountain.

Pierre Honoré, in his *In Quest of the White God*,[5] claims to discover almost identical links between the ancient Central and South American civilisations and those of the Middle East. In considerable detail, he traces characteristics of Central American Aztec civilisation back through the Toltecs and Mayans to the Olmecs and the La Venta civilisations of around the beginning of our own era. The South American Inca roots are similarly traced back through Tihuanaco and the Chimu to the Chavin civilisation of around 700 BC. Honoré also discerns constant artistic and cultural links with China, and the ancient Middle East. His most notable revelation is that 15 ancient Mayan glyphs are almost identical to the Cretan script known as Linear A. As regards China, I have already drawn attention to the existence of many very large pyramids there (see plates), covered in earth and visually identical to both those of the Americas (see plates) and Silbury Hill (see plates) in England.

Across the ancient world, root words are linguistically almost identical, suggesting a common source. It would be unwise to claim that this was just pure coincidence, as they all carry the same mathematical codes as well. The linguistic similarities of the ancient Americans and the ancient Hebrews is clearly demonstrated by the supposed last words of Jesus when he was crucified, as reported by Matthew (23: 46): 'Eli, Eli, lama sabachthani' ('My God, my God, why hast thou forsaken me?'); these are almost identical to the Mayan 'Hele Hele Lamah Sabac Ta Ni' – 'I faint, I faint and my face is hid in darkness'.

Revealing Old Testament etymology

One of the most intriguing elements in the Old Testament is the name of the unspeakable Lord God Almighty, 'Jehovah', which means 'I am that I am'. The true sacred vowels of Jehovah are unknown; we only have the consonants YHWH of which the construction Jehovah is the most widely used. The same applies to the Egyptian pharaoh name KHUFU, which some have translated as 'The Lord protects me' (he was, *according to orthodoxy*, the pharaoh who built the Great Pyramid). In Greek, this is 'Cheops'. Again the vowels are absent, the actual word is HWFW. It is well known (the Hebrew texts are quite explicit on this point) that YHWH derives from the Hebrew verb HAVA(H) meaning 'I am'. From HWFW (Khufu) to HAVA(H) is linguistically an extremely short step, shorter than the northern English pronunciation of 'brother' is from its southern pronunciation. The ancient Egyptian form from HWFW is historically the older of the two and in YHWH we appear to have a Hebrew version of HWFW. Further support for this is that Jehovah is, above all, the God of the Exodus, and the name appears to have been in free use only during the few weeks between the beginning of the Exodus and the moment when the Israelites arrived at Mount Horeb, probably in the Sinai desert, where Moses promptly imposed a strict taboo on the name *he had himself revealed only a short time before.*

There are many links with the name Jehovah and the Great Pyramid. The Great Pyramid was known as 'the building of light' and 'the way'; we have already seen earlier how these same two words are related to Hermes and the Great Pyramid by way of gematria. How many times does the saying 'I am the way and the light' (or 'the life') occur in the Bible? In Isaiah 26, a reference to Jehovah is very suggestive of the Pyramid and its symbolism; what's more, within the Great Pyramid itself the angle of 26 degrees is repeated several times. This is that description: 'We have a strong city where walls and ramparts are our deliverance, open the gates [an identical allusion to the Osiris ritual of the chamber of the open tomb], to let a righteous nation in, a nation that keeps faith.' The text then mentions an everlasting rock, and asserts that the path of the righteous is level and 'thou markest out the right way for the upright'. This is a clear reference to the Pyramid's passages and symbolism. Jesus likewise, knowing the symbolism of the Pyramid, also spoke about it, in particular in Matthew 21: 42: 'The stone which the builders rejected has become the chief corner stone.' You will recall that Jesus later declared that Simon/Peter was to become the chief corner stone of his Church, and we also know (Chapter 22) that Peter in gematria equals 755, and the perimeter base length in feet of each face of the Great Pyramid is 755 feet.

The 'nameless' pharaoh

To add weight to the theory that Moses was a Pharaoh himself, we shall have to look at why this new theory is gaining credibility. But first, it must be noted that much Egyptian chronology is far from accurate – or indeed complete – *especially* in regard to Akhenaten, about whom probably the least is known. In *Act of God* Graham Phillips makes this clear, and covers most of what follows in considerable detail (though he is of the opinion that Moses was not a Pharaoh but lived during the time of Akhenaten).[6]

In 1907 an American archaeologist, Theodore Davies, discovered a new tomb in the Valley of the Kings in Egypt, listed as Tomb 55. Even with 20th-century technology it took days to break in, as its entrance was protected by a double barrier of a thick stone wall reinforced by huge blocks of limestone set in mortar and coated with an incredibly strong cement. Nothing like this had ever been discovered before. The inner doorway seal was still intact, so the tomb had not been disturbed. However, the seal bore no name. Also, unlike other royal tombs, there were no wall decorations and the usual burial goods were absent. All this tomb contained was an elaborate stone coffin and canopic* jars containing the occupant's entrails. The name plates on the coffin had all been damaged beyond recognition, which meant that there was no way of establishing the identity of the mummy, which didn't even have a gold portrait mask, as was custom. Davies initially suspected tomb robbers had been at work but this was discounted as the seal to the tomb was intact and there was no other entrance. The conclusion drawn from the evidence was that whoever buried this person wanted his identity (it *was* possible to ascertain that the mummy was male, from basic physical characteristics) concealed. What's more, from the funeral amulets and incense burners that remained, Davies concluded that the final rite had not been a funeral ceremony, but some form of exorcism.

For over half a century, the nameless Pharaoh was the subject of much controversy. Only in the 1960s, after scientific dating techniques were applied, did researchers manage to date the mummy to the period of the mid-14th century BC, a date corresponding to the reign of the Pharaoh Akhenaten. Egyptologists continued to try to solve the mystery of Akhenaten, because each time excavations unearthed new artefacts contemporary with his reign, all hieroglyphs detailing his life and reign were defaced; Akhenaten's successors had attempted to destroy all record of his existence. Just as in the tomb inscriptions, even his name had been obliterated from statues and carvings all over Egypt. In consequence, practically nothing is known of Akhenaten – less than any other aspect of ancient Egyptian history. Because of all this, Egyptologists concluded that Akhenaten had been proclaimed a heretic after his death, so labelling him 'The Heretic King'.

What *is* known about him? This is a period of great opacity where rulers and their dates are concerned, but Akhenaten apparently ruled for 17 years during the first half of the 14th century BC and was the father-in-law to the famous Tutankhamun. It is believed that in the fifth year of his reign he became inspired – for reasons as yet unknown – by a new monotheistic religion, which caused him to leave his capital at Thebes and establish a new religious centre at Amarna 200 miles to the north. His new religion was completely revolutionary as he denounced the pantheon of ancient Egyptian gods (chief of whom was Amon), and began to preach the philosophy of a single God, the only one, the Aten. Aten was an invisible and omnipresent deity, pictorially represented as the rays of the Sun. This sounds very similar to the omnipresent single God Jehovah as proclaimed by Moses, doesn't it? It must be remembered that until Moses appeared, the early Hebrews worshipped a variety of gods themselves, only converting to the single deity Jehovah during the Exodus.

* The term is derived from the town of Canopus, which we have seen in another context (Chapter 8).

Monotheism was unknown in Egypt before this time. Akhenaten's new religion must have created resentment amongst the priesthood and ruling élite of his day. However, this fact alone would not account for the reaction after Akhenaten's death, nor would it justify the obsessive lengths to which his successors went to eradicate not only his teachings, but also his very memory. Such actions suggest that Akhenaten was feared even after death. The tomb evidence clearly indicates where the Egyptian priests appear to have tried to imprison Akhenaten's actual spirit for eternity.

To go to these extreme lengths, the priesthood must have had good reason. They must have held him personally responsible for some huge wrongdoing, on an unprecedented scale. Phillips argues[7] that Akhenaten was the actual Pharaoh of the Exodus, and as Egypt suffered on a scale never before experienced as a direct result of the Pharaoh's apparent actions against the God of Israel, they held him personally responsible. Although the scholarship here is first-rate, I think we can take the subject one step further.

But, if we challenge the reasoning above, *why* was he so feared? It cannot be argued that he was a religious fanatic responsible for the savage persecution of his opponents, as all the limited available evidence is very much to the contrary. It appears that he was the opposite of a tyrant, since hieroglyphics that *have* survived attempts at effacement record his decrees ordering the mass release of slaves and banning blood sports. Hymns and writings by Akhenaten himself have been discovered which preach the sanctity of life. It also appears that he was a dreamer, a romantic and possibly an inefficient ruler; yet there is nothing to account for the anti-Akhenaten purge that followed his death and swept the entire land of Egypt.

As Phillips points out,[8] even his religion, Atenism, does not appear to have been enforced upon his people. Most citizens continued to worship as they pleased, and outside Akhenaten's religious city of Amarna, religion seems to have been largely ignored. Yet I repeat, no other Pharaoh is known to have aroused such posthumous hostility. Even these who instigated new religions, persecuted opposition or committed acts of heinous cruelty, did not, after death, endure attempts to obliterate their memory; their policies were simply annulled and their followers executed. So again, we have to ask ourselves: What was so different about the mild-mannered Akhenaten?

There is considerable evidence that Egypt suffered socially and politically during Akhenaten's reign, but it must be noted that some sources imply that an ill-defined personage, probably male, named Smenkhkare, had been made co-ruler and continued to rule after Akhenaten's death. As co-ruler, why wasn't Smenkhkare also blamed and held jointly responsible, alongside Akhenaten? Akhenaten, it seems, was held *singularly* responsible for the plight of Egypt.

As I have said, Akhenaten is thought to have ruled sometime between 1400 and 1350 BC and the dynastic records indicate that he reigned for 17 years. As Tutankhamun's tomb and mummy were uniquely preserved, precise dating enabled *his* reign to be established around 1350 BC, *apparently* preceded by Smenkhkare who ruled for 15 years. With so much uncertainty surrounding Smenkhkare, it is obviously not known exactly how long Smenkhkare ruled alone. Paintings of Akhenaten tentatively linked to his early reign show him alone, whereas later depictions show him enthroned alongside another person, presumably Smenkhkare. However, it would seem that at some time after Akhenaten's move to Amarna, the co-regency began. If this co-regency began immediately, Akhenaten's reign would have ended around 1353 BC, but it is more likely that Smenkhkare was appointed co-regent toward the *end* of Akhenaten's life, in a political manoeuvre to avoid civil war. It could therefore be assumed that Smenkhkare ruled alone for most of his 15 years, thus dating Akhenaten's rule to around 1382 to 1365 BC. Is this significant in any other way? Yes. It just happens to tie in with the dates now accepted for the eruption of Thera.

The feared pharaoh

Fascinating though that coincidence is, we still come back to why Akhenaten was so feared. When he came to power, Egypt was one of the most effective, if not the most effective military force on Earth. By the time he died, Egypt had lost control of half its empire and was in turmoil. It had been believed by scholars that this turmoil was caused by civil war and political upheaval. However, modern archaeology heavily suggests that a series of natural catastrophes was ultimately responsible. Excavations throughout the Nile Delta have shown that around 1380 BC intensive flooding destroyed crops and left the nation on the brink of starvation. It is my firm belief that the natural disasters that befell Egypt (and at the same time affected the entire globe) were the direct result of the near passing of the tenth planet Nibiru, which in turn shunted both Mars and the Earth dangerously close to each other's orbit, thus causing huge electromagnetic discharges to be exchanged between the two planets, which in turn momentarily affected their rotations. Hence the eastern hemisphere was in total darkness whilst the western hemisphere was in constant daylight for the same period of time. If the Egyptians contemporary with Moses/Akhenaten blamed *him* for these cataclysms, this is dramatic confirmation that they – *unlike* Moses – had entirely lost the ancient knowledge needed to predict such celestial phenomena, as well as any awareness of inherent codes within and relating to the Great Pyramid, including the secret king-making ritual. I argue, then, that *Akhenaten is Moses*, hence the fear of him even after his death. Remember that nobody knows where Moses is actually buried. I am also not alone in making this assumption.

It must be realised that biblical chronology is prone to gross numerical exaggeration, symbolic in meaning, and can vary in this from one version of the Old Testament to another. We are informed, as if it were an absolute fact, that Rameses II (who ruled *c.* 1290 to 1224 BC) was the Pharaoh of the 'oppression', yet there is no firm evidence to back up this bold assertion, and I will soon declare my candidate for this role. Nonetheless, all the information provided in the Old Testament indicates that the Israelites' 40 years in the wilderness (which was so described more for symbolic reasons connected with 40 than to chronicle a real time period) occurred some time between *c.* 1450 BC and the middle years of Rameses II's 67-year reign. However, a growing body of evidence suggests that all these events were in some way connected with the tumultuous period of Egyptian history known as the Amarna age. This period was marked by the accession to the throne of the enigmatic king named Amenhotep IV.

Following the reign of Amenhotep III, his son Amenhotep IV, became Pharaoh and took unprecedented steps to introduce a form of monotheistic worship. Amenhotep IV not only transferred his seat of power from the old city of Thebes to a new site 200 miles down river on the east bank of the Nile (known today as Tell el Amarna), but he also changed his name from Amenhotep – which honoured the god Amun – to Akhenaten: 'Glory' or 'Spirit'. This monotheism is identical to that of Moses. Now, if Moses was contemporary with this, surely he would not have opposed such a like-minded Pharaoh. I am sure he would have been foresighted enough to see the value of embracing such a concept jointly, not entering into a confrontation; the longterm benefits for all, striving for the same goal, would be enormous. This is why *I* feel that Moses is one and the same person as Akhenaten.

From the extensive archaeological excavations at Amarna, many scholars have concluded that Akhenaten was a great artist, poet, mystic and philosopher. He was totally unlike any other Pharaoh, before or since. Akhenaten ruled for just 17 years with fewer than 13 of those based at Tell el Armarna. After this, he simply disappears completely from the pages of history. Some scholars have argued that he died from the plague that was thought to have swept the entire Near East, including Egypt, in his later reign. He was, as we saw earlier, possibly replaced at some unknown date by the mysterious figure named Smenkhkare, his co-regent, who was followed by the boy-king, Tutankhaten. After *he* succeeded to the throne, the priests of Amun at Thebes quickly changed this young king's name to Tutankhamun, a name that honoured their god.

Tutankhamun only reigned for 9 years, then died in mysterious circumstances at the age of 18. At this point Egypt's throne fell firstly to Akhenaten's old vizier, Aye, and then to Tutankhamun's military commander, Horemheb, who immediately set about erasing all trace of not only Akhenaten's reign, but also every other Amarna king, i.e.

The Giza pyramids as viewed from the South.

The enigmatic Sphinx at Giza.

A few of the remaining polished white lumite stones on the Great Pyramid.

Severe weathering pattern caused by rainfall inside the Sphinx enclosure, whic indicates a time scale for this erosion dating back to at least 8-10,000 B.C. Note th Operation Hermes team members on horseback in the background.

A later–constructed pyramid. Note its crumbled state even though it was built much later than the Great Pyramid. This clearly shows a backward step in construction techniques.

he bent pyramid at Dashur in Egypt. Supposedly from the fourth dynasty, it is far lder, and directly related to the Giza pyramids. Unlike orthodox theory, which states at its shape was changed during construction because of engineering problems, this ook shows that there is very good reason why it was planned to have this structure.

Clearly visible water erosion on the Great Pyramid's platform stones indicates scientifically provable date of around 9,000 B.C. for its construction, which tallies with the latest dating of the Sphinx, based on weathering.

The main entrance to the Temple of Horus at Edfu in Egypt. Notice its two raised entrance door columns and the lintel of solid stone that straddles both, identical in image to the symbol Pi (π) and the Trilithons at Stonehenge. Indeed the entire facade very suggestive of the uprights of the Trilithons, since it tapers upwards from a wide base

The Grand Gallery within the Great Pyramid. Why such a massive over-engineered passage when all the others are so small? Within its dimensions are carried several essential mathematical values that contribute to the overall plan of symbolic codes. It even contains values found in the New Testament.

An ancient Egyptian depiction of the Great Green God of Egypt: Osiris. The green complexion of his face connects Osiris with many later green fertility Gods.

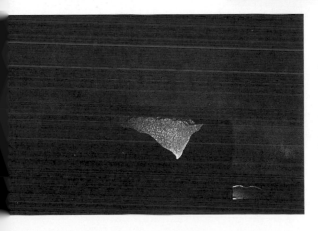

The King's Chamber of the Great Pyramid. Its sophisticated numerical layout is formed by ratios that play a part in my search for the Hall of Records. The 'sarcophagus' was drilled out using a drilling speed and bore rate faster than anything available today, a mystery that remains unexplained.

Hieroglyphic relief from the walls of a temple at Abydos in Egypt that clearly show: modern-looking aircraft, especially the helicopter image that has defied an explan ation from Egyptologists to date.

Sumerian cylinder seal showing planets of our solar system, plus a tenth planet!

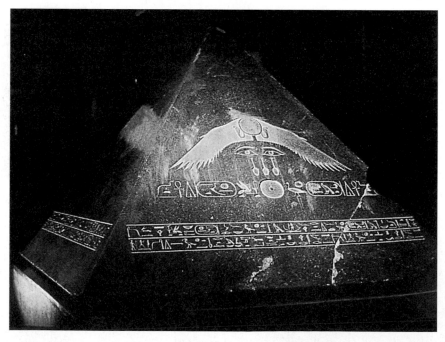

A Pyramidion (Ben Ben of Anomhet III) inside the Egyptian museum. Pyramidion were placed on top of pyramids to cap them. The Great Pyramid's capstone, howeve: has always been known to be missing, even from the depths of antiquity. Its restoratio: has many sacred meanings, according to various esoteric traditions.

Above: Zoser's step pyramid, built in six steps. Classical history agrees that this pyramid was built at the same time as Silbury Hill.

Below: Side elevation of Silbury Hill surrounded by water.

Silbury Hill on the Marlborough Downs – like Zoser's pyramid – is constructed in six steps with a seventh forming the platform summit. It is covered in earth, just like the Pyramids of Central America and the enigmatic pyramids of China, to protect it over the course of time. Silbury Hill is directly linked to both Avebury and Stonehenge in celestial symbology. It can be conclusively shown that Silbury Hill is far older than current orthodoxy allows.

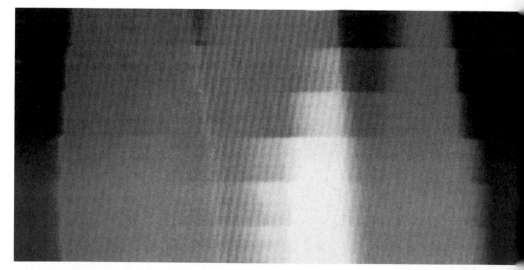

The spectrum recorded on film. The red area of the spectrum, which is to the right, is identical to the image and outline of the enigmatic corner niche in the Queen's Chamber inside the Great Pyramid. Sirius was often referred to as being red and hot. The image of the corner niche is also identical to a spectographic image of light from Sirius. Furthermore, one of the so-called air shafts within the Queen's Chamber pointed directly at Sirius. Is someone trying to tell us something?

Clearly visible pyramids covered in earth rise from the almost flat Chinese landscape. This type of formation does not occur in nature, so suggestions that these structures are of natural origin are absurd.

Just one of the pyramids near the city of Xian, Qui Chan Province, China, which local legends maintain were built by 'the Sons of Heaven', who came down to Earth in a fiery Dragon. Like Silbury Hill and pyramids in Central America, this pyramid was covered in earth for protection.

The Stonehenge Sarsens with the heel stone just visible beyond them. The Sarsens with their encoded mathematical value, directly connect the site of Stonehenge with the position of the Giza plateau in Egypt.

The Trilithons at Stonehenge are finished in a rough manner, yet the central Trilithon is constructed with a smooth finish, denoting its importance. The Trilithon is also a perfect representation of the universal symbol of Pi (π) with its two upright columns and cross lintel at the top slightly overhanging its edges. In addition, it is the key to the greater mystery that connects Stonehenge to the Giza Pyramids of Egypt.

The constellation of Orion was connected in Egyptian myths with Osiris, and, in Biblical symbology, with both Samson and Elijah. The three major Giza pyramids have also been proved to represent the three belts of Orion.

The Pyramid of the Sun at Teotihuacan in Mexico, with its rectangular base of 720x760 feet. The steps of the pyramid rise at an angle of 45 degrees to a height of 216 feet, a number of great importance within ancient hidden codes.

The six-tiered pyramid base for the Temple of Quetzalcoatl, the feathered serpent god. The pyramid stands inside the Citadel, a sunken so-called ceremonial square at Teotihuacan.

The Pyramid of the Niches at El Tajin, Veracruz. The pyramid takes its name from the unique feature of its seven levels which are decorated by 365 square niches, one for each day of the year.

The Temple of Inscriptions at Palenque.

The White Horse at Uffington is carved out of the hillside revealing the white chalk below. It and Stonehenge are equidistant from Avebury. Note that the horse is actually more feline than equine, and resembles celtic images of cats. Could this be a representation of the constellation of Leo, the Lion?

Above and below:
Two views of the actual projected site of the alignments of Sirius. Will this become one of the most sacred sites on Earth?

Raiders of the lost archives 'find pharaohs' records'

by Cherry Norton

TWO British Egyptologists believe they have found the site of an ancient underground chamber containing evidence of a lost civilisation.

Nigel Appleby and Adam Child, already dubbed the "raiders of the lost archives", are preparing an expedition to investigate a site near the great pyramids where they say the Hall of Records lies buried in the sand.

They have been given permission by the Egyptian authorities to survey an area north of the Great Pyramid of Cheops using sensitive scanning equipment capable of detecting underground chambers.

The Hall of Records, according to legend, is made of granite and sheathed in gold; it is said to contain artefacts and documents on the history of mankind whose discovery will herald a new dawn for civilisation. It is alluded to in the Bible and other ancient texts such as the Book of the Dead, Appleby said last week.

He spent many years examining astronomical and astrological data and the position of the stars in relation to the pyramids before arriving at a location for the hall. He claims to have discovered and deciphered codes in ancient writings that describe the importance of

when the three stars of Orion's belt are lined up directly over three of the great pyramids, the star Sirius is directly over the hall. By projecting its position on to the earth, the approximate site of the hall can be found.

"A Japanese team has spent the past 20 years on the Giza plateau trying to find it and an American team is there now looking under the paw of the Sphinx. But they are looking in the wrong place. I know I am right. It is very exciting," he said.

Academic experts acknowledge there are passageways under the Sphinx that have never been fully excavated. However, Appleby said the Hall of Records was further away, probably inside a small pyramid buried by shifting sands. He has calculated that the secret chamber is about eight miles north of the Sphinx and at least 30ft underground.

He and Child plan to spend about a month with a group of geophysical specialists on the site. A team of 18 people including paramedics, scientists and archeologists will submit a scientific report of its findings to the Egyptian authorities. If the search proves

allow them to be involved in any excavation that follows. The two men are unlikely adventurers: Appleby, 33, is an engineering designer who runs his own publishing company and Child, 28, is a development manager for BT.

Despite earlier discoveries of fabulous wealth, such as in the tomb of Tutankhamun, Child does not believe the hall contains treasure. "It was built as a centre of learning. Its value will be in terms of knowledge, not money," he said.

Academic experts remain sceptical. Dr Richard Parkinson, an assistant keeper in the department of Egyptian antiquities at the British Museum, said: "We have had some inquiries about the Hall of Records. It is something people are looking for but there is no firm evidence that it exists.

"There are certainly tunnels under the Sphinx that people have tried to excavate in the past but there are not, as far as anyone knows, any secret chambers."

However, other ancient sites thought by many to be mythical have eventually turned out to be real. For years scholars dismissed the city of Troy as the fiction of Homer; but in the 1870s Heinrich Schliemann, the German archeologist,

HOW STARS LEAD THE WAY

British Egyptologists have used stars to locate the mythical 'Hall of Records' buried beneath sands. When the stars of Orion's Belt are aligned over the Pyramids of Giza, the star Sirius is said to be directly over the missing haul of artefacts and documents

Milky Way

SIRIUS

ORION'S BELT

POSSIBLE SITE OF HALL OF RECORDS

Great Pyramids

THE RIVER NILE
The river is said to follow the trail of stars in the Milky Way

Site of Hall of Records within a mile radius

Giza · Cairo

Great Pyramids

EGYPT

10m

River Nile

N

HALL OF RECORDS

Legendary chamber, alluded to in the Bible, is made of granite and sheathed in gold. Inside it contains documents on the history of mankind which 'will herald a new dawn for civilisation'

THE HIDDEN PYRAMID

Explorers believe the Hall of Records is inside a

How the news broke. Following this article in The *Sunday Times* phones were ringing off the hook at Operation Hermes' headquarters.

Smenkhkare, Tutankhamun and Aye. He even outlawed their names, and Akhenaten's years on the throne became known as the time of the 'Rebel' or 'Rebellion'. Horemheb attacked everything connected with Amarna and the now reviled faith of Aten: he destroyed its temples, defaced its reliefs and chiselled out the inscriptions. All of Akhenaten's family tombs were looted, their mummies desecrated and cast out to disintegrate in the desert. Horemheb even went as far as destroying Akhenaten's gleaming white citadel, carting off the material for other building projects. Why weren't Akhenaten's remains treated in the same manner as the rest of his family and his courtiers and thrown into the desert? I believe the answer is that they feared Akhenaten with an intensity that went above and beyond simple hatred. This means that whatever he did must have been absolutely extraordinary. In view of this, I maintain that Horemheb is a more tenable opponent of Moses than Rameses II, around whom considerable debate still rages.

If he *had* been held responsible for the disasters that befell Egypt during the Exodus, his successors would have stated so and simply thrown his remains to the ravages of the scorching desert. The reason is, I think, this: subsequent rulers did not desecrate Akhenaten's body for fear of a reprisal from his God. Remember that it is not known where Moses was buried, and there is *certainly* no proof that he was interred along the route of the Exodus. The anger and fear felt about Akhenaten would certainly have been felt about Moses with his all-powerful God who had caused such destruction; *that* is very easy to understand. This is why I think that they are both one and the same person.

Certainly, because of this, some scholars have begun to note the comparisons between Akhenaten's new radical, single-God Aten faith and the new single-god faith of Moses, concluding that the Israelites adopted the Aten faith as they left Egypt. It is definitely significant that the hymn to Aten bore distinct parallels to the verses of Psalm 104, first recorded in Solomonic times, *c.* 980 BC. It seems likely that one influenced the other, or both were of direct origin from a common source.

Although it appears that the peaceful, introspective Akhenaten is a direct opposite of the image of the decisive Moses, we must remember that the stories about Moses himself were written long after his death, complete with all the later distortions and embellishments added to create a more forceful and autocratic leader under the direct command of God. (The same, indeed, could be said of the Pharaoh who allegedly opposed the Israelites with such venom; the killing of the first-born, for example, could easily be a later attempt at vilification.)

Further points need to be made. Firstly, the era in which Akhenaten ruled, was, as we have seen, a period of civil upheaval, possibly requiring a co-regency; this coincided with Akhenaten's lack of responsibility

213

towards his state duties, in pursuit of his own enlightenment. Secondly, his learning from God that he was to liberate God's enslaved people, to the detriment of Egyptian policies, would have brought opposition to him to boiling point. In essence, what he was doing undermined both the political and religious status quo of Egypt.

In the 1930s Sigmund Freud published a work (*Moses and Monotheism*)[9] in which he proposed that Moses had been an Egyptian linked to the court of Akhenaten and provided much evidence in support of his argument. One fact he pointed out was that the Jewish word for Lord, 'Adonai', becomes 'Aten' when its letters are transformed into Egyptian. Freud also pointed out that circumcision, a requirement of Hebrew law for every newborn male child, was first practised by the ancient Egyptians – apparently for reasons of hygiene – but not by any other Asiatic or Middle Eastern culture. In other words, the Jews had inherited the tradition, via Moses, from the Egyptians. It was Freud's research that set the scene for more scholars to begin reassessing Akhenaten's life and reign. In 1990, perhaps the most influential book on the subject was published: *Moses Pharaoh of Egypt* by Ahmed Osman,[10] who states categorically that Moses and Akhenaten are in fact one and the same individual. I am *prepared* to believe that Moses and Akhenaten are one and the same person though I concede that it cannot be proved conclusively as yet.

The real significance of Moses?

Another meaning for Moses is simply 'Born of', and usually requires another name to be added to it; for example, Thothmoses means 'born of Thoth', Rameses means 'born of Ra' and Amenmosis means 'born of Amen'. The Moses element may vary when rendered into English, but they all mean the same. Because of this, some scholars have argued that either Moses himself or some later scribe dropped the name of an Egyptian god from his full name. Another story similar to that of Moses is the birth-narrative of Sargon I, ruler of Babylon and Sumer hundreds of years before Moses; this states that Sargon's mother set him in a basket of rushes. She sealed the lid with bitumen and put him into the river. How similar to the story of Moses can you get? I believe that Moses's birth story (which links with the Isis/Horus tales) is almost undoubtedly a fiction created in the later 6th century BC for the birth of the Jewish nation relying heavily on the ancient theme of creation emerging from the waters. Again, this indicates that these events were all symbolically designed to carry the same information and any inherent codes; they were simply adapted to a new era, place and peoples.

Sir E. A. Wallis Budge, in *From Fetish to God in Ancient Egypt*,[11] declared that the miracles that Moses wrought suggested that he was not only a priest, but a magician of the highest order, and perhaps even a Ker Heh, an Egyptian High Priest. This is implied in the Bible, Acts 7: 22: 'And Moses became learned in all the wisdom of the Egyptians, and was mighty in words and in deeds.' In addition, the Egyptian 3rd-century High Priest Manetho stated the following:

> Moses, a son of the tribe of Levi, educated in Egypt and initiated at Heliopolis, became a High Priest of the Brotherhood under the reign of Pharaoh Amenhotep/Akhenaten. He was elected by the Hebrews as their chief and he adapted to the ideas of his people the science and philosophy which he had obtained in the Egyptian mysteries; proofs of this are to be found in the symbols, in the initiations, and in his precepts and commandments. The dogma of an 'Only God' which he taught was the Egyptian Brotherhood interpretation and teaching of the Pharaoh who established the first Monotheistic religion known to man.[12]

This quote emphasises the idea that Moses was an initiate of great mysteries. It might be argued – against my theory – that Manetho here proves that Moses and Akhenaten were *not* one person, but it is highly unlikely that Manetho would have been privy to information that would connect Moses and Akhenaten.

The essential element of the Moses story, however mysterious, is this: his laws and his teachings and all the inherent codes within them have survived so that we can use that information to recover the lost wisdom of the ancients. Sir Isaac Newton believed that Moses understood that matter consisted of atoms, and that these atoms were hard, solid and immutable; gravity accrued to both atoms and to the bodies they composed; gravity was proportional to the quantity of matter in every body. Newton even wrote the following:

> The Egyptians concealed mysteries that were above the capacity of the common herd under the veil of religious rites and hieroglyphic symbols. It was the most ancient opinion that the planets revolved around the Sun, that the Earth, as one of the planets, described an annual course about the Sun, while by a diurnal motion, it turned on its axis, and that the Sun remained at rest.[13]

If there are indeed codes stemming from ancient Egypt via Moses and Jesus, how were those codes then carried on until the present?

To answer this we need to look closely at the organisations that continued after Jesus, carrying the myths and legends into the present – the Knights Templar, supposed guardians of the Holy Grail, and the Freemasons.

Chapter 24

Arthurian Myth, the Holy Grail and the Templars

Many people are aware of King Arthur and his connection to the Holy Grail. Less well known is that the Grail myths are mainly symbolic, intended to carry on encoded information through the Middle Ages and up to the present. It is through the Grail romances connected with King Arthur that many sacred details, particularly measurements, were brought out of Egypt via King Solomon's Temple and eventually to England.

The telling of the legend

The first transmission of the mysterious information was via Joseph of Arimathea. Grail myths relate that Joseph of Arimathea was a follower of Jesus Christ who escaped to England, just prior to the Jewish uprising (AD 70). Some aspects of the myth derive from the *Gospel of Nicodemus*,[1] generally thought to be a 5th-century compilation of earlier Hebrew and Greek texts. (John 19 says: 38 '. . . Joseph of Arimathea, being a disciple of Jesus, but secretly, for fear of the Jews, besought Pilate that he might take away the body of Jesus: and Pilate gave him leave. He came therefore, and took the body of Jesus. 39 And there came also Nicodemus which at the first came to Jesus by night, and brought a mixture of myrrh and aloes . . . 40 Then took they the body of Jesus and wound it in linen clothes with the spices, as the manner of the Jews is to bury.') Subsequent elements derive from Templar, and later Freemason, esoteric sources. These accounts say that Joseph led a group dispatched by Saint Philip, which escorted the Holy Grail. They travelled in a boat named *Stella Maris* ('Star of the Sea'). After various adventures, the group reached Britain.

Here, the travellers were soon granted land in 'Ynys Vytrin' (Isle of Glass) or 'Ynys Afalla' (Isle of Apples), which, of course, legends persistently link with Glastonbury. After setbacks during missionary work in other parts of Britain, Joseph founded a monastery at Glastonbury. Subsequently, various monarchs added to the monastery's

216

estates, which became generally renowned as the 12 hides of Glastonbury.

Unexpected pyramids

It is feasible that Joseph of Arimathea brought with him sacred units of measure from Jerusalem, where the sacred measurements had been introduced by Moses, from Egypt. At Glastonbury, there are two small enigmatic tombs; they are both small pyramids – a strange choice of style for a Christian abbey, especially as it would have been an anathema to the early Church of Saul. This could well indicate that the early Church that founded the Abbey at Glastonbury was the Church of James, the brother of Jesus. Moses brought many Egyptian religious influences with him on his flight from Egypt, and we can see evidence of many of those influences even to this day. For instance, Christians all around the world still finish their prayers with an intonement to the Egyptian god Amen. Thoth, known as 'Three times great', is identical to the Holy Trinity. Moreover, the Ark of the Covenant bears many similarities to the ark of Tutankhamun. So as an initiate and disciple of Jesus (who was in turn a direct descendant of Moses), it is more than probable that Joseph of Arimathea was well educated in the ancient secret rites and sacred measurements.

Not just a cup?

The Holy Grail was reputed to be the cup that Jesus used during the Last Supper (and recovered from Pontius Pilate by Joseph of Arimathea); this eventually became the cup which caught his blood when he was crucified; it then became the vessel containing his blood. It has been argued by such books as *The Holy Blood and the Holy Grail*[1] and *Bloodline of the Holy Grail*[3] that the meaning of the words Holy Grail derive from 'Sang Raal' meaning 'Royal Blood'. It was also argued that the Holy Grail is a blood line from Jesus Christ himself, with the inference that when Mary Magdalene fled to France with Joseph of Arimathea 'with the Holy Grail', this meant she was with child, Jesus's child. From this bloodline, a long line of heirs was to flow resulting in the Frankish Merovingian bloodline. The cup of the Holy Grail was then brought to England by Joseph of Arimathea and was believed to have miraculous properties. Its subsequent loss by the British was deemed to have disastrous consequences for King Arthur's kingdom. King Arthur's sword Excalibur is linked to the Great Pyramid, as we shall see. Excalibur is returned to the Lady in the Lake at the end of Arthur's reign. Once again, water is symbolic. The sword represents wisdom, knowledge, spiritual awareness and compassion, as it could only be drawn from the stone by the truly worthy. It could be then, that this conveys that only the truly worthy and enlightened can draw from the stone (i.e. the Great Pyramid) its secrets and knowledge, which is only to be used for good.

The true meanings behind the legends of the Grail and its hidden wisdom and knowledge had very little to do with any 'historical' King Arthur, yet the quest for the Holy Grail is one of the most haunting themes in Christian history. As it was apparently either buried or lost in Britain, it became the object of search that lasted many centuries. Legend has it that King Arthur's knights found the Grail, by which time it was not only viewed as a holy relic but also as a magical vessel that contained secret wisdom and knowledge. It is my belief that the cup was purely symbolic, and that the actual Holy Grail was a bloodline as mentioned above, one that would ensure that the ancient secrets would continue across time. Such a bloodline was feasible, some say, because Jesus *survived* the crucifixion and went on to father children who became the bloodline; in this way, as has been shown, the San Graal, translated as 'Holy Grail', can also be Sang Raal – 'Holy Blood'. If Mary Magdalene arrived in Southern France carrying the vessel of the Holy Grail (as *symbolised* by the cup) with Joseph, she could well have been carrying a child; in a very real physical sense, then, she was carrying the Holy Blood/Holy Grail.

Connections with England

It has been suggested that Joseph of Arimathea was Jesus's uncle, or at least related in some way; thus he was able to recover Jesus's body. Since Jesus had been sentenced and crucified as a common criminal, his body would, in normal circumstances, have been buried in a reserved area for criminals. In such circumstances, under Jewish and Roman law only a relative could claim the body and dispose of it accordingly. Joseph must have been a wealthy man, to provide Jesus with a tomb. He is supposed to have made his fortune from dealing in the tin trade. Is it a coincidence, therefore, that the traditional journey of Joseph with his delegates, Mary and the Holy Grail follows the trade routes for tin, as described in detail by the Greek writer Diodorus Siculus shortly before the birth of Jesus? He states that tin was transported at low tide to the island of Ictis (thought to be St Michael's Mount) in a bay off Southern Cornwall, after which merchants would transport it on to Gaul, from where it then took 30 days' carrying it, in sacks on horseback, to the mouth of the River Rhône.

Traditions in France, western Ireland, Gloucester, North London and the Cornish tin-mining region all tell of Joseph's involvement in the tin trade. Cornish folklore is emphatic in stating that Joseph made voyages to Cornwall in his own ships, and that he once brought the young Jesus with him and Mary Magdalene when they landed at St Michael's Mount. Accounts suggest that, persecuted by the Jews, Joseph, after being released from prison, left Israel in a boat without oars or sails, accompanied by three Saint Marys, Lazarus and a host of other saints. They left, according to different medieval traditions, from either Caesarea, Mount Carmel, Askalon or Jaffa.

The historian Edward Foord lucidly stated the following:

> Was is possible that Joseph of Arimathea could visit Britain shortly after the death of Christ? To that question the answer must be in the emphatic affirmative. In the Ist century of the Christian era it was much easier to travel from Palestine to Britain than it was in the xiith – or the xviiith, for that matter. The Mediterranean world was resting securely beneath the shield of Rome: there was peace: there were good roads and plenty of vehicles and riding animals to be obtained by anyone who possessed the means. The Jews were spread all over the Roman Empire: there were many of them in Italy. If Jews could settle in Italy a Jew could certainly travel thither, and from Italy to Britain is no lengthy journey for a far-travelling Oriental. Britain, long before the beginning of the Roman Conquest in 43, was within the circle of Roman civilisation and economic influence, and there was nothing to prevent any Jew from visiting the country, much less a wealthy and powerful Jew such as Joseph of Arimathea. After 45 or thereabouts the entire south of the island was directly under Roman rule, and it is at least likely that Jews were among the traders and speculators who flooded the newly-conquered region. There is nothing impossible or even improbable in the central statement of the legend . . .[4]

Furthermore, Jesus visiting Britain is historically very feasible. Very little is known of his early life from the age of 12 to 30, when his ministry started. It is certainly widely believed that he travelled extensively abroad. There is even a 'Jesus Well' at the mouth of the River Camel in Cornwall, *en route* to Glastonbury. At Priddy, 8 miles north of Glastonbury, there is a prevailing legend that Jesus once stayed there, and a church there is the subject of a story relating to a strange energy emanating from a cave beneath it. Indeed, a common saying in the area is: 'As sure as our Lord was at Priddy.'

The above suggests early links between the Holy Land and Britain, and is supported by the fact that the Christian religion was practised in Britain very shortly after Jesus's death. The 6th-century writer Gildas records that it began in the last year of the reign of Tiberius – only 4 years after Jesus's crucifixion. Furthermore, Glastonbury, known by its ancient name of Glastonia, is specifically mentioned in religious texts as already having a church even before Christian missionaries of the

Catholic Church arrived in the 6th century AD, although, of course, Christianity was well established in late Roman Britain, and Augustine's mission was really one of *re*conversion.

If there was no real substance behind the legends of Joseph why, from being such an insignificant figure, has he taken on such an esteemed and important position within the Grail legends? The writer Geoffrey Ashe pointed out that Joseph's presence on British soil is too odd, under the circumstances, to have the air of pure invention. It is certainly possible that Joseph was indeed Jesus's uncle and that after the crucifixion he *did* bring the Holy Grail to England.

On the other hand, a life of St Dunstan written around 1000 and William of Malmesbury's *de Antiquitate* of around 1125 both mention traditions relating to Glastonbury as an early Christian church, but make no mention of Joseph. This is a striking omission if he was indeed responsible for founding the original church in the first place. A much later edition of Malmesbury's book, current after the Arthurian Grail legends had become popular in France, has a reference to Joseph added to the text. Some scholars have argued that this indicates that Joseph was a later invention. Certainly it was not until the 15th century that the story of the Grail became embedded within English folklore, after Thomas Malory's Arthurian legends were widely read. Malory himself had drawn heavily upon French sources, entitling his version of the quest for the Holy Grail as 'The Tale of the Sankreal'.

Whatever the outcome, I maintain that the essential point here is the continuity of a story that deals with knowledge and wisdom and hidden occult information, carried over into medieval times and 'updated' to suit that period. For a start, while Malory's exact sources are not known, it is likely that they were not very ancient themselves. The earliest Grail legends were chronicled by the Burgundian, Robert de Boron, in his *Roman de l'Estoire dou Saint Graal* (*c*. 1195). His writings tell the legends and explain them in a manner that suggests to me that a cryptic and occult meaning lies behind the romantic Christian legends of the Holy Grail, and that the original Grail legends were of a *pre-Christian Celtic symbolism*, disguised to keep it alive within the trappings of Christianity itself.

A rival to Joseph of Arimathea?

According to some legends, the real bearer of the Grail was not Joseph, but a powerful pagan god named Bran. In ancient Celtic myth, he was the possessor of a magical cauldron capable of bringing people back to life. I contend that this does not necessarily mean physically bringing back to life from the dead; rather it implies a return to a spiritual life – just as the later Qumranians referred to those outside of their community as being 'dead'. They meant a symbolic death; newly baptised members could be raised from the 'dead' symbolically, when they became full members of the community.

In Robert de Boron's work, Bran is disguised as Bron, the brother-in-law of Joseph. Bron also appears in all later works about the Grail. Therefore he must have been invented for some very good reason; one which becomes clear only towards the end of the story when Bron, also described as the 'Rich Fisher' (or 'Fisher King'), takes over guardianship of the Grail from Joseph, subsequently becoming more important than Joseph himself. Again we see fisher symbolism. The Grail remains in the hands of the 'Rich Fisher's' descendants until King Arthur's quest to recover it is successful. The scholar Roger Sherman Loomis has traced the similarities between Bron, the Rich Fisher, and Bran, the Celtic god; they are practically identical and must both be references to the same individual. Interestingly, according to various sources, the Rich Fisher was wounded through the thighs or legs with a javelin in battle; Bran was injured in the same manner when he invaded Ireland. Both entertained their guests lavishly and both led their followers westwards (to the Americas, argue the authors of *The Holy Blood and the Holy Grail*[6]), to a place where many years were spent in idyllic peace, unaware of the passage of time. Even the title 'Rich Fisher' is paralleled by Bran, who was once known as a sea god. The link here to the symbolic likeness of Oannes, the Babylonian sea god, is striking. I believe this shows that the same imagery and symbolism were deliberately carried over and simply adapted to suit any particular era.

Descriptions of the Grail

Confusion and mystery certainly surround the *appearance* of the Grail itself. Early Christian documents generally depict it as a large dish containing the host for some unnamed person. The Grail only became a dish much later. Earlier it had been more common to associate it with the vessels and cups of Celtic myths. Bran apparently was in possession of one, of which it was said: 'The virtue of the cauldron is this; a man slain today cast him into the cauldron, and by tomorrow he will be as well as he was at best, save that he will not have the power of speech.' This cauldron could also determine the weak from the brave with the following statement: 'If meat for a coward were put in it to boil, it would never boil; but if meat for a brave man were put in it, it would boil quickly.' There are several other Celtic myths relating to dishes, including one that belonged to the King of Rhydderch. On this, any foodstuff requested instantly appeared. Other relevant legends include that of the horn of Bran, the Niggard from the North, and the crock and dish of Rhygenydd the Celtic, all of which claim the same miraculous powers. These have direct parallels with Malory's description of the knights watching the entrance of the Grail at Arthur's court, after which every knight had whatever meat and drink he most desired.

From the information relating to the Grail romances, it seems that the Grail legends as we know them today were concocted around the 12th and 13th centuries by roving clerics and *conteurs* known as bards, who used Celtic source material and disguised it within Christian doctrines. The question that begs an answer is: Just *what* was it they wanted to preserve? To me it appears obvious: they were trying to guarantee that the ancient knowledge pertaining to some great secret – *which was itself not known to them* – was woven into a new palatable story suited to their time, thus ensuring its survival. Clearly it was being preserved for a much later generation. As we shall see, *we* are that generation.

Robert Graves has convincingly shown in *The White Goddess*[7] that there was a Druidic revival in Wales at the very time when the Grail legends were being developed. It would be too simplistic, however, to state that they were simply resuscitating old pagan religious ideas that had defied earlier Roman attempts at suppression and also those of the early Christian missionaries, as they were in fact *maintaining* the flow of the esoteric wisdom of the ancients. It is no coincidence that Bran, the magical cauldron and the story of a miraculous child who possessed a secret doctrine were all part of the same revival. This revival has almost identical symbolism both to that of Jesus as a child and that of the Egyptian god Horus, the son of Isis and Orion.

Guardians of the Grail

At the same time as the Grail romances were being disseminated across Europe, came the rise of a powerful occult organisation associated with the Holy Grail – the Templars, the so-called guardians of the Grail. A German version of the Grail romances entitled *Parzifal*, composed between *c.* 1200 and 1220, specifically refers to a movement practically identical to the Templars as the guardians of the Grail. *Parzifal* is the most enigmatic of all Grail stories. It clearly describes a spiritual quest to provide a key to enlightenment. A chaste order of knights is depicted who reside in the Munsalvaesche (the Grail castle), and are sustained 'by virtue of a stone most pure'. I couldn't help but wonder if there was a connection here with the Great Pyramid, which as I have said was known as a building of stone most pure and undefiled in an adulterous land (Isaiah). *Parzifal* continues:

There never was a human so ill but that, if he one day sees that stone, he cannot die within the week that follows. And in looks he will not fade. His appearance will stay the same, be it maid or man, as on the day he saw the stone, the same as when the best years of his life began, and though he should see the stone for two hundred years, it will never change, save that his hair might perhaps turn grey. Such power does the stone give a man that flesh and bones are at once made young again. The stone is called the Grail.[8]

Identical allusions have been made by mystics and occultists concerning the magical properties of the Great Pyramid. In view of all the many other gematria connections relating to the Great Pyramid, I am more than inclined to suspect that the Grail legends point towards a connection between the two.

The Templars were founded as a religious order around 1118 as a type of military police-force to protect the pilgrim routes to Jerusalem that had just been freed from the domination of the Turks. There is overwhelming evidence that suggests that the 9 original Templars never actually defended the pilgrim routes – to do so with just 9 men would have been impossible. All Templar knights took the same vows as monks: of poverty, chastity, obedience. They were a religious as well as a military force; they called themselves the 'Poor Knights of Christ' and adopted the device of 2 knights riding on 1 horse as their symbol. The 9 original knights stayed in Jerusalem for 9 years and King Baldwin II of Jerusalem granted them the use of the Al Aqsa Mosque on the Temple Mount of Jerusalem as their headquarters.

The Knights Templar were a secretive and very mysterious chivalric order. They held the deeds and titles to many tracts of land across Europe, including England. The order was founded by French knights led by one Hugues de Payns (meaning 'of the pagans'), after being inspired by St Bernard of Clairvaux (leader of the austere Cistercian order). After the knights had taken residence near to the Church of the Holy Sepulchre (built on the site of the Temple of Solomon), they immediately started searching for some buried artefact or treasure. They certainly did not fulfil their ostensible *raison d'être* – to protect pilgrims. The order became one of the most powerful forces in the Christian world, mainly because it owed allegiance to the Pope alone and was thus beyond lesser jurisdiction. Many nobles and wealthy landowners joined the order, handing over the deeds to their lands. Due to the Templars' international connections, they soon became the first *de facto* bankers, introducing the system of bonds and cheques that could be exchanged for goods and services in parts of the Christian world. This only served to further increase their wealth.

Savage suppression

Although they swore sole allegiance to the Pope, the Templars were nonetheless strangely independent of his authority and were, in real terms, led by their Grand Master. The Grand Master of the Prieuré de Sion (which to all intents and purposes was the political arm of the Templar organisation, and the secret continuation of the society after it was officially dissolved) was often referred to as the 'Nautonnier', an old French word meaning 'navigator' or 'helmsman'. This connection immediately struck me as an almost identical representation of the image of Osiris, who was depicted as sailing in the royal bark that traversed the heavens to the constellation of Orion. It also has direct parallels with the ancient myths of Jason and the Argonauts, as we saw in Chapter 8. This was yet another clue that the hidden information from antiquity was still being transmitted in a new format to our era intact. During the Templars' existence, they were constantly involved in high-level international politics dealing with nobles and monarchs throughout Europe. In Britain, the Master of the Temple regularly attended the king's parliament and took precedence over all priors and abbots of other religious orders. For example, the Master of the Temple stood by the monarch's side at the signing of the Magna Carta. Their political influence even extended to the Muslim world.

The Templars were known to keep close ties with the Islamic Sufis and other mystical organisations and shared their wisdom and esoteric knowledge of alchemy and the Kabbalah. Perhaps because of this, in time false stories began to circulate about their secrets, doctrines, mystical pursuits and mysticism, just as similar accusations would eventually beset the Freemasons. King Philip IV of France (known as Philip the Fair) became suspicious of their activities and their continued growth of wealth and on Friday 13 October 1307, just 189 years after the order's formation, his men seized the Templars' Grand Master, Jean Jacques de Molay, and 140 of his knights. They were charged with heresy, blasphemy and witchcraft, which resulted in the order being persecuted throughout Christendom. Many of its members were tortured by the Inquisition, leading to forcibly extracted false confessions of idolatrous practices.

The order was officially abolished in 1312 by Pope Clement V, who also transferred their estates to the Knights Hospitalers. These were experts in matters of medicine and hygiene and were responsible for starting the first true hospitals in the Western world (hence the use of the word hospital). The Templar Grand Master, still protesting his innocence, was roasted alive. Before he died he summoned Philip IV and Pope Clement V to appear before the judgement seat of God, to answer for their crimes against the Templars: Philip was given a year, Clement a month. It may just be coincidence, but both died within the time stated.

At the time it was thought that the order had dissolved completely but there is overwhelming supporting evidence (outlined in detail in *The Holy Blood and the Holy Grail*[9]) that it evolved into the Freemason organisation. This still embodies many Templar traditions and rituals, though without fully understanding what they mean or represent. Whatever the original Templar knights discovered buried in Jerusalem, one thing is clear; it opened the way for the foundation of two organisations which would carry the hidden codes of antiquity to our present era. It has been speculated that the Templars' find was somehow connected with the Ark of the Covenant; that the Templars became aware of hidden powers or messages within the landscape that invoked energies through their rituals; and that their esoteric knowledge was subsequently incorporated into the hidden geometry within the proportions of Gothic cathedrals.

One of the accusations levelled at the Templars was the worship of an idol named Baphomet, usually described as a skull, a human head or 3 heads. Such worship was certainly deeply enshrined in the Celtic religion, which was being revived at the time of the Grail romances. Could it be that whilst outwardly serving the Pope, the Templars were in fact secretly protecting a very different form of religious doctrine and ritual? The typical image of the Knights Templars is the familiar one of fanatically fierce warrior-monks clad in a white mantle with a splayed red cross emblazoned upon their chests, who played such a crucial role within the Crusades. They were, in effect, the storm troopers of the Holy Land, fighting and dying for Christ in their thousands. Yet at the end of their two-centuries-long existence, these warrior champions of Christ were accused of denying Christ himself and of trampling and spitting on the cross. Obviously they had powerful enemies. Numerous scholars have argued that the prime mover against them was the Roman Catholic church, fearful both of the Templars' power and wealth and of their holding secrets relating to Jesus that could seriously jeopardise Papal power. That secret was, of course, that Jesus survived the crucifixion and went on to father children, thus creating a bloodline that resulted in the Merovingian dynasty.

Templars have been depicted as greedy arrogant bullies, abusing their power and even worshipping the Devil. It is now becoming clear that they were hapless victims, sacrificial pawns in the high-level political machinations of the Church and State. Similar to the later traditions of Freemasonry, they were regarded as initiates and mystical adepts and the custodians of ancient arcane wisdom that transcends Christianity itself. I was intrigued to know what these secrets and wisdom were and what they stood for and to find out about the cover-up that cloaked the real reasons for the Templars' brutal suppression.

The ideal lives on

After the Templars were officially dissolved, many German Templars (who had openly defied their judges by threatening military action) found a haven within the Hospitalers of Saint John and in the Teutonic Order.

(Many years later, Hitler himself tried to portray himself as a Grail knight and even went as far as having posters printed and distributed showing him dressed in a suit of armour astride a horse.) In Portugal the Templars were cleared by an inquiry and simply changed their name to the 'Knights of Christ'. They continued as such under this name well into the 16th century, when they devoted much of their time to maritime pursuits. It is therefore striking that Vasco da Gama was a Knight of Christ and Prince Henry the Navigator was Grand Master of the order. Ships of the Order sailed under the very familiar Red Pattee cross on white sails. The same emblem was used by Christopher Columbus's 3 caravels. Furthermore, Columbus was married to the daughter of a former Knight of Christ and had access to his father-in-law's charts and diaries. Many Knights Templar found refuge in Scotland, and it is even reported that they sailed to the Americas prior to Columbus.

Templar symbols and numerology

Whilst investigating the charges made against the Templars, I read that a number of them referred under interrogation to something known as Baphomet, which I have already mentioned *en passant*. Baphomet, revered to a degree that bordered on idolatry, was apparently associated with an apparition of a bearded head. Some early scholars believed that this was a reference, in a corrupted form, to the name Muhammad, but it appears to be more like the Arabic 'Abufihamet' – pronounced 'Bufihimat' in Moorish Spanish – which literally means 'father of understanding' or 'father of wisdom'. These are identical titles to those given the Egyptian god Thoth, the Greek Hermes. Father in Arabic also implies 'source'.

Here I had made a definite connection between the Templars and the ancient Egyptian myths.

- We saw earlier the connection of the head symbolism in relation to the Grail legends and the Celtic Bran.
- I have commented on the connection of the small woman's head that was found amongst confiscated goods from the Templars' Paris preceptory (a preceptory was a Templar community).
- I also pointed out that another bearded head, which was apparently a totally separate relic, was listed as 'Caput LVIIIm' meaning 'Head 58m'.
- I have demonstrated the Giza Pyramid's layout as connected to an 8× 8 grid square layout which has a Golden Mean Proportion on a ratio of 5:8, and that these two numbers are consecutive numbers of the Fibonacci series (Chapter 16).
- It has also been speculated that the 'm' is actually the Zodiac sign for

Virgo, ♍. Soon we shall see the connection of Virgo in the positioning of cathedrals in Europe that mirror the star constellation of Virgo.
- We shall also see the significance of the value of 58 relating to the star Sirius in 10,500 BC, and to the Great Pyramid.
- With all the other gematria values connected with Christian doctrines, parables and esoterica, *plus* all the Holy Grail connections with the Templars, I felt more than justified in assuming a direct link between the hidden meaning of the enigmatic 'Caput LVIIIm' and the Giza complex, especially in view of all my previous interconnected research, which also appeared to be constantly pointing back to Giza.

The Templars used the sign of a skull and crossbones on the sails of their ships. This was later taken to represent the Jolly Roger of pirate ships (which in all probability only came about after the Templar Order was officially dissolved). The skull and crossbones are still used as a Freemason symbol. A story relates how a great lady of Marcela was loved by a Templar, a Lord of Sidon; but she died in her youth, and on the night of her burial, this wicked lover crept to the grave, dug up her body and violated it. Then a voice from the void bade him to return in 9 months' time, when he would find a son. He obeyed the instructions and at the appointed time opened the grave. Inside he found a head on the leg bones of the skeleton – the skull and crossbones. The same voice from the void said: 'Guard it well, for it would be the giver of all good things', and so he carried it away with him. It became his protecting genius, and he was able to defeat his enemies merely by showing them the magic head – rather a rich reward for an original act of defilement. In due course it passed into the possession of the Templar Order. The story is almost a grotesque travesty of the Immaculate Conception but, in part, is also a garbled account of some form of initiation ceremony, which involves a figurative death and resurrection. It is very similar to the still-practised Freemason initiation ceremony of symbolic resurrection from the dead. One chronicler names the woman 'Yse', which could well be a derivation of the ancient Egyptian name Isis, who as we know is directly associated with Sirius.

The mingled bloodline

The symbolism behind the Grail related to blood, and led circuitously to the Merovingian bloodline. Baigent, Leigh and Lincoln have this to say about it:

> Although deposed in the eighth century, the Merovingian bloodline did not become extinct. On the contrary it perpetuated itself in a direct line from Dagobert II and his son, Sigisbert IV. By dint of dynastic

alliances and intermarriages, this line came to include Godfroi de Bouillon, who captured Jerusalem in 1099, and various other noble and royal families, past and present – Blanchefort, Gisors, Saint-Clair (Sinclair in England), Montesquieu, Montpézat, Poher, Luisignan, Plantard and Habsburg-Lorraine.[10]

During the Crusades, the Merovingian heads wore the crown of the Kingdom of Jerusalem and were protected by both the Order of the Temple and the secretive Prieuré de Sion, the Templars' political and administrative arm. Furthermore, the Merovingian Kings were referred to as the 'long-haired monarchs' as they did not cut their hair, just like Samson in the Old Testament. Their hair supposedly contained their virtue, the essence and secret of their power. The Merovingians took this belief very seriously, and in AD 754, when Childeric III was deposed and imprisoned, his hair was ritually shaved off at the express command of the Pope. This demonstrates that the ancient codes and wisdom of antiquity – that related, in one way or another, to Orion and Sirius – were indeed modernised and continued into the millennium after Christ.

It is important to realise that the Merovingian kings were not regarded as kings in the modern sense of the word, but were 'Priest-Kings'; the embodiment of the divine. This status is identical to that of the ancient Egyptian Pharaohs and the Judaic Messiah. It is also revealing that the Merovingian kings were accepted as rightful and duly acknowledged kings without any prior upheavals, turmoil, usurpation or extinction of an earlier regime, in marked contrast to the rise of other bloodlines across Europe.

The Merovingian line takes its name from a unique and elusive ancestor known as Merovee, Merovech or Meroveus. He was apparently a semi-supernatural figure; even his name bears witness to his miraculous origin and character as it echoes the French word for 'mother' as well as both the French and Latin words for 'sea'. Once more we have a connection with water. Not only that; according to tradition, Merovee was born of two fathers. When pregnant by her husband King Clodio, Merovee's mother supposedly went swimming in the ocean where (it is said) she was seduced or raped by an unidentified creature known as a Quinotaur, apparently some form of Neptune. This beast managed to impregnate the lady a second time, so when Merovee was born, there allegedly flowed in his veins a commingling of two different bloods, the blood of a Frankish king and the blood of a mysterious aquatic creature. How similar is this to the accounts of King Arthur and his connection with the Fisher King, as explained earlier? In fact, this type of legend was quite common in the ancient world as well as across Europe, as though they were an allegorical masking of some concrete historical fact. The above clearly indicates some form of intermarriage of two bloodlines, one of which is related to aqua (water, which as we know is symbolic for the spiritual). The tale, I think, really shows that the Franks became allied by blood with a special bloodline that originated from beyond the sea, i.e. the bloodline that Mary brought with her accompanied by Joseph of Arimathea from the Holy Land. The historical facts of this union became symbolised in the subsequent fable of the sea creature, which was intended to be esoteric and so understood only by those initiated into its secret meanings.

The symbolism of water

It is worth looking at one of Jesus's teachings in Matthew 13: 47–8. Here Jesus likens the coming kingdom of God to the lowering of a net into the sea, after which the good fish are put into pails and the net thrown away. We already know that the parables are symbolic, and in Jesus's case, deal with fish as his ministry occurs during the Piscean age. Pails were only used for carrying water; here we seem to have a direct link with both the Piscean symbolism and Aquarian symbolism. Aquarius is pictured as a man carrying a pitcher of water, a deliberate symbol since water carrying was, in most contemporary societies, strictly women's work. Jesus was fully aware of the symbolism, as indicated in John 13: 5, where Jesus carries a pitcher of water to wash the feet of his disciples. He does so by pouring out the water – this seems expressly part of a baptismal/ rebirth ritual, involving the Aquarian pouring of water rather than the Piscean immersion.

This incident occurred during the Last Supper, just 24 hours before Jesus's apparent death. Jesus declares to his disciples that their continued fellowship with him must somehow be a function of their participation in this Aquarian initiation ceremony, even though they cannot understand its full significance yet. In short, Jesus is saying that if their association is to be continued with him after his death, then that association must become an Aquarian one. They would all have to be physically reborn together again to experience the Golden Age of Aquarius, which Jesus, as the ceremonial and symbolic 'water carrier', would personally inaugurate. Only then would their fellowship be resumed, whether symbolised by the breaking of bread or the sharing of wine; in Jesus's own words, 'Never again will I drink from the fruit of the vine until I drink it new with you in the Kingdom of my Father' (Matthew 26: 29). If we refer back to the fish being separated into pails with only the good being kept, and the net being thrown away; we see that this would be symbolic of the men and women of the Piscean age who will all be subjected to scrutiny with the coming Aquarian, or spiritual age.

Many ancient myths and legends tell that their civiliser gods walked on water (as Jesus did), and continue by stating that in every case, the god or great civiliser was conspired against, attacked, and either was killed and later resurrected, or departed on a boat or vessel across water (as King Arthur did). Two gods with almost identical stories, although separated by thousands of miles, were the Egyptian Osiris and the South American Thunupa/Viracocha. Both were known as great civilisers, both were conspired against, both were struck down, both were sealed inside a container or vessel of some kind and cast into the water, both then drifted away on a river, eventually reaching the sea.

Those who have studied Arthurian legend will immediately see identical similarities. King Arthur was born of two fathers, and was expressly linked to the Fisher King, born of water (i.e. spirit); the other father was a mortal man, Uther Pendragon. He was also referred to as the 'Once and future King' just as Jesus and Osiris/Orion were. Legends also say, rather startlingly, that King Arthur was a direct descendant of Jesus Christ himself; hence 'Holy Grail' which comes from the word 'Sangraal', itself from 'Sang Raal' meaning 'Holy blood'. In gematria, Excalibur, King Arthur's mystical sword that came from the lady of the lake (water again!), is equal to 773. Jesus likewise spoke (Luke 2: 35) of a two-edged long sword (ῥομφαια) that he had brought with him; in gematria this equals 772. By the convention of gematria, which allows a 1 digit difference to be of no consequence, these are symbolically identical. Furthermore the constellation of Orion has a few faint stars that point downwards from the 3 main belt stars of Orion, and these are known as the 'Sword of Orion'. Yet another symbolic connection!

Here are more connections. Excalibur in its original spelling (Caliburn) equals 755; 755 is the average mean distance in feet along each face of the perimeter base of the Great Pyramid. Excalibur was drawn from the stone; the Pyramid is the greatest stone monument on Earth. King Arthur also had 12 Knights of the Round Table; as Jesus had 12 disciples. Remember too, there are 12 signs of the Zodiac, 12 months in a year, 12 essential mineral salts, 12 precious stone gates in the New Jerusalem and 12 hides at Glastonbury (a place steeped in Arthurian myths and legends) that deal directly with the numbers and figures quoted in Revelation.

Wolfram von Eschenbach

As a final note on the Holy Grail I would like to draw your attention once more to the story of *Parzifal*, written by the Bavarian knight Wolfram von Eschenbach sometime between *c.* 1200 and 1220. Wolfram claimed that his Grail story is based upon privileged information that he obtained from one Kyot de Province, who in turn had supposedly received it from one Flegetanis. As this is significant I will quote Wolfram directly:

Anyone who asked me before about the Grail and took me to task for not telling him was very much in the wrong. Kyot asked me not to reveal this, for Adventure commanded him to give it no thought until she herself, Adventure, should invite the telling, and then one must speak of it, of course.

Kyot, the well-known master, found in Toledo, discarded, set down in heathen writing, the first source of this adventure. He first had to learn the abc's, but without the art of black magic . . .

A heathen, Flegetanis, had achieved high renown for his learning. This scholar of nature was descended from Solomon and born of a family which had long been Israelite until baptism became our shield against the fire of Hell. He wrote the adventure of the Grail. On his father's side, Flegetanis was a heathen, who worshipped a calf . . .

The heathen Flegetanis could tell us how all the stars set and rise again . . . To the circling course of the stars man's affairs and destiny are linked. Flegetanis the heathen saw with his own eyes in the constellations things he was shy to talk about, hidden mysteries. He said there was a thing called the Grail, whose name he had read clearly in the constellations. A host of angels left it on the Earth.

Since then, baptised men have had the task of guarding it, and with such chaste discipline that those who are called to the service of the Grail are always noble men. Thus wrote Flegetanis of these things.

Kyot, the wise master, set about to trace this tale in Latin books, to see where there ever had been a people, dedicated to purity and worthy of caring for the Grail. He read the chronicles of the lands, in Britain and elsewhere, in France and in Ireland, and in Anjou he found the tale. There he read the true story of Mazadan, and the exact record of all his family was written there.[11]

This immediately told me that the Grail was linked to hidden mysteries associated with the constellations, and that a host of angels had been somehow involved in leaving it on Earth. It also contained a clue about the setting and rising of the stars, and their direct link to the affairs and destiny of man. Just how accurate this was to later prove I could never have guessed or imagined at the time. Having just studied the Egyptian Edfu texts (which I shall assess later) I was also struck by the startling similarity between their account of something falling from heaven from the gods to Earth, and the statement of the Angels in this. It was an almost identical symbolic allusion.

In the *Parzifal* account, Parzifal's hermit* uncle expounds to him about the Grail. Earlier I cited some of the following quote. I am repeating it, as it is of great symbolic importance in describing the Grail as stone:

---

* Hermits, it should be noted, were originally mystical characters who took their name from Hermes.

Well I know that many brave knights dwell with the Grail at Munsalvaesche. Always when they ride out, as they often do, it is to seek adventure. They do so for their sins, these Templars, whether their reward be defeat or victory. A valiant host lives there, and I will tell you how they are sustained. They live from a stone of purest kind. If you do not know it, it shall here be named to you. It is called Lapsit Exillis. By the power of that stone the Phoenix burns to ashes, but the ashes give him life again. Thus does the Phoenix molt and change its plumage, which afterwards is bright and shining and as lovely as before. There never was a human so ill but that, if he one day sees that stone, he cannot die within the week that follows. And in looks he will not fade. His appearance will stay the same, be it maid or man, as on the day he saw the stone, the same as when the best years of his life began, and though he should see the stone for two hundred years, it will never change, save that his hair might perhaps turn grey. Such power does the stone give a man that flesh and bones are at once made young again. The stone is also called the Grail.[12]

Here we not only have a definite connection of the Templars with the Grail itself, but also an account that identifies the Grail as a stone. Some scholars have argued that 'Lapsit Exillis' might be a corruption of 'Lapsit ex Caelis' which means 'it fell from heaven'. Remarkably, this phrase is *absolutely* identical to the phrase within the Edfu Texts that states 'It fell from heaven', the 'it' being a sacred stone. Equally memorable is the reference to the Phoenix, a purely Egyptian myth. Why include it here, unless it was a deliberate symbolic clue that the Grail is in some way connected to Egypt?

The Templars' heirs . . .

After my studies into the Templars, the Holy Grail and Arthurian myths, I had to extend my investigation to the obvious progression from them – the Freemason order which, after the Templars' dissolution, would carry the information from antiquity on into new centuries.

Chapter 25

Freemasons and the Hiram Key

Having had an interest in knights sparked off by tales of ghostly apparitions of battle when in Cyprus, I became very curious about all chivalric orders. Over the years I had studied the Templars and I was aware of the Freemasons from an early age – mainly because of comedy sketches about them, both in newspapers and on television. My uncle was also involved in the movement; indeed, he is now a Master Mason. I myself had wanted to be part of a noble and chivalric order if one existed, but could I find such an organisation? Not easily!

Army experience

When I was 16 I went on an Army cadet exercise where, with the rest of them, I had to play the part of a civilian evacuee. We had been moved to an airfield ready to be flown out by an RAF C130 Hercules, and as we waited the distinguished-looking white-haired senior officer running the exercise approached. Was everything all right? Did we need anything? he asked. Several lads asked for food, as we hadn't eaten for over 24 hours. I had immediately noticed a very strange-looking set of parachute qualification wings in two-tone blue on his arm. I liked the look of them as they were very Egyptian in style. 'Can I have your badge sir?' I asked in all seriousness. He smiled and said that if I wanted them, I would have to earn them. 'How?' By doing a gruelling selection course and that only a very few actually passed. Shortly after the officer left we were deluged with 24-hour ration packs and hot tea, courtesy of the man himself. That man was Peter de la Billière, then brigadier, later to be knighted, who went on to command the SAS Regiment, the Special Forces Group and the British Forces during the Gulf War.

When I returned home I wanted to find out more about the Regiment, and was told all sorts of things:

- half of its members (especially the officers) were Freemasons;
- their winged 'dagger' badge actually depicted King Arthur's sword, Excalibur;
- the number of the regular regiment – 22 SAS – was deliberately chosen

for its many esoteric connections and was related to the 22 articles of Freemasonry.

Because it was the Regiment's number, I was drawn to 22 every time I came across it in myths and legends. (I found out later that the number was really 'chosen' by adding the numbers of 2 former SAS Regiments when they were amalgamated.) All this certainly fired my imagination; at 16 I thought I had found a modern equivalent of the Knights Templar. To me, the SAS were undeniably the ultimate Special Forces – bar none. They had their own Regimental prayer, a strong sense of loyalty, shunned all publicity, and actively sought to save lives rather than take them. I had to be a part of this. When I approached the Territorial Reserve 21 (another important value) SAS Regiment in London, I was told that I was too young (17). This did not deter me. I phoned up the training wing every month and visited the permanent staff instructors even more frequently. Then, at the beginning of October 1981, I received a letter from the PSI (Permanent Staff Instructor) of training wing, informing me that a huge recruitment drive was under way: and with over 1,500 applications, one extra (mine) wouldn't hurt. I was now 17 years 9 months, the minimum age allowed for joining the reserve forces in England. After a gruelling medical and physical test, amazingly I was accepted for selection; apparently the youngest ever.

After many weeks and numbing selection weekends I found myself lying on my back, my bergen (rucksack) digging into my waist. I was freezing cold somewhere in the middle of the Brecon Beacons in Wales, rain pouring down on to my face, in total darkness at 3 o'clock in the morning. The rain was so heavy that even my waterproof combats had no effect and I was soaked to my underclothes. I was navigating across what is termed 'Moon country', which is made up from huge clumps of grass, a nightmare to cross. Physically and mentally exhausted, I had fallen over for about the 20th time. As I lay there, I knew that if I didn't get up and move (even though the blisters upon the blisters on my feet were agony), I would – as the training instructors had told us many times – die. They didn't particularly care if I died (they had joked), but it would be annoying for them as it meant a lot of extra paper work. I asked myself just *what* exactly I was doing. It was then that I started to have a strong feeling that this wasn't for me. Initially I dismissed it as the result of extreme tiredness, but over the following weeks I continued to fight overwhelming instincts telling me that this was not a course my life should follow. I was getting repeated pressure from the PSIs to transfer to the regular Regiment as I was young, so could improve upon my physique to an even better standard, and with no bad military habits from other units, I could be moulded easily.

Half of me wanted to go for it, then the other half would kick in, saying, No! Eventually one weekend we were practising unarmed combat techniques against members of the regular regiment by playing British Bulldog. Using all of our training we had literally to fight our way from one road to another. Towards the end it got down to just another guy, named Andy, and myself. We had to run a gauntlet of 20 opponents. I had got so far because I could outrun everyone else, but this time I knew I was going down, so I ran like a mad man possessed. I very nearly made it when 2 opponents dived for me. I tried to jump over them but one of them caught my ankle and I went down hard on to the road, with a huge hole in my elbow that bled everywhere and a dislocated shoulder and collar bone. As a result I had to have an operation on my shoulder and collarbone to put it right, ending up in Woolwich Military Hospital for some time. In fact, I missed several important college exams and had to spend a further year there. I took this as a hint that I shouldn't be doing this, but the more I felt that way, the harder I fought my 'silly' instincts. Then a PSI told me that I should always trust my first gut instincts, as the Regiment had learnt that this had saved lives more than once.

I have recounted the above episode as the events would eventually lead me to very good contacts and I would get to hear several strange stories, one of which I shall relate later. As for my continued involvement with the Regiment, my shoulder injury meant that I could no longer carry a full bergen, so partly for that reason I eventually transferred out into a normal infantry unit – mainly, however, for the money to pay my way through college. I came to this decision as I was travelling up an escalator at the Sloane Square tube station. I was all fired up and ready for the rigours of the training weekend but as I approached the top, I simply walked across the walkway to the other platform, down the escalator and back on to a train for Liverpool Street Station. Only when I arrived did I relax from a very rigid state. I ached painfully all over. Without a shadow of a doubt, I knew there and then that I was not going to stay with the Regiment. It was as if I had suddenly just thrown a switch in my head to off mode. Should I stay or shouldn't I? The decision was absolute. Of course, I had a few problems trying to explain to the Regiment, my parents and friends.

What has never left me, though, are the principles, ideologies and philosophies of the Regiment, which I have tried to maintain ever since: honesty, integrity, honour, professionalism, fairness, justice and simple common sense.

Freemasonry – the essentials

After my experience with the Regiment, I again started to research into the Freemasons and Templars to see if I could find any similar organisations. In consequence I embarked on a quest that would ultimately link up seemingly totally unrelated facts about the Knights Templar and the Freemasons with ancient Egyptian history, Moses and the Bible.

Freemasonry is a fraternal order whose basic tenets are brotherly love, relief and truth. Its members actively seek out each other's company and assist each other in times of stress or need; furthermore, they also reinforce essential moral values. A Freemason saying about itself declares: 'It takes good men and makes them better'.

Underlying this is the belief that all men are the products of what they have seen, heard or come into contact with: if they meet with men of good character, their lives and personal development will benefit accordingly. To maintain a friendly and open fraternity, discussing politics and religion within any Freemason lodge is forbidden, viewed as having caused too many divisions between men in the past. Each Mason is, however, expected to believe in a form of God. Freemasonry encourages its members to be religious without advocating a single religion, and to be active in the community without advocating a particular political persuasion.

Freemasonry takes the 'Operative' (i.e. practical) work of the medieval masons and uses it as an allegory for moral development. This is achieved by the use of the symbolism of stonemason's tools such as the gavel, the rule, the compass, the square and the level. Each has a specific meaning; for example, Masons are said to meet 'On the Level', which means that all Masons are brothers – regardless of social status, wealth or position within the order.

Masonry is differentiated from other fraternal organisations by its emphasis on moral character, its strange rituals, and its very long tradition and history, which dates back at least to the 17th century in documented form. Modern Freemasonry has a continuously documented paper history from lodge to lodge since 1717. In addition, there is written evidence of its precursors from the 14th century, while its origins apparently reach far back into the mists of antiquity. As Christopher Knight and Robert Lomas demonstrate in *The Hiram Key*,[1] the rituals and symbolism of Freemasonry stretch as far back as biblical and ancient Egyptian times.

Degrees and rules

There are 3 basic stages, called degrees, in Freemasonry (though other bodies within Freemasonry confer additional degrees up to the 32nd – or, in the Scottish Rite, a 33rd honorary degree). As the Blue Lodge (the name for key regional lodges), Masons receive degrees of entered apprentice (the first degree); fellowcraft (the second degree); and Master

Mason (the third degree). The time taken progressing from entered apprentice to Master Mason varies from lodge to lodge and from country to country. In America it can take as little as under 3 months to become a Master Mason, whereas in England it takes the minimum of a year. No matter how long the period, promotion within the order always requires that candidates memorise certain material. This material however is not fully understood, yet Masons continue to use it. In fact, as we shall see, the rituals carry a symbolised message that has remained almost intact through thousands of years.

The Scottish Rite

There are various different lodges of Freemasons around the world, an example being the Order of Amaranth, open to Masons and their wives, mothers, daughters, widows and sisters, which confers only 1 degree. Perhaps the most notable independent body of Freemasonry is the Scottish Rite, which is not part of the standard 'Blue Lodge' system *per se*, but is closely associated with Masonry, and requires that a man already be a Master Mason before he can join it – any Master Mason is eligible. The Scottish Rite degrees continue the symbolism of the first 3 Masonic Degrees and have a 33rd degree, but also confer the 4th through 32nd degrees.

The 33rd degree is only achieved by those the Scottish Rite feels have made an outstanding contribution to Masonry, the community as a whole, and to mankind. There is no way to achieve this degree or take it; it is purely an honorary one, very rarely bestowed and greatly admired. I was immediately drawn to this degree because 33 has links to Jesus Christ (his apparent age at death) and Stonehenge – as I pointed out earlier, I was able to obtain a latitude marker of 33 degrees east of the monument.

The York Rite

The York Rite, like the Scottish Rite, is an independent body of Freemasonry conferring degrees beyond the Blue Lodge's 3 degrees. It consists of 9 additional degrees: Mark Master; Past Master; Most Excellent Master; Royal Arch Mason; the Cryptic Degrees of the Royal Master; Select Master; Super Excellent Master and the Chivalric Orders of the Order of the Red Cross; Order of the Knights of Malta; and the Order of the Knights Templar. This immediately grabbed my attention – a connection to the Knights Templar.

The history of Freemasonry

Freemasonry's history has given rise to many books detailing many provocative theories. It is my opinion, shared with others, that they originated from *both* the Knights Templar *and* their administrative and political arm, the Prieuré de Sion (an argument exhaustively presented in *The Holy Blood and the Holy Grail*[2]).

The antiquity of Masonry is clearly demonstrated by the so-called Regius Manuscript, written around the year 1390, when King Richard II ruled England, and eventually presented to the British Museum by George II in 1757. It consists of 794 lines of rhymed English verse and claims that Masonry was introduced into England during the reign of Athelstan, who ascended the throne in AD 924. It sets out the regulations for the society with 15 articles and 15 points and rules of behaviour at church, teaching duties to God and Church and country, and promoting brotherhood. Here then is a datable recorded history going back well over 600 years. Further proof is furnished by English Statutes; for example, one of 1350 (the reign of King Edward III) regulated a Master Mason's wage at 4 pence per day.

The Masons of the Middle Ages, the builders of cathedrals and churches throughout Europe, carved enduring stone images telling impressive stories within these structures. These were also frequently chiselled with symbolic markings. Christopher Knight and Robert Lomas argue that it was not from the actual stonemasons that Freemasons derived their name and origins. It is the case that research I have accumulated shows a direct evolution from the Knights Templar. However, the link is that where cathedral-building programmes were concerned, Templars played a key role as regards financing and the logistics of the work – *and* esoteric layouts and designs within the churches' fabrics. It was therefore a logical step to incorporate the stonemason symbology into nascent Freemasonry. Moreover, the Templars, or 'Poor Fellow Soldiery of the Holy House of the Temple', intended to rebuild the Temple of Solomon, in Jerusalem, and took as their models the Warrior-Masons of Zerubbabel from the Bible, who worked holding a sword in one hand and a trowel in the other. Therefore the sword and the trowel were the insignia of the Templars, who subsequently concealed their continued existence under the name of the 'Brethren Masons'. This name ('Frères Maçons' in French), adopted as a secret reference to the builders of the second Temple, was corrupted in English into 'Free-Masons'.

Masons and the New World

By 1700 many lodges had existed for centuries; 4 of the 'Old Lodges' met in London on St John the Baptist's Day (24 June) 1717. The saint is significant: John the Baptist was a known initiate of the Great Pyramid in esoteric circles. These 4 joined together to form the first 'Grand Lodge of England'. No longer actually working as masons, the Masons carried on the traditions of the craft and used its tools as emblems symbolising principles of conduct in a continued effort to 'build' a better world. From this 'Grand Lodge of England' the American Colonial Masonic organisation stemmed, formed soon after 1717. There have been many arguments over the years that the American constitution was directly influenced by Freemasons and that the entire United States of America was founded upon Mason principles; certainly it is intriguing that the following US Presidents were all Masons:

George Washington	Theodore Roosevelt
James Monroe	William Howard Taft
Andrew Jackson	Warren G. Harding
James Polk	Franklin D. Roosevelt
James Buchanan	Harry S. Truman
Andrew Johnson	Lyndon B. Johnson
James Garfield	Gerald R. Ford
William McKinley	

Ronald Reagan is not an actual Craft Mason but was made an honorary 33rd degree. Bill Clinton was rumoured to be a Mason due to his association with the De Molay Order.

The 'International Order of de Molay' is the world's largest fraternal organisation for young men aged between 13 and 21. It was founded in Kansas City, Missouri on 24 March 1919 by Rank Sherman Land. De Molay Chapters are sponsored by Masonic Lodges. De Molays are taught the 7 (note 7!) Cardinal Virtues of the Order of Filial Love: reverence for sacred things; courtesy; comradeship; fidelity; cleanness; patriotism; and the importance of practising these in their daily lives. The Order takes its name from Jacques de Molay, last Grand Master of the Knights Templar, who was executed in France by the Inquisition in 1314.

Is it surprising to realise that the US star, as painted on all their military vehicles and flags, is identical to the 5-pointed star of ancient Egyptian origin? It has been established that the Great Pyramid has been referred to as having a summit platform with no apex (as will be explained in detail later), a fact memorialised on the back of the Seal of the United States and reproduced for many years on the dollar bill (see figure 83).

To the designer of the 1782 official seal of the USA, the Great Pyramid's capstone was obviously of special interest and significance, as it is reminiscent of the medieval alchemical symbol for the divine Tetragrammaton YHWH, or Jehovah. The upper inscription apparently means, 'He has looked with favour on the beginnings'. The capstone's final installation atop the 13 courses of stones depicted is clearly taken to represent, in the designer's own words, 'A new order of ages' (NOVUS

Figure 83.

ORDO SECLORUM). This is symbolically identical to the myths and legends which state that after the Hall of Records is located (its central part being the actual capstone), the stone that the builders rejected, once repositioned on top of the Great Pyramid, will herald the dawn of a new golden spiritual age. Several major buildings in the US have been laid Masonically, including the US Capitol, The Smithsonian Institution, the House of Representatives Office Building and the Washington Monument. The last, in Alexandria, Virginia, honours the first President and a Mason, George Washington.

A New-World Tribe of Israel?

Because of all these American Masonic connections, I became aware of what initially appeared to be a predominantly American religious movement founded by a Joseph Smith, born in Vermont in 1805, who, it has been argued, was a Mason. He founded the Church of Jesus Christ of Latter Day Saints, otherwise known as Mormons. What caught my attention about this man was his claim to have uncovered hidden buried plates of brass that revealed the history of one of the 12 tribes of Israel who had sailed to the Americas hundreds of years before Columbus. This immediately made me think of how the biblical Moses and Aaron* stories paralleled Central American Gagavitz and Zactecaum myths (see Chapter 23).

Smith claimed that he had located, and eventually translated, the plates of brass after a vision of an ancient prophet appeared to him revealing their hidden location – the 'Hill of Cumorah'. Smith used the Urim and Thurim (a biblical device used by Moses to communicate with God) given to him, to translate them. After he had deciphered the plates (the results of which became the *Book of Mormon*[3]), the Urim and Thurim returned whence they came. Joseph Smith described the plates of brass as being bound on metal rings. As nothing like this had ever been uncovered from any ancient site his claims were derided. Many years later, however, several similar brass plates of Babylonian origin, with inscriptions, were uncovered in modern Iraq. The whole episode suggested that there could be other hidden sacred books and writings, anywhere in the world.

Was Smith really a Mason? It's hard to prove either way. It is said that he was made a Master Mason at sight by the Grand Master of Illinois, and that Smith, a very flamboyant individual, subsequently had a disagreement with the Grand Lodge of Illinois over the way the Nauvoo lodges (a Native-American name used for Illinois lodges) were operated. Accordingly the Grand Lodge revoked their charters. What *is* known is that in 1844 he was murdered by a mob. Brigham Young, his close friend and colleague, felt convinced that it was the result of a Masonic conspiracy so forbade all Mormons from becoming Masons. This embargo remained in effect – with ill feelings both ways – until 1984

Templar confessions

With so many Masonic connections linked with America, it has been proposed that Templars sailed west to the Americas – prior to Columbus. We now need to see if there is any evidence to substantiate the claim.

Christopher Knight and Robert Lomas point out[4] that after the Templars had been outlawed by Philip the Fair of France, 15,000 of them were all arrested on the morning of Friday, 13 October 1307. The Inquisition was given firm orders to extract confessions that they were carrying out evil practices from the Templars, using any torture necessary, including the use of the hideously ingenious 'Foot oven' which inflicted maximum pain without causing death. As a result, mutilated Templars apparently 'admitted' they had denied God, Christ and the

* Moses's brother.

Virgin Mary and that they had carried out bizarre sexual initiation ceremonies.

In England, King Edward II eventually complied with the Papal order, though his torturers were not as efficient as those in France. However, a Templar named Stephen de Straelbrugge admitted that he was informed during his initiation ceremony that Jesus was just a man and not a God, and another, John de Stokes, stated that Jacques de Molay had told him that Jesus was just a man and that he should believe in the 'Great omnipotent God' who was the architect of the heavens, and *not* believe in the crucifixion. This surprised many experts, as no such theological belief system then existed.

The comments from de Molay make sense if they are the *true* teachings of Jesus, which predate the crucifixion-cult of Paul as later adopted by the Romans. As Grand Master, de Molay's statements ring true; they do not reject Jesus at all, they simply reinforce the view that there is only one God, i.e. one supreme being. In James's Church, the teachings of Jesus were certainly revered, but the crucifixion was considered to be merely a powerful symbol of 'faithfulness unto death'. This was then closely associated with the murder of Solomon's Temple architect, Hiram Abif, whom we shall look at a little later. Although the Templars undeniably used *a* cross as their emblem, there is some argument that the cross itself was originally a Sumerian and Babylonian symbol that represented the all-important 'Planet of Crossing', Nibiru (Chapter 6).

Throughout their existence the Templars had been a faithful Catholic Order. They had had the military might to establish their own form of Christianity had they so desired. Evidently they were more than content to simply hold on to their special knowledge. I believe this indicates that whatever the true nature of the secret they were guarding, it was obviously not intended to be revealed during that era. The information was being safeguarded for later generations, through symbolism and ceremonies, which the Templars saw as *complementary* to their faith. In short, a Church and a Pope they had served well betrayed the Templars.

Grand Master Jacques de Molay was tortured horribly and, though a physically powerful man, broke down and confessed to crimes he had not committed. Nonetheless he retracted them 7 years later, just prior to being burned at the stake. Knight and Lomas argue that after de Molay's original torture, his body was wrapped in a cloth after he had been crucified by the Grand Inquisitor of France, Guillaume Imbert. Guillaume had a thorn of crowns prepared and thrust upon de Molay's head, drawing blood from his scalp and forehead mimicking the crucifixion of Christ. Guillaume further mimicked the crucifixion by wounding de Molay in the side with a knife. After de Molay confessed, he was wrapped in a cloth and taken to the home of a non-Templar friend, Geoffrey de Charney, where the cloth was washed and put away. The cloth had become impregnated with de Molay's sweat, blood and high concentration of lactic acids produced by his body whilst under extreme physical pain, a mixture of fluids that literally painted de Molay's image on to the cloth. The de Charney family removed the shroud, dressed de Molay's wounds and slowly brought him back to reasonable health. Many years later, in 1356, when the cloth was publicly revealed, many saw, in the image of de Molay's face, that of Christ, and the cloth became known as the Turin Shroud. Only in 1988 did the Vatican release a small piece to be analysed and carbon-dated. The result? Late 12th or early 13th century. Coincidentally, the carbon-daters released the information on 13 October, the date on which de Molay was arrested and crucified. Furthermore, the Vatican has always denied that the shroud is a holy relic, a stance that many might find surprising. The only plausible reason for this conviction would be that they know its *true* origins.

The destruction of the Templars, and the survivors' subsequent encoding of their secrets within the new order of Freemasonry, can be seen as a central event in history – perhaps the greatest water-shed in the course of Western social development. As Knight and Lomas explain:

> The attack on the Templar Order by a greedy unimportant French King, proved to be the first vital step in the long process of releasing the Christian world from the prevailing principle of intellectual castration, exercised by the Vatican, and allowing it to build a civilisation driven by a desire for knowledge and a recognition of the worth of the individual. This drive from autocracy to democracy in government and aristocracy to meritocracy in social structure, within a framework of theological tolerance, has nowhere been so conspicuously sought, and in part achieved, than in the United States of America.[5]

While many Templars were being arrested and tortured, many others managed to slip the net. A large part of the Templar maritime fleet, in harbour at the French Atlantic sea port of La Rochelle, was obviously tipped off – on 13 October, the arresting guards found only water where the night before ships had been tied up. There is evidence to suggest that these ships sailed to Portugal and Scotland. From Portugal they set out on a voyage that had often been discussed but never undertaken. Being privy to ancient source maps (which we shall look at later), these Templar mariners headed exactly due west on the 42nd parallel in search of a land marked by the star that they knew from Nasorean* scrolls was called 'Merica'. The French Knights referred to this land as 'La Merica', which later simply became America. There is further evidence that they

---

* Nasorean: a term used for the original followers of Jesus, who constituted what was known as the 'Jerusalem Church'. Nasorean scrolls would therefore be very early Christian texts.

landed in the Cape Cod area or Rhode Island area of New England in the early weeks of 1308, nearly two centuries before Christopher Columbus; and he too, you will recall, was privy to ancient charts and maps, supplied by his father-in-law.

Once settled in America, it has been suggested that Templars journeyed to and from Scotland. In Westford, Massachusetts, there is an image of a knight carved into a slab of rock; he can be seen wearing a helmet and the habit of a military order, and his sword has a pommelled hilt in a European 14th-century style. His shield bears the motif of a single-masted medieval ship sailing *west*, towards a star. On Rhode Island there is a tower constructed in the style of a Templar round church. In 1524, it was noted by the Italian navigator, Giovanni de Verrazano, as an 'existing Norman villa'. Its (admittedly sparse) architectural details date it to the century when the Templar fleet disappeared.*

There is no record of the seizure of 18 Templar ships at La Rochelle, or of any Templar ships anchored in the Thames or at any other seaports in Britain. Most Templar ships were galleys, and so were ideally suited for piracy after the order was outlawed since they were not dependent upon the wind and could easily attack a becalmed ship. (I pointed out earlier the connection of the Skull and Crossbones of Templar origins and the Jolly Roger pirate flag.) It is striking that in Freemasonry, a Master Mason just newly admitted as a candidate is told that this degree 'will make you a brother to pirates and corsairs'. This statement makes no sense in the context of a society supposedly descended solely from medieval stonemasons; but it does when assessed for its connections to the Templars. Another link: when Templars processed around their circular churches, they only had one way to move; in a circle. Today's Masons process in their 'Circumambulation' of the lodge in identical fashion.

The Scottish connection

Many Templars escaped to Scotland. One well-known Templar chapel (which survived intact during the purge that saw most monasteries destroyed) was Rosslyn Chapel. This elaborate building took 40 years to complete, or so it is stated – and we have seen the importance of 40 with its biblical connection to the Exodus and Noah. Of course, this could be pure coincidence, but why make such an issue about how long it took to construct? It was completed in the 1480s by Oliver St Claire, predating Columbus's arrival in the Americas by several years (his *mainland* landing was not until 1 August 1498, in South America).

* This is illustrated in *The World's Last Mysteries*, Reader's Digest, London, 1977.

Unique to Rosslyn Chapel are the strange decorations carved into its pillars and walls. The archways and ceiling feature corn cobs (Indian maize) and aloes carved into them, yet at the time of construction, no one in Europe had ever seen these. They had been totally unknown until after 1492, yet the carvings are accurate. As they are an integral component of the chapel, constructed prior to its completion in its present form, the logical explanation is that the men who instructed the stonemasons must have visited America nearly a quarter of a century prior to Columbus. In fact, there are indications that a number of European mariners had successfully travelled to the Americas; furthermore a red-haired and white-skinned tribe was documented as already living in North America. In view of this, the Westford Knight and the Newport Tower can be seen as Templar remains in what is now the United States of America.

Essentially, the starting place for Freemasonry was the construction of Rosslyn Chapel. Historical records confirm this as the St Claire family of Rosslyn became the hereditary Grand Masters of Crafts and Guilds and Orders of Scotland, and later held the post of the Master Masons of Scotland until the late 1700s. Also, as Sir John Bernard Burke stated in his *Vicissitudes of Families and other Essays*, 'no other family in Europe, beneath the rank of royalty, boasts a higher antiquity, a nobler illustration, or more romantic interest than that of St Claire.'[6] The St Claires were often classed as the Scottish branch of the Norman Saint Claire/Gisors family. I was immediately struck by the name Gisors and how linguistically similar it is to Giza. It encouraged me to investigate further.

The naming of America

The mainstream view is that America is named after an explorer named Amerigo Vespucci; however, it is more than probable that it actually derived its name from the star of the West, 'Merica'. The Nasoreans believed that this star was a marker of a perfect land of the setting Sun across the ocean. As Knight and Lomas explain,[7] the standard version stems from a misunderstanding by a clergyman named Martin Waldseemüller, who lived in a monastery on the French/German border. He gathered information about the world, including amazing reports about the newly discovered continent across the Western Ocean. In 1507 he created a 103-page work titled *Cosmographiae introductio*, a treatise on traditional cosmography that included the divisions of the planets, distances between key locations, winds, climates, and so on. Waldseemüller had found a number of mariners' accounts of a landmass to the West, describing it as 'America', but as he also had accounts of the travels of an Italian explorer named Amerigo Vespucci, he conflated the 2 pieces of unrelated information and wrote:

Now, these parts of the Earth (Europe, Africa, Asia) have been more extensively explored and a fourth part has been discovered by Amerigo Vespucci. . . . Insomuch as both Europe and Asia received their names from women, I see no reason why any one should justly object to calling this part Amerige (from the Greek 'ge' meaning 'land of'), i.e. the land of Amerigo, or America, after Amerigo, its discoverer, a man of great ability.[8]

So Waldseemüller's book featured a giant map marking the new continent as 'America', and once in print the error was transmitted widely in a very short time. Shortly after writing, Waldseemüller realised his mistake and retracted his statement, but by then it was too late.

The Chapel shares its secrets

As for Rosslyn Chapel, it is credible that it was designed by William St Claire using the plans of Solomon's Temple, incorporating many Templar and Masonic motifs. It has been argued by the likes of Knight and Lomas,[9] that the Chapel also contains a copy of the vaults of Solomon's Temple and its hidden treasure. Learning this, I became curious what the treasure actually is. As I was to discover, there may well be a physical treasure, but the Chapel's design and layout also incorporates a *hidden geometrical treasure*, as we shall see. William St Claire would have had the problem of security with his actual stonemasons, who would be privy to the layout of any vaults. As a consequence (say Knight and Lomas), he devised the First Degree of Craft Masonry and the Mark Mason Degree – to give his stonemasons a code of conduct and an involvement in the secret. Only the great secret of living resurrection was reserved for speculative Masons. It is a matter of record that he had two grades of stonemasons on the site:

- a 10-pounds-a-year 'Standard' mason, or apprentice;
- a 40-pounds-a-year 'Mark' mason honoured by the possession of a personal mark which that mason would chisel into his work.
  (Note that 40 has appeared again.)

Rosslyn Chapel is just a few miles away from the former headquarters of the Templars in Scotland. Also – and this is what really intrigued me – there are carvings everywhere of the 'Green Man', the Celtic figure that represented fertility – just as Isis and her husband, Osiris, were represented as being green (see plates). Here we have Egyptian, Celtic, Jewish, Templar and Masonic symbolism linked together in profusion. Vegetation grows out of the mouths of the 'Green men'; other remarkable motifs include entangled pyramids (totally out of character for a Christian church), images of Moses, towers of the 'Heavenly Jerusalem', engrailed crosses, and squares and compasses. The Chapel also has a star-studded ceiling, drawing my attention to celestial connections. The only truly Christian imagery is found in Victorian alterations; the stained-glass windows, the baptistery and a statue of the Madonna and Child. Now, I interpreted these images (and all that is contained within the Templar and Freemasons' symbology) as pointing directly back to ancient Egyptian myths, especially those connected with Isis/Sirius and the green god Osiris/Orion.

From the outside, Rosslyn Chapel appears to be a representation in stone of the biblical Heavenly Jerusalem, with the finials of its flying buttresses resembling towers. These are extraordinarily dominant and ornate, and adding weight to the theory that they are representational rather than functional, *Lothian* in *The Buildings of Scotland*[10] Series comments that they are 'purely decorative ... the flyers, particularly such thin flyers, are useless'. Furthermore, the same book has a telling remark about the windows: the tracery (i.e. the pattern of stone members in the head of the window) is 'mostly simple and flowing, but several windows have the odd motif of a saltire cross'.[11] This cross is, of course, a Templar motif. Inside, the layout is a reconstruction of Solomon's Temple. There are 14 pillars arranged so that the eastern 8, including the two pillars referred to as Boaz and Jachin, were laid out in the form of a Triple Tau. The formation and the portions are exactly those depicted in the Royal Arch degree today (see figure 84).

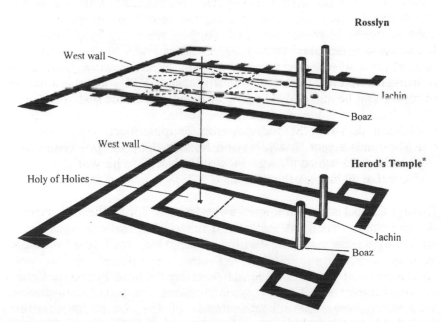

*Figure 84. *Herod's Temple was built to* replicate *the previously destroyed Solomon's Temple.*

To understand the meaning of the Triple Tau, we first need to look at the Star of David. David did not invent it, but Jesus used it and positioned himself to be the 'Star of David' as prophesied of old, which held many esoteric meanings. It is formed by overlaying two triangles (see figure 85).

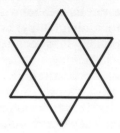 

Figure 85.

This symbol does not appear in any ancient Hebrew books on religious life, and is only in use in the distant past of Judaism as an occasional decorative motif, along with Middle Eastern images including the Swastika. During the Middle Ages it became popular on a large number of Christian churches, especially on those erected by the Templars. It only came into use within Synagogues much later. Alfred Grotte, a noted synagogue builder of the early 20th century, wrote the following about it.

> When in the twentieth century the construction of architecturally significant synagogues was begun, the most non-Jewish architects strove to build these houses of worship according to the model of church construction. They believed they had to look around for a symbol, which corresponded to the symbol of the churches, and they hit upon the hexagram. In view of the total helplessness (of even learned Jewish Theologians) regarding the material of Jewish symbolism, the Megan David was exalted as the visible insignia of Judaism. As its geometrical shape lent itself easily to all structural and ornamental purposes, it has now been for more than three generations an established fact, already hallowed by tradition, that the Megan David for the Jews is the same kind of holy symbol that the Cross and the Crescent are for the other monotheistic faiths.[12]

Knight and Lomas point out[13] that if the two lateral lines of the Star of David are removed, leaving the upward- and downward-pointing arrows of priest and king, the result is the Freemasons' square and compasses. The priestly or heavenly pyramid (here represented by the apex of a triangle) becomes the stonemason's square, an instrument used to ascertain the trueness and uprightness of buildings, and figuratively, human goodness. The kingly or Earthly pyramid is depicted as the compasses which, according to Freemasonry, mark the centre of the circle from which no Master Mason can materially err; that is the extent of the power of the king or ruler. I immediately associated this with the overlapping circles of the Vesica Pisces and the circles involved in sacred geometry, which the Templars were certainly familiar with. As we shall see, the Great Pyramid is directly linked with this symbolism, firstly in the sense of the compasses and square representing the pyramid shape, and secondly, in the sense that the Star of David is made up from two pyramids, as shown above. We shall see further connections between the Great Pyramid and Star of David later. It would be logical, in view of the above, that the symbol of the unified Messiah-ship of Jesus should be the mark of Christianity itself (i.e. the star of David), which of course it was for a short while; and the symbol for Judaism was the cross – not the 4-pointed cross of later Christian design, but that known as the 'Tau', the shape of the cross upon which Jesus was crucified (see figure 86a).

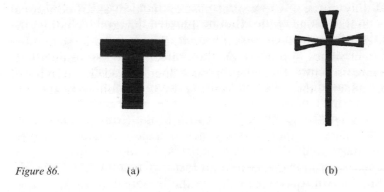

Figure 86.   (a)   (b)

This 'Tau' was the acknowledged mark of Yahweh (God), which the Kenites (an itinerant northern sect of Jewish origin) bore on their foreheads long before Moses came across them in the wilderness of the Sinai. It was also the magical mark painted on the doors during the Passover. The actual Christian cross was derived from an ancient Egyptian hieroglyph (Ankh, see figure 86b), with the very precise meaning of 'Saviour'. This is translated into Hebrew as 'Joshua', which in turn translates into Greek as 'Jesus'. So the shape of the crucifix is not a symbol of Jesus, but his name itself! Intriguingly, the most important symbol of the Royal Arch Degree in Freemasonry is the 'Triple Tau' which represents the power of King, Priest and Prophet. Again here is the symbolism of two upright pillars crossed at the top with a horizontal pillar – like the trilithon image and the Boaz and Jachin pillars.

The other main symbol from early Christianity is the sign of the fish, the Vesica Pisces.

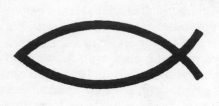

Figure 87.   *Figure 88.*

This symbol is an ancient badge of priestliness and was reputedly the symbol of the Nasorean party. It was used by Christians to identify their Holy places in Jerusalem at the end of the first century AD, the only symbol open to them at the time. If Jesus *was* an initiate of Great Pyramid symbolism, he would have known the Vesica Pisces's importance. John the Baptist was an initiate of the Great Pyramid (as I will show) and it has been argued that he adopted the symbol. The name 'Nasorean' is a form of the word 'Nazrani', which means both 'little fishes' and 'Christians' in modern Arabic, exactly as it did in Aramaic 2,000 years ago. James the Just became the first bishop (Hebrew 'Mebakker' – 'Guardian', as given in the Qumranian *Damascus Rule*[14]), and took to wearing a mitre as a badge of office, as all Bishops do now. The motif must have come out of Egypt with Moses (see figure 88).

My earlier arguments that Moses and Akhenaten were one and the same take on more credibility when it is realised that the mitre, with its split front and rear sections and its tail, is identical to a modern Bishop's headdress and known to have come – via the Nasoreans – from Egypt. Not only that, but the hieroglyph shown above stood for 'Amen', the creator god of Thebes, who was merged later with the Lower Egyptian Sun God Re, as in Amen-Re.

The 'Triple Tau' signifies, among other occult things, 'Templum Hierosolyma', meaning 'The Temple of Jerusalem'. It also means 'Clavis ad Thesaurum' ('a key to a treasure'); 'Theca ubi res pretiosa deponitur' ('a place where a precious thing is concealed'); and 'Res ipsa preciosa' ('the precious thing itself'). In Freemasonry's Royal Arch Degree, the companion jewel of the Royal Arch is a double triangle, sometimes called the seal of Solomon, placed within a circle of gold. At the bottom is a scroll with the words 'Nil nisi clavis deest', which means, 'nothing is wanting but the key', and on the circle the words 'Si talia jungere possis sit tibi scire posse' ('If thou canst comprehend these things, thou knowest enough'). As we have seen, the 'Triple Tau' can be constructed from the 14 pillars; equally interesting, a seal of Solomon can also be produced along with the pillars of Jachin and Boaz (see figure 89).

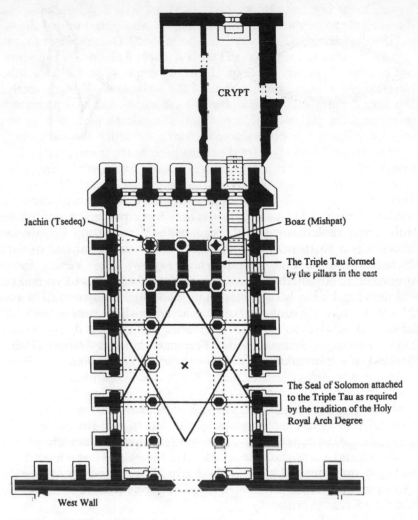

Figure 89. Rosslyn Chapel.

I knew that the Star of David could be formed from the alignment of pillars between the entrance and the Triple Tau formation. This suggested a connection to the pyramids, as represented by the dual triangles of the Star of David. In addition, at the very centre of this invisible Seal of Solomon, in the arched roof, there is a large suspended boss in the form of an arrowhead that points directly downwards, straight to the keystone in the floor below. It is believed that this stone has to be raised in order to enter the reconstructed vaults of Herod's Temple to recover a treasure. I couldn't help but connect this with the fact that the Hall of Records (or to quote the Edfu texts, the 'chambers of creation') is *buried*; with all the connections to the Giza plateau in

251

Egypt, I was beginning to suspect that the codes and symbolism were directing me to *that* area and that a treasure was indeed buried there.

Why does Rosslyn Chapel *appear* unfinished? The answer is that here we have a very carefully executed reproduction, as far as the foundations are concerned, of the ruins of Herod's Temple. This is the symbolic purpose of the unfinished sections of the western walls. Apparently, in the 19th century, other foundations were excavated, which seemed to imply that the present building is only the eastern part of a projected larger cruciform (i.e. cross-shaped) church, of which the visible ragged west walls are the barely started eastern parts of the transepts (the 2 arms of a cruciform church running north and south from the crossing, usually much shorter than the western arm, called the nave). However, the preparations for such work could easily have been a time-consuming device to distract the general workforce from the real purpose of the building as built. All Rosslyn's arrangements fit what is known about Herod's Temple including the placing of Boaz and Jachin, which stand at the eastern end of what would have been the inner Temple. The spot identified at Rosslyn as being at the centre of the seal of Solomon corresponds exactly with the centre point and the middle of the Holy of Holies, the spot where the Ark of the Covenant was placed in the Temple of Jerusalem.

It is worth pointing out that Freemasonry is concerned with the building of a spiritual temple following the design of Ezekiel's version of Solomon's Temple. The 'Address in the North-East corner' is as follows:

> At the erection of all stately or superb edifices, it is customary to lay the first or foundation stone in the North-Eastern corner of the building. You, being newly admitted into Freemasonry are placed in the North-East part of the lodge, figuratively to represent that stone and, from the foundation laid this evening, may you hereafter raise a superstructure, perfect in its parts and honourable to the builder.[15]

I had no idea what this meant when I first came across it but as I learnt more it began to make sense. Why else make such an important point about the north-eastern aspect and the stone? We have already seen the significance of the statements in the Bible about the 'Stone that the builders rejected'. Numerous researchers argue that this stone was symbolic of the capstone of the Great Pyramid. Certainly I sensed that this was a clue indicating that whatever the hidden treasure was it was not only buried, *but also somewhere in a north-eastern direction from a start point*. I believe that this was the Great Pyramid itself, based upon all the information pointing back to the Giza plateau.

The Moses connection again

Knowing that the Hall of Records was linked to Thoth/Hermes, and that he had hidden sacred books away, I was not surprised to discover an almost identical symbolic enactment by Moses. Apart from the surviving books attributed to Moses, it is known that a far larger collection originally existed. One such survivor is the *Assumption of Moses*, identified as an Essene work, in which the following instruction is given by Moses to Joshua:

> Receive thou this writing that thou mayest know how to preserve the books which I shall deliver unto thee; and thou shalt set them in order and anoint them with oil of Cedar and put them away from the beginning of the creation of the world, until the day of repentance in the visitation wherewith the Lord shall visit thee in consummation of the end of the days.[16]

This talk of secret books, which Moses gave Joshua to keep hidden, is clearly a *symbolic* reference to sacred hidden books of antiquity, as it cannot be the case that they were made 'from the beginning of the creation of the world'. The point is that Moses, privy to all the secrets of the ancient Egyptians, would have been well aware of the sacred books hidden away by Thoth/Hermes. As he had clearly used many other symbolic stories of Egyptian origin, I could immediately see in this passage his intention of carrying over the myth of sacred buried books into his new monotheistic religion.

The original Mason himself?

Finally on the subject of Freemasonry, it is important to assess briefly the central character of its teachings – 'Hiram Abif', builder of Solomon's Temple, who was murdered by 3 of his own men. The stylised death and resurrection of the candidate in Freemasonry is the act that makes one a Master Mason when raised from the symbolic tomb.

It seems that the actual murder of Hiram Abif is re-enacted during these Freemason initiation ceremonies. Hiram Abif, an Egyptian King (detailed by Knight and Lomas in considerable detail[17]), was murdered as he refused to reveal his secret king-making rituals, which were used to validate a pharaoh's right to possess the throne, and which also enabled the pharaoh to become a star and join Osiris in the stars after death. Knight and Lomas endeavour to prove that the Hiram Abif of Freemason lore was the Egyptian King Seqenenre Tao II, whose mummified remains show injuries consistent with those described in Freemason rituals. What is apparent from all the available information on the subject, however, is that the story of Hiram Abif appears to be a symbolic amalgamation of 2 important stories, deliberately linked to form a basis of a moral code. The Hiram of biblical origin is of Israelite blood by his mother's side and Tyrian (from the port of Tyre) on his father's side. He therefore symbolised the union of two peoples who were both antagonistic towards each other and opposed in religion, yet now united in one man. 'Hiram' is short in Hebrew for 'Ahiram', meaning 'My brother is exalted'.

In addition, the Bible describes Hiram Abif as 'Most wise',[18] imbued with prudence and understanding. Hiram Abif also derives from the Hebrew 'Av' meaning 'father' or 'leader', implying a connection with the chief builder of the Temple of Jerusalem. The biblical scriptures are very quiet about Hiram Abif's death and merely hint at his mysterious demise. A man so important in his position as to have been called the favourite of 2 kings, of Israel and Tyre, would hardly have passed into oblivion when his labours were complete without so much as a mention – *unless* his death had taken place in such a manner as to render a public account of it improper. As a consequence, it was kept secret within a society, and later adopted as a symbolic vehicle for moral conduct and rituals. However, even if the all-important account of Hiram Abif within Freemasonry proved to be entirely a myth from 2 amalgamated sources, it would not affect the validity of its message. His legend (just like that of King Arthur) is of no real narrative value, but is of immense importance from a symbolic point of view, illustrating one of the most vital philosophical and religious truths, namely the dogma of the immortality of the soul. If the soul is immortal, this would give us another very good reason why the ancients went to such lengths to preserve their wisdom and knowledge for future generations; for *they would be those very later generations themselves*.

Fact and imagination, the real ideal, may be closely united when the goal permits. Undoubtedly the Solomonic Freemasons of the Temple wished to utilise Hiram Abif as the symbol of a man developed in the life here and in the life to come, thus emphasising that the experience of closeness to the Almighty, begun on this Earth, is continued and intensified by all who deserve it in the eternal world of spirit and heaven. Put simply, the Hiram Abif story ensures that key elements of a code are carried across time, *as they have been*. The morning star in the east is significant and the position relating to a north-easterly direction is of major importance. Symbolism within the order that carries the story also keeps pointing back to Egypt and the Giza plateau, and certainly pyramids in one form or another.

We can also note that just as there are 3 major Degrees within Freemasonry, the second Book of Chronicles[19] tells that 3 distinct categories of workmen were involved in the construction of Solomon's

Temple: (a) the bearers; (b) the hewers of stones; and (c) the overseers. As we shall now see, the sacred codes of antiquity were encoded within the dimensions of ancient temples across the world, as well as cathedrals in Europe. All these connect to a single theme; one that is primarily celestial in its symbolism and relates to a sacred hidden treasure.

Chapter 26

Sacred Geometry
and Sacred Sites

Now we need to look again at certain numerical figures, encoded in the book of Revelation in the New Testament, regarding measurements of our planet. These show that the mysterious authors of the text were fully aware of the Earth's dimensions. We shall also look at the connections between ancient Central and South American temples and their inherent hidden information.

The meaning inherent in Glastonbury Abbey

In Revelation, we are told that the New Jerusalem is constructed in the form of a large square with the perimeter being 12,000 furlongs. 12,000 furlongs is equal to 31,680 feet; if we draw a square around the Earth's circumference to fit exactly around its equator, the distance is 31,680 miles. At Stonehenge the width of each of its lintels, the top sections that form a circle on top of the sarsens, is 31.680 inches, and the circumference of the lintel ring, if it was still complete, would be 316.8 feet (the radius is 50.4 feet). This radius figure, with an added zero, can also be obtained from the sequence $1 \times 2 \times 3 \times 4 \times 5 \times 6 \times 7$: 5,040; moreover, $7 \times 8 \times 9 \times 10$ gives 5,040. What's more, 5,040 is the exact measurement of the ancient Greek mile in Imperial feet.* As we shall see later, these details have direct relevance to the ancient Edfu building texts.

The measurements 3,168, 316.8 and 31,680 are all prominent in the construction and layout of Glastonbury Abbey. Glastonbury is known as a prehistoric site of worship, and of Celtic Druidism. It can also be seen as the site of the first Christian church anywhere in the world. As we saw in Chapter 24, Joseph of Arimathea journeyed to Britain after the crucifixion, arriving eventually at Glastonbury. On Weary Hill (a hillock next to the Tor) he struck his pilgrim's staff into the ground. It took root and blossomed into the Holy Thorn, the descendants of which still grow

---

* Our mile is slightly longer, at 5,280 feet.

there to this day. On a site below this, Joseph built a church on a plot of land consisting of 12 hides or 1,440 acres (1 hide equals 120 acres), which the early Christians dedicated to the Virgin Mary. According to the Domesday Book (*c.* 1086), the 12 hides of Glaston were to be forever exempt from taxes. The King's writ did not run within its boundaries up until the Dissolution of the monasteries *c.* 1540. Glastonbury has always been held in special regard and was unique amongst sanctuaries in Britain. To this day, it is still a place of constant pilgrimage. Indeed, Glastonbury has often been called the English Jerusalem.

'Appalling in their dead eloquence'

Although it was, for well over a thousand years, arguably the holiest place in England, the main sensation one gets from the site of Glastonbury Abbey now is one of emptiness. Unassailed by the everyday life of the encircling market town, it is a place of fragments. Isolated creamy pieces of superb medieval masonry are scattered over the green lawns like exhibits in a sculpture park. Once described as 'appalling in their dead eloquence' these thoroughly dismantled survivals do not easily conjure up the final magnificence of the church and its monastic buildings as they were on the eve of their destruction in the Dissolution of the monasteries *c.* 1540. At that point the church itself, read from west to east, comprised: the sumptuously ornate St Mary's Chapel, begun in 1184 and dedicated two years later; then the main vessel of the church, built and rebuilt between 1184 and *c.* 1380, with nave, then crossing topped almost certainly by an immense central tower, then the eastern parts, the choir and retrochoir; and finally the long Edgar Chapel (a shrine for the remains of the Saxon King Edgar) built as late as the 16th century, at the far east end. Including the two chapels at its extremities, the church, with its unique nave in the Transitional style of the moment when Romanesque gave way to Gothic, and its lavish 15th-century remodelling of the eastern parts with panelling that probably resembled similar work at Gloucester Cathedral, was longer than any surviving medieval cathedral in Britain.

The original St Mary's Chapel was laid out to incorporate the dimensions of the Vesica Pisces, and the 12 hides, overlaid with a grid of 74-foot squares, were later incorporated into the Abbey itself (see figure 90).

The ground plan of the New Jerusalem as given in the book of Revelation is almost identical to the 12 hides of Glaston, and the ground plan of Stonehenge. Below are the dimensions of the ground plan of the first Christian settlement at Glastonbury.

There are 12 small circles arranged in groups of 3 that represent, in an

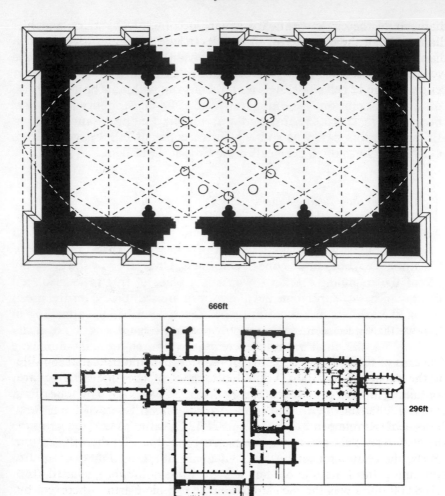

Figure 90. Glastonbury Abbey. (a) St Mary's Chapel; (b) The entire abbey church, with cloisters and monastic buildings to the south (at the base of the image)

astronomical context, the seasons of the Moon (remember how 1,080 was important in gematria and also equalled the radius of the Moon, giving a diameter of 2,160 miles?) and the months of the Great Year, each of which consisted of 2,160 years. 2,160 equals one complete Zodiacal precession of 30 degrees. Each of the 12 circular cells measures 21.60 feet. The circle that passes through the middle of the cells measures 316.8 feet in circumference, or a hundredth part of 6 miles (see figure 91). The circle through the centre of the small circles has a diameter of 100.8 feet; that within the square a diameter of 79.20 feet. As a scheme of cosmology, the diagram can be measured in units of 100 miles instead of feet, so the

258

diameter of the circle within the square becomes 7,920 miles (Earth's diameter) and the diameter of the small circles 2,160 miles (the Moon's diameter). When 79.20 feet is multiplied by 4 (the 4 sides of the square) we get 316.8 feet: the circumference of the circle that runs through the centres of the 12 cell circles.

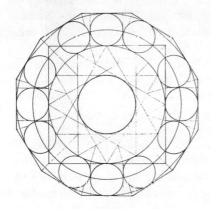 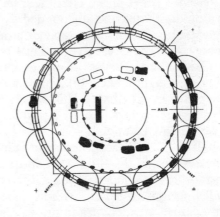

Figure 91. 'The New Jerusalem.' 　　　　*Figure 92*. Stonehenge

The area of the square is equal to 0.144 acres, which means that the side of the square is equal to a hundredth part of the side of a square containing an area of 12 hides (this equals 7,920 feet). 7,920 *thousand* feet equals 12,000 furlongs – and this is the length of the side of the New Jerusalem (Revelation 21). So (4 × 7,920) 31,680 feet is the perimeter of the New Jerusalem and is also the perimeter of the 12 hides of Glaston. The figure has more meanings: 31,680 miles is the perimeter of the square containing the Earth, and Pliny, in his *Natural History*,[1] stated that 3,168,000 miles was the measure round the whole Earth – incorrect by just 2 zeros.

The circles of the New Jerusalem diagram, projected with the exact dimensions of Glastonbury, define the measurements of the concentric stone rings at Stonehenge. This indicates a universal understanding of advanced mathematical science in antiquity, derived from a common source (see figure 92).

In figure 93 the circle of diameter 79.20 feet is shown contained within a square, the western side of which coincides with the interior of St Mary's Chapel wall, which *also* measures 79.20 feet. The diagram is so proportioned that its perimeter, of (4 × 79.20) 316.8 feet, is the same as the circumference of the circle which runs through the middle of the ring of cells. Its significance, here in relation to Glastonbury Abbey itself, is that the area of the square is 0.144 acres – a microcosm of the 12 Hides of Glaston, which cover 1,440 acres.

We have only very recently (the past 50 years) established the exact dimensions of the Earth, so how is it possible that the ancient compilers of the New Testament knew the exact measures?

Glastonbury is unique for many reasons. It stands on a minute hummock that makes it a virtual island rising from the surrounding marshlands. This area was once an inland sea, as geologists and archaeologists confirm. Here then, we have an image of a sacred place on a mount, isolated and surrounded by water. This is exactly how ancient Egyptian myths describe their primordial mound of creation; the same mound that the Great Pyramid was built upon.

Glastonbury Tor, set to the east (note the East connection again?), rises as a great conical hill, and between it and the town is the Moon-shaped dome of Chalice Hill, closely associated with the Holy Grail. At its foot are springs and a holy well, protected by a lid with the Vesica Pisces engraved upon it.

Glastonbury's earlier names, Avalon and the Isle of Glass, reflect the ancients' belief that this was a most sacred site and a place of mystical visions. It was reputed to be a gateway to another world, ruled by a King called 'Gwyn ap Nudd', with his palace beneath the Tor. Here we have an almost identical tradition to the ancient Egyptian belief of an underworld. During the Reformation, around 1540, when the power of the state prevailed over the interests of the Church, the last Abbot of Glastonbury, Richard Whiting, was hanged on a gibbet on the top of the Tor. This was done as he refused to reveal the Abbey's treasures to the commissioners of the State who had been ordered to loot them: this apparent treasure has remained lost to this date. In my view, it isn't a treasure in the usual sense of gold, jewels and so on, but *knowledge*, encoded within the Abbey's geometric dimensions. Many legends talk of underground vaults beneath the site and surrounding it. These Glaston-bury legends parallel accounts of buried treasure at Rosslyn Chapel, the Temple of Jerusalem and the Great Pyramid. The treasure in all the above accounts lies in what they state and where they all point, i.e. to the Great Pyramid.

Many ancient prophecies identify Glastonbury as a place of regeneration, a quality shared by the Giza Pyramids. One prophecy, recounted from a 6th-century work known as the *Book of Melchin*, states that the tomb of St Joseph and a Grail talisman will one day be discovered, and that 'Thenceforth nor water nor dew of heaven shall fail the dwellers on that ancient isle'.[2] This prophecy is remarkably similar to the Holy Grail legend of the lame Fisher-King (also associated with the surrounding marshes of Glastonbury), which declares that when he is healed, his barren kingdom will also flourish again and the primeval golden age will be restored. What's more, this same prophecy has been made about the Great Pyramid's missing capstone: its eventual restoration, too, will herald the dawn of a new golden age.

Two very resonant manifestations also link Glastonbury Abbey and the Pyramids: firstly the highly unusual presence of two pyramids; and secondly, an enigmatic pillar. These were excavated by Bligh Bond,[3] who was director of excavations at Glastonbury in the early half of this century. Pyramidal shaped tombs were and are unheard of on Christian sites, especially one of such antiquity. Yet if Joseph of Arimathea was indeed the originator of the site, it makes plausible sense, since he was very much aware of the symbolic importance of this shape (see figure 93).

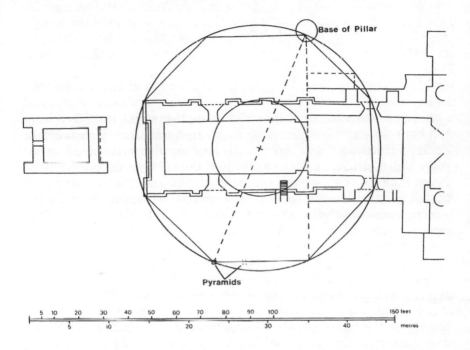

Figure 93. St Mary's Chapel and the pyramid tombs.

The two pyramids and pillars are clearly marked. A line can be drawn between the centres of the two monuments outside the Chapel that cuts the central axis of the Chapel at the mid-point of the Glastonbury scheme. The monuments and two corners of the Chapel mark angles of an octagon within a circle of a radius of 50.4 feet. How many times have we already come across this value? Jesus was often referred to by the Gnostics as 'the Ogdoad', i.e. 'the eightfold'. In gematria, as we saw earlier, Jesus equals 888. Also note that the 12-fold symmetry of the New Jerusalem diagram, when laid over the plan of the Chapel, defines its proportions and the positions of the original 12 cells and central church (see figure 94).

261

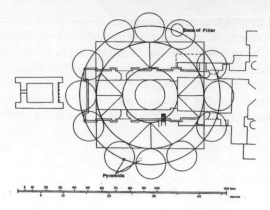

Figure 94.

The Vesica Pisces*

Jesus composed many parables with fish-related symbolism. When Jesus was born the Earth was just finishing its precessional cycle through the Zodiacal constellation of Aries the Ram (previous parables related to goats and rams) and it then passed into the next precessional cycle of Pisces, the Fish. Also, the early Christians' symbol of a fish denoted their church. What is essential to take on board now is that the geometric and esoteric symbol of the Great Pyramid happens to be the 'Vesica Pisces', meaning 'vessel of the fish' (see figure 95).

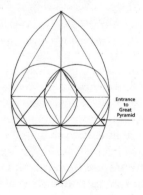

Figure 95.

The illustration of the Vesica Pisces is formed by the intersection of two equal circles, the circumference of each of which passes through the centre of the other. The Pyramid profile is placed within Vesica Pisces's geometric makeup by joining up the lines that cross each other. It is not merely an abstract illustration; it occurs frequently in nature and

*Further information on the arcane and esoteric aspects of the Vesica Pisces is to be found in Mark Hedsel and David Ovason's *The Zelator*, Century, London, 1998.

represents perfect equilibrium between two equal forces. In the words of the ancient geomancers, it was an image of the interpenetrating worlds of Heaven and Earth, of Spirit and Matter. The dimensions and geometry of the Great Pyramid relate directly to the Vesica Pisces and symbolically to what esotericists call the 'number of fusion', 1,746. Let me explain. The Great Pyramid's height, not counting the base platform, is 481 feet and forms the longer axis of a Vesica Pisces made from two intersecting circles of equal circumference of 1,746 feet. The perimeter of the large rhombus (diamond shape) contained within the Vesica Pisces is 1,110 feet, and the area of the rhombus equals 66,600 square feet. The 'height' of the Vesica Pisces, when formed from circles with a circumference of 1,746 feet, is the same as that of the Great Pyramid's 481 feet.

The diameter of each of the two circles forming the 'inner' Vesica Pisces is equal to that number (481) divided by half the square root of 3, or 555.5 feet, giving the circumference of each circle as 1,746 feet. When the two circles are enclosed in a greater Vesica Pisces, the base angle of the Great Pyramid can be formed almost accurately to scale of its 51° 51″ slope. This can be achieved when a line is drawn across the points where the two circle lines meet on the centre line. The horizontal line is extended outwards, passing over the points where the two circle lines again are crossed by the intersecting line that cuts through them, until it finally stops at the outer line of the Vesica Pisces. Two lines are then drawn upwards to converge where the central axis line passes through the two circle lines where they meet. The two inner circles that intersect at the Pyramid's tip and the centre of its base accurately illustrate the form of a magnetic field. This is very important. A known feature of the Great Pyramid is its display of magnetic peculiarities supported by both myths and modern scientific experimentation – miniature pyramids are sold today as razor-blade sharpeners, since magnetic fields produced inside these rearrange the crystalline structure of the blades back to the original sharpness. Moreover, meat placed inside a Pyramid does not rot but simply dehydrates and dries out completely. Later it can be rehydrated, cooked and eaten with no ill effects to the consumer.

The numbers and values obtained from the Vesica Pisces are found in Revelation: the area of the Vesica Pisces is 144,000 feet, the number of souls in Revelation; the rhombus of 66,600 square feet parallels the mark of the Beast, 666. But what of these numbers in other cultures? If they can be found elsewhere, it adds weight to the argument that the mathematical code is indeed a global one.

The finds at Palenque

If we journey to Central America, to an area between the Mayan highlands on the Pacific coast and the lowlands of the Yucatan to the

North in the Gulf of Mexico, we find ourselves at the ancient Mayan city of Palenque, with its beautiful limestone palaces and temples. In 1952, after 3 years of digging, the archaeologist Alberto Ruz Lhuillier finally cleared the entrance passage into the Temple of Inscriptions. As he moved the huge triangular monolith blocking the way into the inner chambers, he was confronted by an enormous empty room that appeared as if it were covered in ice. On top of an altar lay a great slab carved with ornate details (see figure 96).

Figure 96. The Temple of Inscriptions.

The great slab covering the tomb weighed 5 tons and was completely covered with carvings, showing the image of a man sitting on top of a 'monster', falling from this life into the next. On top of the slab were some fragments of a ceremonial belt that carried 3 small human masks and hatchet-shaped pendants; goblets and plates were also discovered. Two stone heads were found on the floor, one of a woman and one of a man. When the lid was removed, another mummy-shaped inner lid, again of stone, was found; under *that* were the remains of a man aged about 40 when he had died. The entire inside of this sarcophagus was painted in red cinnabar and the man's face was covered by fragments of a green jade mask. When I first learnt of this, I immediately recalled that Sirius had been described as red in colour in ancient times, and that Osiris was originally portrayed as being green-faced as well as black (see plates). The 'green man' image is a theme that occurs all over the world, though often it is only seen as a representative of fertility (see figure 97).

Figure 97.

The man in the tomb wore a crown of jade discs, complicated ear hoops, various necklaces of jade, jade bracelets comprised of individually strung jade beads, and jade rings, one for every finger on each hand. One jade bead had been placed in each hand and one in the mouth. By his side lay 2 miniature jade figurines. There were also 9 brightly painted figurines adorning the crypt walls, which represented the 9 'Lords of the Night' – important figures in Mayan theology. In addition there was a square boxed conduit, known as the communications channel, which allowed the dead man to keep in touch with the living, running from the crypt up every step to the top of the pyramid. The man was the Priest-King 'Lord Pacal', who according to the inscriptions in the temple was born in AD 703 and died in AD 783 aged 80; so how was it the body was that of a 40-year-old?

Maurice M. Cotterell asked some very probing questions about these Palenque finds in *The Supergods*.[4] I have listed them below, as we shall need to look at the answers:

- Why did the pyramid have 9 levels (storeys) but only 5 staircases? (It would have been much easier to have built a short staircase up every sloping level.)
- Why did the 5 stairways amount to 69 steps?
- Why were there 5 porchways and 6 pillars at the top of the temple?
- Why were there 4 sets of double holes in the paving slab on the temple floor? (Why not simply 1 hole in each corner?)
- Why was the entire staircase filled with rubble and mortar, so that it took 3 years of digging to reach the tomb?
- Why were there 620 carved inscriptions in the temple?
- Why 26 steps down the first level of the inside staircase?
- Why 22 steps down the second staircase?
- What was the reason for the stone box containing the items at the foot of the stairs?
- Why were there 5 male skeletons and 1 female?
- Why was the door to the tomb triangular?
- Why were there 4 steps down, just after the triangular door?
- What was the meaning of the carving on the lid? And why had the corners been removed?
- Why was one corner missing from the sarcophagus?
- What did the 9 'secret codes' on either side of the lid represent?
- What was the significance of the 2 stucco heads on the floor? And why did 1 head have a high hairstyle while the other had a low hairstyle? And why did one of them have 2 ears, but the other only 1?
- What was the significance of the jade jewellery? Why did the jade mask have peculiar dot markings in certain areas?
- What did the other jade pieces represent?
- Why use jade instead of gold?
- How come the bones of the man in the tomb show he died at 40 whilst the inscriptions suggest a man twice that?
- Why was the inside of the tomb painted with red cinnabar?
- Why were 9 'Lords of the Night' painted on the wall?
- What was the true purpose of the 'Communications Channel'?

Just before arriving at the Temple of Inscriptions, the visitor comes to the Palace, at the foot of which lies a tablet carrying 96 inscriptions. It was demonstrated that there are 96 micro-cycles in the 187-year Sunspot cycle. The 97th micro-cycle was described by Maurice Cotterell as 'the Rogue Cycle'[5] which causes an even longer cycle of 18,139 years. The 96 glyphs on the tablet represent these 96 micro-cycles of solar activity. Maurice Cotterell also demonstrated that the Sunspot cycle is divided into 5 segments and that these corresponded with the 5 doorways of the Temple. He further explains that the Temple of Inscriptions pyramid has 9 levels, to emphasise the most important number of the Mayans (and also important in relation to Fadic values). There are 5 landings to stress the value of the number 5. This number was also of great importance to the ancient Egyptians, as we shall see later.

In *The Mayan Prophecies*,[6] Maurice Cotterell compiled a numerical table, which, when used in conjunction with the Maya cycles, threw up the birth of Venus as he understood it: see figure 98.

144,000	7,200	360	260	20 days
1	1	1	1	1
2	2	2	2	2
3	3	3	3	3
4	4	4	4	4
5	5	5	5	5
6	6	6	6	6
7	7	7	7	7
8	8	8	8	8
9	9	9	9	9 = 1,366,560 days
				(Sunspot cycle)

Figure 98.

Cotterell had arrived at this table through a mathematical inquiry into the revolutions of Venus against the base number of the Mayan counting system, 360. The Mayans were trying to communicate something by their use of numbers within the Temple of Inscriptions. All the numbers in the above table are encoded within the clues in the pyramid. As we have seen, the 96 glyphs related to the 96 micro-cycles of Sunspot activity. Furthermore, by simply reversing the 69 steps of the Temple itself, we get 96. There are 620 inscriptions in the floor of the temple; this can be viewed as an important anagram of the Mayan year of 260 days. Subtracting 260 from 620 gives 360. As 360 mattered so much, it is worth seeing how the Maya actually counted. However, it must be noted that this presupposes that the Mayan mathematicians were sophisticated, which they certainly appear to be, in that they used their vigesimal – base 20 – system to make numerical puns (just like the ancient Egyptian priests) that will only work if you first translate into the decimal system.

Mayan mathematics

The position of figures in a Mayan number was vital. When the Romans were using a clumsy system of addition, the Maya had a positional system, even more concise than our own way of numbering, with only three symbols: a dot, a dash and a shell-shape representing zero. Modern arithmetic, which was developed in India and the Middle East, is based on 10s, with the figure on the right representing units, the next figure to the left showing tens, the third showing hundreds and so on. The Maya, however, counted in 20s and wrote large numbers in columns reading from the bottom to the top. A number up to 20 was expressed by a single hieroglyph, as shown in the table. Each hieroglyph was a combination of dots and dashes, or bars, each dot standing for 1, each dash for 5 (see figure 99).

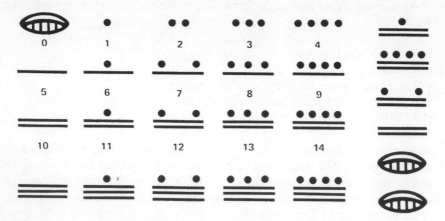

Figure 99.

For numbers higher than 20, a new row was started above the first to mark the number of 20s in the total. Thus the number 234 would be expressed by only two Mayan symbols: the sign for 11, meaning 11 sets of 20, or 220, followed by the sign for 14. Similarly, the third row from the bottom in Mayan numbering stood for multiples of 400, or 20 × 20, the fourth row down for multiples of 8,000 (20 × 20 × 20), and so on. 100,000, for example, required only 4 digits: the sign for 12 (meaning 12 sets of 8,000 – 96,000), followed by the sign for 10 (10 sets of 400 – 4,000), followed by two of the shell-shaped zero signs.

On dates (the form in which most large Mayan numbers have been found), the Maya modified this 20-based system slightly to make the years easier to count. They defined all their dates as the number of days since the start of their calendar; many Mayan experts see this as 11 August 3144 BC. Under this system, the groups in each succeeding row had special names. The 360-day year, shown in the third row, was called a 'Tun', and contained 18 months each of 20 days. The fourth row showed 'Katun', or 20-year periods, each of 7,200 days (20 × 18 × 20), and the fifth showed 'Baktun', or 400-year periods, each of 144,000 days (or 20 × 20 × 18 × 20).

Looking back at figure 98 we can now reconcile each of the numbers in the table with clues from the tomb, as follows:

• First 1 from 11 (i.e. 1 followed by 1) jade pieces inside stone chest found inside the square chamber just outside the triangular entrance door

- Second 1 from above 11
- 1 pearl
- 1 female skeleton
- 1 shell.

Also, every other line on the table is represented, as for example in line 9:

- 9 steps at the bottom of the pyramid (outside)
- 9 levels of the pyramid
- 9 steps on the top stairway of the pyramid (outside)
- 9 Lords of the Night painted on walls of tomb
- 9 Codes on each side of the tomb lid.

Note also that there were 4 sets of double holes in the temple paving-slab, amounting to 2222, and that there were also 2 heads on the floor of the tomb, and 2 jade figurines accompanying the bones of Lord Pacal, as well as 22 steps on the lower internal staircase. (We have seen the importance of 22 many times.) The first section of the internal stairway has 26 steps; 26 is the duration of the revolutionary period of the Sun's equator, in days, and 26 is very important within the Great Pyramid – the significance of the 26-degree angles within its construction, for example. For the third row of 3s, we note that there are 3 sides to the door of the tomb, 3 clay trays, 3 red shells in the stone chest and 3 jade beads, one placed in each hand and one in his mouth. A further significant fact is that the dead man also wore a 3-tiered necklace, which we shall look at in a moment.

From the 4s row, there were 4 sets of double holes in the paving slab, 4 steps down into the crypt and 4 rings on the man's left hand, 4 rings on his right hand and 4 plugs in the sarcophagus. Row 5: 5 stair levels, 5 temple doorways, 5 ceiling beams inside the crypt, 5 sides to the sarcophagus and 5 male skeletons outside in the square chamber. Row 6: 6 pillars to the temple entrance and 6 sides to the Lid of Palenque. Curiously, the remaining 3 6s are missing but as Maurice Cotterell demonstrated,[7] these could be found in conjunction with the 7s and 8s in the jade necklace found around Pacal's neck. The necklace shows the 3 missing 6s from the tomb as a factor of higher numbers in the necklace itself (assessed in the next paragraph). Once found, the 7s and 8s also appear. The necklace's second row of beads adds up to 37, which is the number of days in the Sun's Polar revolutionary periods. The top two tiers add up to 71, which (as Maurice Cotterell again demonstrates[8]) is a critical factor in the mathematical computerised calculation that leads to the Sunspot cycle period of 11 years (11 jade beads) $\times$ 71 $\times$ 87.4545 = 68,302 days; this equals one 187-year Sunspot cycle. After 20 of these, i.e. 1,366,040 days, the Sun's magnetic field reverses. This is an important point to remember, as we shall have cause to come back to it again.

As for the missing 6s, these can be found in the number of strips of 13 beads, which provide 6 + 7, 6 + 7 and 6 + 7, thereby also providing 3 of the required 7s. The second row shows a 7. The next 7 is found as a factor in the next level of numbers, the 8s. 7 + 8 = 15, which can be found on the centre strip of beads. The lower strip runs 1 long bead followed by 3 round beads, then 1 long bead followed by 3 round beads, then 1 long bead followed by 3 round beads, and once again 1 long bead followed by 3 round beads. In Mayan numbers this is 8888 (see figure 100).

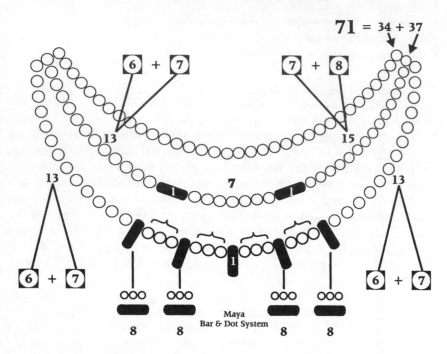

Figure 100. The mathematics of the Palenque necklace.

Cotterell explains the single oblong bead in the centre of the bottom row of the necklace and the 2 single oblong beads on the centre row, either side of the 7 (which have yet to be accounted for), as follows: When attempting to accommodate the first row of the number matrix shown in figure 105, the 11111, he included 11 jade beads found in the square chest as well as the 1 single pearl found in the seashell on a bed of cinnabar. The 3 remaining oblong beads on the necklace indicate that a slight mistake appears to have been made: the 11 jade beads from the chest do not belong in the first line of the matrix after all, but belong with the 71 in the necklace, $11 \times 71 \times 87.4545 = $ a single 187-year Sunspot cycle as just described. Likewise the single pearl in the shell has also been incorrectly included into the matrix. When this is understood, we can see that the

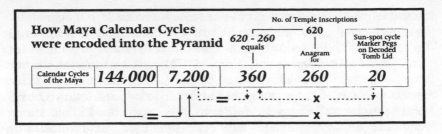

	No. of Temple Inscriptions			
How Maya Calendar Cycles were encoded into the Pyramid	620 - 260 equals	620 Anagram for	Sun-spot cycle Marker Pegs on Decoded Tomb Lid
Calendar Cycles of the Maya	144,000	7,200	360	260	20

Decoding the Clues of the Pyramid and Temple of Inscriptions

1 Pearl in sea-shell	1 Female skeleton in ante-chamber	1 Single long bead on necklace	1 Single long bead on necklace	1 Single long bead on necklace
2 Holes in paving slab	2 Holes in paving slab	2 Holes in paving slab	2 Holes in paving slab	2 Plaster heads on Tomb floor
3 Clay plates in stone chest	3 Red shells in stone chest	3 Sided Tomb door	3 Jade beads (1 in each hand 1 in mouth)	3 Tiered jade necklace
4 Steps down into Tomb	4 Jade rings on left hand	4 Jade rings on right hand	4 Sets of holes in paving slab	4 Cylindrical plugs in Sarcophagus
5 Pyramid stairway landings	5 Temple doorways	5 Male skeletons	5 Ceiling beams	5 Sarcophagus sides
6 Temple pillars	6 Sides to Tomb Lid	missing [6]	missing [6]	missing [6]
missing [7] + [8]=15 Necklace beads	7 Necklace beads	[7]=13 + Necklace beads	[7]=13 + Necklace beads	[7]=13 + Necklace beads
	8 Dash Dot beads ●●● ▬▬	8 Dash Dot beads ●●● ▬▬	8 Dash Dot beads ●●● ▬▬	8 Dash Dot beads ●●● ▬▬
9 Bottom steps of Pyramid	9 Pyramid levels	9 Top steps of Pyramid	9 Lords painted on Tomb walls	9 / 9* Codes on left / right sides of Lid

| Decoding in relation to calendar cycles used by the Maya | 9 x 144,000 + | 9 x 7,200 + | 9 x 360 + | 9 x 260 + | 9 x 20 |

= 1,366,560 days

9 of each of the Maya Cycles amounts to the sun-spot catastrophe period of 1,366,560 days. The extra 9*, in the row of nines, is the final clue to the sun-spot number:
1+3+6+6+5+6+0 = 27;   2+7 = 9*

Figure 101.

clues point to a numerical matrix, the conclusion of which is 99999. Taking 9 each of the Mayan cycles and 9 of the 260-day Mayan years, we will arrive at the Temple of Inscriptions' final numerical value: 1,366,560 (see figure 101).

I would again like to draw your attention to the value of 144,000; and to the total value of 1,366,560 being 27, which in Fadic terms is 9. I mention this because 27 is also evident within the Great Pyramid, as we shall see.

In *The Mayan Prophecies*,[9] Maurice Cotterell and Adrian Gilbert demonstrate what is communicated by the Lid of Palenque (see figure 97). Its engraved border image could be decoded, and many ancient Mayan prophecies and myths were seen to be represented in illustrative form once an acetate image had been drawn of the lid and then repositioned in various positions marked by the missing corner and various other means. One of the composite images revealed the 'Physical Death of Lord Pacal', and also showed the number 144,000 on Lord Pacal's forehead (see figure 102).

Figure 102.

The picture is made up of two halves which are reflected either side of the centre line of the drawing. Because of this it is not possible to reveal the number 144,000 from left to right or from right to left. To overcome this, 1,440 is written from left to right. The mirror image of 1,440 can be seen from right to left. The missing 2 zeros (zero, as I explained earlier, is represented by an oval with three lines) are shown above this number, making the eyes of the mask.

I began these two subsections 'The finds at Palenque', and 'Mayan mathematics', to demonstrate that other cultures knew the vital significance of 144,000. But having examined this Mayan example in detail, I must now point out another highly remarkable link to the Old World. In the Bible, there is a further paragraph that deals with the number 144,000 as being associated with a seal and mark *on the forehead*:

> And I saw another angel ascending from the East, having the seal of the living God: and he cried with a loud voice to the four angels, to whom it was given to hurt the Earth and the sea, saying 'Hurt not the Earth, neither the sea, nor the trees, till we have sealed the servants of our God in their foreheads'. And I heard the number of them which were sealed; and there were sealed an hundred and forty and four thousand of all the tribes of the children of Israel. [Revelation 7: 2–4]

Furthermore, Revelation 9: 4 states: 'And it was commanded them that they should not hurt the grass of the Earth, neither any green thing, neither any tree, but only those men which have not the seal of God in their foreheads'.

The imagery is extraordinary, in the light of the finds at Palenque.

Central American pyramids

Now we have looked at the Temple of Inscriptions, can Teotihuacan and its sacred alignments and geometry tell us more? Let's see what we know of it. Teotihuacan emerged from the local Valley of Teotihuacan and Valley of Mexico populations, but its cultural antecedents seem linked to preceding peoples. When Frenchman Désiré Charnay[10] first uncovered a small part of the city, he believed it was of Toltec origin, but later studies showed that the Toltecs had begun in the 10th century AD, by which time Teotihuacan was already in ruins, and anyway, the Toltecs had their capital further north, in Tollan (now Tula). However, the Toltec theory shouldn't be entirely discounted. And it is instructive that the Aztecs, in their legendary epics and chronicles, used the general name of Toltec to refer to the ancient race whose religious traditions and learning they claimed to retain; furthermore the Aztecs themselves thought that Teotihuacan was the Toltec capital.

To the Aztecs, the word Toltec came to mean 'great craftsmen', which is highly sensible in view of the prodigious architecture of Teotihuacan. One Aztec work states that the city was 'The City of the Gods', purposefully built to mark the Fifth Sun, or Fifth Renewal of the World, after its last destruction. This Sun, the Aztecs maintained, rose in

Teotihuacan to climb to the centre of the universe, and the city's founders were considered the founders of a new era, the era of motion. The site's most dominant building is the Pyramid of the Sun, standing at the city's centre like a celestial signpost. As we know, the main 'road' is the so-called Avenue of the Dead, which stretches for exactly 7,920 feet (significant because 7,920 miles equals Earth's diameter, remember). The Pyramid is 216 feet high; add a zero to get our all-important value of 2,160. Its base measures 720×760 feet – again, two important values.

Are there other Central American pyramids we should analyse? Yes. However, pyramid is not strictly an accurate description of these temples, as they are more truncated and never had an apex. Instead they had a temple built on the flat summit. It has been suggested that there could perhaps be as many as 100,000 pyramids, *in the Mexico region alone*, that have yet to be uncovered. One that caught my attention many years ago was the Pyramid of the Niches at El Tajin, rising out of the jungle in the land of the Totonacs, in what is now the Veracruz area. It stands 80 feet high on its square base, each side measuring 118 feet, and takes its name from the unique feature of its 7 levels decorated by 365 square niches; one for each day of the year (see plates). This is a clear indication that these pyramids are encoded with celestial information – in the most obvious of ways, as well as in hidden ones.

In addition to the hidden information encoded within temples there is something else that, I believe, further demonstrates the existence of a global plan. It would also appear that many ancient sites across the world are intrinsically linked, in regard to celestial information and the constellation of Orion. Moreover, this information is somehow linked back to the Giza pyramids, especially the Great Pyramid. During my years of research I was constantly being made aware of so-called Ley lines or 'Paths of the Dragon' which were also linked to these ancient sites; in consequence I had no option but to study them, to evaluate the many claims made about them. Some of my findings weren't what I expected.

Chapter 27

Ley Lines and Cathedrals

Paths of the Dragon

Perfectly straight roads or paths are found all over the ancient Mediterranean world, linking many of the ancient sites governed by magic squares (for which, see Chapter 15). These paths are often called 'Ley lines' or 'Paths of the Dragon' (especially in China) as the dragon represented, in symbolic form, the energy within the Earth which the ancients believed they could harness and use. They were marked out by Hermes stones, which were directly linked to Omphalos and oracle centres. If you refer back to the section on magic squares, you will notice that the total sum for the square of Mercury/Hermes equals 2,080, which is $1 + 2 + 3$ etc. up to 64.

Although alignment of ancient sites across the world has been noted for many years, especially by geomancers, it is only during the past century that researchers have again started to seriously look at the phenomenon, especially following the publication of *The Old Straight Track* by Alfred Watkins in 1925.[1] Watkins had discovered an extensive network of alignments of straight lines connecting ancient prehistoric earthworks, standing stones, henge monuments, stone circles and medieval churches that had been built over earlier ancient pagan sites. He named these alignments Leys. I soon discovered that many of the sites in England I had studied were in fact sited on these so-called Leys. I *also* learned that the churches that appeared on these lines were built upon old pagan sites as a result of Pope Gregory I specifically ordering in AD 601, that all such places should be sought out, purified and converted into churches.

A cathedral's secret code

In relation to sacred squares, I would like to give one remarkable example, which reveals connections between a magic square (with its inherent geometry) and the construction of Lichfield Cathedral in

Staffordshire. As I explained earlier, and as John Michell expands upon in his book *New View over Atlantis*,[2] every ancient site was associated with a particular planet or star, which in turn corresponded to a colour, a sound and also the human body. The numbers and magic squares associated with the site were incorporated into its ground plans and elevations. Though small – over 200 feet shorter than the final form of Glastonbury Abbey, for instance – Lichfield Cathedral is unique amongst its English peers in retaining all 3 spires, 2 at the west end and a third taller one over the crossing. Trios of spires existed, or were planned, at several medieval cathedrals – Lincoln had 3, timber-framed and covered in lead, all now gone; Durham lost 2 similar spires from its west towers and may have intended a third on the crossing tower – but only here does the scheme survive. That the west front is materially as much restoration work as medieval masonry doesn't undermine the essential power of the composition. (The central spire collapsed after Civil War damage in the 17th century, when the church was besieged, and had to be rebuilt, while much of the ornament of the West Front is Victorian.) The 3 towers with their spires were built in the late 13th and early 14th centuries, but the original founder of the see was St Chad, Bishop of the Mercians (the dominant kingdom in Saxon Central England) 669–72.

Lichfield Cathedral is built upon a levelled prehistoric site, sanctified, according to Christian legend, when 888 early martyrs were massacred there (888, we know, is the value in gematria of Jesus). Lichfield Cathedral is dedicated to St Chad, whose feast day is also that of Mars, 2 March. Is it therefore a coincidence that the design of the cathedral is proportionally identical to the geometric pattern formed by the magic square of Mars (see figure 103)?

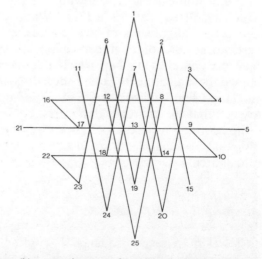

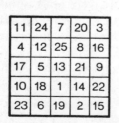

Figure 103. (a) the magic square of Mars; (b) geometric pattern formed by the magic square; (c) engraving of Lichfield Cathedral from the west (*opposite*).

276

The use of these magic squares was a part of the ancient kabbalistic practice dealing with geometry and mathematics, secretly preserved by medieval craftsmen's guilds. These guilds were undoubtedly those of the Freemason order, as they were in most cases directly behind the financing and construction of the great cathedrals of England and Europe.

For each project, appropriate numbers were chosen according to the nature of the site and the dominant astrological sign of the country it was in. Hence in many parts of Germany and in Hanseatic cities such as Lübeck, the great churches were usually laid out according to the square of Mars and built in red brick. Lichfield Cathedral is likewise constructed from red sandstone. Furthermore, the planet Mars is red. Revealingly, according to a medieval document in the church archives, quoted in Britton's *The History and Antiquities of Lichfield*,[3] Lichfield was formerly called 'Liches', meaning 'War'. Mars was the god of war, and the cathedral's patron St Chad was also considered a warrior.

Further clues in great churches?

I assessed earlier the connection between the Templars and the idol head that they were accused of worshipping. This head legend states that it is CAPUT LVIIIm, and as I showed, this has generally been interpreted as meaning 'Head 58'. We know the importance of 58 and also that the m could actually represent the astrological sign for Virgo. The cathedrals of Europe were the pinnacles of architectural achievement. In less than a century the entire landscape of Europe was changed for ever with these, at the time, unbelievably huge inspiring buildings, only equalled in size by the Great Pyramid of Egypt. I would not be at all surprised if part of what the original Templars found under the Temple of Jerusalem proved to contain documents on construction methods from antiquity. This would explain the sudden explosion of technical expertise that flooded Europe shortly after the Templars returned to France with whatever secrets were now in their possession.

The true origins of Gothic architecture?

On their way to the Crusades in 1147, King Louis and Queen Eleanor of France were accompanied by a contingent of Knights Templar. It was around this time that the King adopted the symbol of the *'fleur de lys'* as his heraldic device, which soon became the Royal Coat of Arms of France, and some have speculated that this followed the King's initiation into the Templar Order. The *'fleur de lys'*, which is a lily, was a very popular symbol in both Egypt and Byzantium. *'Fleur de lys'* derives from *'fleur de Luce'*, or Iris. This is the European version of the lily or lotus as given to the Virgin Mary by the Angel Gabriel. It is the same as the sheaf of the Virgo figure and esoterically represents the flower from which the soul of a new King will emerge. Apart from the Templar speculation, just *why* the *'fleur de lys'* became so important in France has never been satisfactorily answered. However, further esoteric meanings are confirmed in *The Mysteries of Chartres Cathedral*, written by a man named Louis Charpentier, published in 1966. However, the copyright holder to this book is listed as Robert Laffont, which would imply that the author's name is a pseudonym.

Adrian Gilbert argues in *The Magi*[5] that the name stands for 'Louis the Carpenter' and that the book betrays knowledge of a living esoteric tradition that links the Templars with the building of the great cathedrals of France (I happen to agree with him on this point as I have already proffered the same argument). The book was originally published in French, but later an English version appeared, with a foreword by Janette Jackson, who remarks:

> M. Charpentier opens a fresh vista of possibilities. He says in effect that Chartres and other cathedrals, like the great monuments of Egypt and Greece, were the manifestation of a secret communicated to mankind by occult or mystical means.[6]

The precise nature of this secret is not spelled out. However, Charpentier's[7] book claims that the original 9 Templar Knights were responsible for bringing the Ark of the Covenant to France, having been instructed by St Bernard* to do so. Apparently the Ark was buried somewhere on Mount Moriah (very close to the Temple in Jerusalem) prior to the destruction of the first Temple of Solomon in 597 BC. The evidence of the actual Ark literally being taken to France is very thin. It is probable, however, that the Ark, as a *symbolic* notion – along with ancient sacred books and scrolls containing ancient wisdom, technical skills and building techniques as well as the genealogical records of Jesus – was indeed recovered. Charpentier continues to argue that the Ark represents the true Gnosis, 'knowledge', as brought to France by the Templars and shows that the cathedrals of Northern France were laid out to a definite plan. As I had already deduced that the symbolic Ark/treasure recovered by the original 9 Templars related to documents that revealed technological wisdom from antiquity, I had to agree with Charpentier's conclusion that his symbolic Ark contained what can only be described as building plans. (Of course, we have already seen Templar connections to building in such designs as Rosslyn Chapel in Scotland.) Charpentier argues that after the Templars had brought these details to

---

* St Bernard of Clairvaux, leader of the Cistercian order.

France, medieval masons set about building them, and they thus became eventually the Gothic cathedrals, such as that at Chartres.

Prior to the arrival back in France of the Templar Knights, only Romanesque churches and cathedrals existed. Then suddenly, after the second Crusade, a totally new form of building appeared, known as Gothic. Adrian Gilbert[8] demonstrates how this new technique was not developed in France but originated in the East, and he names various sites that have a profusion of the typical pointed Gothic arches such as those at Edessa and Mardin in the Middle East. Whatever the true sources, Charpentier's book went on to detail that the cathedrals of France were laid out across the country, following a vast plan: the cathedrals of Rouen, Chartres, Laon, Reims and others each *represented a different star*. This sat very well with my previous researches relating sacred sites to stars and constellations. To be precise, when viewed together the cathedrals make up the image of the main body of stars that form the Constellation of Virgo (see figure 104).

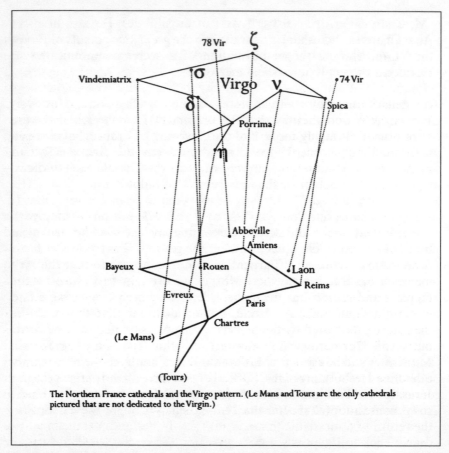

The Northern France cathedrals and the Virgo pattern. (Le Mans and Tours are the only cathedrals pictured that are not dedicated to the Virgin.)

Figure 104. The Northern France cathedrals and the Virgo pattern.

280

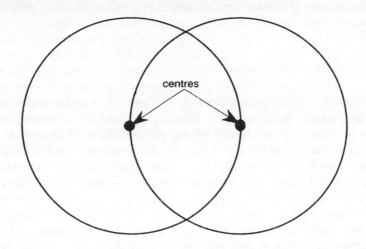

Figure 105.

Apart from Le Mans and Tours cathedrals, all of them are dedicated to the Virgin Mary. Here we have a startlingly apt manifestation of the Hermetic dictum 'As above, so below'. This definitely suggests a continuity of an ancient tradition to represent the patterns of constellations as physical realities on the Earth. My question was: *Why*? What exactly were they trying to tell us? The builders of these cathedrals were obviously highly motivated and inspired by a vision of awesome scale; building just one involved an enormous amount of time, effort and money, but to build *several* they must have a very good reason to convey this message. We shall see later just what that message is.

Adrian Gilbert points out in *The Magi*[9] that in the Virgo figure, Reims Cathedral represents the star Spica, the one that seems to be symbolised both by a sheaf of wheat and a lily flower. Owing to its Royal connections, Reims, not Chartres, was the most important cathedral in medieval France. It was where Kings of France were crowned. Reims therefore, *practically and figuratively*, represents the place of the *'fleur de lys'* and it signifies the Annunciation, the selection of a woman to bear the future prophesied Messiah. In a subtle way, the Virgo figure spread out across Northern France was indicating an expectancy that the next Messiah would be French and of Royal Blood, i.e. from the Merovingian bloodline (see Chapter 24). So his advent was no longer expected in Jerusalem, but in France. This may be one of the reasons why the French royal house adopted the *'fleur de lys'* as their symbol. However, awaiting the return of a messianic figure is not the whole story. Yet again we are drawn back to Egypt when we realise that the symbol of Osiris was the *'fleur de lys'*. Once more, my belief that a message endured from antiquity was reinforced. We shall look closely at the Osiris myths in the next chapter.

Revealing patterns across England

To further my belief that all these details are connected and point back to Egypt, I shall introduce more information relating to sacred sites in England, *which are of **direct** relevance to Egypt*. Over the years I constantly heard rumours about sacred alignments on the Marlborough Downs in Wiltshire. My studies had revealed Templar connections, evident in the presence of Temple Farm, an old Templar holding. Try as I might, I could not make any significant headway or see any irrefutable connections. I had made extensive studies of Avebury, as we saw earlier, which is situated in the area in question, but that was as far as I could take things. Then I came across a book by David Furlong, titled *Keys to the Temple*.[10] He had spent many years researching the Marlborough Downs looking for sacred connections, much as I had. However, he made the unique discovery of sacred alignments formed as two over-lapping circles, creating a central device almost identical to the layout of the Vesica Pisces (see figures 105 and 106).

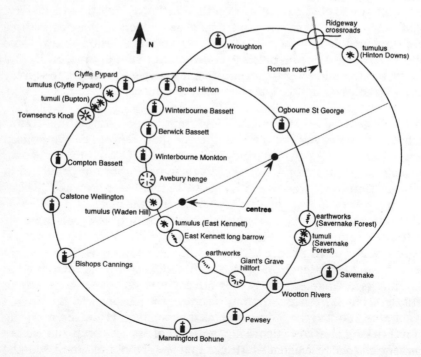

Figure 106.

Furlong backed up his thesis with maps that showed beyond any shadow of a doubt that he had *not* simply fudged the alignments to fit his theory. As we have already seen, the Vesica Pisces became central to Christian mysticism in the Middle Ages. It is also the geometric pattern used to define accurately the layout and proportions of the Great Pyramid itself, as we saw earlier. A typical Vesica Pisces is formed when two circles are intersected at their centres, as in figure 105.

Furlong[11] could not make his two circles match this exactly, as their centre points were in fact off centre. However, his circles' joint 'equator' recalled the 'Long Ley Line', as proposed by Alfred Watkins,[12] which ran across the width of England from St Michael's Mount, through Glastonbury Tor, Avebury and on to Bury St Edmunds Abbey. This ley is not actually dead straight in the true sense of the word, but is certainly straight enough for a projected line on a curved surface such as that of the Earth. I was initially interested by this line due to its connections with Joseph of Arimathea, but also noted that it ran in a north-easterly direction across the country. I assumed this, and not that it was a reverse south-westerly direction, because of the importance laid upon Joseph of Arimathea's landing at St Michael's Mount. Furthermore, I was already away of the significance of the 'north-easterly' aspect from Freemason rituals (see figure 107).

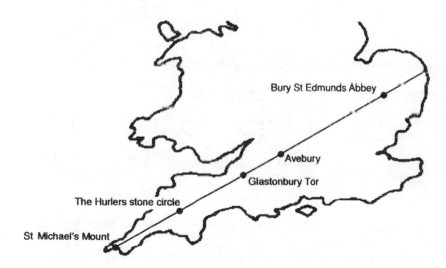

Figure 107.

As for Furlong,[13] as Avebury is an important site on both the circle alignment *and* the St Michael's Mount Ley line, he plotted the Ley line against his circular alignment circles very precisely. When he did, it

283

immediately became apparent that the Ley line ran *parallel* to the centre of axis line of the two circles (see figure 108).

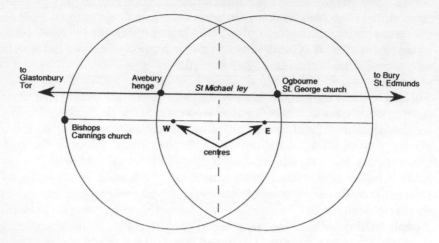

Figure 108.

After many hours hunched over his drawing board, Furlong thought of including an equilateral triangle on his maps within the circles, starting from the two circles 'central points (see figure 109).[14]

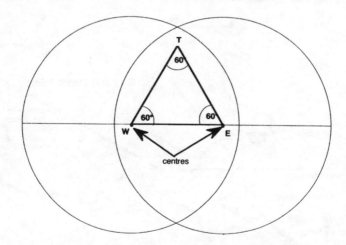

Figure 109.

He then drew two further lines from the apex to the edges of the central axis line where they cross the circles. The final image was an almost exact scale representation of the dimensions and angle of the Great Pyramid of Giza (see figure 110).[15]

284

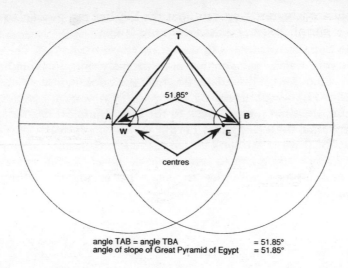

angle TAB = angle TBA   = 51.85°
angle of slope of Great Pyramid of Egypt   = 51.85°

Figure 110.

Even the angle produced was 51.85 degrees, which has often been quoted
as the mean average of the Great Pyramid's angle. (Its *exact* angle is, as
we know, 51.51 degrees.) I could readily accept this information and I
was more than intrigued. What's more, I was enthralled when it was also
demonstrated that when a scale representation of the Great Pyramid
itself is superimposed over the circle's layout, the King's Chamber falls

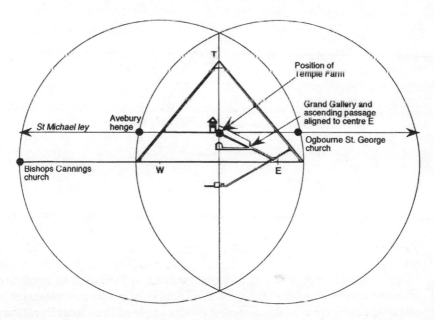

Figure 111.

exactly on the St Michael Ley at the place of the Templar holding, Temple Farm. Furthermore, the junction of the ascending and descending passages aligned to the centre (E on the figure). The chances of this happening by pure chance are extremely slim. Furlong had been very meticulous with his calculations, as his book demonstrates, and I was inclined to accept his theory, especially in view of my own research. Yet again, the clues pointed back to the Giza complex, primarily to the Great Pyramid itself (see figure 111).

However, if we are to look closer at the Giza complex in view of the above, we are first going to have to look closely at ancient Egyptian myths and legends, in order to get a better understanding of the pyramids.

Chapter 28

The Role of the Osiris Ritual

November 1993. Germany. I was very damp and tired, and the drone of the Landrover's engine combined with the whine of the tyres was sending both Bill (whom I'd just met) and me to sleep. Sleet was washing down the windscreen as the rather pathetic wipers fought a losing battle to keep it clear. We were on a major NATO exercise and had been in the field for 2 weeks. At 2.00 a.m. we had received a signal to move out from our hill-top location. In freezing cold temperatures and a wind chill of nearly minus 14 degrees, decamouflaging our 2 main trucks was no mean feat. One 4-ton truck got stuck in the mud, which meant nearly 2 hours of agonising effort trying to free it, getting totally soaked in the process.

Once on our way, we had a 270-mile journey to complete in atrocious weather. I was navigating as Bill drove. This was my first exercise with a Signals unit. I had tried the Special Forces and the Infantry, and after a break from the reserve forces I had re-enlisted, this time into the Signals. I felt pulled to go to Special Forces again but I had to be honest with myself; I was no longer a very fit spring chicken. Doing selection would probably kill me this time around. Besides, my wife was very opposed to my even joining the reserves again, let alone Special Forces. It was my father who polarised everything: 'There's plenty of trouble in the world already. Why go looking for more?' And so I found myself being attached to Bill, who was a Captain in the Signals, to learn all the procedures of running a Signals troop.

I was almost dozing off when Bill wound down the window to let in the freezing air. 'Talk to me Nigel . . . or we die,' he muttered, very matter-of-fact but meaning it. And so I did; all about pyramids, ancient technology, the Templars, Stonehenge, and just about anything else I could think of on the subject. I gave my theories of the Orion constellation lining up with the 3 Giza pyramids as I had noted back in 1983. Instead of assuming that I was obviously off my head, Bill was quite intrigued, despite being a hardened sceptic. I even proffered the notion of a so-called 'Hall of Records' and that I thought I knew where it was; to which Bill replied, 'Why haven't you gone and proved it?' The inference was, if I was so certain of its existence and location, plus the possible benefits to mankind, I had a moral duty to at least attempt to uncover it. My excuses fell on deaf ears – I was told to put my money where my mouth was. As a consequence of this freezing, miserable journey, and my attempts to keep Bill awake, 'Operation Hermes' was eventually conceived – and Bill is a director of the company itself.

The Orion story breaks

Nearly 3 months later I was sitting next to my mother on a packed commuter train from London to Colchester. My mother had had to attend a hospital appointment, after which I dragged her off to the British Museum, to do some research. As we sat chatting, I looked down the aisle of the train and saw a man was reading the *Independent* newspaper. As my mother talked, he folded his paper to a new page revealing a large graphic of the 3 Giza pyramids with the stars of Orion's belt projected above them: 'Trying to build heaven on Earth' was the headline. My heart missed several beats as I stared, transfixed, at this diagram at the other end of the carriage. I felt as though I had developed tunnel vision, and seemed to zoom in on the article. Keeping a firm look at it I got up and walked towards the newspaper reader.

Next thing I was kneeling down next to the poor man, pulling his paper up straight to view it properly. He looked at me in total surprise. I apologised for appearing rude and pointed out that I had just noticed his article, which was of direct relevance to research I was working on. I offered to buy his paper, by which time all the occupants of the carriage were looking at me, wondering what was going on. Red-faced, the city gent simply folded his paper and offered it to me for free. It was Tuesday, 1 February 1994: I know, because I still have the paper to this day.

As I read the article, half of me almost felt cheated; someone else had independently certified what I had been arguing, *and* managed to get his research published. But then I realised that this could only serve my purpose. Perhaps now, friends and family wouldn't think of me as totally 'out there' with the other 'Space cadets' – as my elder brother would often term them. When I had made the connection with Orion's belt stars to the 3 main pyramids in Giza, I had tried to marry up the other stars of Orion with other pyramids but with no result. Here 2 researchers, Robert Bauval and Adrian Gilbert, claimed to prove that Orion's stars *did* marry up with other pyramids – except one. I was amazed. What had I done wrong to miss the connection? I had to get their published research asap. The very next day I bought their book, *The Orion Mystery*.[1]

In it, Bauval and Adrian Gilbert demonstrate very convincingly that the Giza pyramids, plus a few others, were deliberately built as a giant map of the heavens. They had used an astronomical computer to recreate the night skies over Egypt 4,500 years ago, when the pyramids were built. I had argued this for years but met with total indifference and ridicule, especially from the academic world, so I was more than surprised to read that a leading British Egyptologist, Dr Jaromir Malek of Oxford University's Griffith Institute and Ashmolean Museum, was prepared to concede that perhaps Bauval and Gilbert could be correct, but the theory would need to be assessed properly if it was to be taken seriously. Dr Geraldine Pinch of Cambridge University's Oriental Studies faculty was also quoted in the *Independent*'s article as being prepared to take the new proposal seriously.

Was my error not considering whether the stars in 4,500 BC could be in a slightly different position, one that *did*, then, marry up to the other pyramids? No. After reading their book I soon realised that I was not wrong in my earlier assumptions, as I shall explain later. This does not mean that Bauval or Gilbert's theories were in error. Bauval had realised that one of the 4 shafts inside the Great Pyramid, that pointed upwards, would have pointed straight at the highest point in the sky reached by the star Zeta Orionis, which is one of the 3 belt stars of Orion. As we have seen Orion was known to the ancient Egyptians as Osiris, the Lord of the Afterlife. Moreover, a second shaft pointed straight at Sirius, identified as Isis.

Bauval said that all 7 Fourth-Dynasty pyramids were arranged on the ground to match exactly the 7 key stars of the constellation of Orion and its neighbouring star group, the Hyades. My own personal researches, however, had *not* matched up these other sites exactly. The point here is that the stars' positions did not alter as regards their distances apart; only their position as a constellation relative to the background night sky altered when viewed in 4,500 BC. Hyades is often identified with Osiris's evil brother, Set. As I read *The Orion Mystery* I could see that the stars of Orion and the Hyades did, to all intents and purposes, marry up with these Fourth Dynasty pyramids, but not *exactly*. There was a discrepancy of a couple of miles in some cases. Knowing how exact the ancient builders of these sites had been, and that the 3 main Giza Pyramids married up *exactly* with the 3 belt stars of Orion, with each pyramid's size being relative to the star's brightness, I couldn't help but think that the only *true* pyramid/star alignments were those of the Giza 3 alone. What's more, keeping in mind my researches relating to the sites in England and the Americas, it seemed to me that it was always the 3 main belt stars of Orion that were reproduced – across the globe. If you look at the projection of the constellation of Orion over the other pyramids, you will note that the distances apart are not identical (see figure 112).

When I actually took out my map of Egypt and overlaid a projection of the stars, the difference was of nearly 2 miles, both for the Zawiyet El Aryan pyramid and the Abu Roash pyramid, as I had noted back in 1983 when I had tried desperately to make them fit. The Bent and Red pyramids that represented the Hyades group when projected in exact proportion and distance were several miles off as well; the stars were

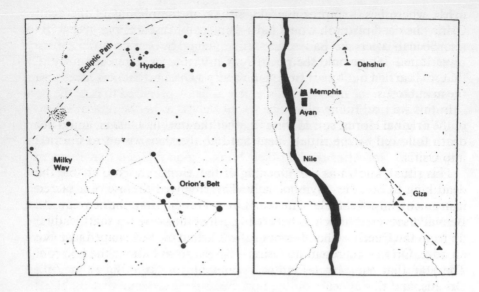

Figure 112. Note the shape and distances between two diagrams of Orion are different. They do not match exactly.

projected over barren desert to the west. This reinforced my belief that the 3 main Giza pyramids alone demanded closer inspection. In view of the ancients' use of symbology, I also felt that the other pyramids were indeed built to represent the constellation – but purely in a symbolic manner, so exact distances for these were not essential. The Nile was also used to represent the Milky Way in *The Orion Mystery*,[2] which made perfect sense. So in effect, then, what Bauval and Gilbert were arguing is not necessarily incorrect simply because the other minor stars of the Orion and Hyades groups didn't exactly marry up. If anything it reinforces their argument, as it makes one look even closer at the Giza pyramids, *because* they are so precisely aligned.

The Osiris ritual

In *The Orion Mystery*, Bauval and Gilbert[3] explain the purpose behind the construction of the pyramids. They believe that the Great Pyramid was built as a place of ritual ceremony where re-enactments of the ancient Osiris myth were carried out. This, they believed, involved placing the dead pharaoh (having already completed a symbolic journey, first across the Nile – representing the Milky Way – to Heliopolis, then to Letopolis and finally back to Giza) inside the Queen's Chamber, opposite the shaft that pointed to Sirius. Just as in the original Osiris myth, where Isis is impregnated by sitting on the phallus of the dead Osiris, the dead pharaoh would have then symbolically impregnated Isis (i.e. Sirius), after *she* had semi-revived *him*. The symbolically 'semi-resuscitated' king would then be reborn into the next world by a ritual that was carried out by his son, who in turn would be the next king, and the next Horus.

In this way, all ruling pharaohs were believed to be the reincarnation of the original Horus, son of Isis and (posthumously) of Osiris, and after death followed by the rituals mentioned above, they were transformed into Osiris.

This ritual, known as the 'Opening of the Mouth', was to enable the dead king to breathe — symbolically. This involved the use of a sacred instrument, an adze made of meteoric iron, i.e. iron from the heavens. As Bauval discovered (much to his credit), when the northern shaft leading up from the Queen's Chamber points to a group of stars shaped just like an adze, Orion – representing Osiris – is seen to rise above the horizon. The star that the Great Pyramid represents in Orion's belt is Zeta Orionis, and this appears on the horizon at the exact moment the shaft points to the adze in the sky. Bauval believes that immediately after the 'Opening of the Mouth' ritual in front of the Queen's Chamber northern shaft, the 'reborn' king was taken higher up inside the pyramid to the King's Chamber, which has a shaft that points to the central belt star of Orion – Epsilon Orionis. Bauval had been able to confirm his conclusion (i.e. that the dead pharaohs believed they would be reborn as stars in the constellation of Orion) from the many references in perhaps one of the world's oldest corpuses of religious writings, known as the 'Pyramid Texts', which come from the walls of burial chambers built in the period of the Old Kingdom, during the latter half of the 3rd millennium BC.

It is my firm belief that these myths and rituals were acted out in order to preserve the message behind them – that is, to highlight the constellation of Orion and the star Sirius. As I have frequently mentioned, the use of symbolism is an essential part of the way information from the ancients has been transmitted, even though the exact thing symbolised has become obscured. This means that the Giza pyramids were not *exclusively* constructed as a place to act out the rituals described above. If that *was* their sole purpose, a far less complicated construction in both size and precision would have sufficed to achieve the same end. There must be another reason why a unified plan was executed – *on such a monumental scale*. We shall see why later.

My many years of research had made one thing blindingly obvious: Orion's special importance was global, and so its symbology had evolved and adapted to be incorporated into many religions and ancient sites across the world. What also became increasingly apparent (though it was not immediately obvious at first) was that the *purpose* of Orion was its function as a pointer to the brightest star, i.e. Sirius. In his book *The*

Magi,[4] Adrian Gilbert maintains that the star which guided the 3 Kings to the birth of Jesus, as detailed in the Gospel of Matthew, was Sirius. Writers such as von Däniken tried to explain the phenomenon as a hovering spaceship; others have argued that it was an exploding supernova. I incline to Gilbert's thesis, that it was indeed Sirius, portrayed symbolically. Matthew, it must be remembered, wrote his account nearly a generation after the events he describes. As Gilbert explained, Matthew's readership would have been more Gentile and Egyptian than Jew, so he needed to prove to the Egyptians, Greeks, Syrians and others that his Messiah, Jesus, was not just another Jewish prophet, but a universal saviour. In order to establish Jesus's credentials, so to speak, Matthew would have had to associate him with Sirius, the royal 5-pointed star of Isis and Horus.

As we have seen, the ancient Egyptians based their calendar upon the movements of Sirius. Sirius is associated with Isis and her son, Horus, who, we have seen, was conceived magically from the seed of the dead Osiris. Another important element here is the image of Isis as mother and Horus as child, a very popular icon in ancient Egypt. This imagery is remarkably similar to the Christian iconography of the Virgin Mary with the baby Jesus. However, reconsider my earlier research relating to Mary Magdalene carrying the Holy Grail (i.e. the child of Jesus) and the similarity becomes even more potent, as Mary Magdalene would also, unlike the virgin, have been a widow. Horus is often pictured sitting upon Isis's lap and either suckling her breast or, more commonly, raising one finger to his lips, a gesture meaning, 'Keep the Secret'. As Christianity spread, Isis, the mother goddess, who was popular in the Roman Empire of the time as well as Egypt, became Mary, the Queen of Heaven. As Gilbert pointed out, the latter's title of 'Stella Maris' ('Star of the Sea') betrays the origins of her cult. The sea in question is not the Mediterranean Sea but the ocean above, i.e. the sky, and the 'Star of the Sea' is the brightest star in the heavens, Sirius, the star of Isis. Earlier I pointed out that when Joseph of Arimathea journeyed across the Mediterranean accompanied by Mary Magdalene and the Holy Grail, the ship that carried them, also named the *Stella Maris*, was one with no oars or sails. The lack of these typical nautical elements clearly denotes its esoteric importance, i.e. its connection with, and symbolic representation of, Sirius.

Ancient perceptions of the Great Pyramid

We shall look at the Sirius connection in regard to the Great Pyramid later, but now I would like to explain further biblical links to the Great Pyramid. One of the links deals with the name Jehovah and the Great Pyramid, which was known as 'The building of light', and also 'The way';

we have already seen how these same 2 words are related to Hermes and the Great Pyramid by way of gematria. As I pointed out, the saying 'I am the way and the light' (or 'the life') occurs regularly in the Bible.

Jesus, knowing full well the symbolism of the Pyramid, spoke about it; in particular as in Matthew 21: 42. 'The stone which the builders rejected has become the chief corner stone.' You will recall that Jesus later declared that Simon/Peter was to become the chief corner stone of his Church. We also know, as mentioned earlier, that Peter in gematria equals 755, the perimeter base length in feet of each face of the Great Pyramid. In addition, the perimeter in *metres* equals 921.44, which not only equals half a degree of equatorial latitude, but also is the same duration of Jesus' ministry in days as we saw earlier.

The Great Pyramid has always been the focus of astrologers and esotericists, since way before the Middle Ages. The ancient Egyptians claimed that it was nothing less than a 'Temple of Initiation'. Its apparent function was to bestow supernatural powers and magical knowledge on all candidates who were prepared to submit themselves to its mysteries. As Peter Lemesurier points out in *The Great Pyramid, Your Personal Guide*,[5] there is no lack of circumstantial evidence to support this. The ancient Egyptian *Book of the Dead* is full of identical references to the Pyramid's initiatory role. In the Saïte version, it even contains what seem to be direct references to passages and chambers within the Great Pyramid. Each of the following appears to be associated with some specific stage in the initiatory process. Again, this is a clear indication that hidden information about the actual layout of the Great Pyramid is being carried through time in sacred teachings and doctrines.

These resemblances are so convincing that the eminent late 19th-century Egyptologist Gaston Maspero declared: 'The Pyramids and the *Book of the Dead* reproduce the same original, the one in words, the other in stone.'[6] (See figure 113.)

Knowing this, years later when I started researching the Edfu Building Texts, I could not help but believe that the description of the 'Chambers of Creation' outlined therein likewise referred to a real location. I shall reveal this later in detail.

Objections could be raised to the connections between the *Book of the Dead* and the Pyramid's passages, as the 'chapters' of the *Book of the Dead* were originally found inscribed upon burial papyri and sarcophagi, and as such are viewed as more to do with the progress of the soul through the underworld after death than with an initiation ceremony of the living. However, it must be remembered that the so-called *Book of the Dead*'s real title is *The Book of Coming Forth by Day*, which is more suggestive of an application to the living. From my point of view, this debate is irrelevant, as it is the actual hidden information that is

BOOK OF THE DEAD	GREAT PYRAMID
Gate of the North	Entrance to Great Pyramid
Double Arched Gate of the Horizon	Double gable over entrance passage
The Descent	Descending passage
The Hidden Lintel	Roof-block formerly concealing entrance to ascending passage
The Door of Ascent	Entrance to ascending passage
The Hall of Truth in Darkness	Ascending passage
The Hall of Truth in Light	Grand Gallery
The Double Hall of Truth	Ascending passage and Grand Gallery
The Crossing of the Pure Roads of Life	Intersection of upper passageways
The Well of Life	Well shaft
The Orbit	Grooves in Grand Gallery's side walls
The Throne of Radiance/Judgement	Great Step
The Royal Arch of the Solstice	Entrance to King's Chamber Passage
The Passage of the Veil	King's Chamber Passage
The Chamber of the Triple Veil	Antechamber
The Chamber of the Open Tomb/Resurrection	King's Chamber
The Path of the Coming Forth of the Regenerated Soul	Queen's Chamber Passage
The Chamber of the Moon/Regeneration/ Rebirth	Queen's Chamber
The Chamber of the Shadow	Lesser Subterranean Chamber
The Chamber of Ordeal/Central Fire	Great Subterranean Chamber
The Gate of the West	Upper or lower entrance to well-shaft, or recess in west wall of Subterranean Chambers
The Secret Places of the Hidden God	Construction chambers

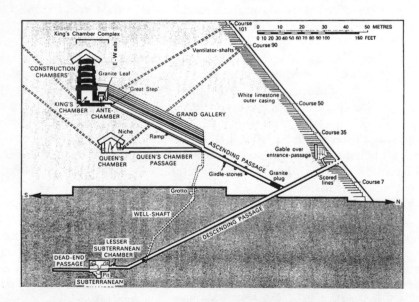

Figure 113. The angle from the Queen's Chamber niche vertically upwards to Great Step is exactly 64° to the angle of the Grand Gallery and ascending passage.

important regardless of how it was initially interpreted. Nonetheless, it is worth noting that the whole basis of the *Book of the Dead*, and the central motif of ancient Egyptian religion, was the life, descent into Hell, struggles, death and resurrection of Osiris himself. As Graham Hancock relates in *Fingerprints of the Gods*,[7] he suspected that the myth of Osiris was much more than just a myth: it was deliberately employed by 'the long-dead mythmakers' to guide initiates through a maze of clues to secret reservoirs of lost scientific knowledge. As such, the Osiris myth as dramatised and acted out each year in ancient Egypt in the form of a play, was in reality a secret message passed down as a treasured tradition since prehistoric times, and also included the values of precessional cycles and other celestial calculations.

Chapter 29

Dates in Turmoil

Dating the Sphinx

The Sphinx, the guardian built next to the 3 pyramids on the Giza plateau, is a time enigma; for centuries various cultures have tried to explain and date it. Conventionally, the Sphinx is dated to the Fourth Dynasty (*c.* 2565 BC) simply because a stele (a commemorative pillar or tablet) was found that had been erected by Thutmosis IV in around 1,400 BC, which mentioned Pharaoh Khafre (or Chephren). However, it has been shown that this much-eroded stele actually relates to *restoration* carried out on the Sphinx during the time of the Pharaoh Khafre, not the *building* of the Sphinx itself. Even the eminent Egyptologist Sir Wallis Budge stated that, 'This marvellous object was in existence in the days of Khafre, and was, most probably, very old at that early period.' However, geological evidence conclusively proves that it was constructed at least as long ago as 10,000 to 11,500 BC. This was the time when the Earth's precessional cycle was passing through the zodiacal constellation of Leo the Lion, hence the Sphinx has a lion's body with a humanoid head. Earlier I pointed out how I made the simple connection of dating the Sphinx to the Zodiacal time scale of Leo, but as we shall cover in a moment, there is now hard scientific fact to back up this argument; certainly it is significant that the Sphinx is set to face the Leo constellation as it rises (see figure 114). The Sphinx is also related to phoenix myths and legends that deal with celestial phenomena and stellar alignments, alignments that are apparently due to occur soon. The Sphinx has the front paws and chest of the lion, the hindquarters of a bull, the head of a man and originally had side boxes in its body, the remnants of which are still visible, which were filled with burning oil that at night forced out a huge plume of flame, giving the impression of wings. The Phoenix myth and its connection with Earthly cycles relates to the reversals of the Earth's magnetic poles at regular intervals of time that are triggered off by Sunspot and solar activity when the Sun's magnetic polarity reverses. The Mayans detailed these events in their ancient prophecies, as we shall see later.

How did this radical reappraisal of the Sphinx come about?

The man who fixed the attention of the world's media – and orthodox

296

Figure 114(a). As seen in 10,450 BC.

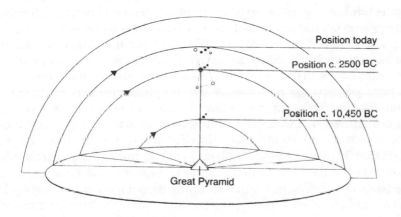

Figure 114(b). Precession and the stars of Orion's belt.

Egyptologists – on the fact that the Sphinx could be scientifically proved to be at least 11–12,000 years old was an American scholar, John Anthony West.[1] It was the French mathematician R. A. Schwaller de Lubicz[2] who first noticed the signs of weathering on the Sphinx and its enclosure, and a simple statement to this effect in one of his books caught West's eye and led him to investigate the matter further. He maintained

297

that other specialists had missed the clues to this, not because they had failed to find them, but because they had failed to interpret them correctly. West's evidence had primarily focused upon certain key structures such as the Sphinx, the Valley Temple at Giza and the mysterious Osireion (a temple to Osiris) at Abydos. (Abydos, remember, is the location of the strange hieroglyph that looks like a modern aircraft – see plates.)

Many previous claims that the Sphinx, Osireion and other related temples were far older than the accepted view allowed had been dismissed as over-imaginative and unfounded speculation. West's theory could not be so easily dispelled. He argued that scientific geological evidence clearly indicated erosion of these sites by water falling upon them vertically. The only time that such a quantity of water was available to cause this was during the 'Pluvial' period, immediately following the last Ice Age, *c.*11,000 BC. In simple terms, the weathering on these structures (this is particularly evident on the Sphinx enclosure walls – see plates), which shows distinctive precipitation-induced (i.e. rainfall) erosion, means that these structures must have been constructed prior to 10,000 BC. West's view was later validated by the American geologist, Dr Robert Schoch, a Professor of Geology at Boston University.[3] Schoch's findings on West's theory were endorsed by nearly 300 of his peers at the 1992 annual convention of the Geological Society of America. At the time, as Graham Hancock revealed,[4] a rather acrimonious dispute began between geologists and Egyptologists. This was perhaps understandable; what was at stake was a complete upheaval in accepted views about the evolution of human civilisation. As West stated:

> We are told that the evolution of human civilisation is a linear process – that it goes from stupid cavemen to smart old us with our hydrogen bombs and striped toothpaste. But the proof that the Sphinx is many, many thousands of years older than archaeologists think it is, that it preceded by many thousands of years even dynastic Egypt, means that there must have been, at some distant point in history, a high and sophisticated civilisation – just as all the legends affirm.[5]

Since West's and Schoch's findings were publicly aired in 1992, much of the animosity between geology and Egyptology has diminished considerably, especially among the young and newly qualified. This is very encouraging.

West's chronology is this. Around 10,000 BC the Sahara Desert was a relatively green savannah, with lakes and plenty of animal wildlife, that extended across much of upper Egypt. The Northern Nile Delta was marshy, with many large fertile islands, and the climate was far cooler and rainier than it is now. Between 13,000 and 9,000 BC it rained almost constantly. This period of constant rain ended after severe flooding – as

Graham Hancock suggests, 'as though marking an ecological turning-point'. This period coincides remarkably closely with the myths and legends that relate to a worldwide deluge in antiquity, the flood of Noah recounted in the Bible being just one. From then onwards conditions became increasingly arid and warmer, until *c.* 7,000 BC when the Neolithic Subpluvial period began, causing 1,000 years of heavy rainfall followed by 3,000 years of moderate rainfall. It was during this moderate period, when the desert bloomed, that humans colonised it.

However, by the time of the early Egyptian Dynasties (*c.* 3,000 BC) the climate had changed *again* – to its present arid and hot state. Archaeological evidence shows early agricultural experimentation during the period between 13,000 and 10,000 BC. This epoch was marked by dramatic Earth displacements, climate shifts, rising sea levels, volcanic eruptions and floods. It is because of the weathering on such sites as the Sphinx, the Osireion and the Valley Temple that West and Schoch argue[6] that their construction dates must have been prior to 10,000 BC, because in order to suffer the water erosion so clearly evident, they had to have experienced centuries of exposure. Professor Arthur Posnansky of the University of La Paz argues the same for the astonishing Bolivian city of Tiahuanaco, which in his opinion, based on scientific research, was constructed prior to the immense floods of the Andes, *c.* 11,000 BC.[7] In fact, Posnansky demonstrates that this exceptional South American site was most probably built around 15,000 BC.

If the likes of West, Schoch and Posnansky are correct – and I agree with them, as I have further evidence to support their claims – history will have to be rewritten. It's that simple.

The Pyramids – kicking over the traces . . .

If the real age of the Sphinx has provoked debate heated to boiling point, where does that leave the Pyramids? Presently accepted history tells us that the pyramids of Giza were constructed during the Fourth Dynasty era. This alone presents itself as an obvious anomaly that Egyptologists have not answered properly. I will explain why. Zoser's Step Pyramid at Saqqara, about 8 miles from Giza (see plates), was built, so the current view holds, during the Third Dynasty – this I can agree with. It is rather small in comparison with the magnificent structures at Giza and was built from small manageable blocks. Then all of a sudden, the Fourth-Dynasty pyramids of Giza and at Dashur appear, constructed to an unsurpassed level of technical ability that we cannot duplicate today. Then, in the Fifth and Six Dynasties, pyramid technology took a huge backwards slide; the results were so poorly constructed that most of them are now just mounds of rubble and brick; one near Dashur (see plates) is a depressingly prime example. Yet the Giza and Dashur pyramids still stand intact, despite the ravages of time and despite having their outer casing stone being stripped for other building projects. Surely there is a mystery here? Undoubtedly this freakish sequence of accomplishment followed by the second-rate – or worse – provoked my thought processes. I *had* to establish their true ages. Before I outline how I did so, I would like to introduce you to just a few of the enigmatic facts surrounding the Great Pyramid.

As I have explained, when the 3 belt stars of the Orion constellation are projected onto the Giza Pyramids, the layout is identical, with each pyramid's size directly proportional to its allocated star's brightness, and the River Nile runs a course in relation to the Pyramids that is almost identical to the placing of the Milky Way (see figure 115).

Stars
1   Epsilon Tauri
2   Aldebaran
3   Gamma Orionis
4   Delta Orionis
5   Epsilon Orionis
6   Zeta Orionis
7   Kappa Orionis
8   Rigel
9   Betelgeuse

Pyramids
A   The Bent Pyramid
B   The Red Pyramid
C   Zawiyet El-Aryan
D   Pyramid of Menkura
E   Pyramid of Khafre
F   The Great Pyramid
G   Abu Roash

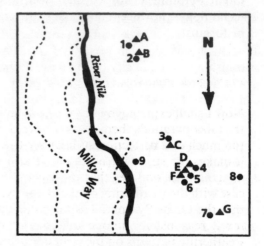

Figure 115. Symbolically, Orion is represented by the pyramids' relative positions only.

The Great Pyramid contains over 6,000,000 tons of stone, some 2.5 million blocks of various sizes, some weighing over 200 tons, though the majority weigh around 2.5 tons. We are taught that it took 100,000 men over 20 years to construct, but there is no archaeological proof to support this. Simple mathematics will also show that this cannot be correct. If 100,000 men were to work 24 hours a day, 7 days a week, 52 weeks of the year for 20 years (as the historian Herodotus claimed to have been told and which is today taught as fact) they would have to lay an average of over 342 of the typical 2.5-ton blocks *a day*. (Furthermore, to build a ramp up the side to drag the huge blocks up as theorised, would only exacerbate the problem, demanding more time. If you read Mark Lehner's book *The Complete Pyramids*,[8] you will note that on page 216, several theorised ramps are displayed. This demonstrates that Egyptologists do not know for certain how it was constructed. There is evidence of ramps being employed on far later and smaller constructions, but not at Giza.)

Now, to lay well over 300 2.5-ton blocks a day is an impossible feat; all modern attempts at moving and positioning just one or two such blocks have taken a full day to achieve with any degree of accuracy. To further compound the problem, how were the huge blocks transported from their quarries at Tura on the east bank of the Nile, about 10 miles away? Today we can only just manage to lift and position a 200-ton block of stone, and that is with a machine that has a 120-ton counter weight, and is manned by 20 engineers; what's more, it takes several days to organise. (We can just about lift heavier weights up and down, but cannot move them any distance). And there are only 2 of these machines in existence anywhere in the world. To understand that it was possible to build the Great Pyramid at all, we shall need to look at the realities of ancient technology, however unsettling the result might be for orthodox historians.

Proving the great age of the pyramids

Now I shall explain why I am so convinced of the enormous antiquity of the Giza pyramids themselves. I have been accused many times of being too much of a perfectionist, but I see this as beneficial to my research, as it makes me strive for accuracy; it also means that I sometimes notice nagging little oddities that most people miss. This was particularly the case with the weathering on the Great Pyramid itself. I became suspicious that the Great Pyramid was far older than accepted chronology states, for 2 reasons: its unique qualities of construction, and the peculiar weathering patterns on the remaining facing stones and platform stones. As with the Sphinx, the weathering had been caused by prolonged rainfall over thousands of years. If accepted chronology is to be believed, giving the Great Pyramid a Fourth-Dynasty origin, when was the period of rainfall that caused the erosion? Since the first dynasties (nearly 3000 BC), Egypt has been arid and dry. As we saw earlier, the only tenable period of continual rainfall was *c.* 11,000 BC.

Before looking more closely at the Great Pyramid's weathering, it is instructive to consider the other so-called Fourth-Dynasty pyramids at Dashur – the Red and Bent pyramids (see plates). There is considerable debate as to who exactly built these. The Pharaoh Sneferu has been traditionally described as the builder of both, and credited with building a third pyramid at Meidum. Sneferu only reigned for 24 years, so it stretches credibility to believe that he had the time or resources to construct all 3 during his lifetime. In fact, there is evidence that pharaohs did build directly over existing mastaba tombs (square mausolea, up to 200 feet high), turning them into pyramids and claiming them for themselves, as 19th-century authority Sir William Flinders Petrie confirmed: 'From the successive coats of the mastaba-pyramids of Meidum, and Saqqara, it shows that the buildings quoted were completely finished and cased many times over, probably by successive kings.'[9]

The entrance to the pyramid at Meidum shows 3 distinctive styles. In any case, the fact that Sneferu is associated with 3 different pyramids is contrary to established orthodox principles of building a pyramid as a personal tomb. Was he going to have himself cut into 3 parts? Or can we accept what Egyptology tells us – that he simply changed his mind (*twice*) and fancied another tomb elsewhere? The root of the problem lies with the initial impetus to such attributions. All references that connect these pyramids with Sneferu were found *outside*, in the mortuary temple, on carved reliefs or on shards of pottery. By contrast, the *interiors* of the Fourth-Dynasty pyramids were completely devoid of any such markings (or indeed, any other kind; even the red quarry marks inside the Great Pyramid's relieving chambers have been shown to have been faked). It is only the pyramids of inferior design that feature inscriptions and carved reliefs – in total contrast to these pyramids and the equally unmarked Osireion. Why?

To return to the Great Pyramid, we should consider how the original casing blocks were positioned upon the basement paving. The casing blocks stopped short of the pavement blocks, meaning that a portion of the pavement slab was exposed whilst the rest was covered and thus protected from the elements. As a result, we can see that the exposed sections of pavement are more obviously weathered than the protected covered portions (see figure 116 and plates).

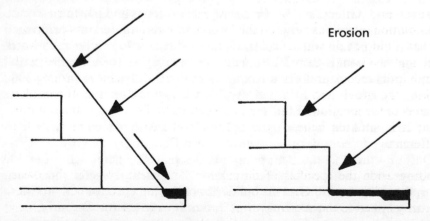

Figure 116. Notice area protected by outer casing stones is only 5 mm eroded, whilst exposed area is up to 250 mm (erosion rate not to scale in this diagram).

As the stone used on the Great Pyramid was of superior quality, the rate of erosion would be minimal over long periods of time. The mere 4,500 years presently cited as the Pyramid's age would not be sufficient to allow such erosion. For a start, the desert climate has been very dry for the past several thousand years, so any erosion would be of the absolute minimum and very slow. To compound the issue, the Great Pyramid was still covered in its polished white casing blocks of lumite (a durable form of limestone) until the 8th century AD, when it was removed for other building projects. The pavement slabs underneath the original casing would therefore have only been exposed to sun and sand erosion, with practically no water erosion as the region has been arid. Once the casing blocks had been removed, there would naturally be a large differential between the erosion of the exposed slab and the newly exposed portion of slab. This, it must be noted, is visible on the same single slab.

Compare the long-exposed portion and recently exposed section in the plates. The difference is immediately visible. The covered portion has been eroded to just less than 5mm since it was exposed in the 8th century AD – just over 1,000 years. This means an erosion rate of 5mm every 1,000 years, maximum. So, if the Great Pyramid was 4,500 years old, its original exposed pavement slabs should have been eroded only to a depth of 22.5mm. So why, then, do we find that they are actually eroded to a depth that ranges from a minimum of 50mm to nearly 250mm? If a constant erosion rate is presumed, relative to when the casing stones were removed just over 1,000 years ago, then the time required to erode the exposed pavement slabs to the present depth (at least 50mm) would be in the region of 10,000 years, and most likely longer.

Giza and the heavens

Bauval and Gilbert's *The Orion Mystery* certainly kick-started the commotion over links between the Giza pyramids and the stars of Orion. What it did not do was reveal the symbolic meanings behind the whole site and the rituals themselves. Bauval's later book (co-authored with Graham Hancock and titled *Keeper of Genesis*) did achieve progress in taking the rituals and Pyramid layout clues further, relating the hidden secrets to the location of the 'Hall of Records'.[10] They are of the opinion that it is situated beneath the Sphinx itself. My argument is rather different.

Setting aside the specifics of dating for a moment, what is the basic purpose of the entire Giza complex? It acts as an astronomical marker directly linked to the ancients' most important star, Sirius. We have seen just how important this star is within the ancient myths and that their encoded celestial information relating to Sirius itself is factually correct.

So, *why* is there nothing represented on the ground where Sirius should be, in relation to the way the Giza pyramids replicate the alignment of the belt stars of Orion? Its omission – and remember, Sirius was the most significant star to the ancients – screams at us to ask why. As we shall see, it is *not* missing; just hidden.

To recap, then, there are many reasons to believe that the Giza site is an astronomical marker, representing the constellation of Orion in the year *c.* 10,500 BC. We have seen that the weathering pattern certainly agrees with this period. But is there more evidence to prove that the original builders were able to tell us exactly what time period they were speaking from? I believe there is.

The Sphinx, with its leonine elements, is one good indicator for marking the epoch of Leo the Lion, but this is not totally reliable and sceptics can argue against this hypothesis. However, if we were to use precessional information, we have a more reliable mechanism for marking a set time period. As we have seen, a full cycle of precession takes nearly 26,000 years; as such, it affords far fewer opportunities for confusion, when used as a marker, than shorter periods such as centuries or even millennia.

We also saw that the equator of the Earth, when drawn out in space, forms a circle around the visible universe. This is known as the celestial equator and appears constant during the course of a normal human lifetime, so we see the same stars directly overhead on the same dates each year. Then, at 90 degrees to the celestial equator, we have what is referred to as the celestial pole (and on Earth, the North Pole). This presently points at the star Polaris. As I demonstrated earlier, the celestial equator is at a slightly different angle to that which the solar systems planets revolve around. This plane is known as the ecliptic and can also be drawn out into space to form a circle, one that is more constant than the celestial equator and will remain fixed in its position for millions of years. At 90 degrees to this circle, there is another pole, which is known as the Ecliptic pole; it is the Sun's pole, again constant over millions of years. Here, then, we have a larger version of the Earth's pole against that of the Earth's equator, thus giving us the Earth's pole and the pole of the Sun displaced from each other by 23.5 degrees.

Since the Sun's pole appears constant, it can be viewed as a fixed point within a circle, with the Earth's pole located on the perimeter travelling in a circular direction anti-clockwise. It takes nearly 26,000 years for the Earth's pole to complete one revolution around the Sun's pole. In other words, it takes 1,000 years to complete one of the 26 equal segments around the Sun's pole. Knowing this, we can start to use this method to date the Giza pyramids conclusively, without the need for the corroborative evidence of weathering or the clues inherent in the Sphinx.

Rather disconcertingly for those new to it, in the mythology of Egypt it was common for the gods to have a multitude of names as well as composite images, hence Ra was known also as Ra-Atum or Ra Horakhti (meaning 'Horus of the Horizon'), or Atum-Ra-Horakhti. So when the stele of Pharaoh Amenhotep II refers to the 'Pyramids of Hor em Ahket' it also means 'Pyramids of Horus in the Horizon'. Now, the hieroglyph representing horizon is two triangles looking like two pyramids on the horizon; moreover, that for the planet Earth is a single triangle tilted by 45 degrees. In addition, the stele of Thutmosis IV which stood between the paws of the Sphinx refers to the Sphinx as 'Atum Hor em Ahket', meaning 'Father God of Horus in the Horizon', and to the Giza plateau as 'Horizon of Heliopolis in the West'.

So here – as Bauval and Gilbert demonstrate in *The Orion Mystery*[11] – the Giza plateau is clearly being compared to a horizon. The question is, *which* horizon, and why is it of such importance? As I have already shown, the allegedly Fourth Dynasty pyramids of Giza, and the Red and Bent Pyramids, are unique in the superiority of their construction, compared with later pyramids. This suggests a unified plan linking the sites of Giza and Dashur, as Bauval and Gilbert propose. I had a suspicion that this was of great importance but as I could not match the other pyramids exactly, I had taken the investigation further, in regard to the Dashur pyramids' celestial context, only to the point of a speculative theory.

A stellar horizon?

Giza can be considered as having its own horizon, *a stellar horizon*; that is, a horizon at the edge of a planisphere, or star chart. As such, Giza in this symbolic position is a representation of the layout of this planisphere, with the constellation of Orion, married up to the 3 main Giza pyramids, sitting at the base of the chart. The horizons being referred to in this symbolic context are the celestial equator and the ecliptic equator, which the ancient Egyptians saw as 'Horizons'. This Giza planisphere theory has been overlooked in the obsessive fervour surrounding the Giza plateau site, to the detriment of the Dashur sites. Over the past 2 years, however, several people that I have come into contact with have started to suspect that the Dashur pyramids were also of great importance, and that they were part of a great key.

Before continuing on this argument it must be noted that of the 90-plus pyramids in Egypt, not one has ever been conclusively shown to contain a body. All recovered mummies have been found within tombs, such as those in the Valley of the Kings, or the huge funerary site near Helwan that has nearly 5,000 tombs of various sizes dating from the First and Second Dynasties. Some of these are pyramidal in shape, but are simply very basic structures built directly above a tomb. In 1953, Professor

Walter Emery[12] discovered a large tomb in the archaic cemetery of North Saqqara, attributed to a pharaoh of the First Dynasty – thought to be Uadyis. Apart from the main tomb, there were 72 other tombs arranged in 3 rows. In these tombs lay the servants who had voluntarily been buried along with their king.* This raised a crucial question: Why, if the pharaohs felt compelled to bury their servants and wealth along with themselves at death (as is evident from many tombs), weren't the Giza pyramids, supposedly the largest tombs ever built, similarly filled with treasures, servants and the bodies of the pharaohs who allegedly built them? The answer is obvious: they were not built as tombs in the first place.

In view of these facts we must put aside all the preconceived and inaccurate theories that the pyramids at Dashur and Giza were tombs, and accept them for what they are: components of a clearly and precisely executed single plan that deals with mathematics and celestial precession, both of which are constant.

The Dashur enigma

Whilst undergoing Special Forces training, we had to be very familiar with the constellations and how to determine our position accurately, anywhere on Earth, entirely without instruments. Naturally I buried myself in navigation and astronomy books. It was whilst doing this that I first of all noticed a connection between the Queen's Chamber's enigmatic corner niche and Sirius, (as I shall explain later), and I also became aware of the various phenomena relating to the Earth's celestial poles and the Sun's celestial poles, outlined earlier in this chapter. I had suspected that the Dashur pyramids were somehow connected with this phenomenon, but again, proving so was difficult. Then, in 1994, when poring over Bauval and Gilbert's research and their presentation that the Dashur pyramids married up to the Hyades stars, I again took a closer look, since I had not been able to establish this fact due to the large margin of error. Then it hit me in a rare moment of euphoria: the Dashur pyramids didn't marry up with the stars, *because they were not representing stars at all*. This was one of the most crucial discoveries I made. Instead, they represented points in space as marked by the Earth and Sun's celestial poles.

When researching the Bent Pyramid and its peculiar shape (see plates), I became aware that orthodox Egyptology holds that the angle was

* One aspect of this which caught my attention was the fact that the all-important number 72 was present. Not only that, but 64 of the bodies were male and the other 8 were female. The numbers here, apart from being symbolic, equal the values of 64 and 8 inherent in DNA and RNA.

changed halfway up because of construction problems. From an engineering point of view this is absurd, as it would prove far more difficult to change the angle than it would to continue the original one. No, the change was a deliberate feature of the design from the very start. Why? Let's look at the mainstream case in more detail. The Egyptologists' argument, that the change was due to construction problems, is based upon a few cracks within the pyramid itself. However, Egyptologists also state that early earthquakes caused the cracks found inside the Great Pyramid. Why can't this also apply to the Bent Pyramid? The Great Pyramid is actually constructed with alternating layers of stone of different thicknesses. It starts off at the base with thin layers and small stones then a thick course made with bigger stones, in total contrast to post-medieval building techniques, for example, where stones would get smaller as layers were built up. The reason why the ancient architects did this is simple. The alternating levels of thickness reduce the frequency and strength of any vibrating forces caused during an earthquake. This alone demonstrates a very high understanding of the frequency transmission of forces, indicating a technological ability not even equalled today.

In the Bent Pyramid, the lower angle is almost identical to that of the Great Pyramid, while that of the top half is identical to that of the Red Pyramid. Once more, it is mathematics that speaks to us from the Bent Pyramid – not unsubstantiated theory, or assumptions based upon fragments of pottery that supposedly date the pyramid to the Fourth Dynasty. If you look at figure 117, and extend the bottom portions of the Bent Pyramid upwards until they touch, a complete but taller pyramid is formed, with a base-length-to-height ratio of exactly 10:7, representing the Great Pyramid. If we extend the lines from the Bent Pyramid's actual apex downwards to the ground (as illustrated) a wider pyramid is formed, identical in size and angle to its close neighbour, the Red Pyramid. A logical plan was evidently being followed from the very beginning.

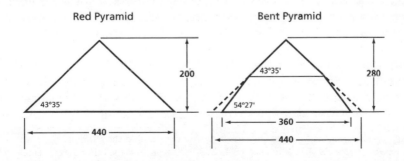

Red Pyramid   Bent Pyramid

Figure 117.

307

The Bent Pyramid has a smaller satellite pyramid constructed close to it. Now the interesting point here is that the ratio of the Bent Pyramid's base length of 360, in relation to the smaller satellite pyramid, is exactly 3.6:1, and the Earth, in relation to the Moon, also has a ratio of exactly 3.6:1. The Bent Pyramid represents the Earth and its satellite pyramid represents the Moon.

The Red Pyramid

The Red Pyramid at Dashur has a unique angle, compared with all other pyramids of similar size. This would indicate that it should be viewed differently from the Giza pyramids, which (as a whole complex) represent stars. In fact, the Red Pyramid actually represents a point in space marking the Sun's pole. The pyramid is representative of the Sun, so was constructed to resemble it by the use of red limestone. The Sun's pole, an extension of its axis into space, happens to point to the constellation of Draco, the Dragon. Dragons have frequently been symbolically represented as red, an obvious example being the Welsh dragon. It is piquant in the light of this that inside the Great Pyramid the north-pointing shaft from the Queen's Chamber points directly at the 5th star, Kochab, in the constellation of Ursa Minor, and that the shaft from the Queen's Chamber south wall points to Sirius. Sirius is a binary star, as we have seen made up from 2 major bodies – Sirius and the 'newly discovered' Sirius B – and Kochab is the 5th star; from this we get the important number 7 once more. In addition, the south-facing shaft of the King's Chamber points directly at the 3 belt stars of Orion, and its north-facing passage points directly to the star Thuban in the Draco constellation. Thuban is the 4th star and adding the 3 belt stars of Orion gives 7 yet again. Then, adding these 7s together, we get the recurring value of 14 (see figure 118).

Notice the shape of the constellation of Draco is serpent-like. As the angle of the upper portion of the Bent Pyramid is the same as that of the Red Pyramid, both can be associated with the Sun's pole. It follows, then, that the Bent Pyramid represents both the Sun's pole and the Earth's pole.

Things start to come together

To sum up: we already have our representations of the 3 belt stars of Orion – the Giza pyramids. In addition we also have the representation of both the Sun's pole and the Earth's pole by the Red and Bent pyramids at Dashur.

From the above, we are now in a position to be able to draw these

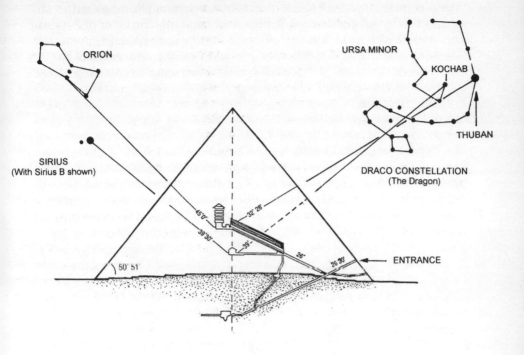

Figure 118. Alignments at 2,500 BC. Notice the King's shaft pointing at Thuban in the Draco constellation. This is an important indicator for back-dating the construction of the pyramids at Giza and Dashur.

points on a star chart and also find a date for the pyramids, since we have all the data required for a precessional dating, as I will explain. An angle formed between a line drawn through the stars of Orion's belt and a line drawn from the Sun's pole down to Orion is the same as the angle formed between a line through the pyramids of Giza and a second line drawn that joins the Great Pyramid to the Red Pyramid at Dashur. The angle is 65 degrees. This we have already seen earlier, in figure 77. A chart drawn showing this looks very much like a planisphere chart, but not of our present era. Looking at the angle from Giza/ Orion to the Red/Sun's Pole Pyramid, and then on to the Bent/Earth's Pole Pyramid, the angle is very different from what we have today. This is to be expected, as the Earth's pole moves (as will be shown later).

In Chapter 1 of the 1998 revised edition of *The Sirius Mystery*, Robert

Temple opines that the Sphinx (and its enclosure) is related to Sirius. He argues this by saying that the Sphinx was originally the form of Anubis, the dog-headed god associated with Isis/Sirius. Knowing that the ancients used multiple symbolism I would not like to argue that this is definitely not the case, as it could have well been used to represent Anubis symbolically at one point in its history. I will, however, argue that its original function was, and is, to provide an astronomical marker denoting the constellation of Leo, the Lion. In support of this (and *regardless* of the weathering patterns linking the Sphinx to the period of the Earth's precession through the Zodiacal sign of Leo), if you look at the position of the constellation of Leo on a star chart, you will notice that it is situated off to the left of a line running up from Orion to both of the poles. This exactly mirrors what we find at Giza, with the Sphinx positioned out to the left of a line drawn from Giza to Dashur (see figure 119).

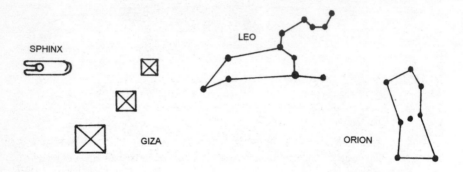

Figure 119.

If we refer back to Chapters 19 and 20, we can make the same connection with Avebury, Stonehenge and Silbury Hill. The reason that these links have not been seen before is their apparent remoteness from each other; yet, as we have seen, they are indeed closely connected and sited apart purposefully. We have 2 sets of monuments, thousands of miles apart, one in Egypt, the other in England, plus the third site in the Americas, all showing the same inherent design. Further supporting evidence comes from the Uffington Horse; it is situated in an identical position, in relation to Avebury, Silbury and Stonehenge, as the constellation of Pegasus is to the Earth and Sun's pole to Orion.

Knowing all that, we can now start the nittygritty of actually dating the monuments themselves. Using the Giza and Avebury planispheres, we can achieve this with a great degree of accuracy. For centuries, orthodox academics have insisted that the henges and the pyramids of

Giza were built around 4,500 years ago – the Fourth Dynasty period. A stele was found bearing Khafre's cartouche at Giza, so the pyramid it was found next to became Khafre's pyramid. Once a senior historian has agreed upon this (as has been the case to date) then heaven help the career of any academic who dares to suggest otherwise. Our Western technology cannot date stone at present, so Egyptologists and archaeologists are forced to depend upon the inefficient method of carbon-dating (C14) to date any organic materials found at these sites. Furthermore, orthodox history has still to answer how it is that later Egyptian pyramids have crumbled into dust whilst the Giza and Dashur pyramids of the far earlier period are still standing almost intact, even though their outer casing stones have been ripped off for other building projects over the past 1,000 years.

(a)

(b)

Figure 120. (a) Sketch by the antiquarian William Stukeley of the North Circle, at Avebury. The 3 stones to the right of the Cove have since disappeared. (b) William Stukeley by the Obelisk at Avebury.

Figure 120. A 14th-century manuscript depiction of Merlin 'building' Stonehenge. Its significance lies in showing the evident fascination exerted by Stonehenge over many epochs.

We can now understand why such sites have been held to be of immense value from antiquity, and also why they were so carefully maintained by the initiates who guarded them across time. So we can see now that the astronomical dates, based upon mathematical principles and pre-cessional time signatures that are not open to misunderstanding as they are fixed and constant, also tie in with the weathering dates established by geologists.

False leads and further confirmation

Obviously, these findings will have their opponents. It will be argued that the sites have been positively dated to around 4,500 years of age because artefacts found at Giza and Avebury have been carbon-dated to that period. The problem is that radio-carbon dating, though fairly accurate (up to a point) when applied to objects from the past 1,000 to 2,000 years, is unreliable for earlier dates, as there are too many variables to consider, which are often simply ignored in the interests of maintaining a theory. Heat can have an effect on an artefact that will cause it to give a false reading, since more carbon 14 is depleted from the object as it becomes agitated by heat extremes. Tellingly, when artefacts have been recovered from around Stonehenge that indicated a date of 10,000 BC they were immediately dismissed as not belonging to the site in question. This is very selective thinking, wouldn't you say? An example of this attitude occurred when wooden posts were recovered from under the present-day car park at Stonehenge and dated to 8,820 BC – i.e. they were nearly 11,000 years old. The solution? Label them as being from some kind of wooden totem poles, erected long before Stonehenge even existed.

To validate further the proposed dates – should you still be in any doubt – we need only look at the causeways on the Giza plateau. These causeways mark out the cross quarter sunrises during the year. This means that they mark the dates between the equinoxes and solstices, i.e. the dates that lie in the middle of the summer and autumn, autumn and winter, winter and spring, and spring and summer. What is so important about the cross quarter sunrise? We have seen that the number 14 is important, but for no apparent reason. We also saw at Stonehenge that the original designer, being aware of precession, built into its design the Heel Stone, positioned in such a manner that at the appropriate time in his long distant future (i.e. now), the Sun would have to rise 14 degrees above the horizon before sitting on top of it. According to our dates, Stonehenge was constructed prior to Giza. So it would appear that 14 is important. When we look at the angles of the causeways on the Giza complex we immediately see that the causeways of the Great and Khafre pyramids are set at 14 degrees. And notice how the Khafre causeway points directly at the cross quarter sunrise between the winter solstice and spring equinox at 14 degrees south of east during the epoch of 10,500 BC (see figure 121(a)).

Also, make a specific mental note of the position of Orion, and that Sirius is hidden below the horizon. It should be further remembered that in the Osiris myth, Osiris was cut into 14 pieces. Here we have the value of 14 carried across time within the myth itself. If it was simply a numerical value of no real significance, why wasn't the more common symbolic figure of 12 used instead?

As we saw earlier, the ancient Egyptian word Zep Tepi stood for 'The

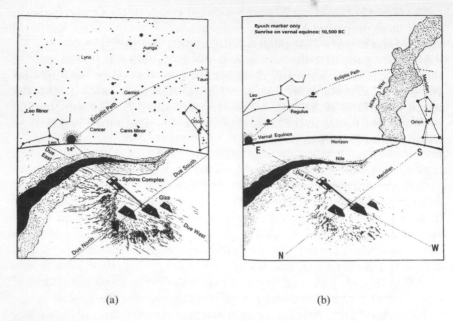

(a)   (b)

Figure 121. Cross-quarter sunrise of 10,500 BC (winter and spring). Note the position of Sirius is hidden below the horizon. Is this a clue? And is the 14° linked symbolically to the 14 parts of Orion?

first time'. We also saw that this referred directly to the first part of a period of time dealing with Sirius, its orbit and the prow of a celestial boat often depicted with Osiris/Orion and Isis/Sirius standing in it, accompanied by Nephthys/Sirius B. Throughout the ancient world, the moment of sunrise and its conjunction with other celestial events was always looked upon as very important. On the spring equinox of 10,500 BC a particularly spectacular conjunction occurred when the sunrise, the constellation of Leo and the meridian transit of the 3 belt stars all aligned exactly to the Giza site, for the first time. What is its vital significance? This conjunction happened to mark the beginning of the age of Leo, i.e. the Zep Tepi, 'first time' of Leo (see figure 121b).

The most important star Sirius is again hidden, but its presence is felt by its obvious omission. If you refer back to figure 121 you will note that in 10,500 BC, the constellation of Orion was at its lowest point, with Sirius hidden from view. During this period the declination of Sirius was exactly 58 degrees and 43 minutes (the numbers 58 links to the Templars and the Freemasons; 43 has the Fadic value of 7). When the constellation of Orion reaches the highest point of its precessional cycle in the years between AD 2000 and 2012, it will be exactly 58 degrees and 6 minutes above the horizon. Don't forget, we have already seen that the entire Giza complex was set out within a 5:8 square, forming 64 squares.

314

The Great Pyramid has 27 notches on either side of the Grand Gallery, which have perplexed historians for centuries. We saw earlier the total value of the height of the pillars of Solomon's Temple: $18 + 4 + 5 = 27$. Remember, too, that the northern circle at Avebury has 27 stones. It should come as no surprise, therefore, to note that when we apply an angle of 27 degrees from due south to the Giza pyramids during the epoch of around 10,500 BC, a line passes through the 3 small satellite pyramids and points to the horizon point exactly where the 3 belt stars of Orion appear (see figure 122).

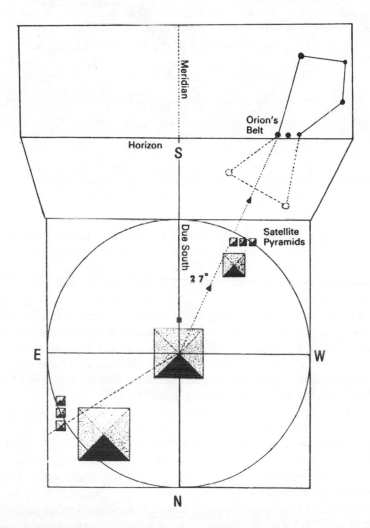

Figure 122. Remember the 27 notches within the Grand Gallery and that mankind is separated genetically from our nearest 'relative' by 27 differences. Notice again that Sirius is hidden, buried beneath the horizon.

At this point we need to look again at the dating process. As I have argued, the Sphinx denotes the constellation of Leo from the period of 10,500 BC. Although Graham Hancock and Robert Bauval[13] were in agreement about this, accepting the weathering evidence, they still thought the Pyramids of Giza were constructed much later – around 2,400 BC, during the 4th Dynasty. Whereas I, as we have seen, maintain they come from the same period. Graham Hancock and Robert Bauval believed the Sphinx, as it sat in the ground, mimicked the constellation of Leo in 10,500 BC *as it appeared sunken on the horizon* just prior to the equinox sunrise in what is known as Zep Tepi. They further believed that as Leo sat slightly sunken on the horizon, the Sun's position below it (by some 12 degrees) marked the position of the 'Hall of Records'. Zep Tepi was evidently something I had to investigate in detail, and I soon realised I had to look at the *Book of the Dead*, to see what it was *really* telling us.

Chapter 30

The *Book of the Dead* and the Hall of Records

Zep Tepi

As I've said, we are living in the era of Pisces the Fish and about to enter the Age of Aquarius sometime between AD 2000 and 2012. As there is a slight discrepancy of exactly when each zodiacal precessional cycle begins and starts, we need to establish an exact reference date, which at present is accepted as being 24 March, the spring equinox. Unfortunately, this date appears to have been slightly altered over time, as evinced by the fact that the Giza pyramids point at the cross quarter sunrises, not the equinox. This means that if we take the equinox of Leo and its position at sunrise on the Zep Tepi date of 10,500 BC, we will see that Leo is already high in the sky. Because of this, Bauval and Hancock adjusted their rising of Leo to nearly an hour prior to sunrise in order to keep Leo sitting on the horizon and the Sun marking the position of the Hall of Records. This is another reason why I feel that their interpretation of the Hall's position is not entirely correct. That said, however, if we accept the idea of the Zep Tepi as occurring when the Giza and Dashur sites were actually constructed in *c.* 11,500 BC (which is further represented by an additional 14-degree movement in the stars around the night sky) we can see that instead of using the equinoxes, we can now use the winter and spring cross quarter sunrises, as indicated by the Khafre causeway. When this is done, Leo does indeed sit on the horizon and actually rises with the Sun. This then is the proper Zep Tepi, the 'first time' (see figure 123).

I believe that this era simply marks the construction date of the site. The *later* date of 10,500 BC marks the true alignments of Leo and the constellation of Orion at the beginning of its upward precessional cycle. This is not a contradictory statement; what it shows is that the designers of the site were well aware of the cycles ahead of them and could calculate the detail accordingly. In this respect then, Hancock and Bauval were not strictly correct, but neither were they wrong.

317

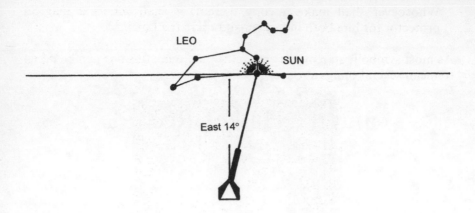

Figure 123. Khafre Pyramid. Cross quarter Sunrise *c.* 11,500 BC

The Duat

The Egyptian *Book of the Dead* has something very relevant to say:

> Sothis [Sirius] is swallowed up by the Duat, pure and living in the Horizon. The reed floats of the sky are brought down to me that I may go up on them to Horakhti at the Horizon. I go up on the Eastern side of the sky where the Gods are born, and I am born as Horus, as 'Him of the Horizon', Sothis is my companion.[1]

As this is all symbolic allegory, I saw that this passage was actually saying that Sirius is hidden beneath the Duat. As Bauval and Hancock have demonstrated, the Earth's Duat is associated with the Giza complex and the Earth itself with its own counterpart in the heavens. I could not help but feel that this was yet another clue; a key, perhaps, telling us that the Earthly counterpart of Sirius is beneath the ground, hidden in the Earthly Duat, the underworld. It was a logical assumption to make, as the Pyramids at Giza represented the Earthly counterparts of Orion's 3 belt stars. So, instead of concluding that it was absent because there was no trace of it on the surface, I decided that it – i.e. the counterpart of Sirius – was likely to be present after all; but *underground*. But *what exactly* would be underground? A temple to Isis, perhaps? The *Book of the Dead* certainly convinced me that the Giza complex was, indeed, a representation of the constellation of Orion when I read the following passage from it:

> Whosoever shall make an exact copy of these forms, and shall know it, shall be a spirit and well equipped in heaven and earth, unfailingly and eternally. The hidden circle in the Duat, in the body of Nut [the sky].

Whosoever shall make a copy thereof, it shall act as a magical protector for him both in heaven and upon the Earth.[2]

As most symbolic statements are multi-functional, this one can be taken to mean several things at once.

Figure 124. Worship of Re when he rises in the eastern horizon of the sky. From the Egyptian *Book of the Dead* (Ani).

We are also told in the ancient Egyptian *Shat Ent Am Duat* ('The Book of What Is in the Duat' – a section of the *Book of the Dead*) to build on the ground a replica of a special part of the sky called the Duat. Sir E. A. Wallis Budge commented on this with the following: 'A material heaven, on the banks of the heavenly Nile, whereon they built cities.' When I read the comment about the 'hidden circle in the Duat',[3] I immediately thought of the symbolic geometrical circle (as illustrated in figure 91) and the subsequent connections that this image contained, relating to the biblical New Jerusalem, and to both the Earth and the Moon. At first I didn't pay much attention to this connection, as it seemed rather tenuous. However, it would prove to have direct relevance later in regard to the Hall of Records and information gleaned from the Edfu Buildings Texts.

The mysterious capstone

Before we move on to the Edfu texts, we need to look at more enigmatic connections, relating to Sirius, that are encoded within the Great Pyramid and its capstone.

We saw earlier the 5-pointed star of Sirius; interestingly, the capstone

319

to the Great Pyramid is 5-pointed, if one counts 4 corners, plus the apex. In esoteric traditions, the 5 points have particular attributes. The top point is 'Time/Eternity'; the second point 'Air'; the third 'Water'; the fourth 'Gravity'; and the fifth 'Fire'. Actually, 5 is an important number in relation to the Great Pyramid as the structure is made of 5 corners and 5 faces: i.e. the 5 corners and apex, and 4 sloping faces and a base. Each of its faces contains a one-fifth scale inset triangle. However, the Great Pyramid will not *truly* be a 5-sided building until its 5-sided capstone is in place.

It is almost certain that the Great Pyramid never had its capstone added when completed. Indeed, speculation abounds as to whether it was even cut and transported to the site. Nonetheless, symbolically the capstone would have rested upon the existing summit-platform, which we know to be 153 courses above the King's Chamber floor. Not only that, the dimensions of the capstone are of considerable importance to us as they contain critical numerical values. For a start, its base length across each face is 47.1 feet, which means that it has a diagonal value of 66.6 feet. So here we see a symbolic connection as we saw earlier when 666 is added together with the number of Jesus (888) and Mary (192) to give the value of fusion, the joining of good and evil – 1,746. We have seen (Chapter 22) how this value is connected by gematria with several passages from the Bible, and how the Great Pyramid's exact dimensions can be formed, plus its entrance located, when two circles are joined together with a circumference of 1,746 feet.

It has been argued that the ancients did not complete the Great Pyramid as the capstone would be far too heavy to move, never mind put into position. On the contrary, however, the technological expertise apparent in the Pyramid's construction shows that this would not have proved to be a problem. Moreover, we need only look at the huge platform terrace at Baalbek in the Lebanon, which is estimated to weigh nearly 2,000 tons. It is there for all to see, as is the hole from where it was quarried in antiquity. Support for my view that the Great Pyramid was completed with its capstone deliberately omitted comes from the fact that the other two Giza Pyramids, of Khafre and Menkura, are complete to their apexes. Why should the Great Pyramid be the only one missing a component? Successive reports of the 17th, 18th and 19th centuries, by such observers as John Greaves and Nathaniel Davison, chronicle that the summit platform was clear except for a very few minor blocks.[4] These were no doubt part of a substandard false apex later added. We can be sure of this as the classical historian Diodorus Siculus (1st century BC) describes the building as being practically apexless in his day, even though it was still covered in its 21 acres of white polished lumite. With the smooth faultless facing blocks set at their steep angle, it would have been impossible to reach its summit, unless of course you were to make a ladder over 650 feet long.

In fact, Diodorus Siculus insists that the Great Pyramid of his time was in perfect condition, apart from its missing capstone.[5] I see this as confirmation that the original capstone (which myth and legend state is gold-sheathed) was never installed in the first place. Even if an adventurous climber was able to scale the heights or remove enough casing blocks to gain access to the summit, that could not explain how the capstone was removed. Even if we assume that the actual capstone was made of several blocks and not one solid piece of stone covered in gold, surely the damage caused to the facing stones as the capstone blocks were hurled off down the sloping sides would have been evident. No such damage has been reported.

Though this next is pure speculation and not provable, it is nonetheless worth noting that in esoteric circles, the eventual installation of the Great Pyramid's capstone is deemed to mark the dawn of a new age for mankind. Some see this as taking place just prior to the return of a Messianic figure, whilst others see it as marking the return of the Gods, whoever they prove to be. As the capstone has been linked to the Hall of Records (as we shall see) some have drawn the conclusion that the Hall of Records is actually a beacon that, once uncovered, will set off a signal to the gods – or extraterrestrials, depending upon which viewpoint you subscribe to.

I have already mentioned the saying from the Bible about the chief corner stone being rejected. In Matthew 21: 42, Jesus appears to apply the very same words to himself as follows: 'The stone, which the builders rejected, has become the chief corner-stone.' (I brought to your attention the connections of this stone within the Grail legends, as recounted in the epic of *Parzifal*.) The extraordinary thing about this statement by Jesus is the clear indication from the author that he is associating Jesus with the Great Pyramid. We can be sure of this, as not just any building has a 'chief corner-stone' that differentiates it from the others, except for the apex corner of a pyramid, because it is set above all the others. What's more, this sentence represents Jesus as *symbolically different*. Also note, however, that 'corner-stone' can be, and often is, translated as 'head-stone', which also fits the purpose and function of the capstone.

Further biblical references to the Great Pyramid are numerous. Here are 2 more.

- A passage adding weight to my argument about Jesus's connection with, and awareness of, the Great Pyramid's symbolism comes from Luke 19: 37–40: 'And when he was come nigh, even now at the descent of the mount of Olives, the whole multitude of the disciples began to rejoice and praise God with a loud voice for all the mighty works that they had seen; Saying Blessed *be* the King that cometh in the name of the Lord: peace in heaven, and glory in the highest. And some of the Pharisees from among the multitude said unto him, Master, rebuke thy

321

disciples. And he answered and said unto them, I tell you that, if these should hold their peace, the stones would immediately cry out.' This is clearly a cryptic statement, evidenced by the deliberate reference to stones that will 'shout aloud'. The Great Pyramid certainly and most definitely falls into this category.

• In John 6: 51, Jesus describes himself as 'that living bread which has come down from heaven'. As I explained earlier, the Egyptian hieroglyph for bread is identical in shape to the King's Chamber seal/boss (see figure 66).

We have already noted previously that the Grand Gallery is 153 feet in length. The number 153 has a long Christian tradition associated with the notion of enlightened souls, primarily drawn from the symbolism of 153 fish as outlined towards the end of John's Gospel. Here the disciples are told to cast their nets to the right, which they promptly do – and so catch the said 153 fish. The King's Chamber floor is exactly 153 courses of masonry below the summit platform. Years after reading about the connections of 153 within the Great Pyramid, and biblical passages that outlined the number in relation to fishing and the specific term of casting the nets to the right, I was not surprised to read almost identical symbolism within the Egyptian *Book of the Dead*.

Pyramid rituals

The basic concept behind the ancient Egyptian initiate trying to get from this world into the next focused upon passing through 4 frontiers of the sky. This required the departed spirit to convince the guardians to grant a free passage, only granted by knowing secret words and names, which, when repeated, were guaranteed to ward off any aggressor or evil apparition. As a consequence, any person daring to venture into the underworld would require magical skills of the very highest order. In ferrying oneself across the 4 frontiers of the sky the services of a ferryman were essential, and the initiate needed to know the correct answers to the ferryman's questions in order to use his boat, which was of course a celestial boat. The knowledge required involved knowing mythology, the gods' names, and the magic of Egypt, as well as possessing mathematical and practical scientific skills. I see in these rituals a memory that the hitherto unknown pre-dynastic priests, from whom the Egyptians obtained their knowledge, were scientists, technologists and perhaps even metaphysicists.

The Pyramid, nets and Jesus

What also struck me in these rituals was the similarity to later Christian symbology as regards the casting of nets. In Egyptian magic one of the most important symbols is that of the net. Moreover, in Greek traditions this same net is represented by the net of Hephaestus, with which the vengeful Olympian smith ensnared his beautiful wife Aphrodite and her lover Ares, the god of war. Net symbology nearly always entails 2 linked deities or persons and special knots for undoing the net. In Egyptian myths these two deities are Neith (known as Net) and Thoth. Wallace Budge informs us that in a group of titles, Thoth is called 'Great God in Het Abtit', or the 'Temple of Abtit', which was one of the chief sanctuaries of the god at Hermopolis. As Murry Hope[6] points out in *The Sirius Connection*, Wallis Budge further states that the hieroglyphs with which the name 'Het Abtit' are written actually mean, 'House of the Net', or more precisely, 'A temple wherein a net was preserved and venerated'. According to the *Book of the Dead*, a dreaded net was thought to exist in the underworld, greatly feared by the dead themselves. The dying were required to know the name of every single part of it, including ropes, weights, cords, hooks and so forth. Reading this I could not help but see connections with the symbolism displayed within Masonic Lodges. Furthermore, in the Babylonian mythical battle between Marduk and Tiamat, Marduk ensnared Tiamat *with his net* before cutting her open. Therefore, we see that when Jesus told his disciples to cast their nets to the right and catch 153 fish, it was a continuation of ancient esoteric wisdom which connected the Great Pyramid with Jesus himself, and which included important mathematical values.

Further links between Jesus and the Great Pyramid occur in the book of Isaiah as we saw earlier. In Chapter 19, the future Messianic figure's return is described as follows: 'See how the Lord comes riding swiftly upon a cloud, he shall descend upon Egypt.' What caught my attention was the very fact that he would descend *upon Egypt*; why not the Holy Land? Later in the same chapter, we are informed that when that day comes, there shall be an altar to the Lord in the heart of Egypt, and a sacred pillar set up for the Lord upon her frontier. In addition, it is stated that it shall stand as a token and a reminder to the Lord of Hosts in Egypt, so that when they appeal to him against their oppressors, he may send a deliverer to champion their cause, and he shall rescue them (Isaiah 19: 19–20).

I pointed out earlier that this passage was extraordinary as it describes exactly the site, nature and significance of the Great Pyramid itself. Please note here that the word translated as altar had two distinct meanings for the Hebrews. It could mean either the familiar sacrificial stone or the commemorative altar of witness. In the above context, the meaning is clearly that of the commemorative altar of witness. According to *Cruden's Complete Concordance to the Bible*,[7] great heaps of stones were raised up as a witness to any form of memorable event and to preserve the remembrance of some matter of great importance, and were the most ancient of monuments among the Hebrews. Such were allegedly built by Moses, Jacob, Joshua and Gideon, to name but a few. Evidently, the Great Pyramid must be the greatest 'heap of stones' bar none. Note, too, that the second sentence uses the word 'it' to refer to both an altar and a pillar. How can a pillar look like a heap of stones? Perhaps, as Peter Lemesurier points out in *The Great Pyramid Decoded*,[8] the word for pillar is a misleading translation from the Hebrew. In Hebrew it is 'Matstsebah', which means almost any kind of monument. Intriguingly, it is linguistically very close to the Egyptian word 'mstpt' meaning 'funeral bier', and almost identical to the Arabic 'mastaba', a funerary monument.

Chapter 31

The Great Pyramid and King Lists

I have used Christian (and pre-Christian biblical) traditions regarding the Great Pyramid to demonstrate that the secret wisdom of the ancients was updated into each new age. For example, when the age of Pisces dawned, the information was incorporated, and carried forward, in the new religion of Christianity. Prior to that, when Moses left Egypt, he likewise incorporated the information into what became the Jewish nation, even down to the formation of the Star of David, made from 2 triangles, one inverted, laid upon each other. If we turn to Egyptian history we can also even find the Great Pyramid's dimensions set out within the chronologies of the 'king lists'. I pointed out earlier how inaccurate these are from an historical perspective, and they seem so contradictory to archaeological finds. The reason is quite simple. They have been deliberately altered to include the mathematical values of the Great Pyramid.

Manetho (3rd century BC)[1] compiled a list of kings and their dynasties but only his king lists were accepted as fact; the other lists, stretching back many thousands of years, were totally ignored by Egyptology. Manetho's actual writings have not survived but have come down to us through the works of later authors, such as Sextus Julius Africanus, Eusebius, Syncellus and others, and as such, have been interpreted in a variety of ways. To give one example, the lists of Eusebius can push the dating of the reign of Khufu back by nearly 2,000 years. Why is it that Manetho's figures in the dating of the chronological tables have been taken as a basis by Egyptologists, who seem able to accept Manetho's work as regards the First Dynasty, but not what he said of kings earlier than that? And what are *we* to do with the preceding 5,813-year dynasty of Manes, for example, or the even earlier dynasties, such as the 5,124-year line of the Demigods, or the 13,900-year era presided over by gods? To add further to the conundrum, there are claims by such classical authors as Plato, Berossus and Diodorus that the history of Egypt – *as recorded by the Egyptian priesthood* – went back *hundreds of thousands of years*.

Figure 125 shows the Great Pyramid with dimensions in Sacred Pyramid inches and Royal Cubits. These are units of measurement that are derived directly from the Great Pyramid itself. The point is: the figures can *also* be derived from the chronologies of the ancient Egyptian

Dynasties, as reported by Herodotus and Manetho. In his chronology, Herodotus refers to 8 gods known as Hephaistos, Helios, Agathodaimob, Kronos, Osiris, Isis, Typhon (Set) and Horus (Ares). There were 12 further gods: Anubis, Heracles, Apollo, Ammon, Tithoes, Sosos, Zeus, and 5 others. There were 4 dynasties of the demigods and 30 human dynasties. Manetho detailed the number of years in each reign, whose figures were tabulated by Davidson and Aldersmith[2] on page 77 of their book *The Great Pyramid*, published in 1925. From this list, we have our present-day king list, still taught as if absolute fact. Fortunately the likes of David Rohl have advanced a more plausible chronology which shows that progress to reinterpret the evidence is beginning to surface.

As Peter Lemesurier noted,[3] these parallels between the Great Pyramid and the lists could be coincidental, but the similarities seem too numerous to allow that *all* of them are. In view of this, it would seem that the king lists were devised or remodelled on the basis of the known measurements of a Standard pyramid, as shown in figure 125.

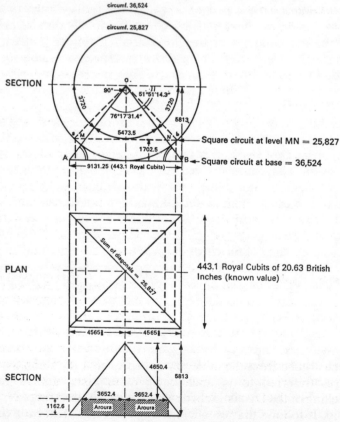

Figure 125. All the Great Pyramid's basic external measurements are presented in ancient Egyptian fictitious king lists. (Aroura is is a unit of measure derived from a roller.)

The Pyramid in question is of course, the Great Pyramid. The application of the king list figures clearly indicates that the unit of measurement is equal to 1 Primitive Inch (P″), which is in turn equal to 1.001 Imperial inches. 1.001 was the standard measure of the Imperial inch until it was altered during the reign of Queen Elizabeth I. A Royal Cubit is fractionally smaller, therefore, than a modern yard but originally identical in length prior to the 16th century. The following table compares the values (see figure 126).

Source	Figure	King-list attribution	Pyramidal application (full-design)
Syncellus	36,525	Total years, divine and human dynasties to Amasis II (end of 30th dynasty)	Base perimeter in P″
Manetho	5,813	Total years, dynasty of Manes (Ghosts)	Height in P″
Manetho	29,220	Total years, gods and kings	Circuit at 35th course axis in P″
Let aMNb subtend at O an angle of 90° in outer circle (centre O) circumference 36,524 P″.			
Manetho	25,827	Total years, divine dynasties	Circuit at level MN in P″
Africanus			Sum of base-diagonals in P″ Circumference of inner circle, centre O, to touch MN
Manetho	1,702	Total years, dynasty 3 of demigods	Height of level MN from base in P″
Africanus	5,474	Total years, human dynasties 1 to 31	Length in P″ of arc subtending at O the Pyramid's apex-angle (76° 17′ 13·4″) in inner circle (centre O, circumference 25,827 P″)
Castor	8,720	Total years, human dynasties 1 to 18	Length in P″ of arc subtending at O the Pyramid's angle of slope (51° 51′ 14·3″) in inner circle (circumference 25,827 P″)
Eusebius	4,565	Total years, human dynasties 1 to 31	Half base-side in P″
Syncellus	443	Total in years of the 15 generations of the Cynic (Sothic) cycle after the divine dynasties	Length of base-side in *Royal Cubits*
Africanus	5,151	Total years, first 26 human dynasties	Side of square equal in area to Pyramid's cross-section, in P″

Figure 126.

It can be argued from the table that it proves that the standard Pyramid measures (referred to in ancient Egyptian texts, and used for the remodelling of the Dynastic chronologies) were indeed those of the Great Pyramid. It follows that even if the Great Pyramid had been destroyed, we would still be able to reconstruct an accurate representation of it by using the figures in the king lists.

The enigmatic Queen's Chamber

I refer to the Queen's Chamber as enigmatic, and that is precisely what it is. I was initially drawn to this room because of the significant fact that it has 7 sides to it: 1 floor, 4 walls and 2 parts to its vaulted ceiling. Its so-called airshafts, and the very mysterious corner niche (which has defied any suitable explanation to date), also intrigued me, and I shall offer my conclusions on these in a moment. We have seen how important the value of 7 is, both in its biblical and other religious connections, and also in the Fadic numbering system. The ancient Egyptian rituals that were apparently carried out within this chamber hinted strongly at its link to the processes of procreation and regeneration. As the southern shaft in the chamber pointed to the star Sirius in *c.* 2,450 BC, I was immediately fascinated by this connection. At this same period, the southern shaft in the King's Chamber pointed at Al Nitak (that is, Zeta Orionis), in the constellation of Orion. I had suspected, from my personal researches, that Sirius played an important role, but it wasn't until the publication of Bauval and Gilbert's *The Orion Mystery* that I felt convinced of my supposition that the Chamber was linked directly to Sirius.

Knowing that the encoded information within the Great Pyramid was repeated many times over, and that it was also expressed symbolically, I immediately thought that as the shafts in the Queen's Chamber had been sealed at both ends – thus proving that they were not air shafts – then they must have been intended to convey that whatever related to the shafts was a secret, and hidden. The shafts were covered by 5 inches of stone that was part of the facing block (and only opened in 1872), meaning that they had been sealed since the Pyramid's construction. Their exit points have still not been found. As the southern shaft pointed at Sirius in *c.* 2,450 BC, I perceived that this was a clue indicating that something *connected with Sirius* was hidden. I had already thought that as Sirius was not represented by a temple or pyramid (as was the case for the Giza pyramids and the Orion belt stars) it would be worth while to investigate whether there was a buried temple or structure hidden and sealed, just as the texts had stated (i.e. the hidden circle within the Duat).

Remember that I demonstrated (Chapter 20) that the angles between the pyramids at Teotihuacan and its causeway, *and* between the Giza site and that of Dashur, were both 65 degrees? Imagine then my surprise on learning that in 1993, a German engineer, Rudolf Gantenbrink,[4] had sent up a miniature remote-controlled robot, appropriately named 'Upuaut' (since that means 'Opener of the ways'). At exactly 65 metres up it ran into a miniature portcullis slab. Attached to it were 2 copper fittings, one of which was broken. This area of the shaft was lined with Tura lime-stone, which was only used, normally, for the lining of the Pyramid's chambers. This was seen to indicate that a hidden chamber would be present (see figure 55, where I indicate the proposed position). There may very well prove to be a chamber behind the door, but it is a very *small* door and access up the shaft is impossible for any human. It is feasible that another, as yet unknown, entrance passage might lead to it from another direction, but in view of the symbolic nature of the entire Giza site, I believe that this is another symbolic code, carefully placed as part of a key. Essentially the former hidden shaft – indicating that the message was a secret from the start – pointed to Sirius. Then, at 65 metres, we find a sealed portcullis; furthermore the fact that the immediate area is lined with Tura limestone indicates the existence of something important – something again hidden from view and connected with Sirius.

The cryptic niche and the colour of Sirius

The reason that I argue that the connection with Sirius is the overriding message from the Queen's Chamber is due not only to the extreme importance that the ancient Egyptians placed upon Isis/Sirius, or the fact that the Great Pyramid was originally dedicated to Isis at the dawn of Egyptian history; but primarily to the scientific information that *positively identifies Sirius with the enigmatic corner niche*. The corner niche has perplexed Egyptologists, historians and engineers alike, ever since it was entered in the 9th century AD. It serves no practical purpose whatsoever. Orthodox Egyptology simply states that a statue was placed there. Because of this theory, all subsequent niches found in tombs or temples are assumed to have the same original purpose. It is held that the Queen's Chamber was abandoned after the designers changed their minds, and decided upon the King's Chamber instead as the final resting place of the dead pharaoh. The fact that no body was ever found when it was first entered still does not stop the story being told that the Great Pyramid was constructed as a tomb. Not only that, but when the King's Chamber was first entered by Caliph Al Mamoun's crew in the 9th century AD, the so-called sarcophagus didn't even have a lid.

The Egyptian *Book of the Dead* (see above) seems to associate the Queen's Chamber with the Moon, which is specifically related to rebirth. Could this further mean that whatever the hidden secret is – that relates somehow to Sirius – it actually indicates something to do with regenerating or a specific rebirth? In view of its apparent connection with the Moon and the Moon's effects upon women's menstrual cycles – and indeed, its effects upon the very element of all life on Earth, water – this is not merely a wild assumption. As we have seen already, Thoth/Hermes is firmly equated with the Moon, as are the periods of time for each precessional cycle of 2,160 years, having the same value as its 2,160-mile diameter. Nonetheless, this is, realistically, speculation on symbolic meanings that could conceivably be misinterpreted. Hence I believe the inclusion of the corner niche was deliberate, since that positively identifies the chamber with Sirius, regardless of when specific periods cause its shafts to align with Orion and Sirius.

The value of 5 is important, as we have seen, so it is relevant that the niche is 5 steps high. I had spent much time pondering on what this niche could represent. The statue-location theory was, I felt, insubstantial. During the 19th century, excavations were carried out to see if the niche was some kind of secret door, and damage caused by the drilling involved is still very evident. Many different theories have been proposed for the niche, to little avail. Certainly I tried everything I could think of, from assessing mathematical values within its design to trying to fit musical frequency values to it, but nothing fitted conclusively. I was dissatisfied with anything I came up with, so the niche enigma had to simmer on the back boiler for several years. I could accept that its 5 stages might represent the 5-pointed star of Sirius, with all its inherent symbolic and esoteric connotations, but that good (though at times annoying) old instinct was telling me there was more. If the niche had been designed purely to convey this, a simple 5-pointed star engraved into the Queen's Chamber walls would have served as a far better marker.

The red star, or the yellow star?

It was not until Christmas 1994 that I finally understood what I believe to be the purpose behind the niche. Knowing I was a keen astronomer, my parents-in-law bought me a book titled *Colours of the Galaxies* by David Malin and Paul Murdin, published by Cambridge University Press.[5] Years earlier I had read reports in ancient chronicles stating that Sirius was 'red'. In astronomy circles, these details had caused a considerable debate, and many theories were proposed to explain how Sirius could have changed colour from a red to a blue/white star in just 2,000 years. The 18th-century scientist, theologian and writer Thomas Barker sparked off the controversy by declaring that the present colours of the stars and planets, as we see today, were the same as those the ancients had observed. Ptolemy compiled a catalogue of stars in his classic work on astronomy, *Almagest*, which marked as distinctive the colour of only 6 of them, which he named *Hypokirros*, a word that actually means 'Somewhat yellow'.[6] However, 5 of the named stars are in fact so reddish in colour that Liddell and Scott's classical Greek dictionary notes that the word can means red when applied to stars. The oddest star of the 6 listed is Sirius (Canis Major, the Dog Star), which, as we know, is the brightest star in the night sky. As such, it can be plainly seen to be a whitish blue colour that flickers brightly; certainly not red. Yet because of Ptolemy calling it *Hypokirros*, the implication was that Sirius had previously been red. Barker inflated the controversy by adding the comments of Seneca (4 BC – AD 65) as follows: 'The red Dog Star divides its children.'[7] As a consequence, many astronomers accepted Barker's argument. Among these was Sir John Herschel, who explained Sirius's red hue in his hypothesis that space contains opaque matter in clouds, which travel in front of stars and cause their colour, as we perceive it, to change.

Chinese observations made by Sima Qian in the 1st century BC describe Sirius as white. Here then, we find that the classical observations are contradicted. It would appear from all the evidence (too long to include here but readily available in Malin and Murdin's book), that Sirius was never seen as red, and that the only reason it was thought so previously was due to Ptolemy's error in recording Sirius under the title of *Hypokirros*. As Malin and Murdin memorably conclude,[8] such astronomers as Herschel (1839), Newcomb (1902), Eddington (1911), Osthoff (1927), Gundel (1927), Kopal (1959), Lauterborn (1970, 1971), Rakos (1974), Lindenblad (1975), Maran (1975), and D'Antona and Mazzitelli (1978) may all have been stimulated to investigate the redness of Sirius 2,000 years ago by a slip of a pen, a careless translation and an unconsidered adjective. In short, then, it appears that the change of colour in Sirius constitutes a red herring for astronomy.

All this explains why I was so excited when I encountered a colour spectrum, as illustrated in the plates. I was aware of the arguments regarding 'red' Sirius, and I had wrongly assumed the colour to be correct, so when I noticed that the spectrum image produced for the colour red is identical in shape to that of the Queen's corner niche, I was exhilarated. I had both found a positive connection to Sirius *and* solved the enigma of the niche as well, I thought jubilantly. Sadly my excitement was shortlived and I had to temper my enthusiasm once I confirmed that the 'red' Sirius of antiquity derived from error. I was stuck. Nonetheless, looking at the red spectrum pattern and assessing the niche really got me thinking, and I couldn't let go of the idea that there was a connection with Sirius.

At this point, I was doing an Open University degree in maths and science, and since part of my studies involved spectrographic analysis, I was made aware of charts that present a bar-graph image of spectral types and colours of stars. Whilst studying one chart, I noticed that the bar graph for the image presented by whitish-yellow stars looked very similar to the Queen's corner niche, but with only 4 levels instead of 5. It also had a small depression box below the main image. Again, this is very similar to what *appears* to be a depression immediately below the corner niche. Without going into the full scientific technicalities, I approached a friend at the University of East Anglia and asked her to run a little test for me. I asked her to do a spectral analysis of Sirius and produce a bar-graph chart accordingly. The result can be seen next to the image of the Queen's Chamber corner niche in figure 127.

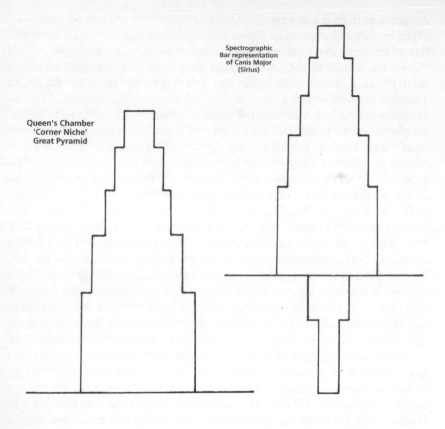

Queen's Chamber 'Corner Niche' Great Pyramid

Spectrographic Bar representation of Canis Major (Sirius)

Figure 127.   (a)   (b)

Notice the exact dimensions in height, width and number of levels. Note also the lower protrusion on the Sirius bar chart. It has been speculated that this is also a feature just below the corner niche, so it would be instructive to see this confirmed. Naturally there will be some who will insist that there are many variables that can be either added or taken away from any spectral analysis of the light from Sirius, but it could be argued that the red bar graph is evidence supporting the notion that the corner niche is representative of Sirius. I certainly believe it to be so.

Pyramids in the Orient

Meanwhile, I would like to bring us back to the huge, enigmatic pyramids in China. As we have seen, these structures are buried in earth and have unmistakable similarities to Silbury Hill and the pyramids of Central America (see plates). Immediately I must demolish the contention that these were gradually (over many millennia) covered in earth by natural processes. These enormous structures are situated on a flat plain and the only way earth could have covered them was by deliberate human effort, moving vast quantities of earth onto them, and then packing it down heavily. The vital question is: *Why* would the ancients here have felt compelled to bury these structures, just as the ancients in Central America had done? I propose, in view of the Earth's magnetic polarity and the Sun's magnetic polarity reversing on a regular, predictable basis (with all its destructive implications), that they were buried to protect them from physical damage, and weathering, and especially from the massive amount of solar radiation that bombards the Earth during the Sun's magnetic polarity reversal.

When I joined the military reserve, I was issued with what is known as an IPK pack – an Individual Protection Kit. It consisted of a length of string, several aluminium pegs and a 6 by 8 feet sheet of material. After an intensive training period learning all about nuclear, chemical and biological warfare, I became immersed in the subject. Because it worried me, I learnt as much as I possibly could about it. One of the first things I learnt was that with my IPK pack I could dig a hole in the ground, stake out the pegs, stretch the strings across the hole (connected to the pegs), lay the sheet covering across the strings and then cover that with earth to the minimum of 18 inches. This simple design, and the use of only 18 inches of earth, is sufficient to absorb gamma radiation following a nuclear explosion. It was also sufficient to absorb later radioactive fallout, thus offering sustained protection; the more earth on top, the more protection was afforded. If the cataclysms of antiquity were predictable, as I maintain, then the ancients would have been aware of imminent cosmic disaster, which would have included massive amounts of solar radiation. This, I suggest, is why monuments were buried in earth. In addition, this would also afford considerable protection against intense heat. Various sites around the world that haven't been covered in earth certainly bear the marks of intense heat, which has even vitrified and fused building materials together. Authors such as Erich von Däniken have argued that this melting of rocks on ancient sites is evidence of a nuclear war in antiquity. I feel my reasoning is more plausible.

As for the Chinese pyramids (see plates), they were first observed in 1945 by a US Air Force pilot named James Gaussman, during a reconnaissance mission over the Qin Ling Shan mountain range southwest of the city of Xian. Flying over a valley he suddenly saw an enormous pyramid in front of him.[9] Realising that he would not be believed back at base, he took photographs of it. When developed, these showed a pyramid at least 300 metres high and with a side length of nearly 500 metres. This was far bigger than the Great Pyramid in Egypt. Tellingly, these photographs were then held in the US Military Secret Services vaults for 45 years, but fortunately for us, another US pilot, Maurice Sheahan, flew over the same area and photographed the pyramid again, only this time the photos were published in the *New York Times* on 28 March 1947. As is the case all too often within academic circles, the photos were deemed to depict something of natural origin, and were consequently dismissed, as archaeologists denied the existence of pyramids in China – especially ones purportedly larger than those of Egypt.

Nearly 50 years after the original story was published, the German author Hartwig Hausedorf[10] was the first Westerner to be granted permission to visit the area of the Chinese pyramids. During his visit, Hartwig was able to photograph them, and he has very kindly allowed me to reproduce the results in this book – see plates. He was also able to meet and talk with the Chinese archaeologist Professor Wang Shi Ping,[11] who believed that all the pyramids were laid out to represent constellations. What is obvious is that the entire site is witness to an incredible knowledge of geometry and mathematics. This was emphasised in January 1994, when archaeologists discovered several pyramids standing near the River Wei Ho north of the city of Xian; one of these is located on the geometric centre of the ancient Chinese Imperium. Exact calculations show the pyramid to be off centre by a few metres.

One aspect of this that really intrigued me was the account of an old monk living in a nearby monastery. He claimed that the monastery's oldest records date back 5,000 years, and state that even in those remote times the region's pyramids were considered extremely old. Note how the tops of the pyramids are flattened, just like those in Central America. Now another aspect of the Chinese pyramids that should concern us from an historical point of view, is the fact that Hausedorf's companion Peter Krassa was told by Professor Xia Nai from the Beijing Academy of Sciences, when he asked about opening the tombs: 'That's a job for future generations.'[12] Mysteriously, and perhaps alarmingly, the pyramids in the area of Mao Ling near the township of Xian Yang have had fast-growing conifers deliberately planted over them. Just what lies waiting to be discovered beneath these pyramids? And why the concealment? Only time will tell.

Chapter 32

The 'Chambers of Creation' and the Ani and Edfu Texts

In this chapter we finally find ourselves dealing with the undeniably puzzling and complex accounts from the Edfu Texts. These texts are crowded with mysterious and shadowy deities, and other quasi-supernatural beings, who seem to have various descriptive titles. Nonetheless, behind the superficial image of their nature, elements of great importance, dealing with the very earliest periods of Egypt, are revealed, as well as a layout of a site that relates to certain vital number values, of which (I hope) you are now very much aware.

When I first read *The Great Pyramid Decoded* and learnt for the first time about a 'Hall of Records', I also learnt more about the ancient Egyptian work known as the *Book of the Dead*. This is basically an ancient Egyptian collection of mortuary texts made up of spells or magic formulas which were placed in tombs and believed to protect and aid the deceased in the next life. It is thought that these were probably compiled and re-edited during the 16th century BC. There is a lot of debate as to the exact date of the compilation, as many later additions augmented the core. Some Egyptologists believe that it dates back as far as 2500 BC, as the compilation of the *Book of the Dead* included the Coffin Texts (*c.* 2000 BC), the Pyramid Texts (*c.* 2400 BC) and other later writings. Scribes often copied these texts on rolls of papyrus, sometimes colourfully illustrated and used for individual burial purposes. As a consequence, many copies have been found in Egyptian tombs. However, none has been found to contain *all* of the (approximately) 200 known chapters. The collection, correctly titled *The Chapters of Coming Forth by Day,* only received its present name in 1842 from the German archaeologist Karl Richard Lepsius, who published the first edition of the texts.[1]

The Heliopolitan Recension of *The Chapter For Coming Forth By Day* (i.e. first section) was in use during the 4th and 5th dynasties, dated to 3500 BC. According to Sir E. A. Wallis Budge in his *Books on Egypt and Chaldea*:

The book is definitely not of Egyptian origin for, although it would

335

appear that from pre-dynastic times the aborigines of Egypt possessed tolerably well defined ideas about the future life, they could not be regarded as the authors even of the earliest Recension of the *Book of the Dead*,[2] because the work presupposes the existence of ideas which the aboriginals did not possess and refers to an elaborate system of sepulture which they never practised.[2]

It is worth noting at this point that although the Egyptians must have been fundamentally a dark-skinned people and therefore predominantly brown-eyed, they almost always depicted their Sun gods with *blue* eyes. This was, as Murry Hope, author of *The Sirius Connection*, remarked, 'a folk memory no doubt of a fair and blue-eyed people who, to them, were the original race of Gods'.[3] The *Book of the Dead* reads very much like an oratorio, and although there is no evidence that it was actually performed, the ritual itself is full of theatrical elements. It describes the journey of the soul, brought after death by the jackal-headed god Anubis into the Hall of Truth, where the dead person's heart was weighed against a feather. If the heart, made light by goodness, did not outweigh the feather, then the soul was brought before Osiris and granted immortality.

Once I had managed to obtain a decent copy of the *Book of the Dead*, I was immediately struck by the presence of familiar numbers: 12 gods; 21 pylons; 7 halls; 7 Arits and 7 uraei (serpents of wisdom). I had no idea what the names meant but I recognised the values. Making such connections was something I had done frequently, often with good results.

7 and 12 reappear

Reading the *Book of the Dead*, and being aware of the concept of a Hall of Records, I noted down details about halls whenever mentioned. I took on board the fact that there were 7 halls mentioned, including one called the Hall of Maati (truth), which had 12 constituent parts. These details were very intriguing, so I studied the *Book of the Dead* more closely. I learnt about the scribe of Osiris, known as Ani (hence parts that concern Ani are often referred to as the Papyrus of Ani). Glimpsing the colourful illustrations that detail the stories of Osiris, I counted 12 gods on thrones seated at the top of the illustration. This was the first hint that perhaps these Egyptian papyri held mathematical values, so I read on, looking for further values. Naturally, one can make anything fit a particular value depending upon one's own definitions and what one would class as a countable commodity. I chose to stick only to the most obvious aspects of the texts, such as how many gods were depicted, the pylons, and so on.

I noted that beneath the 12 gods stood Thoth/Hermes, and that after the scribe Ani had had his heart weighed and passed sinless, he was presented to Osiris, at which Ani promptly declares: 'Here I am in your presence, O Lord of the West.' Lord of the West caught my attention as I had read several books claiming that the original founders of Egypt were supposedly survivors from Atlantis, in the west. In chapter 1:22, I read that Osiris had arisen from the egg which is in the secret land and that he speaks with it in the presence of the Great God, Lord of the Duat (the underworld). He adds that as Osiris, he is Lord of Rostau (Rosetjau), which, as Bauval and Gilbert show, is the Giza plateau.[4]

In the Osiris myth there are 7 gateways that have to be passed through, each of which has 3 figures seated within the entrance. Here I perceived my earlier important values of 7 and 21. In chapter 18 I noticed drawings of what look exactly like trilithons; one is even painted green and has an Anubis figure sitting on top of it (and is beautifully illustrated in *Egyptian Book of the Dead (The Book of Going Forth by Day)*, translated by Dr Raymond Faulkner, plate 12).[5] Throughout the book, there are many images that represent both doorways and gates yet look identical to the trilithons of Stonehenge. In view of all the information on Osiris and Isis as we covered earlier, I couldn't help but sense that certain values were indeed being carried over from epoch to epoch, especially in regard to the star Sirius itself. The problem with the Ani papyrus texts was that they are clearly copies of even older information, just as Wallis Budge claimed. Naturally I wanted an earlier source, but this was to prove very difficult to find. Because of the similarity to trilithons I discerned in the *Book of the Dead*, I decided to go back to my original source material on these. It is most likely that the 'trilithon' images in the papyrus actually had absolutely nothing to do with the things themselves, but this nevertheless led in a particular direction of investigation that would yield important information.

As I pored over my old research relating to Stonehenge, I found myself sitting at my desk late one afternoon and sipping yet another cup of tea. It was pouring with rain outside so I enjoyed the rare peaceful moment, hearing the gentle wash of the rain on the window. Then I noticed my pictures of the Temple of Horus at Edfu. As I flicked through the old notes accompanying them, I remembered about the many reliefs and texts inscribed upon its walls. I vaguely recalled that I had read that although the reliefs and hieroglyphs were relatively young, the message they conveyed apparently stretched back into antiquity. And so I began my investigations anew into what are known as the Edfu Texts.

Myths of the Underworld

In the ancient Egyptian myths and rituals, great emphasis was placed upon the 12 divisions of the night that the Sun, symbolised by a ram-headed figure known as the Great God Atum, had to travel through. After enduring various ordeals, supported by other lesser gods and the use of magic spells, the God Atum would eventually exit out of the Duat at the end of the 12th hour in the east, on the horizon. The underworld where the journey had taken place was known as the Tuat, Duat or Dwat (Duat is the usual form). Later, during the 5th and 6th dynasties, Pyramid Texts painted or chiselled onto walls and tombs specifically dealt with the Sun's passage through the Duat as a form of star map that guided the soul of a deceased pharaoh, after which he became as one with the god Osiris in the constellation of Orion. The symbolism inherent within the Osiris myths in relation to celestial phenomena is now becoming apparent, especially in view of the Osiris/Orion and Isis/Sirius connections and the Giza Pyramids. Because of this, we can be quite confident that, at the very heart of these ancient traditions, there is a key element that is telling us a message that has been passed down through many millennia.

The Duat can be viewed as having 2 gates: one where the Sun enters each night and one where it exits each morning. Each of these gates is guarded by a lion or Sphinx, known as an Aker. On the Giza Plateau, we have our guardian in the form of the Sphinx; *but only one*. Does this therefore imply that there could be a second somewhere? I believe it does, and that soon another Sphinx will be located on, or near, the Giza plateau. As for the Aker or double Akeru, it was depicted either as 2 lions back to back, or a single lion with 2 heads. As Andrew Collins points out in his book *Gods of Eden*: 'Since the Aker lions were to be found in the path of the rising and setting sun, and thus on the line of the ecliptic, they must represent one of the 12 zodiacal constellations. It does not take much imagination to realise that the most obvious choice is Leo, but does any of this make sense of what we known about Egyptian astrology?'[6] Yet again, I believe the connection to be valid, especially as my own original deductions linking the Sphinx to the age of Leo were originally based simply on counting back through time to that particular period.

What *is* apparent from the early myths about the 12 periods of the Duat underworld, is that the Duat was segmented into 12 divisions known as hours. These bore no relation to the 12 signs of the Zodiac, however. Now, the priests of Heliopolis saw the Sphinx as a leonine embodiment of Harakhty. Re-harakhty the Sun God, as Horus of the Horizon, represents the Giza pyramids; so the Sphinx was seen as the physical representation of one of the two Aker lions. Again this provokes the question: if this is the case, where is the second one? This direct relationship between Re-harakhty and the Aker lions seems to show the relationship between the Sphinx and a celestial counterpart, the constellation of Leo. As we have already seen, the Sphinx does not gaze out to the position on the horizon where the constellation of Leo and the

Sun were reborn/seen at dawn together on the summer solstice in the 4th dynasty pyramid age, but during the precessional age of Leo, nearly 8,000 years earlier. Only during the age of Leo did the Sun set in the stars of Leo and then rise with them at dawn exactly 12 hours later. This is why the Sphinx was seen as the embodiment of Re-harakhty and one of the Aker lions – *it gazed out upon its celestial counterpart*, on the eastern horizon.

It is my belief that the myths surrounding the Duat amount to information that relates directly to structures that are actually built *under* the Duat, i.e. a literal 'underworld'. This is a logical parallel to the Giza plateau being the Earthly representation of the celestial Orion; why not have the underworld also manifested physically? Let's look at the narrative again. The ancient Sun god had to make his way through the 12 divisions of the Duat firstly by entering via a mountain of the west. The pyramids are on the West Bank of the Nile. In the first hour, the god is within the entrance hall. After uttering his magic spells he enters the second hour. After more trials and tribulations he enters the third hour. After this hour, the story changes in style as the Sun god passed directly over the top of the obstacles of the 4th and 5th hours, which are seen as the central area of the Duat; this is described as the 'Kingdom of Sokar'. Sokar was the patron god of the Memphite necropolis that encompassed all the major pyramid fields, including Giza. The Sphinx stele of Thutmosis IV (*c.* 1420 BC) refers to the Sphinx as sitting beside Sokar in Rostau. Rostau is the Egyptian name for Giza and as the Sphinx sits next to the pyramids, this indicates that Sokar is a pyramid.

The Road to Rostau

Interestingly enough, the 4th hour, or division, of the Duat underworld is depicted as a descending passageway, known as 'The Road to Rostau', which is very like the passages of the Great Pyramid. The text continues to tell us that this particular passage is the road by which 'entereth the body of Sokar who is on his sand, the image which is hidden, and is neither seen nor perceived'. This caught my attention as it infers a passage that leads to something hidden, that is neither seen nor perceived. The stele of Thutmosis IV informs us that Giza (which is Rostau) lay at the end of the 'Sacred Road of the Gods'. This is another indication of an underground passageway along which the ancient gods (known as the Netjeru) travelled. At this stage then, we can assume that a passage leads us somewhere underground that is in 12 divisions. I repeat, although symbolic, it is very likely that, just as the Giza pyramids actually represent celestial counterparts, the Duat underworld does likewise. Once the Sun god has passed the 4th and 5th divisions, he eventually enters the heart of the house of Sokar, where the ground rises forming a hollow mound that looks remarkably like the omphalos stones we looked at in Chapter 8. This omphalos-looking device not only represents the centre of the House of Sokar, but also the precise centre of the Duat and point of the First Creation, the Primeval Mound, which we shall hear more of later. It seems to me that what we are being told within these myths of Sokar and Rostau, is quite simply that beneath the Giza/Rostau plateau, there are indeed many real, physical passages of the Duat/Underworld that are symbolically encoded within the myth. In effect, the 12 divisions and hours of the Duat have nothing to do with 12 actual hours of the night at all, but are symbolic of actual passages and chambers.

As I pointed out at the beginning of this book, rumours of passages beneath the Giza Plateau have been around for as long as the pyramids themselves. These are the syringes, massive passages built underground to preserve the knowledge and wisdom of the ancients, which they feared would be destroyed in a coming deluge. This information was not enough for me; I wanted further proof. I could well accept that there were passages beneath the Giza Plateau, especially as seismic tests had revealed many chamber-sized fissures beneath the surface. But referring back to my researches about Edfu, and in light of what I knew about Giza, I could now look at the Edfu Texts from a different perspective.

Learning the significance of Edfu

The Horus Temple at Edfu is an enigmatic-looking structure built during the reign of Ptolemy III. According to records, building started in 237 BC and completed in 57 BC. It apparently replaced a much earlier structure designed in accordance (the myths maintain) with a divine plan that dropped from heaven to Earth, landing near the city of Memphis. When I read this, I immediately thought of the symbolic geometric illustration of 12 circles around another circle – see figure 91. This geometric diagram was representative of both the Moon and Earth and could be associated with heavenly imagery due to its connection with the layout of the New Jerusalem. At that stage of my investigation, though, I had to play down this connection as it was only an instinctive feeling and totally unfounded; however, I was to find further supporting evidence that it could well be linked to Edfu, after all.

Edfu's architect was apparently none other than Imhotep himself and his father Kaneferre. Together they built the site's first Dynastic temple in the 3rd Dynasty period of Pharaoh Zoser, for whom Imhotep had built the Step Pyramid at Saqqara. As Andrew Collins explains in *Gods of Eden*,[7] other legends state that the origins of the once-important city of Edfu are to be credited to the mysterious 'Shemsu Hor', the followers of Horus. This group had established their cult centre at Edfu long before the arrival of the pharaohs.

Wanting to know more about the Edfu Texts, I visited my local library in Colchester and asked for anything on the subject. I was met with blank faces. It was a specialist type of book that I was requesting, which they did not have. They would have to order anything relating to the subject from elsewhere. Nonetheless, within a week I found myself collecting a book from the library that they had managed to track down for me: *The Mythical Origin of the Egyptian Temple* by Dr E. A. E. Reymond.[8] In it she revealed her interpretations of what the Edfu Texts were saying about a strange world that existed in Egypt prior to any other peoples, or dynasties. The actual Edfu Texts were a compilation of many accounts taken from ancient sources. As I read the details in Dr Reymond's book I began to formulate my own interpretations in light of what I had previously learnt.

For several years I had assumed (wrongly) that my interpretations were unique to me, as only I could see the information for what it was. Although that may sound rather arrogant, it wasn't; it's just that my interpretations didn't agree with orthodox Egyptology, and anyone I spoke to about the subject either expressed embarrassed bafflement or told me that I was utterly and hopelessly wrong. Suddenly, things changed. Within a week of the *Sunday Times* article about Operation Hermes, I was talking, for hours at a time, with Andrew Collins. We both realised that we had independently studied the same source material and had drawn the same conclusions, as he was later to acknowledge in *Gods of Eden*.[9] This was a tremendous boost. I now had independent verification of another theory of mine.

'The Island of the Egg'

All of the Edfu Texts start by detailing the emergence out of the 'Nun' (the primeval waters) of a sacred island. This is identical symbolically with the primeval mound of Heliopolis, but also reminds us of the island of Glastonbury, surrounded by water, the site of Teotihuacan, and apparently the Giza pyramids, as geological evidence suggests. Reymond believed[10] this event happened during 'A first occasion', which relates to Zep Tepi, the First Time. This original island was known as the 'Island of the Egg', and it was surrounded by a circle or channel of water, which is almost identical to a description of Atlantis given by Plato. At the edge of this water was a field of reeds and a sacred area known as 'Wetjeset-Neter'. (Glastonbury Tor was surrounded by water full of reeds, it should be noted.) Sacred pillars, known as Djed pillars (see figure 45), were erected at the Wetjeset-Neter sites that served as perches for the first divine beings to inhabit the area. Numbering 60, they were led by a group known as the 'Drty' ('Falcons') or Sages who, in turn, were ruled by a strange figure known as 'Pn' ('God'). Various other groups were said to be present, but what is of interest here is that these 'enigmatic beings' preceded the Ennead (group of 9) of Heliopolis. These are outlined in Chapter 9.

On the original 'Island of the Egg', a violent conflict breaks out, caused when a serpent known as 'The Great Leaping One' opposes the sacred domain's divine beings. As a consequence of the battle that follows, all the inhabitants are killed and darkness descends upon the Earth again. Alternative names are recorded for the island, such as 'The Island of Combat', 'The Island of Trampling' and 'The Island of Peace'. In the myth, the only thing to survive from this period is a single Djed pillar. In view of all the symbolic connections with pillars, from the (vanished) pillar that Manetho apparently found inscriptions upon, to the pillars of Solomon's Temple and the pillars of Rosslyn Chapel in Scotland, it seems clear that pillars have always had some kind of important symbolic meaning. Eventually a second generation of beings is created known as the 'Shebtiu'. The new leaders, Wa and Aa, are known as the 'Lords of the Island of Tramplings'. Then 8 members of the Shebtiu are given special names, for no apparent reason, other than the probable significance of 8 itself.

The Wetjeset are joined by other divine beings, as well as a figure known as the Falcon. He is known as the 'Lord of the Perch' and 'The Winged One' and commands a group of individuals known variously as 'The Crew of the Falcon', 'The Senior Ones', 'Elders' or 'the Elder Culture'. This second generation of divine beings is known as the Netjeru, who become the new rulers of Wetjeset-Neter. Eventually they build a Temple known as the 'Mansion of Wetjeset-Neter'. The Edfu Temple texts state that this building stood in a vast enclosure which surrounded a second, inner enclosure, which held the temple itself. Exact details are given as to its measurements: 30 cubits west to east, 20 cubits south to north. This temple eventually becomes damaged or destroyed and the Shebtiu Wa and Aa are ordered by the (annoyingly unnamed) God of the Temple to enter a place named 'Place in which the things of the Earth were filled with power', which is yet another name for the water-encircled island. Inside, magic spells cause the water to recede through the use of mysterious power objects known as 'iht'; these had been stored within the temple. After all this, the Shebtiu simply sailed away – to who knows where?

After a period of time, the world begins to evolve again and the Wetjeset-Neters are succeeded by the Shemsu-hor, who were the ancestors to the pre-dynastic Egyptian race led by Horus of Behdet. He led to the first Horus Kings, who in turn led up to the foundation of the 1st Dynasty of a united Egypt *c.* 3100 BC. Dr Reymond is convinced[11] that the Edfu Texts preserve the memory of a forgotten culture that built Egypt's first temples, way before the first pharaohs.

It is resonant that after the 'Island of the Egg' resurfaced from beneath the primeval waters after the period of conflict, it became a tomb for the ghosts of the first divine beings. After this emergence it also became known as 'The Underworld of the Soul' and became the first resting-place of the body of Osiris, the god of the Underworld. The important point to note here is that the term 'Underworld' is that used in the Heliopolitan texts to describe the 'Duat Underworld', whilst the resting-place of Osiris is being linked with the 4th Hour, which forms part of the House of Sokar. As we have seen, Orion is positively linked to the Rostau/Giza plateau, so we can confidently say that Osiris is linked with both Giza/Rostau and the House of Sokar – the region in the Duat that is also linked to the supposed subterranean chambers and passages beneath the Giza plateau. In turn, we can further state that the original first sacred mound of the Wetjeset-Neter, with its field of reeds, water-encircled island and temple complex, was almost certainly the Giza complex.

The Island of Giza?

As I showed earlier, the Giza site marks the centre of the entire Earth's landmass. The 3 main pyramids are indeed made upon a raised mound of stone. Also, as I pointed out earlier, the pyramids are far older than is presently accepted. When they were originally constructed, the entire Giza plateau was a fertile, lush green area with an abundance of water. Not only that, but recent research and excavation work has revealed a broad trench cut into the rock that would have served to channel water from the Nile to the Giza site. The ancient historian Herodotus stated: 'To make it took 10 years, as I said, or rather to make the causeway, the works on the mound where the pyramid stands, and the underground chambers which Cheops intended as vaults for his own use; these last were built on a sort of island, surrounded by water introduced from the Nile by a canal.'[12]

But this doesn't end the story where the Edfu Texts are concerned. I still had questions. I wanted to know where, and if, such things as the Great Pyramid's capstone ever existed. If it did, where was it now? If the Edfu Texts were referring to the Giza site itself, would they contain any information relating to it? So it was back to burning the midnight oil and more research. Dr Reymond went on to state[13] that she thought the Osiris Temple at Abydos was also linked to the 'Island of Creation' as outlined in the Edfu Texts. Its massive structure differentiated it from all the other temples in Egypt. Earlier I stated that this Temple was in fact far older than generally believed and that it was in all probability constructed by the same people who were behind the construction of the Giza and Dashur sites. What is so intriguing about the Osireion, though, is that it has a water channel all around its inner walled enclosure, which is fed by a well – thereby mimicking, in stone, the 'Island of Creation'.

As Andrew Collins observed: 'The prehistoric "Creation Myths" of Edfu appear to recall specific individuals, events, locations and building projects from the epoch of the Elder Gods. Yet encoded in these ancient textual accounts is much more than this – clues that, if interpreted properly, will reveal the nature, appearance and meaning of what has remained in darkness beneath the bedrock of the Giza plateau for the past 11,500 years.'[14]

To both Collins and me, it appears that the 'Underworld of the Soul' can be considered to be the main source behind the legends of the Duat Underworld. If that island is indeed the Giza plateau mound, as all the evidence suggests, what can we expect the physical underworld to look like? The Edfu Texts state that this area can have an alternative title of 'Bw hnm'. This helps me argue that the place is a physical reality, as the prefix 'Bw' actually translates as 'Place' and the suffix 'hnm' has several possible meanings. As Collins points out, it can mean 'Kingship' as in coronation, a 'Coming together' as in royal festival, or it can mean a 'Consecrated well'. This translation led Reymond to term it 'Place of the Well'. The celebrated Egyptologist Joseph Jochmans, however, translated 'Bw hnm' as 'A deep underground place that is constructed'. This is very suggestive of a real 'understructure'.[15]

Relics, guardians and virility

The Edfu Texts inform us that the 'Iht' relics were stored in the 'Bw hnm', with Shebtiu guardians being able to enter and conduct magical spells that continued the act of creation outside. Collins has proposed that at the bottom of the Bw hnm, the underground structure, there could well be the Hall of Records containing the lost legacy of a forgotten race of great antiquity. I mentioned earlier that the earliest form of name for the primeval mound, as outlined in the Edfu Texts, is the 'Island of the Egg'. The egg, 'swht', is never fully explained, but is described as a creative force used for the formation of the Earth. As with all Egyptian names, this egg was known by many different names such as 'bnnt', meaning 'embryo' or 'seed', This was seen as the nucleus of the 'iht' power objects, as used in the underworld. The egg has also been associated as being one and the same as the so-called 'Great Lotus' or 'Throne'. Perhaps here we can see the origins of the symbol of the lotus which was eventually used in France as the *Fleur de lys*, as we have seen.

Next I would like to draw your attention to the word 'bnnt', translated by Reymond as 'Embryo', as this is a female rendering of the masculine root 'bnn', 'To copulate, to beget, to be begotten, virile, phallus'. While this seems an unusual mixing of verbs, adjectives and nouns, the point here is the notion of creation, of sexual energy, of potency. What really interested me was that it also derives from the same root as 'bnbn' or 'benben', the name given to the stone, obelisk or pyramidion which were all associated with the primeval hill. I couldn't help but believe that this particular benben stone was none other than the 'builder's stone that was rejected', the 'chief corner stone', i.e. the Great Pyramid's missing cap-stone. However, I needed further proof before I could seriously offer this as a viable possibility. Still, the implications of what the Edfu Texts were saying are clear: the underground complex, located beneath the original primeval mound of Giza/Rostau, did actually conceal a physical repre-sentation of a benben stone. The fact that the 4th and 5th Hours of the Duat (as covered earlier) very strongly indicate an underworld passage and chamber system – in accordance with the myths and legends – under the Giza complex, only adds more weight to the argument.

In essence, the Edfu Texts are in simple terms telling us that there is some kind of enormous stone buried underground, at the heart of, or at least central to, the Giza complex. From a symbolic perspective, if we view the Giza complex in its celestial representation of Orion, the central and most important star to the constellation is Orion's heel star, Sirius. Yet, as I have said, at Giza and the surrounding area, where Sirius would be projected in relation to the three main Giza pyramids, there is nothing on the ground; just a barely noticeable, very slight mound. This really got me thinking. As I said earlier, the obvious omission of Sirius on the ground must have the greatest significance. But at this point, to be absolutely sure that something could very well be located beneath the projected site of Sirius, I needed more information; not for my own benefit, but in order to convince others.

The indestructible pillars of Enoch

At the beginning of this book I drew your attention to the ancient Egyptian Coffin Texts, in particular the spell number 1,080. To refresh your memory I shall repeat it: 'This is the sealed thing, which is in darkness, with fire about it, which contains the efflux of Osiris, and it is put in Rostau. It has been hidden since it fell from him, and it is what came down from him onto the desert of sand.'[16] This is another indicator of a benben stone lying buried at the heart of the Giza/Rostau subterranean complex. The fact that it has 'fire about it' immediately made me think of a pyramid, since, as we now know, the root word for pyramid is *pyr*, 'fire'. Knowing of the importance of the value of 12 within the 12 Hours of the Night in the Underworld, I took this to be of both numerical value and symbolic value.

Because the values of 12 and 7 recur throughout this book, I would like to bring to your attention the story of Enoch, when he finds himself taken on a visit to the 7 heavens. Once in the 7th heaven, he finds that he is alongside a house built of crystals, surrounded by strange tongues of fire. The floor has the appearance of crystal with a ceiling like the path of the stars and lightning. It is easy to see why some analysts have seen this taking place inside a spaceship. Inside the room there were moving wheels as bright as the shining Sun and beneath it came streams of flaming fire. Collins[17] used the same account of Enoch as it demonstrates an image of 'The sealed thing with fire about it', as mentioned in the Coffin Texts. Collins thought it possible that the fire referred to in both cases was merely the shimmering radiance that could be expected when torchlight, especially orange, is refracted through transparent crystal-line surfaces.

Could it therefore be that a benben stone of the underworld complex is some kind of enormous crystal? Collins certainly thinks so,[18] but in fact this is where we start to differ in our interpretations of the Edfu Texts. He believes that the 'iht' relics could have been hand-held phallic crystals resonating cosmic energy contained within the nucleus located at the heart of the complex. I was instantly reminded of the single large stone that the Babylonian god Oannes was portrayed as carrying in his hand (see figure 1), and also of the curious legends featuring Enoch, where it is claimed that some kind of sacred stone was placed beneath the Giza pyramids.

Relevantly, the Jews of Alexandria during the Ptolemaic period viewed the Great Pyramid as having been made by Enoch himself, who was also equated with Thoth/Hermes. As Collins points out,[19] Enoch was said to have been the inventor of the 12-fold division of the starry canopy which is reflected within the astrological sections of the pseudepigraphic books accredited to the patriarch. Enoch then went on to become confused with later stories circulated among the Copts (Egyptian Christians) of Cairo, featuring the legendary King Saurid Ibn Salhouk who, being warned of the coming deluge, built the pyramids of Giza and then constructed secret chambers in which all the arts and sciences of his race were preserved.

Marble and Laterus

According to one tradition, Enoch constructed vaults in which he sealed away items that included tablets inscribed with strange words that angels had given to him. Once these were sealed, Enoch constructed 2 indestructible columns, one made of marble so that it might never burn, and the other made of 'Laterus' so that it might not sink in water. (It is, I think, worth noting here that on the brick column, the 7 sciences of mankind – the so-called archives of speculative Masonry – were inscribed.) On the second column he placed an inscription stating that a

short distance away, a priceless treasure would be found in a subterranean vault. Now we can, of course, choose to view these stories as
pure fable, but as they all seem to be saying the same thing, and use the
same symbology, I am prepared to investigate them, especially as they
bear no connection at all with Enoch's few brief mentions in the book of
Genesis, nor does he appear in any other Hebrew sources.

We can even gain some idea of the actual layout of the complex from
the account of the Duat underworld, as outlined in Heliopolitan
cosmological tradition, when it speaks of the 1st division or hour
consisting of an 'arrit', which means a hall or antechamber of the Duat.
Once past this entrance, there were 12 more divisions or hours to pass
through. Symbolically, this indicates 12 further chambers or rooms. We
can feel pretty confident in assuming this, having seen the previous
evidence of values, numbers and dimensions being symbolically carried
within religious rituals and myths.

The symbolic journey involves moving from one division into the next,
which suggests that the rooms are connected, and as they are related to
the Sun passing in a circular motion, it is tempting to think of the
chambers being formed in a circle. Further support for this idea comes
from the fact that we know that the twin Aker lions, set as guardians at
the gates to the entrance and exit of the Duat underworld, can be seen as
representative of the equinoctial horizon during the precessional cycle of
Leo. Andrew Collins drew very similar conclusions, suggesting that the
chambers represented the 12-fold division of the ecliptic. Even more
substance for the suggestion that the chambers of the Duat were formed
in a circle comes from the fact that the Duat was itself conceived as being
round like the path of the Sun. Furthermore, the Sun god Re, on 19th-
and 20th-Dynasty wall inscriptions, is referred to us 'Ra, exalted
Sekhem, Lord of the hidden circles, bringer of forms, thou restest in
secret places and makest thy creations in the form of the God Tamt.'[20]

A circle within circles

As for the 'egg of creation' that was in the middle of the Duat, it becomes
clear that it is situated in the centre of a circle formed from 12 smaller
circles. On perceiving this I knew that my earlier instinctive hunch was
more credible, with the actual pyramidion being at the centre of a
complex surrounded by 12 chambers and buried in the Duat underworld.
The image of this layout was easy to visualise as I had already come
across it so many times; for example, the geometrical illustration of the
New Jerusalem, the layout as projected over Stonehenge and the
projection over Glastonbury Abbey – refer back to figures 92 and 94. It
would therefore appear that a design pattern of 12 chambers, all
connected to myths of buried sacred books of wisdom and knowledge

and mathematical codes, had been passed down through millennia, intact from the depths of antiquity.

As we shall see shortly, all we have to do now is locate the actual position. This can be achieved in several ways, using different methods of calculation that still all converge on exactly the same site; and I mean *exactly*. Such is the precision of the ancients and their codes.

Chapter 33

Ancient Technology

This is a short chapter to introduce you to certain artefacts that are, quite simply, out of place according to orthodox history. If we were to ignore the obvious technological achievements of the pyramids themselves, we are still left with many cases of highly technological artefacts that defy explanation. It is becoming increasingly obvious that our ancient forefathers were intellectually and technologically far more advanced than we have given them credit for. It is very unwise to jump onto a bandwagon and label an artefact as being of extraterrestrial origin simply because it is technologically advanced and appears ahead of its time. Until we have conclusive proof of an origin, we must remain open-minded to all possibilities. Sometimes we have to make a leap and take the plunge in order to further the research; if it later proves to be incorrect, then we should at least admit so and reappraise the information, not simply leave the matter bogged down under academic dogma.

A copper cylinder and an iron rod

One of the first ancient artefacts that caught my imagination, many years ago, was one recovered from Baghdad in June 1936 when railway construction workers came across an old grave covered with a stone slab. During 2 months of excavations, the Iraq Antiquities Department uncovered artefacts dating from the Parthian period of 248 BC to AD 226. Amongst the finds was a unique object which consisted of a copper cylinder and an iron rod, which the German archaeologist, Wilhelm König, soon suggested might be a primitive electric cell.[1]

Once back at the Berlin Museum, he related the discovery to similar Iraqi cylinders, rods and asphalt stoppers, plus some slender iron and bronze rods that were all corroded, as if by a mild acid. König even found 10 of these battery cells joined together, which in effect increased the voltage output. Separate experiments in the United States with replicas of the cells produced half-volt batteries, which lasted nearly 18 days. The batteries used an electrolyte of 5 percent solutions of vinegar, wine or copper sulphate. Sulphuric and citric acid, which was readily available at the time, would have worked just as well. This demonstrated conclusively that these were indeed batteries.

In addition, a lot of the jewellery found in the Middle East, especially Iraq, has been found to be electro-plated, for which electricity is needed. For many years it was argued that such pieces couldn't be electro-plated, and must have been plated by some other means. However, here was the answer: this was achieved by the use of these simple cell batteries (see figure 128).

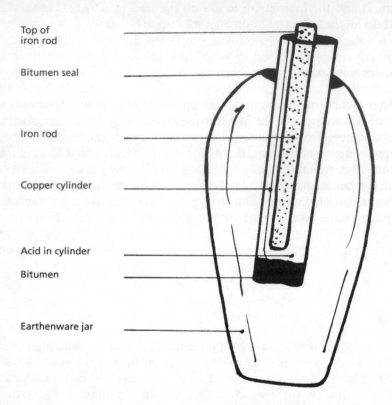

Top of
iron rod

Bitumen seal

Iron rod

Copper cylinder

Acid in cylinder

Bitumen

Earthenware jar

Figure 128.

In this context it is intriguing that King Solomon's Temples were reputedly lit at night by special pearls that glowed without flame. Furthermore, inside the Pyramids of Giza there is no blackening of the ceilings caused by flame torches. This has puzzled scholars, since it indicates that the builders must have had another means of lighting their interiors. Sir Norman Lockyer noted[2] that deep within the later 5th-Dynasty pyramids, very intricate and detailed paintings have been etched in stone. The inner chambers containing these paintings are in total pitch darkness, and there is no sign of blackened carbon on the walls, which would have been present even if well-trimmed torches or oil lamps had been used. Orthodox Egyptology explains the lack of soot deposits on the ceilings by claiming that the ancients used a series of reflective mirrors to shine sunlight into the interiors.

Here's another mystery: engravings on the tomb walls of Dendera show devices that look very much like electrical insulators. Even the Djed pillar amulets seen earlier (figure 45) remind most people of electrical conductors. And, of course, at the very beginning of this book we saw the Egyptian glider found at Saqqara near the first step pyramid of Zoser (figure 2) and the hieroglyph found on the wall at Abydos (see plates). What do all these bizarre anomalies add up to?

Does this compute?

Another technological anomaly was discovered by sponge divers off the coast of Antikythera in the Mediterranean Sea. A corroded fragment of a metallic device of complicated construction with gears and dials was revealed when it was cleaned. In 1959 Derek J. de Solla Price of the Institute for Advanced Study at Princeton, New Jersey, proved the device to be a basic form of analogue computer used to short-cut astronomical calculations. This device, known as the 'Greek Antikythera computer', dates to around *c.* 65 BC (see figure 129).[3]

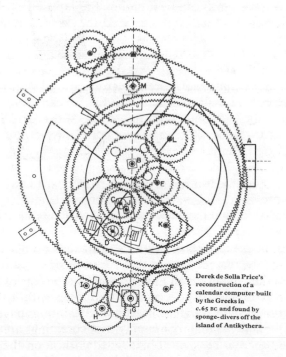

Derek de Solla Price's reconstruction of a calendar computer built by the Greeks in *c.*65 BC and found by sponge-divers off the island of Antikythera.

Figure 129.

Advanced stone-cutting?

We are taught that the Giza pyramids were built using only the most primitive of tools, copper saws and drills. Large stones were cut and quarried by hammering in wooden pegs that were then soaked. As they expanded, they forced the stone to break away in two. This is even the accepted view when dealing with solid granite, one of the hardest stones on Earth. Splitting rock is one thing, but machining it to exact dimensions as in the case of the King's Chamber sarcophagus is another matter.

At Aswan there is a quarry with an unfinished obelisk still present, estimated to weigh nearly 3,000 tons. Egyptologists confidently state that such obelisks were carved out by pommel stones pounding away, thereby gradually chipping away the stone in channels. Yet if one cares to look carefully at the evidence, as American technologist Christopher Dunn did during his visits to the site in 1986,[4] you will also notice that located within one of the channels is a large round hole drilled into the bedrock that measures 12 inches in diameter and 3 feet deep. This is highly suggestive of drilling out many holes around the perimeter and simply removing the webs between the holes later. Of course, this would mean accepting the possibility that the ancient Egyptians possessed such technology. But this may not be so far-fetched as it at first appears.

Identical quarry marks can be found on the exposed parts of the fallen granite casing stones that once sheathed the second pyramid at Giza. Now, archaeology bases a lot of its theories upon the type of artefacts and tools that it finds; tools especially indicate how advanced the peoples who used them were. However, we are expected to believe that the Giza pyramid builders used crude tools – yet constructed buildings that are vastly over-engineered and built to a standard that we cannot duplicate today. The enigma of the Giza and Dashur pyramids is that artefacts have been found with no evidence of the tools that could have produced them. For a start, the King's Chamber sarcophagus exhibits a very high level of technological expertise that we would be hard pressed to match, even with state-of-the-art cutting technology. I will explain why in a moment.

Furthermore, how do we explain complex detailed carvings upon Diorite and granite that have been executed to a very high level of proficiency and accuracy? These are two of the hardest rocks known. Even the British Egyptologist Sir William Flinders Petrie, one of the first and most eminent Egyptologists, recognised that the tools declared to be responsible for making the Pyramids and Temples of Giza were wholly inadequate and insufficient. He even expressed amazement regarding the methods the ancient Egyptians were apparently using to cut hard igneous rock, crediting them with methods that we are only now coming to understand.

It is stated as a matter of accepted fact that the ancient Egyptians – as well as Central American cultures – did not use the wheel. If this is the case, how come there are artefacts in the Cairo Museum that clearly show the distinct markings of lathe work? Sir William Flinders Petrie had two items in his collection that he positively identified as being lathe-turned items.[5] These were bowls that even had indentations where they had been fixed to a lathe. On the sarcophagus inside the King's Chamber, saw marks are still visible (on the north end). These marks, if made today, would be seen as reflecting either the differences in the aggregate dimensions of a wire-band saw, with abrasive wire entraps doing the cutting, or the side-to-side movement of the wire (or the wheels that drive the wire). The effects of either method would be a series of slight grooves with the distance between them determining the feed-rate and either the distance between the variation in diameter of the saw, or the diameter of the wheels. The distance between the grooves on the King's Chamber sarcophagus is 0.05 inches, which indicates quite a high feed-rate; certainly one that would be very difficult to maintain manually. However, as the marks are found on an ancient sarcophagus, they are instead assumed to be the result of a large primitive saw of at least 9 feet in length. This only compounds the saw feed-rate.

The drilling conundrum

There's more to consider. The King's Chamber sarcophagus shows irrefutable evidence that the ancients who built it used a technique known as trepanning, which leaves a central core as it cuts downwards. This is one of the fastest and most efficient drilling methods available today. If the drill didn't need to cut all the way through an object, it was simply sunk to a desired depth and the core broken off. Many of these core cast-offs still show the grooves from the drills. Regarding these granite stone cast-off cores, Sir William Flinders Petrie wrote: 'The spiral of the cut sinks 0.1 inch in the circumference of 6 inches, or 1 in 60, a rate of ploughing out of the quartz and feldspar which is astonishing.'[6] From an engineering perspective, this is a phenomenal feed-rate for drilling into any material, but for granite it is totally astonishing. Petrie noted 3 main anomalous points that he tried to explain. Firstly there was a taper on both the hole and the core; secondly, there was a symmetrical helical groove following these tapers, which showed the drill had to be advancing into the granite at a feed rate of 0.1 of an inch per revolution of the drill; thirdly, the confounding fact was that the spiral groove cut deeper through the quartz than through the softer feldspar – in conventional machining, the reverse would be the case. Donald Rahn of the Rahn Granite Surface Plate Co., Dayton, Ohio, stated in 1983[7] (when asked by Christopher Dunn) that when drilling granite, diamond drills, rotating at 900 revolutions per minute, penetrate at the rate of 1 inch in 5 minutes; this calculates to 0.0002 inches per revolution. This is with the very latest, fastest and most sophisticated diamond drilling system available today. So how is that the ancient builders of the Giza pyramids were able to drill into granite with a feed rate that was 500 times faster?

The other notable anomaly about their cutting skills is the fact that they cut a tapered hole with a spiral groove that was cut deeper through the harder constituent of the granite. We cannot answer *one* of the points raised by Petrie, so how are we to answer *three* of them? Dunn had been puzzled by Petrie's points and set out to find the answers. He challenged a group of toolmakers who had been using drills day in day out for decades to replicate the ancients' work. Of the people he challenged, all but one gave up, declaring that it could not be done. Eventually that one exception declared that he had found the answer but also opined that the ancients couldn't have had the machinery in their times.[8]

In the normal sense of drilling and lathe-turning, you require an element to cut with that is hard enough to cut the object being machined, and also to withstand the tremendous pressures exerted upon it, without shattering – or splintering in the case of rock. Now, the fact that the spiral is symmetrical is quite remarkable, considering the proposed method of cutting. The taper indicates an increase in the cutting surface area of the drill as it cut deeper, hence an increase in the resistance. A uniform feed under these conditions, using manpower, would be impossible. Petrie theorised that a ton or two of pressure was applied to a tubular drill that consisted of bronze inset with jewels. The major drawback with this theory is that it does not take into account that under several thousand pounds of pressure, the jewels would actually work their way into the softer bronze, leaving the granite practically untouched. This also does not explain the faster feed-rate through the even harder quartz sections.

The mystery drill explained?

Christopher Dunn, with many years of research in this subject, seems to have found a solution that explains all 3 of Petrie's points. Before explaining his theory (which I agree with), it has to be noted that ultrasonic machining is the oscillatory motion of a tool that chips away material like a jackhammer, just as a road drill chips away a pavement, only much faster. An ultrasonic tool bit vibrates between 19,000 and 25,000 cycles per seconds (Hertz). Ultrasonic machining has as a consequence found itself in the unique position of being used for precision machining of odd-shaped holes in hard, brittle materials such as hardened steels, carbides, ceramics and semiconductors. To accelerate the cutting action, an abrasive slurry or paste is used.

Using ultrasound drilling also explains why the grooves in the far-harder quartz sections were cut deeper and faster than the softer feldspar, as quartz crystals are employed in the production of ultrasonic sound. Conversely, this means that the quartz sections within the sarcophagus become responsive to the influence of vibration in the ultrasonic ranges, thus inducing the quartz to vibrate at a high frequency. This means that unlike ordinary machining, where the quartz offers more resistance and in turn a slower cutting and feed-rate, by using ultrasound machining the quartz would be induced to respond and vibrate in sympathy with the drill bit and the high-frequency waves, which would then in turn actually amplify the abrasive action, thus cutting faster.

The grooves can be explained in several ways. An uneven flow of energy may cause the tool to oscillate more on one side than the other. The tool may not have been mounted correctly, or a build-up of abrasive on one side of the tool may have cut the groove as it spiralled into the granite. As for the tapered sides of the hole and core, this would be perfectly normal when we consider that the basic requirement for all types of cutting tools is to provide clearance between the tool's non-matching surfaces and the worked piece. This would mean that instead of having a straight tube, we would have one with a wall thickness that gradually became thinner along its length. The outside diameter would get smaller, thus creating the clearance between the tool and the hole, with the inside diameter getting larger, creating a clearance between the tool and central core. This, then, would allow a free flow of abrasive slurry to reach the cutting area, and would also explain the tapering of the hole and core; as the tube drill is of a softer material than the abrasive, the cutting edge would gradually wear away. As a result, the dimensions of the hole would correspond with the dimensions of the tool at the cutting edge. As the tool becomes worn, the hole and core would wear accordingly to form a taper.

The spiral groove can be explained by understanding the methods used to uniformly advance machine components. The speed of the drill is not the major factor, as the drill is merely a means to advance the drill into the worked piece. When using the screw-and-nut method, the tube drill can be efficiently advanced into the work piece by turning the handles in a clockwise direction. As the oscillating drill is forced into the granite, the ultrasonically induced motion of the drill would do the cutting, not the speed of the drill itself. The speed of the drill would only be needed to sustain a cutting action at the work-face.

In short, therefore, we can see that it can be positively proved that only ultrasound resolves all the unanswered questions. Other theories only answer 1 of the questions, never all 3![9] Of course, the problem is that this method is totally anomalous for the accepted period of history the sarcophagus *apparently* comes from. Some would discount it for that reason. But should they?

PART FIVE

CRACKING THE CODE

Chapter 34

The Venus Legacy and
Atlantean Records

Venus

We have seen that Venus is unique in our solar system, since it has an opposite orbit around the Sun (i.e. retrograde), compared with the other presently known planets. We also noted that it is the only planet with a Fadic value of 4 – all the others which have 9. There must be good reason for this individuality. And there is. The planet was deliberately placed within our solar system *to be used as a warning marker*, as I shall explain in a moment. Certainly, the ancients watched it very carefully and with respect, calculating its time periods to (almost) unbelievably accurate figures.

Now, if you look back at figure 121, you will notice that as Leo and the Sun are rising *at the same time*, Venus is visible above them, following the same path. In these particular circumstances, Venus's path forms a planetary loop, lasting for just 6 months in any one year, which takes it across the top of the constellation of Orion. This phenomenon only occurs once every 12,500 years, and the next time it will occur happens to be the year 2012. This is the *exact* year which the Maya predict will mark the end of 'this time' of man – i.e. the end of the age of Pisces. It will also mark the highest point of Sunspot activity as calculated using the Mayan Sunspot cycles. Sunspot activity and solar flares are *already* on the increase and certainly show signs of increasing further. The impact on humans will, I am sure, be dramatic, due to the massive increase in solar radiation, which in turn will directly affect our biological rhythms. Even more worrying, however, are the effects it will have globally. As the Sun's electromagnetic polarity reverses, causing the increase in solar flares, the Earth will be bombarded with massive amounts of electromagnetic particles that will directly affect the Earth's *own* electromagnetic polarity.

This massive influx of electromagnetic particles will cause a short circuit in the Earth's dynamo, as it were. This will cause it to reverse. Since the Earth's geomagnetic field is fairly strong, if it reverses it will generate worldwide magnetic fields. There will undoubtedly be major earthquakes, volcanic eruptions, tidal waves and enormously powerful weather conditions; furthermore, there will be Earth-crust displacements all over the globe, as its thin lithosphere is let loose with no stable geomagnetic forces to keep it in balance. On top of this, it will cause a technological super-disaster. This will happen because as the electromagnetic field reverses, it will generate strong potential differences that will be so powerful that all of our world's very sensitive electronic equipment will burn out *in a single moment*. As the poles reverse strong currents will be induced, capable of destroying most, if not all, electronic appliances. Everything – pocket calculators, watches, radios, computers, televisions, electronic ignitions in cars, electronic controls of ships, planes, communication satellites and more – dependent upon electrical power will simply cease to function.

An author named Michael Mandeville has written a book titled *The Return of the Phoenix*.[1] He sees this period as marking the fifth flight of the phoenix, which is symbolic of the Earth's entire lithosphere loosing itself from its mooring ropes and taking flight, so to speak. In fact, the phoenix story is one of the oldest on Earth; on one level it is used to symbolise regeneration, the cycle of death and rebirth; on another, the phoenix is an ancient symbol for the Earth *itself*, which undergoes a profound change every 10,000 to 60,000 years, when it 'flies'. If Mandeville is correct, then it will fly again on 22 December 2012. When this happens, the Earth's thin lithosphere may shift by as much as 30 degrees of latitude. We will see below the evidence that suggests that this has indeed occurred previously, the last time thrusting the present Antarctica south by nearly 2,000 miles.

But don't lose heart, fearing all is lost. The Giza pyramids act as clocks, to help signal a multitude of events in different times. In any case, it seems totally illogical to me that a code would be designed to span millennia and be *deliberately* kept secret within esoteric traditions and mystery schools until the appointed time, only to be revealed to the world at the very last hour before we meet our doom. No, the codes of antiquity have followed their course as planned. We can now use those codes if we so choose, to help us. Part of those codes will lead to such sites as the Hall of Records in Egypt. The coming geophysical upheavals won't be pleasant, but then, nor is giving birth. Yes, there will be unpleasant effects, but we do have some time to start organising ourselves to minimise as much of the potential destruction as possible. This will be especially essential in areas that will shut down temporarily: nuclear power systems, for example. I'm not naïve and I'm sure that, unfortunately, things being what they are, business will carry on as usual with a head-in-the-sand attitude. This is why I personally feel it is so important to locate and uncover such a find as the Hall of Records. If we find *bona fide* records and artefacts that conclusively show that mankind had once before reached a very high level of civilisation, at least as advanced as our own, but had perished after a predictable natural disaster induced by the Sun's magnetic polarity being reversed, and then *still* choose to ignore the evidence, we only have ourselves to blame. I'm far from melodramatic about this, but I, for one, will certainly start to make serious plans.

Obviously I intend the above comments to be sobering in the extreme. Conversely however, I believe that the outcome for mankind can be greatly improved if the Hall of Records can be located. Finding the Hall of Records will indicate that the ancients intended it to be recovered in our era, just as the myths testify. Never forget that the contents of the Hall of Records were preserved specifically to *help* mankind through a predictable and specified stage.

Edgar Cayce

No book on the Hall of Records would be considered complete without some mention of the American psychic Edgar Cayce. It is mainly due to him that the Hall of Records came to be so popularly known. The American Association for Research and Enlightenment (ARE) is a foundation dedicated to locating the Hall of Records and is an organisation directly inspired by Edgar Cayce; it is often referred to as the Edgar Cayce Foundation.

Edgar Cayce is often looked upon by those who believe in his psychic readings as a 20th-century prophet. There is no doubt that this remarkable, and some say saintly, clairvoyant appears to have had access to limitless knowledge whilst in a hypnotic trance. He was a deeply religious man and initially found it very difficult to accept some of the readings he had given in a trance, especially those which gave details about past lives and reincarnation. Nevertheless, he freely used his gift to diagnose illnesses of people named to him, then prescribe remedies ranging from the orthodox to totally unorthodox. He placed considerable stress on having the right mental attitude and stated, 'Mind is the builder.'[2] Often Cayce himself was unable to understand the medical terminology that he had used in a trance, yet medical methods were judged basically sound after investigation by official medical authorities. In 1932 he set up a research foundation, ARE, in Virginia Beach, USA, primarily to preserve and collate the stenographic records of over 14,000 of his trance readings.

After gaining considerable respect for his psychic readings, especially in America, Cayce turned his attentions to other fields of investigation. He affirmed and explained the reality of reincarnation – much to his own consternation, as he was a Sunday School teacher. He is probably most famous for making predictions for the years up to 1998, many of which have been fulfilled. 1998 is also marked as the date of the Great Initiates' return to Earth. During this time, too, the Great Pyramid would finally be decoded, and an ancient 'Hall of Records' would be discovered, 'at the proper time', somewhere between the Sphinx and the Nile. As I shall demonstrate, the projections of the Hall's site do indeed fall between the Sphinx and the Nile.

Insights into the Great Pyramid's secret

According to Cayce, the building of the Great Pyramid was started in 10,490 BC, nearly 12,500 years ago, which ties up perfectly with the revised construction dates proposed earlier. (This date also agrees – with extraordinary exactness – with the date of the last known reversal of the Earth's magnetic field, as determined in 1971 by Swedish scientists, as I shall explain later.) It took 100 years to complete the Pyramid and within it were recorded, in terms of passage angles, types of rock, colour etc., the future rise and fall of nations and the evolution of worldwide religious thought. Peter Lemesurier's *The Great Pyramid Decoded* demonstrates convincingly how this method of coding in the stone works.[3] Cayce further described the Hall of Records as a *Pyramid* of Records, as follows:

> As the Sun rises from the waters, the line of shadow (or light) falls between the paws of the Sphinx, that was later set as the sentinel or guard, and which may not be entered from the connecting chambers from the Sphinx's paw (right paw) until the time has ben fulfilled when changes must be active in this sphere of man's experience. Between, then, the Sphinx and the river.[4]

Some have seen the Sun rising from the waters as a reference to the ancient time of the High Nile and its annual flooding, which only occurred from late June onwards. On the other hand, it could also mean that the Hall could only be entered during this particular time of the year. We have seen the connection between the Sphinx and the cross quarter sunrises. If Cayce is to be believed, the Hall of Records will take the form of a sealed 'Time Capsule' containing ancient records and artefacts supposedly left by Atlantean refugees and colonists, who founded the Egyptian civilisation and built the Great Pyramid. It is further suggested that its likely form is that of a pit sealed over by a pyramidion. If that pyramidion should turn out to be 30 feet high and 47 feet along the base and have an angle of 51° 51' 14.3, then of course this cultural bombshell will, fittingly, be the missing capstone of the Great Pyramid itself.

The legacy of a lost continent?

As for Atlantis, I feel that it is really just a symbolic name for the previous worldwide civilisation that existed prior to the last reversal of the Sun and Earth's magnetic fields and the subsequent cataclysm that followed. I also believe that a major portion of this civilisation still remains practically intact beneath the ice of Antarctica, as held by Graham Hancock[5] and the Canadian investigators Rand and Rose Flem-Ath.[6] I am inclined to believe this since ancient artifacts such as the Piri Reis and Oronteus Finnaeus maps show the coastline of Antarctica, but free of ice. The Antarctic coastline was not mapped or really known until the late 1950s, yet these ancient maps (which depict not only Antarctica but also the Americas before they were discovered by Columbus) were apparently copied from even earlier sources.

I feel that the Hall of Records may very well contain details about the lost continent of Atlantis, if it ever did exist; conversely, if it *didn't* exist, I am sure there will be information on what it was based on, so we shall have an answer either way. From all the accumulated information it becomes apparent that perhaps part of a former worldwide civilisation was based on what is now Antarctica. Geological evidence shows that it once occupied a position nearly 2,000 miles further north than it occupies today. Its current position was caused by displacement that swivelled a large portion of the Earth's crust in a circular motion. I am more than confident in predicting that beneath the two-mile-thick ice sheet that presently covers most of Antarctica, the evidence of a highly advanced civilisation lies buried, just waiting to be discovered. If this sounds ridiculous, then bear in mind that the Earth crust displacement theory (outlined above), as formulated by Professor Charles Hapgood, was backed and supported by Albert Einstein. This instance of it, including Antarctica, did not occur in a due north-south direction but followed a swivelling course, pivoting (as it were) around what is now the central plains of the USA, so that the North Pole was located in the Hudson Bay. At the same time, the north-western segment of the hemisphere – Alaska and the Yucatan, and large parts of Siberia – swivelled northwards into the Arctic Circle. This happened around 14,500 to 12,500 BC, thus tying in with the 'destruction of Atlantis' as recorded in myths and legends (such as those given by Plato), *and* also with the reversal of the Earth's magnetic field.

A history of turbulence

The Earth's magnetic field has been shown by geological evidence to have been reversed at least 170 times in the past 200 million years alone. The dating of 12,500 BC also accords with extraordinary exactness with the date of the last known shift (i.e. not a full reversal*) of the Earth's magnetic field as established in 1971 by the Swedish scientists N. A. Morner, J.P. Lanser and J. Hospers on the basis of geological core-samples.[7] The end of this shift was calculated to have occurred in around 12,500 BC. This notionally (if we accept the evidence for the construction of the Great Pyramid taking place at this time) ties in with the myths telling of its construction *after a great cataclysm*. The evidence further suggests that the Earth's magnetic field did not so much reverse, but was geologically and astronomically *induced*, by the Earth shifting (by up to 30 degrees) on its axis. This would produce tidal waves and geological upheavals of unimaginable magnitude – again as testified to in all ancient myths and religions. The ancient Egyptian priests maintained that this had actually occurred at least 4 times during the periods to which their records referred, recounting this belief to Herodotus, who then wrote it down. They maintained that without doubt the Sun rose twice where it now sets and twice set where it now rises. In the tomb of Senmut, the architect of Queen Hatshepsut, a panel on the ceiling shows celestial signs and constellations in a reversed orientation of the southern sky. The centre of this panel is occupied by the Orion group constellation, but Orion appears *west* of Sirius, instead of east. A friend suggested that if this was the case, then the Zodiacal signs should now be going the other way relative to the background of space. This is a simple mistake to make, but it must be noted that what in effect has happened is that the Earth has tilted on its axis, not its direction around the Sun, as would have to be the case for the Zodiac to also change in sequence.

One notable piece of evidence comes from the frozen remains of thousands of mammoths in Siberia. These mammoths were frozen to death in an instant, some still standing up with food in their mouths. The surrounding vegetation is that of a temperate warm climate. A *gradual* decrease in temperature would have forced the mammoths to warmer climates; if this had not been possible, they would then have died slowly, not the rapid way that they did. Such mammoths are, even today, being dug up and their meat cooked and eaten, with no ill effects at all. Over 10,000 tons of ivory is still obtained from their tusks every decade. No plausible explanation has yet been formulated that answers how they all died and were frozen immediately. However, the evidence shows that the region in question was thrown, almost instantly, into a polar position during the Earth crust displacement. The Earth shifting, in this way, makes sense of this mystery. After the Earth's last magnetic shift, massive aftershocks occurred at widely separated intervals, until about 9,500 BC. Evidence also shows that the Earth's magnetic field is still altering and could shift again, as it appears to do so every 12,500 years or so. We are

* Full reversals occur only once every 1,176,471 years.

currently nearing the end of the last 12,500-year period. I think it very wise to establish these facts conclusively in order to be prepared, especially as our ancestors appear to be warning us through their myths, legends and mathematical codes. We still do not fully understand the effects of gravity or magnetism ourselves. After all, even the gravitational effects of Jupiter can affect radio signals on Earth, while the Moon is usually at its nearest point to the Earth when earthquakes occur.

These are serious considerations.

Chapter 35

Conclusion

The Alignments

We are now ready to use the information contained within this book to help us locate the fabled Hall of Records. The journey has not been an easy one, and as I pointed out at the very beginning, it was not meant to be. If it had been, the location would have been established a long time ago.

In my argument I have tried to demonstrate – from a practical, logical and scientific perspective – that our past history is not how we imagine it, or how it is taught, as if undisputed fact, in today's schools and universities. I have shown that a mathematical code exists that reaches us today, having been carried intact across the millennia of time. Its journey has certainly been a difficult and bloody one with, for example, countless millions dying in defence of seemingly contradictory religions that in fact carried the same information.

We now know that throughout the universe and creation itself, a comparatively limited set of numbers and values constantly recur, in defiance of the accepted laws of probability, and that these numbers constitute evidence of a unified and coherent plan. The evidence from antiquity further supports the inescapable fact that our ancient forefathers were very much aware of these figures and values. Not only that, but they also understood the fundamental principles of predictable cyclical patterns of events, *which could be calculated in advance*, as everything is governed by a mathematical constant. As a consequence, they were able to leave us messages not only within the religions of the world, but also erected in solid stone.

We have seen that the religions from across the world all recount legends of great civiliser gods and universal floods; all use water symbolism; and all carry a mathematical code. This is indicative of a single source of origin. We have also seen how the same symbolism and values are visible within ancient architecture, such as that of Giza in Egypt, Teotihuacan in Mexico and even Stonehenge, Avebury and Silbury in England. How can we justify any longer our blinkered and narrow-minded approach to history, when so much overwhelming evidence proves our ancient forefathers were technologically advanced?

As a further consequence of the ancients' knowledge and understanding (which *we* are only just beginning to relearn), they were able to use the principles of the universal codes to predict accurately when great cataclysms would occur. Just prior to the last major upheaval, they deliberately buried their accumulated wisdom and knowledge within sealed time capsules around the world. The biggest and by far the best-known of these is the Hall of Records in Egypt, known in the Edfu Texts as 'The Chambers of Creation'.

The very layout of the Hall of Records has been preserved and handed down to us today in enough detail for us to know that it is constructed with 12 circular chambers around a 13th that contains the Great Pyramid's gold-sheathed pyramidion ('the builder's stone that was rejected'). Also within the 12 circular chambers would be various items, artefacts and documents that dealt with a specific aspect of the technology and science of the ancients.

That there was an advanced worldwide civilisation that existed thousands of years before the supposed dawn of civilisation cannot be denied any more. No longer can we view the *verifiable* evidence from the past with the complacency that has been prevalent for so long in academic circles. Once uncovered, the information revealed within the Chambers of Creation will force us to re-evaluate our past, whether we like it or not. Because of the major – and potentially dangerous – aspects of unleashing such information onto an unsuspecting world, happy in its naivety about our true past and what may lay ahead, proper procedures and common-sense guidelines will need to be in force when releasing and interpreting the information. To do otherwise would not only be dangerous and foolhardy, it would also totally undermine the entire *raison d'être* of the site.

During the course of this book, I have tried to convey some of the experience, good and bad, of my journey and my quest. I have outlined just the tip of an enormous iceberg of information that has led me to my conclusions. I am not content to sit back and theorise and debate the issue for countless years; I am a person of direct action, and as a consequence, I will put my hypothesis, to the test, irrespective of the final outcome. I am not afraid of being proved wrong as I have a belief in my own convictions. I do not think I am wrong, far from it, but I am a realist and fully accept the fact that I may be incorrect in my final interpretations. I do not possess the arrogance to state unequivocally that I am absolutely correct. I can only state *that* once the site is confirmed.

So, using all the encoded symbolic imagery from ancient myths, Templar and Freemason rituals and Christian iconography, we can now calculate the exact position of the hidden circle outlined in the Edfu Texts, as follows.

Alignment 1. The 1,746 value and the Heliopolis and Letopolis line

We have seen just how important the value of 1,746 is. We know that the gematria value for Jesus is 888, that for the Devil is 666, and that for Mary is 192. When added together, these total 1,746. 1,746 is also the value for 'Lord God of Israel', as well as for 'Holy Spirit'.

One of the ancient Egyptian rituals involved the body of the dead Pharaoh being ferried across the Nile to Heliopolis then back across the Nile to Letopolis before finally being returned to Giza. This route took a triangular journey to 2 sacred Benben stones, at Letopolis and Heliopolis respectively, and was known as the 'Gateway to the Duat'. See figure 130.

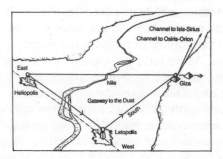

Figure 130.

'Gateway to the Duat' in itself seems like a giveaway, as it clearly refers to, or at least symbolises, a gateway into the Duat, which we know to be the underground complex of the area. Now, if we use this triangulation to Heliopolis and Letopolis and also use our mathematical codes, we can locate a position that would indicate the site of this gateway by using simple projections following standard mathematical principles.

Having seen how the Great Pyramid's passage angle of 26 degrees from due east echoes a line that passes through Bethlehem, the Reed Sea, River Jordan and so on, we know that the ancients were able to use projections across distances and encoded them within their symbolism. Therefore, if we take the all-important value of 1,746 and project a line in a north-easterly direction towards Heliopolis, we can get our first triangulation marker. We have deduced the key importance of a north-easterly direction not only from the rituals that place an initiate in a north-east corner (such as in Freemasonry) but also from the fact that the Sun rises in a north-easterly direction. In addition, alignments from various ancient sites such as the causeway at Stonehenge point in a north-easterly direction – in this instance, 1,746 feet. What's more, the Sun travels 14 degrees above the horizon in a north-easterly direction at Stonehenge before appearing to rest on the Heelstone, and we know the importance of the value of 14 from the many sources I have outlined.

Adding further weight, the Great Pyramid's causeway is exactly 1,746 metres in length on its outside edge, and we know that various key phrases in religion have a gematria value of 1,746.

The very fact that the ancient Egyptian ritual-route heads in a north-easterly direction lets us know that this is the bearing to choose. Moreover, the significance of direction is emphasised in England by the St Michael's Ley line heading in a north-easterly direction, as well as the axis line at Avebury. Yet more evidence is that Stonehenge's trilithon stones also face outwards in a north-easterly direction.

Now we need to multiply our distances by 10 (as is acceptable by the conventions of gematria) to calculate on a global scale, and then move in a north-easterly direction for 17,460 metres from the Great Pyramid's apex. (We could use yards instead, or sacred yards, and only have an overall error of 52 metres. We will use metres, as this is a simple unit of measure, being 1 ten millionth of the distance from the Earth's equator to the North Pole. As we have seen, this is not the best unit of measurement available to us (since it is of recent origin), but it is perhaps the *easiest to calculate*, and hence the ancients, having most probably followed the same path of technological progression as us, correctly anticipated that we would develop the same unit of measures. So, if we then take a bearing due north towards Letopolis until we have a distance of 12,000 metres between the outer limit of the 17,460 line, and the due north Letopolis line, we can draw a line from the midpoint section of each line to each corner of the triangle we have constructed. Where these lines all cross at the centre marks our 'Gateway-to-the-Duat' position, and thereby the central position of our site, i.e. the buried Hall of Records complete with the Great Pyramid's capstone within the hidden circle. The circle, as we have seen, is identical to the symbolic geometric diagram of cosmology with 12 smaller circles about it, just as outlined in the Edfu Texts.

The distance from the Great Pyramid's apex to the spot marked by the crossing lines is equal to 9,210 metres on a bearing of 64 degrees from east or 26 degrees due east of north. 26 degrees is the angle of the Bethlehem line, and remember also that the Sun's equator takes 26 days to complete one complete rotation. Both figures – 64 and 26 – are of great importance, while 921 is also important: the value of Jesus's total ministry in days. 921.44 metres equals half a minute of equatorial latitude as well as the perimeter of the Great Pyramid, and furthermore, the length of the 8 × 8 grid over the Giza site is also equal to 921.44 metres. As for 64, 8 × 8 is an important value within DNA and RNA, while the magic square of Hermes and the Great Pyramid equalled 64.

We have also seen that the entire Giza site is connected with the value of 27. There are 27 notches that run down either side of the Grand Gallery inside the Great Pyramid. The entire site is also aligned with an angle of 27 degrees that points at the 3 belts stars of Orion on the horizon

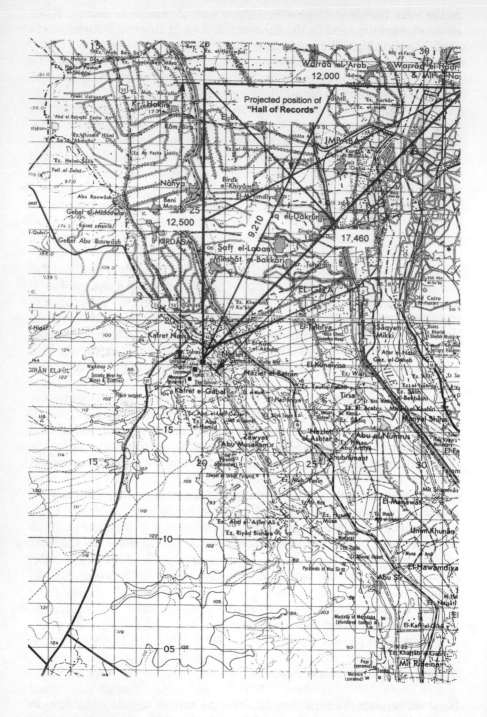

Figure 131. Alignment 1.

in the year 10,500 BC. Elsewhere, there were 27 stones in the northern circle at Avebury, and in the Bible the Pillars of Boaz and Jachin were each 27 cubits high. We know, too, that there are 27 differences between man and our nearest Neanderthal relation. Finally on the value of 27 it must be noted that the Mayan figure for calculating the birth of Venus is 1,366,560, which by Fadic addition equals 27 (Fadic 9).

Could all these details have simply been a product of pure chance? If so, then we would not expect to find further proofs and alignments that converge on exactly the same site. And yet, just as the myths and legends tell, where the lines converge, the area is slightly raised as a barely discernible mound.

But there is more.

Alignment 2. The Pythagorean triangle

We do find further alignments. The angle between the descending and ascending passages within the Great Pyramid forms a Pythagorean triangle when a line is taken from the centre of the Queen's Chamber to the base of the King's Chamber entrance step. The angles produced are 90, 64 and 24 degrees, making a Pythagorean triangle with a ratio of 5, 12, and 13. We have seen the importance of all these numbers, especially in Fadic numbering.

If we take this triangle and place the 64-degree angle corner/point over the apex of the Great Pyramid with its 5-ratio base-line pointing due east, we can then extend its 12-ratio line due north, and the 13-ratio line in a north-easterly direction. The north-easterly line just happens to follow the exact same line angle as that formed by the intersecting line of the previous 17,460 line. In addition, the apex of the 5, 12 and 13 ratio Pythagorean triangle also converges on the exact same spot as the crossed lines marking the centre of the previous triangle.

The north-easterly 13-ratio line measures exactly 921.44 metres as well. If the previous 17,460 triangle had been formed using any other measure of distance, then the resultant intersecting north-easterly line that converges onto the site would have had a totally different length and angle.

Now we have 2 calculations that converge on exactly the same spot. Doesn't this fact alone tell us something?

Alignment 3. The Fibonacci curve

Now we can use the other important numbers, as found in the Mayan numbering system, various world legends, the Bible (Revelation), and

371

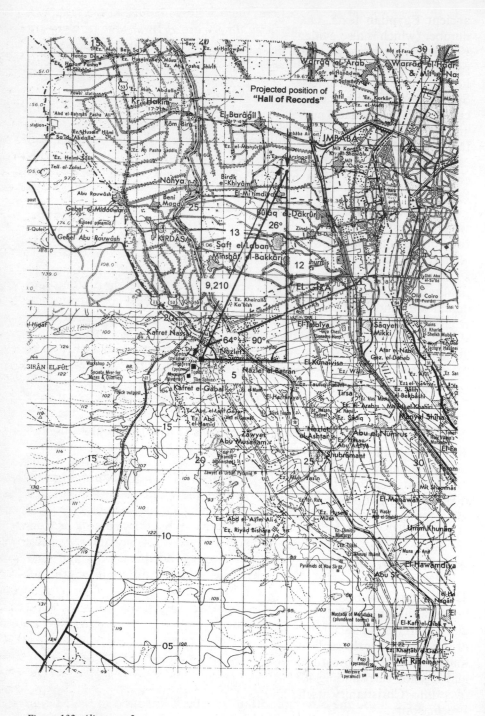

Figure 132. Alignment 2.

372

ancient Egyptian texts. One such is the value of 144,000. From this number (which is also evident within the Fibonacci scale) we can form a Fibonacci curve as we have already seen (figure 41) over the Giza pyramids. We know that the Sphinx plays a part in giving us a clue in how to locate the Hall of Records. If we therefore use the right paw of the Sphinx as a marker point (as various prophecies state we should) then we can project a Fibonacci curve that not only gives other valuable details and values, but also converges on exactly the same spot. What's more, the 8 × 8 grid square of 64 squares over the Giza pyramids means that we can draw a golden mean radius from the Great Pyramid's north-eastern corner that swings right through the shoulder of the right arm of the Sphinx.

If we fix the corner of the central line box with the ratio of 21, we can form the rest of the Fibonacci curve accordingly. Taking the various ratio boxes and stopping after reaching the 144 ratio box, we can see that we have a rectangular box that has the longest side measuring exactly 14,400 metres from north to south. If we were to use Sacred yards, our final position would only be in error by a fractional margin, and as the actual site underground is quite large, we would still end up there regardless. What else do we know about 21? The Great Pyramid was sheathed in 21 acres of white polished lumite stone; in the *Book of the Dead* there were 21 pylons in the sacred Hall of Maati. Note also that the 21 ratio box just happens to measure 1,746 feet diagonally. It is also significant that the 13-ratio box equals 792 feet – the Earth's diameter is 7,920 miles.

So, what does *this* tell us? Obviously, someone is trying to inform us about something regarding this spot, *using different methods*. Just one of the alignments would be sufficient to enable us to locate the position, but the ancients very wisely saw fit to give us *several*, in order to guarantee that the information reached us in one way or another. On top of that, they also used the values taken from the very building blocks of life itself.

Alignment 4: The projection of Sirius

Throughout this book I have demonstrated the celestial connections between the stars and ancient sites. We know that projections across the globe marry up to ancient sacred sites and that the last of the 7 Wonders of the ancient world replicates the 3 belt stars of Orion. We also know that Sirius was the most important star of antiquity, with many myths and legends surrounding it. The symbolism of Sirius was even carried over into Christianity itself, and, via the Knights Templar, reached Freemasonry.

Knowing full well the importance of Orion, and that the Great

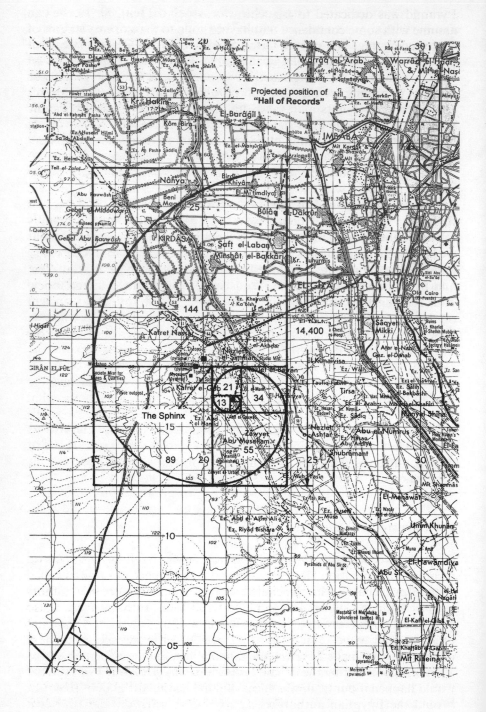

Figure 133. Alignment 3.

Pyramid was dedicated to Isis who was associated with Sirius, we can assume with some confidence that having gone to the extreme lengths of reproducing the 3 belt stars of Orion, the ancients would not totally omit Sirius from their plan. We know that an underground complex exists on the Giza plateau, and also that the architect of the Great Pyramid was directly informing us of the importance of Sirius, since the Queen's Chamber shaft points at it, and the corner niche is a spectrographic representation of the light signature of Sirius. Moreover, we have seen the importance of the value of 58 carried across time for no apparent reason, yet the declination of Sirius in 10,500 BC was 58 degrees.

When we take the ancient saying 'As above, so below', and apply it to the Giza pyramids with the 3 belt stars of Orion, we can project a position of Sirius on the ground in relation to the Giza pyramids. When we do this, as in figure 142, it comes as no surprise to note that it actually projects directly over the position of the 3 previous alignments. Now as we have seen, it has always been the 3 belt stars of Orion that have led us and that are represented in stone by pyramids in Giza, at Teotihuacan, and by alignments in England. We have seen that all the astronomical data relating to Sirius have likewise been encoded within the ancient myths, especially the Egyptian Osiris and Isis myths. Tellingly, when we view the various alignments of Orion, Sirius is always depicted just below the horizon – *hidden and symbolically buried.*

Can we honestly say that all this information is just pure coincidence? No we can't. And as we cannot, we must seriously view the facts for what they are. Furthermore, we have to consider what potential discoveries lie ahead, if we are prepared to act upon the evidence. The only way to do this is to test the information by actually going to the site and checking it out for ourselves. This has been my intention and aim since making the connections.

The Opening. A blueprint for destiny

Over the weekend of 28 and 29 March 1998, I (along with several members of Operation Hermes) attended a conference in London called 'The Giza Debate', which included several lectures by notable authors such as Andrew Collins, Adrian Gilbert and John Anthony West. I also gave one. Dr Ali Hassan, the former Director of the Egyptian Antiquities Organisation, gave 2 lectures that were well received, but more importantly, he made 2 statements that are very encouraging indeed.

At one point during the debate Dr Hassan was questioned about what would happen if our team was successful in locating the Hall of Records. Would the Egyptian authorities sit on the information and restrict it from public view? Much to his credit, Dr Hassan stated (as recorded on

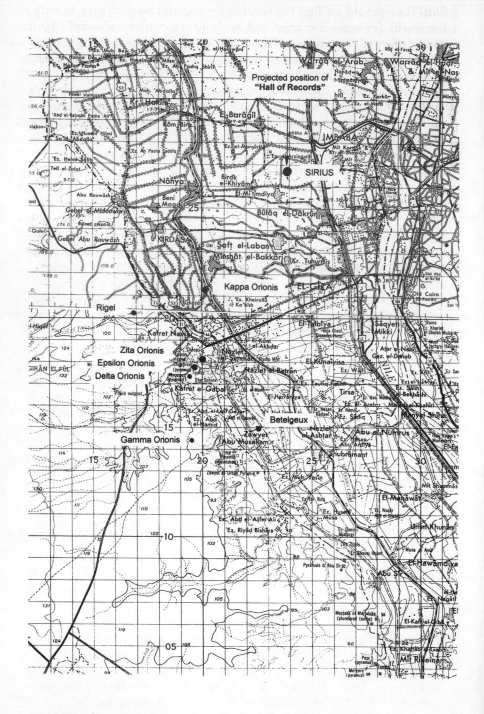

Figure 134. Alignment 4.

film) that should we find the records they would be displayed openly to the world, for academic appraisal, without restrictions or secret agendas being followed. Dr Hassan also stated during his opening address that it was at last time for Egyptology and science to come together in order to move forwards, adding that the entire chronology of ancient Egypt needs total reassessment, as it was very evidently in error – timescales would inevitably be pushed far further back than had previously been thought. This statement from a highly respected and eminent Egyptologist is a landmark comment by itself, the importance of which cannot be over-emphasised.

Once the Hall of Records is found, it will still take some time to analyse fully whatever is recovered. This analysis will have to be thorough in order to do it justice. We cannot expect the information to answer all our present problems, as some people are inclined to believe. Finding the Hall of Records is a beginning, not an ending. If a total re-evaluation of human knowledge is called for, due to the Hall's information being at odds with presently accepted history, so be it.

Whatever the outcome, one thing is becoming perfectly clear. The past as we presently perceive it will never be the same again, and the future may well be beyond our wildest dreams.

Epilogue

I have put my reputation on the line in writing this book. There may well be minor mistakes within it and maybe you will not agree with all my ideas and theories; but at least I am trying to establish conclusively the validity of my research. I am not afraid to stand up and be counted, as it is only from having the courage to face such challenges that breakthroughs will be made. Only by scholarly and scientific processes and practicable application, built upon previous research, will the answers be found. We have a moral obligation to listen to what our forefathers are telling us. It may prove that we cannot afford to ignore them. Certainly it is far wiser to listen to them now, and prove it all wrong, rather than ignore the information and suffer the consequences at our peril.

In order to test my research, I have – with the support and help of my co-directors – put together a team of highly motivated individuals ranging from PhD qualified geophysicists, archaeologists and surveyors to medical doctors. Our aim is simple: to survey the proposed site using the most highly advanced probing and scanning equipment available in the world. After our survey is complete, we will hand over all the scientifically prepared information to the Egyptian Antiquities Organisation for assessment. In time, if this proves agreeable to the Egyptians, we would then like to assist both *financially* and with personnel to excavate the site. This could prove to be a lengthy process. I would urge any conspiracy theorists to bear this in mind, as it would be wholly unjustifiable to condemn the Egyptian authorities for only doing their jobs properly. As Dr Hassan said, putting it into context, they cannot undertake all the projects and answer all the claims made upon them. If they did, they would be forever doing just that and not their actual jobs. Indeed, they are swamped with requests every day. They definitely cannot let just anyone turn up to their sites and start digging, causing untold damage in the process. The monuments of Egypt are their greatest assets and it would be foolhardy of them to drill into them simply to satisfy the whim or claim of whoever chooses to propose a theory.

Operation Hermes is also in the process of organising several other major expeditions that will take us from the deserts of Egypt to the

378

jungles of Central and South America, the plains of China and eventually to the frozen ice fields of Antarctica.

Finally, what will be revealed over the coming years with, for example, the new discoveries of huge pyramids in China? Evidently we are living in a new period of awareness. How we use that new awareness and any new information it brings to light is strictly down to us. We cannot sit idly waiting for some figurehead to come to the world and do it for us. If religion has taught us anything, it is the principles of responsibility, of self-determination, of choice. There is much to think about and a lot of it is sobering, but I for one do not feel that all is doom and gloom, with apocalyptic disasters waiting to destroy mankind and just the few chosen people being spared. As I have said earlier, there are definitely changes ahead, and considerable upheavals. But we are fortunate enough to know about them in advance, and if we listen to the warnings and messages from the past, we can minimise whatever devastation lies ahead, and plan accordingly.

Hermes Foundation International

The Hermes Foundation International is an organisation launched to accommodate the overwhelming responses from across the world that Operation Hermes received, from people of all walks of life who wished to get involved or support us in some manner.

To date, we have members who range from Egyptologists, archaeologists, medical doctors, geophysicists and airline pilots to service personnal and hod carriers. Both the Foundation and Operation Hermes are *non-profit-making*, non-religious and non-political organisations which aim to cross all such divides and self-imposed barriers.

It is our intention to bring together like-minded individuals who have a desire for the truth and a thirst for knowledge. Any monies raised from our endeavours and membership fees will go towards other projects, expeditions and research, to help further our understanding of the past. We also aim to help with the preservation and restoration of ancient sites across the world for posterity.

If you are interested in joining us, or simply wish to find out more about the above, we can be reached via our extensive website detailed below.

Operation Hermes website: http://www./Inter.com/Hermes

Appendix 1

The Colchester Connection

My quest for knowledge started in Cyprus, but really took off whilst living in Colchester, because in 1983 I made the connection between the Orion constellation and this part of eastern England. I had made this connection purely by chance after plotting 135 Ley lines that all converged on a church in Lexden Road, Colchester. This church happened to be on a point known as Beacon Hill, still marked on Ordnance Survey maps (Sheet 168). The number of Ley lines that converged upon the site was huge in comparison with other such Ley-line convergences across England and Europe. I had only plotted lines where there were at least 3 major churches or tumuli or old monument sites, but as I had many other maps, I was able to pin these around my central map, and thereby follow the lines onto adjoining maps.

The area around Colchester is steeped in history, with many Knights Templar traditions and former holdings. I had been aware that Colchester was formerly the capital of England and that it had Arthurian connections, as explained earlier. Whilst studying the Ley lines I began to mark the older churches and monument sites with a small orange dot sticker. I hung my map against my bedroom wall and stood back to view all the orange dots. Many of the dots were located near to place names that contained words such as Knights Hall, Blind Knights, Copt Hall etc. As I lay on my bed listening to music several evenings later, I noticed that the central orange dots, positioned near Beacon Hill, reminded me of the 3 belt stars of Orion (Orion, you will recall, was one of the very first constellations that I had learnt of whilst in Cyprus). As soon as I made this connection, I immediately saw that 4 other orange dots, marking 4 other churches, also mirrored the image of the other 4 stars that form Orion. I had been aware for many years of the significant value of 7 and the constellation of Orion, but I had also recently read an article about cathedrals in Europe being aligned to represent the celestial constellation of Virgo in France. Could this therefore be the equivalent, but in England? I thought. I quickly removed the other orange dots to leave just the 7 that formed Orion.

As I looked closely at the map where the 3 belt stars seemed to be represented, I noticed that 3 ancient causeways were present; one was named Brymes Dyke. This immediately made me think of the causeways on the Giza plateau in Egypt. Having read *The Sirius Mystery* years previously, I was very much aware of the importance of Sirius. As a consequence I projected where Sirius would be in relation to the 3 belt stars. I was excited to note that Tiptree Priory marked that actual position. The very next day I borrowed my younger brother's car (I couldn't afford one, being at college at the time) and dragged my friend, Simon Baldwin, off to the Priory. Upon arrival, we were saddened to see that there were no remains of it; a brick Elizabethan mansion now stood practically on the spot, with some of the Priory's original material having been used in its construction.

After our initial disappointment we noted that the site was situated on a commanding position on a hill with excellent views of the surrounding countryside. Both being military enthusiasts we discussed military strategy and tactics and the positioning of the site. Less than 3,000 feet away from the Priory is the highest point of land on the entire map at 82 feet above sea level (except for a tiny rise in the very top left-hand corner at a place named Deans Hall at 86 feet above sea level).

Naturally we rationalised that this was all just a coincidence, so we set off to check out the other churches in turn. This research showed that the 'monument' signs on my map had marked the positions of ancient dykes that had originally led up to 3 tumuli on Beacon Hill itself – now long since built over, but one is still visible. (Simon had to endure many a visit to churches and monuments up and down the country over the following years. A Sergeant Major in the Reserve Forces, he is now also an integral member of Operation Hermes.)

As a direct consequence of the projection of Sirius marrying up with an old priory just outside Tiptree, and the 3 main Colchester monument sites each being marked by a causeway leading to them (just as at Giza) and appearing to represent the 3 belt stars of Orion, I felt compelled to look more closely at Giza and its pyramids. Using the same logic as the Colchester projections, I eventually projected Sirius in relation to the Giza pyramids. When I did so for the first time, I was truly excited at just how accurately the 3 belt stars of Orion married up to the 3 main Giza pyramids. I was disappointed, however, to see that nothing was represented upon the ground where Sirius was projected. I also noted that the other stars of Orion did not match exactly any other pyramids, as I have explained earlier, but how little did I realise where my initial findings would eventually lead! Not in my wildest dreams could I have foreseen the unfolding of a secret that had been preserved across the millennia of time.

In regard to the Priory at Tiptree, it is worth noting that it was dedicated to St Mary and St Nicholas. One other interesting point that caught my eye only very recently was the fact that in 1281, due to poverty, a licence was issued for the Canons (members of the religious community on the

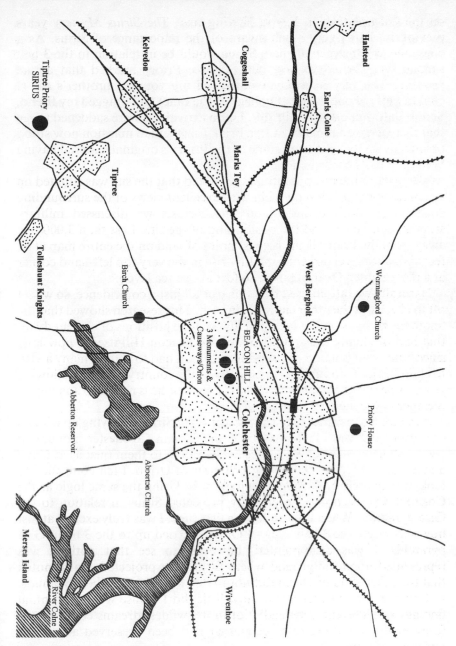

Figure 135. The Colchester area.

site) to enclose 60 acres of forest, and then in 1302 there was the generous gift of 153 acres of land. We have already seen the importance of this value for a number of reasons. This figure seems rather odd, as measuring of acreage was usually rounded off in whole numbers.

As for Colchester itself, it must be noted that it contains many churches of very ancient foundation. Furthermore, the Roman wall that once surrounded it is still very much in evidence. The wall enclosed an area of 108 acres. Again we have seen the importance of this value. In time I shall return to the Colchester research to take the investigation further, but as the information would fill volumes, and as space here does not permit an assessment that would do it full justice, it will have to wait for another day and another book.

Appendix 2

The Solar System

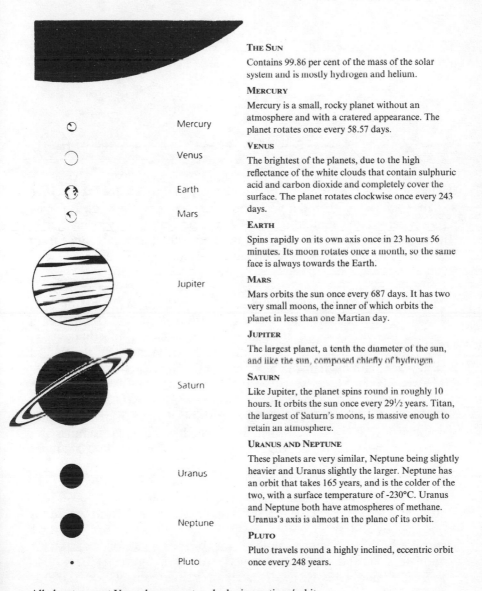

The Sun
Contains 99.86 per cent of the mass of the solar system and is mostly hydrogen and helium.

Mercury
Mercury is a small, rocky planet without an atmosphere and with a cratered appearance. The planet rotates once every 58.57 days.

Venus
The brightest of the planets, due to the high reflectance of the white clouds that contain sulphuric acid and carbon dioxide and completely cover the surface. The planet rotates clockwise once every 243 days.

Earth
Spins rapidly on its own axis once in 23 hours 56 minutes. Its moon rotates once a month, so the same face is always towards the Earth.

Mars
Mars orbits the sun once every 687 days. It has two very small moons, the inner of which orbits the planet in less than one Martian day.

Jupiter
The largest planet, a tenth the diameter of the sun, and like the sun, composed chiefly of hydrogen

Saturn
Like Jupiter, the planet spins round in roughly 10 hours. It orbits the sun once every $29\frac{1}{2}$ years. Titan, the largest of Saturn's moons, is massive enough to retain an atmosphere.

Uranus and Neptune
These planets are very similar, Neptune being slightly heavier and Uranus slightly the larger. Neptune has an orbit that takes 165 years, and is the colder of the two, with a surface temperature of -230°C. Uranus and Neptune both have atmospheres of methane. Uranus's axis is almost in the plane of its orbit.

Pluto
Pluto travels round a highly inclined, eccentric orbit once every 248 years.

All planets except Venus have counter-clockwise motions/orbits

Appendix 3

Further Mathematics

Maths in the solar system

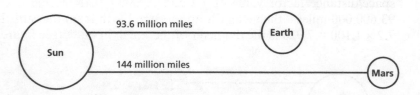

We came across the number 5,040, which is equal to $1 \times 2 \times 3 \times 4 \times 5 \times 6 \times 7$, or $7 \times 8 \times 9 \times 10$, and a very important value to the ancient Greek philosophers. Note that Mars is 50.4 million miles away from Earth. (Interestingly 144,000,000 miles minus 93,600,000, Earth's distance from the Sun, is 50,400,000.) We saw previously the connection of the value of 5,040 and its relevance to the Great Pyramid.

- The Fadic value for the Sun is either 3, 12 or 12,000. When we multiply 12,000 by our space/distance factor of 72 (that all-important number in the Osiris myths), we get 864,000, which equals the Sun's diameter in miles. In consequence we can work out the distance from the Sun of each planet and its diameter as shown in the figure above.
- The first planet, Mercury, will be at a distance of $300 + 100 + 100 =$ Sun + Sun + Moon values, and have a diameter of $300 + 100$. Space values of 5 (500) and 4 (400) can then be multiplied by our space/distance number of 72,000 and 7.2 respectively, which will convert to miles as a perceived measure. Thus, Mercury is $500 \times 72,000 = 36,000,000$ miles from the Sun and has a diameter of $400 \times 7.2 = 2,880$ miles.
- Venus is found by utilising the space/distance numbers of the Sun, Moon and Mercury, in the following manner: $300 + 100 + 500 + 30 + 10 + 50 + 40 + 5 + 3 + 10 + 580 = 1,048$; the distance from the Sun is obtained by adding $900 + 30 + 5 + 3 = 938$ (Fadic value 4). Then if we convert both numbers by multiplying by our space/distance factor number of 7.2 and 72,000 respectively, we obtain figures of $7.2 \times 1,048 = 7,545.6$ miles (this is the diameter of Venus), and $938 \times 72,000 = 67,536,000$ miles, which is the mean distance of Venus from the Sun.

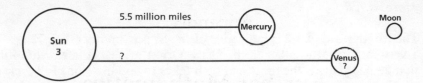

- The Earth can be evaluated in the same manner, by using the distances of the Sun, Moon, Mercury and Venus: 300 (Sun) + 100 (Sun) + 500 (Mercury distance) + 200 (Venus distance) + 30 (Sun) + 50 (Mercury) + 10 (Sun) + 20 (Venus) + 40 (Mercury) + 40 (Venus) + 10 (Moon) = 1,300. Diameter is 1,048 + 20 + 30 + 2 = 1,100. Converting by our space/distance factor value of 7.2 and 72,000 equals 72,000 × 1,300, 93,600,000 miles – the mean distance of the Earth from the Sun. Then 7.2 × 1,100 = 7,920 is the diameter of the Earth in miles (see figure).

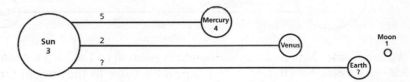

To calculate the distance from the Sun and diameter of Mars, we add 10 + 10 (Sun and Moon), giving 20 for its distance, and its diameter 1,100 + 4,000 + 700 = 5,800. Note that 5 and 8 are evident here. Conversion to miles is again by our distance/space factor numbers of 7.2 and 72,000 respectively, but as Mars is past Earth, further from the Sun, the number factors increase by 10 to the power of 3 for distances and decrease by 10 to the power of minus 1, for diameters. Hence 7,200,000 × 20 = 144,000,000, which is the mean distance of Mars from the Sun in miles, and 0.72 × 5,800 = 4,176, which is equal to the diameter of Mars in miles (see figure).

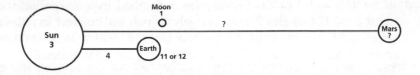

The important point to note here is the figure 5,800, or 58. This is not only found on the layout pattern of the Giza pyramid complex in Egypt, within its 5:8 grid square design, but is also a very important number within the Knights Templar traditions. I think this value has to be telling us something. Its connection to Mars, and also to the Queen's Chamber corner niche, possibly serves as double symbolic representation.

More on 720

The length ratio of 7.2 is indicative of the 'space' number 720; 72 is also a very important number in the Osiris/Orion myths. It is worth noting that 25,920 years is the time the Earth takes to complete one full cycle in the Zodiacal precessional period (i.e., the time our solar system takes to complete one revolution of the galaxy). When divided by the 360 degrees in a full circle, 25,920 is equal to 72. This is the number of years it takes for the Sun to move in its precessional cycle through 1 degree. At Teotihuacan in Central America, the Pyramid of the Sun is exactly 72 feet high. Furthermore, another number we have considered reappears in this context: a shadow cast on the pyramid during the vernal equinox of the year takes exactly 66.6 seconds to move down its face.

More on the Pythagorean triangle and the solar system

Take two 3, 4, 5 Pythagorean triangles and fold them into a 5, 12, 13 triangle. Circles can now be drawn with the diameters 3 and 4; these represent the Moon and Mercury respectively. The distance from Mercury to the Sun is 5.

The line joining the vertices of the two 3, 4, 5 triangles meets AC at D. DC is 2.4 long, and the point Y is marked at a distance of 2.4 from A. A line drawn perpendicular horizontally from Y meets line AB at X. The length of XY equals the diameter of Pluto's Moon, which is 720 miles. When the combined lengths of AY and DC (2.4 = 2.4; total 4.8) are deducted from length AC (that is, 12), the result equals 7.2. The space/distance factor is 720, remember.

Now, if we draw a small circle so that it touches line AC and the vertex of the 3, 4, 5 triangle it would have a diameter of 2. The number 2 represents the planet Pluto. The 11 also denotes the Earth number 11. and, 43 is Uranus (Fadic value 7). A circle with a diameter of line AC (12) would represent the Sun's number, 12, while line AB (length 13) equals the Sun's distance from the Earth. The numbers 3 and 4 plus their Fadic value 7 from the smaller triangles gives us 347, the distance between the Earth and Moon. The inherent geometry of the Fadic numbering system allows for: the formation of Charon (Pluto's moon), important for its 720 diameter value; Pluto, for its 1,440 diameter value; the Earth; the Moon; Mercury; and the Sun; *plus* various distances between the bodies of the solar system. The other planets can be discerned in this construction, but because I appreciate that it is complex and demanding, I have discussed here only those which are important in our quest.

For the mathematically inclined person here follows the necessary mathematical treatment to verify the results stated in the previous part.

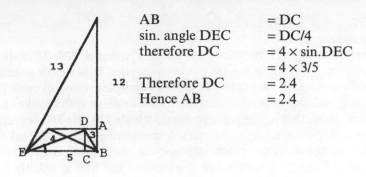

AB	= DC
sin. angle DEC	= DC/4
therefore DC	= 4 × sin.DEC
	= 4 × 3/5
Therefore DC	= 2.4
Hence AB	= 2.4

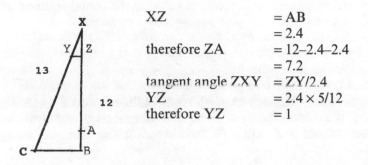

XZ	= AB
	= 2.4
therefore ZA	= 12–2.4–2.4
	= 7.2
tangent angle ZXY	= ZY/2.4
YZ	= 2.4 × 5/12
therefore YZ	= 1

A circle is drawn, centre M and radius r, so that the lines BX and BC are tangents. Thus triangle BCM is right angled, and the angle, between any radius of and tangent to the same circle, is a right angle.

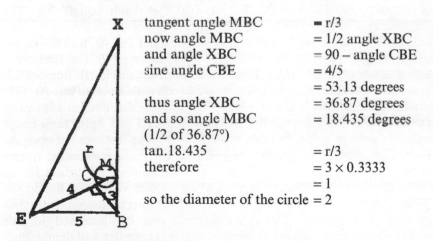

tangent angle MBC	= r/3
now angle MBC	= 1/2 angle XBC
and angle XBC	= 90 – angle CBE
sine angle CBE	= 4/5
	= 53.13 degrees
thus angle XBC	= 36.87 degrees
and so angle MBC	= 18.435 degrees
(1/2 of 36.87°)	
tan.18.435	= r/3
therefore	= 3 × 0.3333
	= 1

so the diameter of the circle = 2

From the mathematical solutions it can be seen that:
1. The radius of the circle near the vertex of the 5, 12, 13 triangle represents Charon, s-1.

2. 7.2 is indicative of the 720 miles factor, which converts s-numbers to perceived ones.
3. The circle of diameter 2. represents the planet Pluto, s-2, and the '1 1' Earth, s-11.
4. Diameters of s-4 and s-3 represent Mercury and the Moon.
5. s-12(00), and s-13(0000) are Sun diameter and Earth distance from it.
6. s-3, 4 and 3 plus 4, that is s-347, represents the distance between Earth and Moon.
7. s-43 represents the seventh planet, Uranus.

Mayan Glyph Maths

If the Mayans did not deliberately use a very sophisticated mathematical system whereby they used their vigisimal system to make numerical puns, then we are left with the following:

69 could be reversed to give 96 and 620 is a numerical anagram of 260, but these numbers are written in base 10, whereas the Mayans used base 20. This means that the elements of these numbers when written in the vigisimal system would NOT break down into 6, 9 and 2.

Example:
The number 234 as expressed by the sign for 11 (meaning $11 \times 20 = 220$) followed by the sign for 14, it looks as if 69 would be the sign for 3 (meaning $3 \times 20 = 60$) followed by the sign for 9 – and then juggling these two elements couldn't possibly produce the number 96.

Likewise, it looks as if the Mayans 620 would be the sign for 400 followed by the signs for 11 (again, $11 \times 20 = 220$) and for zero. No combinations of these signs would take us to 260, which in the Mayan System would be the sign for 13 ($13 \times x\ 20 = 260$) followed by the sign for zero, and you can't get to 620 from those two signs.

In short, this means that the final interpretation is down to the individual concerned.

Bibliographic Notes

Chapter 2
1 Temple, R.: *The Sirius Mystery*, Century, 1998.
2 Blumrich, J.: *The Spaceships of Ezekiel*, Bantam Books, 1973.
3 Alford, A.: *Gods of the New Millennium*, Hodder and Stoughton, 1997.
4 Alford, A., op. cit.

Chapter 3
1 *The Sunday Times*, 20 August 1995.
2 Hawkes, J. (ed.): *The Atlas of Ancient Archaeology*, Michael O'Mara, 1994, p.9.
3 Pablo, S. Anthropologist from the Zoological Institute at the University of Munich. Co-author of article that appeared in the Cambridge Massachusetts, journal, *Cell*.
4 Wolpoff, M., Professor of Anthropology at the University of Michigan.
5 *National Geographic*, 187.6, 1995.

Chapter 4
1 Sitchin, Z.: *The Twelfth Planet*, Avon Books, 1976, Chapter 12, p.349.
2 Sitchin, Z., op. cit., Chapter 12, p.354 and p.358.
3 Sitchin, Z., op. cit., Chapter 11, p.334.
4 Lemmon, R.: *Chemical Reviews*, Vol. 70, 1970, pp.95–109.
5 Pearce, E. K. V.: *Who Was Adam*, Paternoster Press, 1969.

Chapter 5
1 Canup, R.: University of Colorado. *Quest For Knowledge*, Vol. 6, 1997.
2 Kirshvink, J. L., Ripperdau, R. L., and Evans, D. A.: *Science*, 1997.

Chapter 6
1 *Book of Moses*, Moses 1: 32–36. Pearl of Great Price, Church of Jesus Christ of Latter-day Saints, 1830.
2 Neugebauer, G.: *Washington Post*, 30 December 1983.
3 *Newsweek*, 13 July 1987, p.45.
4 Sitchin, Z., op. cit., Chapter 7, p.233.
5 ibid., pp.223–6.
6 ibid., pp.226–7.
7 Van Flandern, T., *Dark Matter, Missing Planets and New Comets*, North Atlantic Books, California, 1993, p.262.

Chapter 8
1 Temple, R.: *The Sirius Mystery*, St Martin's Press, 1976, rev. ed. Century, 1998.
2 Crocker, Dr Richard L., and Kilmer, Dr Anne: *The Times*, 7 March 1974.
3 Heidel, A.: *Epic of Gilgamesh and Old Testament Parallels*, University of Chicago Press, 1970.

Chapter 12
1 Santillana, Giorgio de, and von Dechend, Hertha: *Hamlet's Mill*, Macmillan, 1969.
2 ibid.
3 ibid.

Chapter 13
1 Gilbert, A. and Cotterell, M.: *The Mayan Prophecies*, Element Books, 1994, Appendices 1 and 2.
2 Cotterell, M.: *The Supergods*, Thorsons, 1997, p.192.
3 ibid., p.193.
4 ibid., p.197.
5 *Daily Telegraph*, 1991.
6 Cotterell, M., op. cit., p.199.
7 Alford, A., op. cit.

Chapter 14
1 Herodotus: *Canon of the Kings of Egypt* (from *The Histories*), trans. Aubery de Selincourt, Penguin Books, 1971.
2 Velikovsky, I.: *Worlds in Collision*, Victor Gollancz, 1950, Abacus/Sphere Books, 1972.
3 Herodotus, op. cit.
4 Manetho, an Egyptian Priest *c*.300 BC. It is believed that his writings on papyrus were destroyed in the burning of the Great Library of Alexandria in AD 642. Fortunately many of his writings have been referred to by other contemporary historians, whose accounts have survived.
5 Lockyer, Sir Norman: *The Dawn of Astronomy*, 1894.
6 Hamnuna, Rabbi.: *Zo Har*. The Kabbalah (Meaning, 'That which was received').

Chapter 15
1 Levi, E.: *Transcendental Magic*, W. Rider and Son, 1923.

Chapter 16
1 *I Ching* (the Chinese Book of Changes).
2 Lemesurier, P.: *The Great Pyramid Decoded*, Element, 1977, pp.316–321.

Chapter 17
1 Knight, C. and Lomas, T.: *The Hiram Key*, Century, 1996.
2 Eisenman, R.: *The Habakkuk Pesher*. Qumran. (Dead Sea Scrolls, discovered 1947).
3 Wise, M.: *The Habakkuk Pesher*.
4 *The Manual of Discipline*, Qumran (Dead Sea Scrolls, discovered 1947).
5 Knight, C. and Lomas, R., op. cit.
6 Knight, C. and Lomas, R., op. cit.

Chapter 18
1 Newton, Sir Isaac.: *Lexicon Propheticum* (dissertation, printed 10 years after his death).

Chapter 19
1 Various sources on the Internet discuss this theory, as did Dr Gerald O'Farrell during our many conversations on the subject.
2 R. Ellis did parallel research to mine, as regards Stonehenge and Avebury (see next Chapter), and conceived almost identical results, in *Thoth, Architect of the*

Universe (Edfu Books, 1997). Our *final* conclusions, however, were totally different.

Chapter 20
1 Stukeley, Rev'd Dr W.: *Stonehenge, a Temple Restored to the British Druids*, 1740, and *Avebury, a Temple of British Druids*, 1743.
2 Smith, Rev'd A. C.: *Wiltshire Archaeological Magazine*, Vol. 6, 1860, pp.365–89.
3 Fix, W. R.: *Pyramid Odyssey*, Mayflower Books, 1978.

Chapter 21
1 Baigent, M., Leigh, R., and Lincoln, H.: *The Holy Blood and the Holy Grail*, Jonathan Cape Ltd, 1982.

Chapter 22
1 *The Gospels of the Infancy* (Armenian gospels).

Chapter 23
1 Phillips, G.: *Act of God*, Macmillan, 1998.
2 Phillips, G., op. cit.
3 Velikovsky, I.: *Worlds in Collision*, Victor Gollancz, 1950, Abacus/Sphere Books, 1972.
4 *Mormon, Book of*, The Church of Jesus Christ of Latter-day Saints, 1830.
5 Honoré, P.: *In Quest of the White God*, Futura, 1975.
6 Phillips, G., op. cit.
7 ibid.
8 ibid.
9 Freud, S.: *Moses and Monotheism (Dissertation)* London, 1938.
10 Osman, A.: *Moses: Pharaoh of Egypt*, Harper Collins, 1990.
11 Budge, Sir E. A. Wallis: *From Fetish to God in Ancient Egypt*, Oxford University Press, 1934.
12 Manetho, op. cit.
13 Newton, Sir Isaac, op. cit.

Chapter 24
1 Nicodemus.: *Gospel of Nicodemus* (apocryphal).
2 Baigent, M., Leigh, R., Lincoln, H., op. cit.
3 Gardiner, L.: *Bloodline of the Holy Grail*, Element Books, 1996.
4 Foord, E.: *Wells, Glastonbury and Cleeve*, J. M. Dent and Sons, 1925.
5 de Boron, R.: *Roman de L'Estoire dou Saint Graal*, c.1195.
6 Baigent, M., Leigh, R., Lincoln, H., op. cit.
7 Graves, R.. *White Goddess*, enlarged ed., London, 1977.
8 Eschenbach, Wolfram von: *Parzifal*, c.1200–1220.
9 Baigent, M., Leigh, R., Lincoln, H., op. cit.
10 ibid.
11 Eschenbach, Wolfram von, op. cit.
12 ibid.

Chapter 25
1 Knight, C. and Lomas, R., op. cit.
2 Baigent, M., Leigh, R., Lincoln, H., op. cit.
3 *Mormon, Book of*, op. cit.
4 Knight, C. and Lomas, R., op. cit.
5 ibid.
6 Burke, Sir John Bernard: *Vicissitudes of Families and other Essays*.

7 Knight, C. and Lomas, R., op. cit.
8 Waldseemüller, Martin: *Cosmographiae introductio*, 1507.
9 Knight, C. and Lomas, R., op. cit.
10 McWilliam, C.: *Lothian except Edinburgh*, Penguin Books, 1978 (medieval churches by Christopher Wilson).
11 ibid.
12 Grotte, A.: a noted synagogue builder of the early 20th century.
13 Knight, C. and Lomas, R., op. cit.
14 *Damascus Rule* (Qumran scrolls, discovered 1947).
15 Ezekiel's vision of Solomon's Temple, *c*.570 BC.
16 *The Assumption of Moses* (Qumran, Dead Sea Scrolls, discovered 1947).
17 Knight, C. and Lomas, R., op. cit.
18 ibid.
19 *Book of Chronicles* (the Bible, King James Version).

Chapter 26
1 Pliny, *Natural History*.
2 *Book of Melchin* (6th Century AD).
3 Bond, F. B.: *The Mystery of Glaston*, Glastonbury Publications, 1938.
4 Cotterell, M.: op. cit.
5 ibid.
6 ibid.
7 ibid.
8 ibid.
9 Gilbert, A. and Cotterell, M., op. cit.
10 Charnay, C. (a Frenchman who uncovered the first parts of Teotihuacan).

Chapter 27
1 Watkins, A.: *The Old Straight Track*, Methuen and Co., 1925, rep. Garnstone, 1970.
2 Michell, J.: *New View over Atlantis*, Thames and Hudson, 1983. First published as *The View over Atlantis* in 1969 by Sago Press.
3 Britton, J.: *The History and Antiquities of Lichfield*. Longman, 1820.
4 Charpentier, J.: *The Mysteries of Chartres Cathedral*. R.I.L.K.O., 1972. First published as *Les Mystères de la Cathédrale de Chartres*, Laffont, Paris, 1967.
5 Gilbert, A.: *The Magi, The Quest for a Secret Tradition*, Bloomsbury, 1996.
6 Charpentier, J., op. cit.
7 ibid.
8 Gilbert, A., op. cit.
9 ibid.
10 Furlong, D.: *The Keys to the Temple*, Judy Piatkus, 1997.
11 ibid.
12 Watkins, A., op. cit.
13 Furlong, D., op. cit.
14 ibid.
15 ibid.

Chapter 28
1 Bauval, R. and Gilbert, A.: *The Orion Mystery*, Heinemann, 1955.
2 ibid.
3 ibid.
4 Gilbert, A., op. cit.
5 Lemesurier, P.: *The Great Pyramid, Your Personal Guide*, Element, 1987.
6 Maspero, Sir Gaston – 19th-century Egyptologist.

7 Hancock, G.: *Fingerprints of the Gods*, Heinemann, 1995.

Chapter 29
1 West, Anthony, John: *The Traveller's Key to Ancient Egypt*, Harrap–Colombus, 1989 (proposed weathering and age pattern on the Sphinx).
2 Schwaller de Lubicz, R. A.: *Sacred Science: The King of Pharaonic Theocracy*, Inner Traditions International, 1988.
3 Schoch, Dr Robert: Professor of Geology at Boston University (endorsed West's claims about weathering on Sphinx).
4 Hancock, G., op cit.
5 ibid., p.378.
6 ibid., p.378.
7 Posnansky, A., professor of the University of La Paz.
8 Lehner, M.: *The Complete Pyramids*, American University in Cairo Press, 1997, p.216.
9 Petrie, Sir William Flinders: *Pyramids and Temples of Gizeh*, 1881.
10 Bauval, R. and Hancock, G.: *Keeper of Genesis*, Heinemann, 1996.
11 Bauval, R. and Gilbert, A., op. cit.
12 Emery, Prof. Walter, B.: *Archaic Egypt*, Penguin Books, 1987. It was in 1953 that Emery uncovered a large tomb at Saqqara, attributed to the 1st Dynasty.
13 Bauval, R. and Hancock, G., op. cit.

Chapter 30
1 The *Book of the Dead* (ancient Egyptian collection of funerary texts).
2 ibid.
3 Budge, Sir E. A. Wallis, op. cit.
4 Greaves, Dr J. and Davison, N.: *Miscellaneous Works*, T. Birch, 1737.
5 Siculus, Diodorus, trans. C. H. Oldfather, Loeb Classical Library, 1989. Harvard University Press, 1989.
6 Hope, M.: *The Sirius Connection*, Element Books, 1990, BCA, 1996.
7 Cruden, *Complete Concordance to the Bible*.
8 Lemesurier, P.: *The Great Pyramid Decoded*, Element, 1979.

Chapter 31
1 Manetho, trans. W. G. Waddell, Heinemann, 1940.
2 Davidson, D. and Aldersmith, J.: *The Great Pyramid: its Divine Message*, Williams and Norgate, 1925, p.77.
3 Lemesurier, P., *The Great Pyramid Decoded*.
4 Gantenbrink, R., as cited in Hancock, G.: *Fingerprints of the Gods*, Heinemann, 1995, pp.339, 341, 342, 355, 468.
5 Malin, D. and Murdin, P.: *Colours of the Galaxies*, Cambridge University Press, 1984.
6 Ptolomy, *Almagest* (a catalogue of stars compiled by Ptolomy), AD 140.
7 Seneca. As cited by Malin, D. and Murdin, P., op. cit.
8 ibid.
9 Gauseman, J.: *Quest for Knowledge*, Vol. 1, Issue 6, 1997.
10 Hausdorf, H.: *Quest for Knowledge*, Vol. 1, Issue 6, 1997.
11 Ping, Prof. W. S.: *Quest for Knowledge*, Vol. 1, Issue 6, 1997.
12 Nai, X. N.: *Quest for Knowledge*, Vol. 1, Issue 6, 1997.

Chapter 32
1 Lepsius, K. R.: *The Chapters of Coming Forth by Day*.
2 Budge, Sir E. A. Wallis, *The Book of the Dead* (trans.), British Museum, 1895, Arkana, 1986.

3 Hope, M., op. cit.
4 Bauval, R. and Gilbert, A., op. cit.
5 Faulkner, Dr R.: *Book of the Dead* (professor of Ancient Egyptian Language at University College, London).
6 Collins, A., *Gods of Eden*, Headline, 1998.
7 Ibid.
8 Reymond, Dr E. A. E., *The Mythical Origin of the Egyptian Temple*, Manchester University Press, 1969.
9 Collins, A., op. cit.
10 Reymond, op. cit.
11 ibid.
12 Herodotus, *The History*, trans. David Grene, University of Chicago Press, 1987.
13 Reymond, op. cit.
14 Collins, A., op. cit.
15 Jochmans, J.: *Hall of Records: Part 1, Revelations of the Great Pyramid and Sphinx, Chapter II, A Glimmer at Giza – The Lost Hall and its Secret Brotherhood.* Privately published, 1985.
16 Faulkner, Dr R.: *The Ancient Egyptian Coffin Texts*, Spell 1080, p.147.
17 Collins, A., op. cit.
18 ibid.
19 ibid.
20 ibid.

Chapter 33
1 König, W., cited by Winton, W. in *Baghdad Batteries BC*, Sumer XVIII, 1962, pp.87–9.
2 Lockyer, Sir Norman J.: *The Dawn of Astronomy*, Macmillan, 1894.
3 Price, de Solla, D. J.: 'Gears from the Greeks: The Antikythera Mechanism – a computer–calendar from 80 BC', *Transactions of the American Philosophical Society*, New Series 64, 7, 1964.
4 Dunn, C.: *Quest for Knowledge*, Vol. 1, Issue 7, 1997, pp.26–7.
5 Petrie, Sir William Flinders: *Pyramids and Temples of Gizeh*, 1881.
6 ibid.
7 Dunn, C., op. cit.
8 ibid.
9 ibid.

Chapter 34
1 Mandeville, M.: *The Return of the Phoenix*, self-published, 1997.
2 Cayce, E.: *On Mysteries of the Mind*, ed. Charles Thomas Cayce, Aquarian Press, 1990, Thorsons, 1995.
3 Lemesurier, P.: *The Great Pyramid Decoded*.
4 ibid.
5 Hancock, G., op. cit.
6 Flem-Ath, R. and R.: *When the Sky Fell*.
7 Morner, N. A., Lanser, J. P. and Hospers, J., *New Scientist*, 6 January 1972.

Selected Bibliography

Alford, A.: *Gods of the New Millennium*, Eridu Books, 1996; Hodder & Stoughton, 1997.

Armstrong, K.: *A History of God*, Mandarin, 1993.

Baigent, M., Leigh, R., Lincoln, H.: *The Holy Blood and The Holy Grail*, Jonathan Cape Ltd, 1982.

Bauval, R. and Gilbert, A.: *The Orion Mystery*, Heinemann, 1995.

Bauval, R. and Hancock, G.: *Keeper of Genesis*, Heinemann, 1996.

Betro, M. C.: *Hieroglyphics: The Writings of Ancient Egypt*, Abbeville Press, 1966.

Bible, The. King James Version.

Cambridge Illustrated History; Archaelogy, Cambridge University Press, 1996.

Cayce, E.: *Edgar Cayce on Mysteries of the Mind*, The Aquarian Press, 1990; Thorsons/Harper Collins, 1995.

Clayton, P. A.: *Chronicles of the Pharaohs*, Thames and Hudson, 1994.

Collins, A.: *The Gods of Eden*, Headline, 1998.

Copernicus, N.: *De Revolutionibus Orbium Coelestium*, 1543.

Cotterell, M.: *The Supergods*, Thorsons, 1997.

Däniken, E. von.: *Chariots of the Gods*, Souvenir Press, 1969.

Dawkins, R.: *River Out of Eden*, Weidenfeld & Nicholson, 1995.

Einstein, A.: *Relativity: The Special and the General Theory*, Methuen, 1920.

Ellis, R.: *Thoth, Architect of the Universe*, Edfu Books, 1997.

Furlong, D.: *The Keys to the Temple*, Judy Piatkus, 1997.

Gilbert, A., and Cotterell, M.: *The Mayan Prophecies*, Element Books, 1994.

Gilbert, A.: *Magi, The Quest for a Secret Tradition*, Bloomsbury, 1996.

Hancock, G.: *Fingerprints of the Gods*, Heinemann, 1995.

Her Majesty's Stationery Office: *Stonehenge and Avebury*, 1959

Hitching, F.: *The World Atlas of Mysteries*, William Collins Sons and Co., 1978; Pan Books, 1981; Book Club Associates, 1981.

Flem-Ath, R. and R.: *When the Sky Fell*, Weidenfeld and Nicolson, 1995, Orion, 1996.

Edwards, I.E.S.: *The Pyramids of Egypt*, Penguin, 1980.

Hope, M.: *The Sirius Connection*, Element Books, 1990, BCA, 1996.

Knight, C. and Lomas, R.: *The Hiram Key*, Century, 1996; Arrow Books, 1997.

Lehner, M.: *The Complete Pyramids*, American University In Cairo Press, 1997.

Lemesurier, P.: *The Great Pyramid Decoded*, Element, 1977.

Lemesurier, P.: *The Great Pyramid: Your Personal Guide*, Element, 1987.

Malin, D., and Murdin, P.: *Colours of the Galaxies*, Cambridge University Press, 1984.

Michell, J.: *The New View over Atlantis*, Thames and Hudson, 1983.

Mormon, Book of. The Church of Jesus Christ of Latter-day Saints, 1830.

Morner, N. A., Lanser, J. P. and Hospers, J., in *New Scientist*, 6 January 1972.

North, J.: *Stonehenge, Neolithic Man and the Cosmos*, Harper Collins, 1996.

Osman, A.: *The House of the Messiah,* Harper Collins, 1992.

Osman, A.: *Moses: Pharaoh of Egypt*, Grafton, 1990.

Petrie, Sir William Flinders: *Pyramids and Temples of Gizeh*, 1881.

Phillips, G.: *Act of God*, Macmillan, 1998.

Piazzi Smyth, C.: *Our Inheritance in the Great Pyramid*, 1864.

Plato: *Timaeus*.

Rohl, D.: *A Testament of Time*, Century, 1995.

Scott, A.: *The Creation of Life, Past, Future, Alien*, Basil Blackwell, 1986.

Shaw, I., and Nicholson, P.: *British Museum Dictionary of Ancient Egypt*, BCA, 1996.

Sitchin, Z.: *The Stairway to Heaven*, Avon, 1980.

Sitchin, Z.: *The Twelfth Planet*. 1976.

Temple, R.: *The Sirius Mystery*, St Martin's Press, 1976, Century, 1998.

The Times Atlas of World History. 4 ed., BCA/Times Books, 1993.

Velikovsky, I.: *Worlds in Collision*, Victor Gollancz, 1950. Abacus/Sphere Books, 1972.

Velikovsky, I.: *Ages in Chaos*, 1952.

Velikovsky, I.: *Earth in Upheaval*, 1955.

White, A. J., Dr.: *What About Origins*, BCA, 1983.

Illustrations Acknowledgements

1. From Graham Hancock, *Fingerprints of the Gods*, p.87
2. After Kenneth Smith/Francis Hitching.
3. After Joseph F. Blumrich.
4. Nigel R. Appleby.
5. Nigel R. Appleby/Random House.
6. Nigel R. Appleby.
7. After Zecharia Sitchin.
8. Nigel R. Appleby/Random House.
9. Nigel R. Appleby.
10. Nigel R. Appleby/Random House.
11. Nigel R. Appleby/Random House.
12. Nigel R. Appleby.
13. Robert Kyle Grenville Temple.
14. Robert Kyle Grenville Temple.
15. Robert Kyle Grenville Temple.
16. Robert Kyle Grenville Temple.
17. Robert Kyle Grenville Temple.
18. Robert Kyle Grenville Temple.
19. Nigel R. Appleby/Random House.
20. Mitchell Beazley.
21. After Maurice Cotterell.
22. Nigel R. Appleby/Random House.
23. Nigel R. Appleby.
24. Nigel R. Appleby.
25. Nigel R. Appleby.
26. Nigel R. Appleby.
27. Nigel R. Appleby.
28. Nigel R. Appleby.
29. After Maurice Cotterell.
30. After Maurice Cotterell.
31. After Alan Alford.
32. Nigel R. Appleby/Random House.
33. (a) Nigel R. Appleby/Random House.
33. (b) Nigel R. Appleby/Random House.
34. After John Michell.
35. Nigel R. Appleby.
36. After Kurt Roland.
37. Nigel R. Appleby.
38. Nigel R. Appleby/Random House.
39. Nigel R. Appleby.
40. (a) After Kurt Roland.
40. (b) After Kurt Roland.
41. Nigel R. Appleby/Random House.
42. Nigel R. Appleby.
43. Nigel R. Appleby (After R. Ellis).
44. Nigel R. Appleby/Random House.
45. Nigel R. Appleby.
46. After The Edgar Brothers.
47. Piazzi Smyth.
48. Nigel R. Appleby.
49. Nigel R. Appleby.
50. Nigel R. Appleby.
51. Nigel R. Appleby.
52. Nigel R. Appleby/Random House.
53. Nigel R. Appleby/Random House.
54. Nigel R. Appleby/Random House.
55. Nigel R. Appleby.
56. Nigel R. Appleby/Random House.
57. Kenneth Smith/Francis Hitching.
58. Nigel R. Appleby.
59. Nigel R. Appleby.
60. Bauval and Hancock.
61. Nigel R. Appleby (After R. Ellis).
62. Nigel R. Appleby (After R. Ellis).
63. Nigel R. Appleby (After R. Ellis).
64. Nigel R. Appleby (After R. Ellis).
65. Nigel R. Appleby (After R. Ellis).
66. Nigel R. Appleby.
67. Nigel R. Appleby.
68. Nigel R. Appleby (After R. Ellis).
69. Nigel R. Appleby (After R. Ellis).
70. Nigel R. Appleby (After R. Ellis).
71. Nigel R. Appleby (After R. Ellis).
72. Nigel R. Appleby.
73. Nigel R. Appleby.
74. Nigel R. Appleby (After R. Ellis).
75. Nigel R. Appleby (After R. Ellis).
76. Nigel R. Appleby.
77. Nigel R. Appleby (After R. Ellis).
78. Nigel R. Appleby (After R. Ellis).
79. After David Furlong.
80. (a) After John Michell.
80. (b) Nigel R. Appleby.
81. Nigel R. Appleby.
82. Peter Lemesurier.
83. Peter Lemesurier.
84. After Lomas and Knight.
85. After Lomas and Knight.
86. (a) After Lomas and Knight.
86. (b) After Lomas and Knight.
87. Nigel R. Appleby.

88. After Lomas and Knight.
89. After Lomas and Knight.
90. After John Michell.
91. Nigel R. Appleby.
92. After John Michell.
93. After John Michell.
94. After John Michell.
95. Nigel R. Appleby.
96. Readers Digest.
97. After Maurice Cotterell.
98. After Maurice Cotterell.
99. Readers Digest.
100. After Maurice Cotterell.
101. After Maurice Cotterell.
102. After Maurice Cotterell.
103. (*a*) After John Michell.
103. (*b*) After John Michell.
103. (*c*) After John Michell.
104. Louis Charpentier.
105. Nigel R. Appleby.
106. After David Furlong.
107. After David Furlong.
108. After David Furlong.
109. After David Furlong.
110. After David Furlong.
111. After David Furlong.
112. After Gilbert and Bauval.
113. Peter Lemesurier.
114. (*a*) Bauval and Hancock.

114. (*b*) Bauval and Hancock.
115. Nigel R. Appleby.
116. Nigel R. Appleby (After R. Ellis).
117. Nigel R. Appleby.
118. Nigel R. Appleby.
119. Nigel R. Appleby (After R. Ellis).
120. (*a*) William Stukeley's sketch of North circle at Avebury.
120. (*b*) William Stukeley's Obelisk at Avebury.
120. (*c*) British Library Egerton MS 3028, fo. 140 v.
121. (*a*) Bauval and Hancock.
121. (*b*) Bauval and Hancock.
122. Bauval and Hancock.
123. Nigel R. Appleby.
124. Egyptian *Book of the Dead.*
125. Peter Lemesurier.
126. Peter Lemesurier.
127. (*a*) Nigel R. Appleby.
127. (*b*) Nigel R. Appleby.
128. Nigel R. Appleby.
129. After Derek de Solla Price.
130. Bauval and Hancock.
131. Nigel R. Appleby.
132. Nigel R. Appleby.
133. Nigel R. Appleby. ·
134. Nigel R. Appleby.
Appendices 1 and 3. Nigel R. Appleby.

Photographic plates

Page 1: 1. The Giza Pyramids as viewed from the south. *Operation Hermes Ltd.* 2. The enigmatic Sphinx at Giza. *Operation Hermes Ltd.*

Page 2: 3. A few of the remaining polished white lumite stones on the Great Pyramid. *Operation Hermes Ltd.* 4. Severe weathering pattern. *Operation Hermes Ltd.*

Page 3: 5. A later constructed pyramid, showing decay. *Operation Hermes Ltd.* 6. The Bent Pyramid at Dashur. *Lucien Morgan and Richard Gibson.*

Page 4: 7. Water erosion on the Great Pyramid. *Lucien Morgan and Richard Gibson.* 8. The Temple of Horus at Edfu. *Lucien Morgan and Richard Gibson.*

Page 5: 9. The Grand Gallery. *Lucien Morgan and Richard Gibson.* 10. Depiction of green Osiris. *Lucien Morgan and Richard Gibson.* 11. The King's Chamber of the Great Pyramid. *Lucien Morgan and Richard Gibson.*

Page 6: 12. Hieroglyphic relief from a wall at Abydos. *Operation Hermes Ltd.* 13. Sumerian cylinder seal. *Staatliche Museum zu Berlin – Preussischer Kulturbesitz Vorderasiatisches Museum.* 14. A pyramidion (Ben Ben). *Lucien Morgan and Richard Gibson.*

Page 7: 15. Zoser's Step Pyramid. *Lucien Morgan and Richard Gibson.* 16. Silbury Hill. *Richard Gibson.*

Page 8: 17. Silbury Hill from the air. *English Heritage.* 18. Spectrographic image of light from Sirius. *David Malin and Paul Murdin.*

Page 9: 19. Pyramid in China covered in earth on flat plain. *Hartwig Hausdorf.* 20. Pyramid in China near the city of Xian Qui Chan. *Hartwig Hausdorf.*

Page 10: 21. The Stonehenge sarsen stones. *English Heritage.* 22. Stonehenge trilithons. *English Heritage.*

Page 11: 23. Constellation of Orion. *David Malin and Paul Murdin.*

Page 12: 24. Pyramid of the Sun, Teotihuacan. *Readers Digest.* 25. Six-tiered pyramid of Quetzalcoatl. *Readers Digest.*

Page 13: 26. Central American temple. *Readers Digest.*

Page 14: 27. The Temple of Inscriptions. *Readers Digest.* 28. Uffington White Horse. *English Heritage.*

Page 15: 29. Projected site of the Hall of Records in Egypt, 1st view. *Operation Hermes Ltd.* 30. Projected site of the Hall of Records in Egypt, 2nd view. *Operation Hermes Ltd.*

Page 16: 31 *Sunday Times* article about the team and graphic of the projected site. *The Sunday Times.*

List of Illustrations

Index

Note: **significant numbers** are **emboldened** to distinguish
them from page numbers

405

Index